NATIVE V

Tupelo Press Anthologies

Another English: Anglophone Poems from Around the World
edited by Catherine Barnett and Tiphanie Yanique

Beyond Boundaries: Prose Poems by 24 American Poets
edited by Ray Gonzalez

*Cooking with the Muse: A Sumptuous Gathering of Seasonal Recipes, Culinary Poetry,
    and Literary Fare*
edited by Myra Kornfeld and Stephen Massimilla

A God in the House: Poets Talk About Faith
edited by Ilya Kaminsky and Katherine Towler

Gossip & Metaphysics: Russian Modernist Poems and Prose
edited by Katie Farris, Ilya Kaminsky, and Valzhyna Mort

The Imaginary Poets
edited by Alan Michael Parker

Native Voices: Indigenous American Poetry, Craft and Conversation
edited by CMarie Fuhrman and Dean Rader

New Cathay: Contemporary Chinese Poetry
edited by Ming Di

Xeixa: Fourteen Catalan Poets
edited by Marlon Fick and Francisca Esteve

NATIVE VOICES

Indigenous American Poetry, Craft and Conversations

edited by
CMarie Fuhrman and Dean Rader

Tupelo Press
North Adams, Massachusetts

ISBN 978-1-946482-18-1

Designed and composed in Birch Standard and Garamond by Howard Klein.

Cover art by Laura Calhoun, designed by Diana Walczak. Copyright © 2017. Used with permission of the artist.

First paperback edition: April 2019.

Library of Congress Cataloging-in-Publication Data available upon request.

The sources of the book's epigraphs are: Joy Harjo, from *Crazy Brave: A Memoir* (W.W. Norton, 2012); Simon J. Ortiz, from *After and Before the Lightning* (University of Arizona Press, 1994); Adrian C. Louis, from the essay "Of Craft, Cub Scouts, Mayonnaise, and UFOs," in this anthology.

Tupelo Press

P.O. Box 1767

North Adams, Massachusetts 01247

(413) 664-9611 / editor@tupelopress.org / www.tupelopress.org

Tupelo Press is an award-winning independent literary press that publishes fine fiction, nonfiction, and poetry in books that are a joy to hold as well as read. Tupelo Press is a registered 501(c)(3) nonprofit organization, and we rely on public support to carry out our mission of publishing extraordinary work that may be outside the realm of large commercial publishers. Financial donations are welcome and are tax deductible.

Produced with support from the National Endowment for the Arts and with contributions from enthusiastic and generous Kickstarter donors, especially D.G. Geis and William Prindle.

ART WORKS.
arts.gov

for Adrian C. Louis, 1946–2018

"It is amazing how much knowledge we have of hope.
Whisper bravely into the dark, heart—whisper bravely." —*Simon J. Ortiz*

"'You're coming with me, poor thing. You don't know how to listen.
You don't know how to speak. You don't know how to sing. I will teach you.'
I followed poetry." —*Joy Harjo*

"Poetry is art, period." —*Adrian C. Louis*

Contents

Preface   xx
Introduction   xxiv

Carter Revard   3
OSAGE, PONCA, IRISH, AND SCOTCH-IRISH
Poems:
Indians Demand Equal Time with God
People from the Stars
Driving in Oklahoma
Statement on Energy Policy
Essay:
"Herbs of Healing: American Values in American Indian Literature"

Simon J. Ortiz   30
ACOMA PUEBLO
Poems:
Culture and the Universe
Survival This Way
A Story of How a Wall Stands
Our Eagerness Blooms
Essay:
from "Song/Poetry, and Language: Expression and Perception"

Diane Glancy   41
CHEROKEE
Poems:
The Bat House
Without Title
Buffalo Medicine
He Dressed Me for the Pretend Cold
Until the times of restitution — Acts 3:21
Essay and influence poem:
Federico Garcia Lorca's "From Here"

Ernestine Hayes   48
TLINGIT
Poems:
Shapeshifters
Land otter people
The Spoken Forest
Influence poem:
With Elegant Craft: Nora Marks Dauenhauer's "How to Make Good Baked
     Salmon from the River"

Adrian C. Louis   57
LOVELOCK PAIUTE
Poems:
In Lieu of a Communion Wafer
Prairie Madness
Skinology
The Hermit's Diary
Magpie in Margaritaville
Essay:
Of Craft, Cub Scouts, Mayonnaise, and UFOs

Chrystos   67
MENOMINEE
Poems:
Sky Falls Away
Beauti Full Soft Black Tongues
She Had to Go
Palestinians & Indians Feel
I Still Have the Bullet
The Earth Where I Live
Essay:
War Piece Craft
Influencing poem:
Audre Lorde's "A Litany for Survival"

Linda Hogan   79
CHICKASAW
Poems:
Bones at the River
Creation
The Fingers, Writing
About Myself
Lost in the Milky Way
What I Keep
Essay and influencing poems:
Poetry Is My First Language: Layli Long Soldier's "Whereas" and Craig Santos
    Perez's "understory"

Leslie Marmon Silko   91
LAGUNO PUEBLO
Poems:
Poem for Myself and Mei: Concerning Abortion
Love Poem
The Storyteller's Escape
When Sun Came to Riverwoman
Essay:
from Language and Literature from a Pueblo Indian Perspective
Influencing poem:
Excerpt from a letter to James Wright, September 12, 1979, and James Wright's
poem "Wherever Home Is"

Janice Gould   110
KOYANGK'AUWI MAIDU
Poems:
Indian Mascot, 1959
The Day of the Dead
Kim
A Poem
Poor in Spirit
Essay:
Influences
Influencing poem:
Gary Snyder's "Riprap"

Ray A. Young Bear   119
MESKWAKI
Poems:
To See as Far as the Grandfather World
Our Bird Aegis
John Whirlwind's Doublebeat Songs, 1956
Four Hinterland Abstractions
Essay:
"The Summer of 1969: Children of Speakthunder"
Influence poem:
James Welch's "In My Lifetime"

Joy Harjo   136
MVSKOKE
Poems:
The Woman Hanging From the Thirteenth Floor Window
A Postcolonial Tale
Eagle Poem
Essay:
from "One Song"

LeAnne Howe   149
CHOCTAW
Poems:
Gatorland
Noble Savage Learns to Tweet
The Rope Speaks
Now I Lay Me Down
Apocrypha
Essay:
Inner Conflicts
Influence poem:
W. D. Snodgrass's "Eva Braun"

Luci Tapahonso   170
DINÉ
Poems:
Blue Horses Rush In
The Motion of Songs Rising
It Has Always Been This Way
Daané é Diné
Essay:
from the Preface to Sáanii Dahataał: The Women Are Singing

Ruby Hansen Murray   179
OSAGE
Poems:
The Dark Mother
Nch'i-Wana
Rest Assured
Food Fight at Hanford, No Laughing Matter
The Little Osage Captive, Elias Cornelius, 1824
Essay:
Giving Voice to Place: Where You See Yourself
Influencing poem:
Carter Revard's "Wazhazhe Grandmother"

Louise Erdrich   188
TURTLE MOUNTAIN OJIBWE
Poems:
Dear John Wayne
Indian Boarding School: The Runaways
Captivity
Windigo
Rez Litany
Essay:
Out of the Black Night
Influencing Poem:
Elizabeth Bishop's "One Art"

Gordon Henry Jr.   200
WHITE EARTH OJIBWE
Poems:
When Names Escaped Us
November Becomes the Sky with Suppers for the Dead
Jazz Tune for a Hiawatha Woman
Essay:
Let us be painting painting painter singing singing singer: On the verve of verbs

Kimberly Blaeser   208
ANISHINAABE
Poems:
Captivity
Apprenticed to Justice
Goodbye to All That
Fantasies of Women
Of Fractals and Pink Flowering
Essay:
"Air is Between These Words, Fanning the Flame": Poetry and
Literary Inheritance
Influence poem:
Linda Hogan's "Workday"

C. R. Resetarits   226
CHEROKEE-CREEK
Poems:
Elegy
Arroyo
Hovenweep
Essay:
Lost Tribes, Rain C. Goméz, and the Shadow Arts
Influence poem:
Rain C Goméz's "Mapping Shadow"

Allison Adelle Hedge Coke   234
HURON, METIS, LUSO, FRENCH CANADIAN, AND MIXED
SOUTHEASTERN NATIVE
Poems:
America, I Sing You Back
Taxonomy
Radio Wave Mama
Streaming
Essay:
Beyond the Ballads
Influence poem:
Delmore Schwartz's "The Heavy Bear that Goes With Me"

Elise Paschen   259
OSAGE
Poems:
Oklahoma Home
Under the Dome
Wí'-gi-e
My Mother Descends
Parents at Rest
Essay:
Straddling Two Worlds
Influence poem:
Joy Harjo's "She Had Some Horses"

Suzanne S. Rancourt   270
ABENAKI (BEAR CLAN) / HURON
Poems:
Fabric
Maccha
The Smell of Blood
Essay:
So Glad You Asked
Influence poem:
Ai's "Warrior"

Deborah A. Miranda   280
OHLONE-COSTANOAN ESSELEN / CHUMASH
Poems:
Juliana, 1803
Indian Cartography
Novena to Bad Indians
Erasurepoem
Tears of the Sun
Essay:
Looking for Ourselves in the Poetry of Others
Influence poem:
Wendy Rose's "Excavation at Santa Barbara Mission"

Heid E. Erdrich   298
TURTLE MOUNTAIN OJIBWE
Poems:
Little Souvenirs from the DNA Trading Post
National Monuments
Kennewick Man Tells All
Guidelines for the Treatment of Sacred Objects
Pre-Occupied
Essay:
Real to Me
Influencing poem:
Kimberly Blaeser's "Rewriting Your Life"

Celia Bland   311
CHEROKEE
Poems:
Car Crash
Cherokee Hogscape
Lost Highway
Essay:
Car Crashes, Shootings, and Ghosts
Influence poem:
Natalie Díaz's "When My Brother Was an Aztec"

Margaret Noodin   319
ANISHINAABE
Poems:
Daanisag / Daughters
Nayendamowin Mitigwaaking / Woodland Liberty
Apenimonodan / Trust
Essay:
Like Sedimentary Stone
Influence poem:
Jane Johnston Schoolcraft's "On Leaving My Children John and Jane, in the
Atlantic States, and preparing to return to the interior"

Chip Livingston   327
MVSKOKE
Poems:
Stadium Mocs
Punta Del Este Pantoum
52 Hawks
Essay:
The Influence of Repetition in Chrystos's "Crazy Grandpa Whispers"

Esther G. Belin   335
DINÉ
Poems:
This Is What I Mean
_____ Child(ren) Left Behind
Public Record 1831
Ruby in Me #1
Blues-ing on the Brown Vibe
Essay:
Poem Making as Making Space
Influence poem:
Luci Tapahonso's "That American Flag"

dg nanouk okpik   349
INUPIAQ-INUIT
Poems:
Frightening Acid Flakes Haibun
Fossil Fuel Embers Haibun
Glacial Oil World
Man and the Little People
Influence poem:
Arthur Sze's "The Owl": Thoughts on Word Choice

Sammie Bordeaux-Seeger   355
SICANGU LAKOTA
Poems:
Blue Water
No Water
November
1900
Essay:
Finding Resonance in Roberta Hill's "Star Quilt"
Influence poem:
Roberta Hill's "Star Quilt"

Molly McGlennen   363
ANISHINAABE
Poems:
Three Poems for Ellia
Living the Language
Legend
Essay:
Preface to Fried Fish and Flour Biscuits

M. L. Smoker   369
ASSINIBOINE–SIOUX
Poems:
The Feed
Another Attempt at a Rescue
Letter to Richard Hugo

Mercy
Essay:
Hugo
Influence poem:
Richard Hugo's "Degrees of Gray in Philipsburg"

Sherwin Bitsui   378
DINÉ
Poems:
Atlas
Apparition
Drought
Stepping through the drum's vibration
Essay:
from "The Motion of Poetic Landscape: An Interview with Sherwin Bitsui" by Bianca Viñas

Cedar Sigo   388
SUQUAMISH
Poems:
First Love
The Material Field
The Studio
Essay:
Return to Grafitti Land
Influence poem:
John Trudell's "Rant and Roll"

Julian Talamantez Brolaski   397
MESCALERO AND LIPAN APACHE, LATIN@, EUROPEAN
Poems:
as the owl augurs
in the cut
I had already shuttered an aspect of my vision

Jennifer Elise Foerster   403
MVSKOKE
Poems:
From Coosa
Atlas
Leaving Tulsa
Essay:
The Spiral: Circling Closer
Influence poem:
Joy Harjo's "Speaking Tree"

Laura Da'   416
EASTERN SHAWNEE
Poems:
Perspective
Eye Turned Crow
Leviathan
Essay and Influence poem:
On James Thomas Stevens's "Tokinish"

Bojan Louis   426
DINÉ
Poems:
The Nature of Mortal Illness
If Nothing, the Land
Breach
Essay:
"Between the Abyss and Here, Beauty"
Influence poem:
Lynda Hull's "Studies from Life"

Craig Santos Perez   439
CHAMORU
Poems:
Interwoven
Ode (Ending with a Confession) to the First Mango I Ate on Guam after Decades Away
The Pacific Written Tradition
Essay and Influence poem:
On Writing from the New Oceania and Cecilia Catherine Taitano Perez's "As I Turn the Pages"

Ishmael Angaluuk Hope   456
TLINGIT, IÑUPIAQ
Poems:
Canoe Launching into the Gaslit Sea
from Love Letter to the Future: A Book of the Land in Four Acts
Essay and Influence text:
"A Story of Turtle Island" told by Sequoyah Guess

Michaelsun Stonesweat Knapp   469
OHLONE (COSTANOAN-RUMSEN CARMEL BAND)
Poems:
Manwreck
At What Number Are Numbers No Good?
Essay and Influence texts:
On "At What Number Are Numbers No Good?" and Tecumseh's Speech to the Osages

Michael Wasson   477
NIMÍIPUU
Poems:
Aposiopesis [Or, the Field Between the Living & the Dead]
I Say After-Rain, You Say Hahalxpáawisa
Self-Portrait as 1879–1934
This Dusk in a Mouth Full of Prayer
Self-Portrait as Article 1 [1]. [Treaty With Nez Percés, 1855]: Cession of Lands
    to the United States
Essay and Influence poem:

I Am To Carry This History, This Body: Eduardo C. Corral's "Our Completion: Oil on Wood: Tino Rodríguez: 1999"

Benjamín Naka-Hasebe Kingsley   494
ONONDAGA
Poems:
American Rust
just another horse poem
Run: 2nd Street Harrisburg PA Summertime '17
Essay:
Our Work Is Never Over
Influence poem:
Gail Tremblay's "Indian Singing in 20th Century America"

Orlando White   501
DINÉ OF THE NAANEESHT'ÉZHI TÁBAAHÍ AND BORN FOR
THE NAAKAI DINÉ'E
Poems:
Analogy
Sentence
Writ
Unwritten
Whit
Essay:
from Interview with Orlando White, by Veronica Golos

Layli Long Soldier   509
OGLALA LAKOTA
Poems:
38
Excerpts from "Whereas Statements"
Essay:
from "Layli Long Soldier: interviewed by Kaveh Akbar"

Permissions 522
Acknowledgments 526

Preface

Dear Dean,

I'd like to tell you a story about this book we are working on.

In the spring of 2017, I co-taught a Native Literature course at the University of Idaho with my friend, associate professor Jan Johnson. We wanted to teach through a NODAPL lens so as to expose students not only to contemporary and modern Native American literature, but to show how Native voices have been fighting to be heard for hundreds of years—and were fighting now.

The course consisted of fiction and poetry and we had several guest speakers. Over the semester we cultivated a comfort in that class. Perhaps this is because I am Native and was willing to talk about topics that are sometimes considered unapproachable (offensive mascots and Halloween costumes, pejorative words, etc.), and willing to allow the students (all non-Native, save for one) to openly ask questions while listening to their opinions and confusion. Or perhaps the community had been moved enough by the literature we were studying to want to engage—to try and understand the literature from a Native perspective. In the end, they were not afraid to ask questions, not afraid to look foolish in front of one another, not afraid to admit to the stereotypes they had been raised with and become so used to that they took these as truth. Between the papers they wrote and the class discussions we had, I found this class to be tremendously successful.

Except.

The literature was still being approached, at least critically, through a non-Native lens. Craft was being talked about in terms of how non-Native writers, mainly white writers, approach craft. Reference materials about craft and theory that the students found outside the classroom were not written by Native writers. I would stand at the front of the classroom and look into the eyes of the one Native student, thinking how wrong it was that I needed to deliver the words of our ancestors through the opinions, written in books of craft and theory, of the same people who had colonized them, who had taken their language away. I longed for a text to ac company that course which would teach in a Native way of knowing. From Native to Native, from Native to non-Native. I longed for a text that honored and gave space for poets to talk about their creative processes and inspirations.

A few short weeks later, I would find myself at a table with Tupelo Press publisher Jeffrey Levine, telling him about the lack of such a comprehensive and inclusive guide to Indigenous poetries, and what came out of that conversation, and of a vision that he had, is this book.

I took the draft manuscript of *Native Voices* with me on a camping trip to Hells Canyon, Idaho, in March of 2018. The place where my partner and I camp holds great importance to me. Its occupancy dates back sixteen thousand years. Over the seven years that my partner and I have made this our spring-break destination, we have walked ancient trails and found house pits, lithic scatter, hunting blinds, and art—most notably a pictograph of a salmon painted ochre in the twilit opening of a cave. I am haunted by that painting. I cannot forget that it is the last of so much that once occupied the canyon: one of the very few paintings to still exist, one of the few signs of the Native people who made Hells Canyon their home for thousands of years, and the last remaining salmon present above Hells Canyon Dam, all the rest denied passage when the dam was completed in 1956.

The United States Forest Service has erected signs and a fence to inform and protect two graves at Spring Bar in Hells Canyon. A sign refers to two men, white men, who are buried there, and explains how the orchard they planted on the substantial bar fed miners, and how they lived there until they died.

The sign mentions nothing about the long Native presence in this place. About the lives birthed and buried in the area. About the salmon that once were so many you could hear them spawning. Nothing.

Recently, thanks to an archaeologist at the university where I teach, I learned more about this place I have come to cherish, to need: I learned that the very spot where we camp, the bar that has been orchard, has been trailer park for dam build ers, and that is now a campground replete with pit toilets, is also a burial site. Before the dam was built, nearly two hundred mounds were recorded in the area. Some are still visible; the rest now lay under silt in the murky reservoir water.

I took that information with me, along with the anthology manuscript, when I camped there this past spring. Sitting inside the camper on a cold spring day, rain softly drumming the roof, I read about bones of our ancestors being used for church foundations; traditions lost, whole families lost. I read poems written in multiple Indigenous languages. I read essays that were words escaping choked throats. I read and read and felt something of like a weight being lifted. Something close to a reckoning.

I went out for a walk. The light rain was a reprieve and a cleansing. Watching the drops fall on the reservoir and spill out like sound waves reminded me of the importance of the words I had just read, how they ripple out and out, until they meet another wave or shoreline. And I wondered how far out the voices would carry.

My partner and I walked past the graves of the orchardists, past the inter- pretive sign, to an area that we were told may have held some burial sites. I found myself deeply frustrated. It did not seem fair, it never seemed fair—there was homage paid to the white history, but the people who knew this land, who lived with it for thousands of years were forgotten, along with their stories, along with their voices, their songs. I thought, there must be some way: We have to do some- thing to stop this. People need to know what happened here.

I felt poor, as if I owed this land something.

When I returned to the camper, wet, frustrated, still eager to make amends, I saw the draft of this anthology on the table. Forty-four voices that would not be buried, voices whose ripples would go far beyond these banks. What I saw, through my own tearing eyes, was one way of making amends.

Sincerely,
CMarie

Dear CMarie,

I love what you've said here. Your note appeared in my box at a time when nine people were staying in our house, including four kids between the ages of eleven and six. It was the first reunion of my family since my dad passed away in December. I was thinking of family, ancestors, past generations, future generations, education, race, justice.

Coincidentally (or not), the day your letter arrived we had gone, as an entire family, to Alcatraz. My sons were fascinated by the "INDIANS WELCOME" sign that hangs prominently as visitors approach the dock by ferry. They knew a little bit about the occupation but had a lot of questions. Once we got off the boat, I showed them the RED POWER painting sort of hidden around the corner of the main building, recently restored and now protected behind plexiglass. I probably launched into a bit of a lecture, but this is the burden of having me as a father. A few minutes later, as we started our walk up the hill to the cells, we stopped to watch a bit of a film about the occupation before going into the bookstore across the hall, where my wife found a copy of my book *Engaged Resistance* for sale in the shop. I took the book off the shelf, and I walked the kids, probably with too much detail, through the photos from the Alcatraz chapter. They were getting antsy, but history has learned to be patient.

As you were thinking about our anthology on your hike through the canyon, I was thinking about our anthology as I hiked through Alcatraz. I was thinking how important voices and words are. I was thinking how past and present collapses in poetry. I was thinking about lineage and tradition and influence and community. I was thinking about you in Idaho, the burial sites, the many graves, and my father in Oklahoma in his grave. I was thinking about our work which is not work at all but a kind of honor. A prayer.

I hope to see you soon.

Sincerely,
Dean

Introduction

In the beginning was the story, and within the story was voice, and within voice was hope. Within this book, and these voices, and these poems is hope. There are other things too—anger, despair, interrogation, remembering, healing—but there is a lot of hope, a lot of generosity, and a lot of gratitude.

There is also a great deal of artistry. This anthology is not just a collection of individual poems, it is an exhibition of creation. Too often, critics and teachers look at Indigenous poetry through the lens of *culture*. Or *meaning*. Or *theme*. They look to literature to reinforce assumptions about race, gender, history, nature. They come to this poetry for its *aboutness*. One of the main goals of *Native Voices* is to reframe how Indigenous poetry is seen. We want to highlight craft, foreground form, underscore art.

To this end, we have integrated into the selections of poetry a feature we hope will help readers, including teachers and students, to discover and appreciate the formal components of Native poetics. We asked contributors to choose a poem that was and is especially important to them as poets, inviting them to write about how that poem influenced their own poetry. Some of these craft essays are long, and some are short. Some are formal, while others are colloquial. As you will see, the poems and essays talk to each other in fascinating ways. When read together, they widen the experience of interacting with poetry—they help focus and orient the reader without over-determining interpretation.

Readers might be surprised to see that some of the poets selected poems by non-Natives as their influencing texts. While this means that not every poem between these covers was written by an Indigenous American, it reinforces a truth we know intimately—Native writers read widely. Their sphere of what is influential is as broad, as inclusive, and as global as anyone else's.

The poets included in these pages represent three different but interrelated generations of Indigenous poets. We begin with major foreruners such as Carter Revard, Simon Ortiz, Diane Glancy, Adrian C. Louis, Chrystos, Linda Hogan, Leslie Marmon Silko, and Ray A. Young Bear, who took Native poetry to new levels and helped usher Indigenous writing into anthololgies and classrooms. Featured here are revered and widely read and taught poems and some new work, along with pieces of seminal prose. Born in the 1930s and '40s, most of these poets didn't see their work in print until the 1960s and '70s, but each has emerged as an important presence in American letters and have been, for many of the younger poets in this anthology, invaluable mentors. We are also honored to feature the work of a group of poets born in the 1950s and '60s who have themselves become luminaries, including Joy Harjo, LeAnne Howe, Luci Tapahonso, Louise Erdrich, Kimberly Blaeser, Allison Adele Hedge Coke, Elise Paschen, Deborah A. Miranda, Heid Erdrich, and a host of others. In addition, this anthology presents an exciting sampling of poets emerging now, writers who have published a book or two (or perhaps not yet a full-length collection) but who are already changing the conversation about contemporary poetry.

In editing *Native Voices*, we have tried to be judicious in our selections. We wanted to present a wide variety of poets with a similar number of poems. There are forty-four poets, with three to six poems for each poet. Some of these poems are classic, well-known works; some are in print here for the first time. For most of the contributors, there is also an influencing text and an accompanying essay. In most instances, the essays were written specifically for this anthology, but in a few cases we have reprinted previously published essays or excerpts from interviews. The prose selections reflect the far-ranging contributions these poets have made to world of poetics.

We open the book with a correspondence because the poems and the essays that follow are themselves in conversation with each other. They speak to, respond to, reply to each other. They are texts moving across time and space. But they are not just texts—they are human entreaties written by artists who love and fear and dream and hope. Their poems are a testament to their humanity and creativity.

Indigenous poetry is not just a *field of subject matter*, but a way of being in the world. And this is the other reason we began with a correspondence between the two editors—we are writers, partners, parents, poets, and these poems, this art, is an important part of our worlds. Our hope with this volume is that these Native voices speak to your worlds, as well.

NATIVE VOICES

CARTER REVARD

Osage

"Good language, in both talk and writing, builds a small community in which peopelo can live a little more completely and joyously than solitude allows."

Known for his narrative, conversational poems as well as his lyric riddles based on Old English forms, Carter Revard (1931–)is one of the great elder statesmen of Indigenous literary studies, and a marvelous teacher. Drawing from Osage worldviews, Old English literary traditions, classic storytelling motifs, and contemporary news and political issues, Revard's poems are a thrilling (and often humorous) mix of the ancient and the recent. The Osage believe they are descended from the stars, and Revard sees his ancestors, and perhaps himself, as conduits between the heavens and the earth, figures in whom one finds a balance of terrestrial and celestial. There is a profound directionality in his work, the rhetoric of descending and ascending, rising and plunging. For instance, in a poem like "Indians Demand Equal Time with God," Revard warns us (and God) that despite attempts to take away Indian access to the divine, Natives will ascend. And, in "How the Songs Came Down," Revard suggests that, like light from the stars, and like the Wazhazhe (the Osage people), stories will always make their way to earth to make this their residence. In Revard's impressive poetry, stories and the Wazhaze are the same. Both arrive from stars. Both inhabit this world. Both put us in touch with the divine, because they are themselves divine. The scope and generosity of Revard's intelligence are evident in his essay "Herbs of Healing," which serves as a form of keynote address for the anthology. Carter Revard's poems and prose remind us of our responsibility to this life, this earth.

*See also page 184, for Ruby Hansen Murray's testimony to the influence of Carter Revard's poem "Wazhazme Grandmother."

Indians Demand Equal Time with God

Angry Demonstrators at Funeral

Hey wait a minute—
        you guys that climbed God like
a ladder up to Rome, Zion,
                then Paris, London, Moscow
and Washington, D.C.—
        you're trying to tell us Osages that
he died in Nietzsche's lap, is embalmed
in Lenin's tomb, got shrunk on Sigmund's couch,
                that all his priest turned
        poets then defected to
                        Mad Avenue and worship
the brazen-faced Ms. Liberty?

        Listen, you dirty
        Majoritarians, kicking
                our ladder away
now you've got up, you ought to
                be advised that even old
Coyote comes back to life no matter what
        direction or how far your ladder falls.
                You think because
he sees right through you that he
                just isn't looking?
                        We're not looking
just for careers, fame, money, we want
        to stay alive; hearts die the minute
things aren't life or death, and when
                things die beliefs
                        go radioactive and
can kill with half-lives. But
                we're used to this, our stories
have often killed off God, their chromosomes
                play Job among the potsherds

of our pueblos all the time.
                    We won't let
you kill him even now before
                    we're ready.
        Until then,
                quit stepping on our fingers dammit—
they fit the ladder well enough.

        Look out, Big Dipper—here we come!

People from the Stars

John Joseph Matthews's The Osages, chapter 1

Wazhazhe come from the stars
        by their choice, not by falling
            or being thrown out
                    of the heavenly bars like Satan
                into Europe,
                        and we are invited back
                    whenever we may choose to go;
            but we joined the people of death
            and moved to another village
                            (we call it, Ho-e-ga)
        where time began; we made our fire places
            and made our bodies of
    the golden eagle and the cedar tree,
            of mountain lion and buffalo,
            of redbird, black bear, of the
    great elk and of thunder so that we
            may live to see old age
                and go back to the stars.
    Meantime, the Europeans pay us royalties
        for oil that lights their midnight highways
        dangling across the land in

                    star-strings through the night.
We trade our royalties for time enthroned
                on wings of shining metal
        to look down at the stars beneath
            or up at stars above
                            before we touch down in the desert
        creation of Las Vegas and wheel off
            to shoot craps at the Stardust Inn
    and talk of Indians and their Trickster Tales,
                of Manabozho up
                in Wounded Knee.

Driving in Oklahoma

On humming rubber along this white concrete,
lighthearted between the gravities
of source and destination like a man
halfway to the moon
in this bubble of tuneless whistling
at seventy miles an hour from the windvents,
over prairie swells rising
and falling, over the quick offramp
that drops to its underpass and the truck
thundering beneath as I cross
with the country music twanging out my windows,
I'm grooving down this highway feeling
technology is freedom's other name when
— a meadowlark
comes sailing across my windshield
with breast shining yellow
and five notes pierce
the windroar like a flash
of nectar on mind,
gone as the country music swells up and drops

me wheeling down
my notch of cement-bottomed sky
between home and away
and wanting
to move again through country that a bird
has defined wholly with song,
and maybe next time to see how
he flies so easy, when he sings.

Statement on Energy Policy

It's true we have invented quark-extraction,
and this allows our aiming gravity at will,
it's true also that time
can now be made to flow
backward or forward by

the same process. It may be true as well that
what is happening at the focal point,
the meristem of this process,
creates a future kind of space,
a tiny universe that has

quite different rules. In this, it seems,
whatever one may choose to do or be becomes
at once the case. In short,
we have discovered heaven and
it's in our grasp. However,

the Patent Office has not yet approved and cites
less positive aspects of this invention. First, it
does not generate profit, and
it does make obsolete all present
delivery systems for our nukes. Then,

it wil let private citizens do things that only
a chosen few, that is, OUR sort, should be allowed—
fly freely from one country
to any other, spreading diseases
and bankrupting transportation.

Home-heating, auto-making industries will be trashed,
employment shelled, depressions spread worldwide,
sheer anarchy descend.
For these and other reasons,
no one must know of this. . . .

HERBS OF HEALING: AMERICAN VALUES IN AMERICAN INDIAN LITERATURE

Minority/Majority Considerations

The history of empires is a funny thing, whether we are talking of literary or po-
litical empires. Six thousand years ago, two small "tribes" dwelt at the far margins
of great empires, and unknown elders within those tribes fashioned stories made
to create and preserve those tribes as communal wholes, to keep them in a good
relation to the transhuman powers of the universe, and to give them strength to
handle the great forces of empire that would destroy the special separate cultures
of those tribes. Versions of the stories which they fashioned have survived the fall
of the great empires—and those tribes, having canonized their stories and stayed
themselves by keeping them alive, now dominate Planet Earth economically and
culturally. One of those tribes, of course, was "Indo-European," the other was
"Hebrew." Much revised, reinterpreted, added onto in astonishing ways, the He-
brew stories are now the "Judeo-Christian Bible," while the Indo-European ones
include those of Homer, Shakespeare, Karl Marx, Charles Darwin, and Mark
Twain. I wonder which of the marginal tribes of this last decade of the Twentieth
Century of the Christian Messiah may now be composing the poetry which, six
thousand years from now, will energize our galaxy—and I wonder whether those
tribes now dwell on Planet Earth.

Culture-Wars

There are some Big Guns of American culture and politics who aim to shoot down "Minority Literature," claiming that it is trash unworthy of our classrooms, that conversing with it corrupts and keeps students from the uplifting morality of the "classical" books they ought to be spending time with.[1] Well (Gentle Readers), I want to introduce you to a few members of this family of monsters, so you can judge whether they are fit company for the next generation of Americans, to whom we stand *in loco parentis*. I will do this by setting certain "classic" poems beside others by contemporary American Indian writers, hoping this critical look will prove that the true values of American are just as vividly and richly present in the "ethnic" as in the classic poems. I think the comparison will show why American culture is enriched, not weakened, by opening the curriculum to these "new" regions of our heartland – regions which the Big Guns want us to think are deserts, but which I see as *lands of plenty, filled with herbs of healing*. To show this, I hope, may help end the war fomented by those old Gunslingers between "Minority Literature" and "Great Books." They want, being Gunslingers, to divide and conquer—but (I would ask) why shouldn't we unite, and live in freedom and plenty? Think what Columbus found, five hundred years ago, upon which we now feast, or with which we doctor ourselves: corn, potatoes, chocolate, pumpkins, potatoes, quinine, curare, as well as European wheat and whiskey; coyotes, raccoons, bison as well as imported Black Angus, Norway rats, and Arab steeds; bluejays and scissortails as well as English sparrows, starlings, and pigeons for the shoulders of our bronzed panjandrums. Don't we want an *All-American* curriculum?

Family Values

To begin, we will set a much-anthologized poem, a "modern classic" by Wallace Stevens (1879–1955), alongside one by Simon Ortiz (1941–) of Acoma Pueblo. These are small poems but they hold huge ideas: versions of America itself. Stevens's "Anecdote of the Jar," first published in 1923, has been given much commentary.[2] No such attention has yet been given "Speaking," published in the 1970s.[3]

Anecdote of the Jar

I placed a jar in Tennessee,
And round it was, upon a hill,
It made the slovenly wilderness
Surround that hill.
The wilderness rose up to it,
And sprawled around no longer
    wild.
The jar was round upon the
    ground,
And tall and of a port in air.
It took dominion everywhere.
The jar was gray and bare
It did not give of bird or bush,
Like nothing else in Tennessee.[4]

Speaking

I take him outside
under the trees,
have him stand on the ground.
We listen to the crickets,
Cicadas, million years old sound.
Ants come by us.
I tell them,
"This is he, my son.
This boy is looking at you.
I am speaking for him.

The crickets, cicadas
the ants, the millions of years
are watching us.
My son murmurs infant words,
speaking, small laughter
bubbles from him.
Tree leaves tremble.
They listen to this boy
speaking for me.

Stevens's poem is a terse fable, a kind of bonsai version of how Art conquers and indeed enslaves Nature, or Reality. It is hard to say whether Stevens approves, disapproves, or takes an ironically detached view of this conquest. The poem certainly speaks in a Conqueror's voice, saying just what many American historians have said (with no irony intended) about "civilizing" the "American Wilderness," and compelling deference from its natives. Round, tall, and with an important air, this non-natural Jar defines Wilderness as *slovenly*, effortlessly tames it so that it "sprawl[s] around, no longer wild," as the jar assumes imperial power "everywhere." Only in the last three lines does Stevens seem to turn his irony against the Jar, describing it as "gray and bare," as not allowing any sense of Nature or Vegetation, and showing up the whole of "Tennessee" as being UNlike the Jar—which indeed is "like nothing else in Tennessee."

There is, then, and Idea of Art and America in this poem—and the idea, I think, is as purple, showy and poisonous as loco-weed. Perhaps Stevens is himself appalled or ironically critical of this Empire of Abstract Ideas and the Jar which is their Centurion—yet the poem exalts the magic of Abstraction and Power which enslaves Tennessee and its creatures. One of the poem's crimes, indeed, is its dandiacal condescending to the great abstract "state" of Tennessee—which, before that Jar arrived, was some sort of Tabula Rasa, but after its arrival is cowed into cooliedom, kowtowing to the Imperial—nay, the DIVINE!—Artist. Just one bit of European Craft, wrought by a single sly-and handy poet, has turned an entire country into a subdued and self-alienated place, where his Viceroy refuses all resemblance to any "native" being!

It is of course a "classic" European notion that setting a Jar—or a Cross, or a Crown, or a Write—upon a hill allows one to "take possession" of the whole "territory" surrounding that artifact. What bothers me most, I think, is that Stevens does not really put any America around his Jar. It was Gertrude Stein who wittily complained about Oakland, "There is no THERE, there!" In Stevens's poem, there is no Tennessee in Tennessee: what's "there" is an Easterner's idea that "culture stops at the Hudson" (a phrase actually spoken to me once, with amused seriousness, by a professor of German at Amherst College).[5] Here the European Modern has throned itself at the continent's center, destroying any possible alternative: has, in short, "civilized" America.

But there IS an alternative, and Simon Ortiz has given us an Acoma story that counters this "classic" one. His poem, "Speaking," like Stevens's "Anecdote," is short and profound. Its ideas of America, of Art, of Nature and Humanity, are no less heroic in size, but lack the pompous arrogance, the neurofibromatosis of the artistic ego, which mask the Stevens poem.

One crucial difference is that Ortiz puts two humans into his poem, a father and his son. The poet himself is just as powerfully "there" as in Stevens—but whereas Stevens makes the Jar his Viceroy, Ortiz acts as Intercessor for his son, speaking "for" the infant to the powerful, ancient, and enduring beings whom this poem calls to our awareness. Then Ortiz is in turn "spoken for" by his infant son, whose language is after all older than that of his father, and whose "speaking" is listened to by those future generations to whom, eventually, he will indeed "speak for" his father.

And here we touch the nub of our comparison: it is FAMILY VALUES which dominate the Ortiz poem, *and the family in question is more than human.* "Anecdote of the Jar" narrates conquest, enslavement, culture-wars, class alienation, war between the Civil and the Natural, all as a result of the poet's imagined action. In "Speaking," the poet is not alone, not alienating himself by language or art, but using speech within a family, introducing his new son to other members of that family: trees, ground, crickets, cicadas, ants, and—in a startling leap— Time itself, the "millions of years." As the title tells us, this poem is about the human act of speaking, not just the high-culture *art* of speech or poetry, which is only one part of that more profound act. Here, the act of speaking and the art of listening work together in a mutual effort to gain understanding, support, and blessing for a fruitful life on earth. More remarkably, the poem discovers for its composer that his son's first speech to this great family is as deeply meaningful and important as anything his father can say. That a child's voice utters itself, that it is heard, is after all the most important human truth celebrated in the poem: to continue, to keep the human race alive, is more important than whatever the father might have uttered at that point. Implicitly, the poem humbles its poet AND us, tells us that our best speaking begins with, depends upon, is like that of the tiniest infant in this great universe.

So the idea of America in Ortiz's poem is truly a healing reminder of what is amiss in the remarkable poem by Stevens, where abstraction disdainfully dominates nature. The English of Ortiz is no less metaphysically sophisticated than that of Stevens, but it is "ordinary" English not "artful," it sounds like plain speech, not highfalutin rhetoric. As Wordsworth said in his Preface to the *Lyrical Ballads*, it is the language of real men speaking with deep feeling and not falling into "poetic diction." The result is a sense that Ortiz is just telling us a real story, what happened, what he did, what was said. In the poem, the poet stands not imperiously but humbly, not as lord of all he surveys but as an Acoma father, one member only of this realm of beings, conscious and respectful of those others we might scarcely notice "outside" our homes, including Time itself listening to the child as well as the father. This is no "talking possession" but a ritual of acknowledging smallness and dependency, fellowship and community, shared natural being. Stevens diagnoses an illness, Ortiz enacts a cure.

Speaking of Massacres

Human beings, however, do not always "share natural being" so nicely as the Ortiz poem shows them doing. John Milton (1608–1674), for instance, lived in interesting times, when one tribe of Europeans was apt to massacre another on religious grounds if no strictly economic or political excuse came handy. In 1655, certain Catholic troopers in the Savoy Alps slaughtered a large number of Protestant men, women, and babies, whereupon Milton—a Protestant—wrote a magnificent sonnet of protest, saying some pretty nasty things about the Pope and his forces.[6] Three and a half centuries afterwards, in 1890, a slaughter of similar brutality was carried out in Wounded Knee, South Dakota, by troopers of the U.S. Seventh Cavalry (George Custer's regiment)—their motive for massacre being also, in part, religious: the Lakotas slaughtered there were engaging in a forbidden religious ritual (the "Ghost Dance"), and the Lakota were not merely "heretics" but "heathens." In the 1970s (some four-score and seven years later), the Hopi/Miwok poet Wendy Rose wrote a protest, Miltonic in its eloquence though not in its rhetoric, against the Wounded Knee Massacre. Let's see what we can learn from these two poems, starting with John Milton's sonnet.[7]

On the Late Massacre in Piedmont

Avenge, O Lord, thy slaughtered saints, whose bones
Lie scattered on the Alpine mountains cold –
Even them who kept thy truth so pure of old,
When all our fathers worshipped stocks and stones!
Forget not: in thy Book record their groans
Who were thy sheep, and in their ancient fold
Slain by the bloody Piedmontese, that rolled
Mother with infant down the rocks; their moans
The vales redoubled to the hills, and they
To heaven. Their martyred blood and ashes sow
O'er all the Italian fields, where still doth sway
The Triple Tyrant: that from these may grow
A hundred fold, who having learnt thy Way,
Early may fly the Babylonian woe!

When I talk with students about this poem, I speak of its biblical majesty of sound, of the history that lies behind and within it, its political commitment, the effective propaganda in its picture of mother and baby as they are brutally, callously, sadistically ROLLED down the steep Alpine slopes on those rocks. I marvel at how vividly we hear what happens in these mountain vales, the echoing moans of pain and screams of terror as women clinging to their babies are jerked, thrown, shoved over the precipices to fall down and down onto rocks below, how precisely Milton recreates in the poem's rhythm and cadences what the soldiers did. Then I try to say how much more powerful the poem becomes, how its words light up, when we connect them to their biblical reservoirs of prophetic rage, the thunderous lines of Isaiah, of the Psalms, of the book of Revelations. But I make sure we all remember, in all this, where the poem "comes out" in the end: not in a call for God to slaughter the Catholics in return for their slaughter of Protestants, but in a call for God to RECORD the martyrdom and SPREAD THE NEWS of it, so that the blood of these martyrs will become the seed of a hundred times as many new believers converted by such unjustified suffering. These new Protestants will thereafter, having learned God's true Way, FLEE the coming destruction of the Roman church, which Milton refers to as a *Babylonian woe*—that is, the kind of woe suffered by the citizens of ancient Babylon when it fell, as described in Old and New Testaments. Milton expects his readers to know both the canonical books of the Bible, and the contemporary political uses of that canon. It is a very beautiful poem, majestic in its wrath, angelic in its compassion, apostolic in its looking toward an ultimate triumph of the despised and suffering minority to which its writer belongs.

For let me repeat: though the poem seems at first to call down the wrath of God upon the Roman Catholics, in the end it steadfastly awaits God's grace to draw these criminals into the faith of those they are murdering, and expresses hope that the converted people will then manage to flee the inevitable destruction which (Milton implies) will strike down this "Babylon" – this great imperial city of the Triple Tyrant. We have to see that Milton's great flashing thunderclouds call a gentle rain of mercy down from heaven, not just the thunder and lighting of prophetic wrath.

And now let us look at Wendy Rose's poem of protest:

I Expected My Blood and My Skin to Ripen

When the blizzard subsided four days later, a burial party was sent to Wounded Knee. A long trench was dug, Many of the bodies were stripped...to get the ghost shirts...the frozen bodies were thrown into the trench stiff and naked...only a handful of items remain in private hands...exposure to snow has stiffened the leggings and moccasins, and all the object show the effects of age and long use..." [There follows:] Moccasins at $140, hid scraper at $350, buckskin shirt at $1200, woman's leggings at $275, bone breastplate at $1000. —Plains Indian Art: Sales Catalog by Kenneth Canfield, 1977

I expected my blood and my skin

to ripen,
not to be ripped from my bones;
like green fruit I am peeled,
tasted, discarded; my seeds are stepped on
and crushed
as if there were no future. Now
there has been
no past. My own body gave up the beads,
my own arms handed the babies away
to be strung on bayonets, to be counted
one by one like rosary stones and then
to be tossed to each side of life
as if the pain of their borning
had never been.
My feet were frozen to the leather,
pried apart, left behind — bits of flesh
on the moccasins, bits of papery deerhide
on the bones. My back was stripped
of its cover, its quilling intact; was torn,
was taken away, was restored.
My leggings were taken like in a rape
and shriveled to the size of stick figures
like they had never felt
the push of my strong woman's body
walking in the hills.
It was my own baby whose cradleboard I held.
Would've put her in my mouth
like a snake
if I could, would've turned her
into a bush or old rock
if there'd been enough magic
to work such changes. Not enough magic
even to stop the bullets.
Not enough magic
to stop the scientists.
Not enough magic
to stop the collectors.[8]

Rose's poem differs much from Milton's. His is spoken in the poet's own voice; hers is a dramatic monologue spoken a long time after the Wounded Knee massacre by one of the women killed there. Milton's poem says nothing of the economic forces involved in the Catholic/Protestant wars, though his "Lycidas" and prose tracts had shown his keen awareness of ecclesiastical corruptions in his time. But Wendy Rose prefaces her poem with a prose bit taken from a sales catalog written as guide to buyers and sellers of "Indian artifacts," some of which apparently were taken from corpses at Wounded Knee in 1890. The catalog offers quite a perspective on the teaching of American History in our schools. That the items described could be displayed, bought and sold on the open market, has its own grisly interest. To ask a controversial but (I think) relevant question, would it be possible to catalogue and sell a collection of souvenirs from Belsen, Dachau, or Auschwitz, and not draw a firestorm of outrage from a wide range of United States citizens? The answer to that question might explain why we may build in Washington, D.C., a monument to the Holocaust carried out in Europe by the Germans, but none to the many exterminations on this continent by the United States.

Though Rose's poem has for remote ancestor the biblical laments, it seems closer to the Martyr's Speech, particularly the Lament of Mary, Mother of Jesus. Perhaps the Middle English *Stond well, mother, under Rood* would have been the nearest "classic" poem for comparison—but it goes better with the historically parallel sonnet by Milton, which likewise concerns a particular slaughter for religious (and politico-economic) reasons of a minority group. One great difference between Rose and Milton is that she does not have his confidence that the martyrs' cause will prevail. Her speaker is defeated and lacks the tacit consolation apparent in Milton that form each of the martyred persons there will grow a multitude of "descendants" who will keep to the right way until the Apocalypse. She lacks, too, any sense that this painful death will allow her people to gain some sort of paradise, or regain America as the Ghost Dance had promised. Behind Rose's poem, no scripture looms; it forms its own canon. Milton calls on God; Rose's unvoiced appeal is to her readers, to do the right thing to those who acted and still act against her people.

Rose expects her readers to know the history of Wounded Knee, and to have some remaining belief that what we call Art is linked in some way to the ethical and spiritual aspects of life, not solely to the monetary. As a medievalist, I know that cathedrals were built, in considerable part, by money drawn from saint-seeking tourists: religion, art, money are not separate from each other in

Christian history. But it is less clear how the sufferings of women and children at Wounded Knee are related to the ART of that sales catalog, that "history" of the Collectors, the Museums, the Archaeologists and Scientists. And the only word Rose has for the Indian side of the encounter is MAGIC – not just that of the Ghost Dance, though including it. When I talk about this poem with students, one of the things I point to is the power of her final section's repeating the phrase, "not enough magic to stop . . . ," and how the "enemy list" builds to that final horror, from *bullets* to *scientists* to *collectors*. And with that last term, the poet has come full circle from its epigraph and made its point with the most poignant irony.

Men and Women: Garden and Wilderness

For our third pairing we have a complex sonnet by Robert Frost ("Never Again Would Birds' Song Be the Same") and a vivid, disturbing poem by Louise Erdrich ("Jacklight"). They are subtle in different ways about the relations between men and women: Frost puts a spin on the myth of Eden and our First Parents Adam and Eve, while Erdrich begins with the macho world of deerhunters (who use jacklights to mesmerize their prey) and turns it into the mythic world of Deer Woman (who lures men into a kind of Underworld). Here, first, is Frost's sonnet:

Never Again Would Birds' Song Be the Same

He would declare and could himself believe
That the birds there in all the garden round
From having heard the daylong voice of Eve
Had added to their own an oversound,
Her tone of meaning but without the words.
Admittedly an eloquence so soft
Could only have had an influence on birds
When call or laughter carried it aloft.
Be that as may be, she was in their song.
Moreover her voice upon their voices crossed
Had now persisted in the woods so long
That probably it never would be lost.
Never again would birds' song be the same.
And to do that to birds was why she came.[9]

And here, next, is Erdrich's poem:

Jacklight

The same Chippewa word is used both for flirting and hunting game, while another Chippewa word connotes both using force in intercourse and also killing a bear with one's bare hands. —R.W. Dunning, Social and Economic Change among the Northern Chippewa (1959)

We have come to the edge of the woods,
out of brown grass where we slept, unseen,
out of knotted twigs, out of leaves creaked shut,
out of hiding.

At first the light wavered, glancing over us.
Then it clenched to a fist of light that pointed,
searched out, divided us.
Each took the beams like direct blows the heart answers.
Each of us moved forward alone.

We have come to the edge of the woods,
drawn out of ourselves by this night sun,
this battery of polarized acids,
that outshines the moon.

We smell them behind it
but they are faceless, invisible.
We smell the raw steel of their gun barrels,
mink oil on leather, their tongues of sour barley.
We smell their mothers buried chin-deep in wet dirt.
We smell their fathers with scoured knuckles,
teeth cracked from hot marrow.
We smell their sisters of crushed dogwood, bruised apples,
of fractured cups and concussions of burnt hooks.

We smell their breath steaming lightly behind the jacklight.
We smell the itch underneath the caked guts on their clothes.

We smell their minds like silver hammers
cocked back, held in readiness
for the first of us to step into the open.

We have come to the edge of the woods,
out of brown grass where we slept unseen,
out of leaves creaked shut out of our hiding.
We have come here too long.

It is their turn now
their turn to follow us. Listen,
they put down their equipment.
It is useless in the tall brush.
And now they take the first steps, not knowing
how deep the woods are and lightless.
How deep the woods are.[10]

Frost's sonnet, as I read it, is a love poem, delicately praising the way the natural unfallen voice of one human being has given the whole world a hidden reservoir of partly human, partly animal music.[11] Erdrich's is a poem about sexual confrontation as well as the conflicts in American culture between human and animal, technological and natural—and it may hint at whites "preying on" American Indians as well.

In Frost's sonnet, someone (the poet? A son of Adam and Eve?) "reports" to us what Adam used to say about the way Eve's voice has become "an oversound," which lives on in the song of birds now that (the reporter implies) Eve herself is no longer with us. As Adam asserts in the poem's last two lines, "Never again would birds' song be the same. / And to do that to the birds was why she came." Frost has carefully distanced himself, not only front the Adam who thus reminisces, but from whichever daughter or son of Adam reports the reminiscing. More subtly, Frost has that reporter keep his or her own distance, remarking with wry amusement that HE (Adam, not the reporter) would declare such things. And even Adam seems to be mildly skeptical, since we are not told he *actually believed*, but only that he *could himself believe* what he is saying. So the reporter seems to be hinting wry disbelief or even cynical doubt of any truth in Adam's fancy: it was, well, the sort of thing Adam would say when he was going on about how wonderful things were in the *good* old days. In short, Frost's poem hedges

Adam's fancy with so many thickets of skepticism, amused doubt, lightly patronizing headshakes, that the reader must suspect this Adam is pretty well past it, an old man telling tall tales that he has begun to take more seriously now that he is growing senilely sentimental.

Yet through all these ironic thorns, so carefully planted by Frost around his adamant fancy, there wafts a certain Edenic fragrance. The rhetorical hedges have been planted to guard a private space, not to institutionalize Adam as a loony old liar. Frost is a very subtle and tricky poet and easier to under-read than his sunlit words make it seem. His poem, however wondrous its spins and twists and leaps of poetic rhetoric, is charged with intense and yearning love for a woman who has changed the way the whole universe presents itself to him. This most shy and private man gets it both ways: any sensitive reader who has tried to celebrate his beloved without being a kiss-and-tell fool or (worse) a sentimental pretender, will admire Frost's managing to tell the whole world what he feels with such humorous indirection that he could walk out of any courtroom unconvicted even though the jury would know the poem's "He" is really the poet's "I" in ambush. "He would declare," the poem begins: only after a rereading or two do we realize that this "He" is Adam speaking of Eve, and only after a few more readings do we understand that it is also Robert Frost speaking of his wife.[12] I know no more poignant love poem in English than this, and I would forgive any mistake in tone this poet might have made anywhere—and critics are fond of finding them, or inventing if necessary—for this wonderful sonnet. At any rate—so it seems to me—Frost gives us a beautiful and comforting reminder of what love in the Western tradition might once have been like.

Erdrich, in contrast, gives us a vivid and disturbing reminder of how unlike this ideal the relations between men and women too often are. Her poem's speakers seem to be the animals (for simplicity I will call them "deer") being hunted by humans with the help of a jacklight—illegal but effective since the deer are hypnotized and come slowly and hesitantly out of the dark woods toward the hunters' guns. But when the deer get close enough to smell the hunters, what they learn is not just about these male hunters, but about their women, families, relationships. The deer smell guns, mink-oiled boots, beer-tainted breath; but they also smell the oppressed mothers of these men, their overworked and defeated fathers ("teeth cracked from hot marrow" suggests that the fathers too were hunters, but that the excesses have damaged them), their abused sisters. Something sinister (from the point of view of the hunters) is going on here: the deer are "walking in their souls," learning the nature of their lives beyond this hunting relationship. Even though the deer are sensing the cocked guns, it is to those cocked minds ("like silver hammers"), ready to send a bullet into the first deer to step into the open, that the deer are paying sharpest attention.

And now the poem, and this relationship, begin to turn around. When the speaker, for the third time, says, *We have come to the edge of the woods*, and describes once more, as if hypnotized, where they have come from, "out of our hiding," this time she follows with a very different assertion: *We have come here too long.* For anyone reading this poem aloud, here is the place to change the voice from tranced to grimly alert, here is where the speaker begins to take charge of the situation. "It is their turn now, / their turn to follow us," the woods-creature says—and if I were reading this aloud, I would want to sound like the Godfather making an offer not to be refused: a quiet, deadly, utterly assured tone is what we should hear in these last sentences as the deer describe how the mesmeric hunters have themselves been hypnotized.

And at this point we may wonder just what these "woods" ARE, into which Erdrich's creatures are luring the hunters. Recalling Stevens's "slovenly wilderness," we may think these woods are that very wilderness, rising up like Tecumseh against its "possessors"; and there is partial truth to this. That is, Erdrich's hunters, though more honkytonking Cowboys than hoity-toity Conquistadores, are "talking dominion" just as arrogantly as did Stevens's Jar. It is clear from Erdrich's epigraph that a main theme of her poem will be ways in which male contempt for women is shown in both language and customs of hunting, whether practiced at deer-stand or bar-stool, with jacklight or strobe lights. So luring deer to the jacklight becomes a figure for the luring of women to the sexual encounter, in both cases to "score," or as one might say in Chippewa (according to Dunning as cited by Erdrich in the epigraph to "Jacklight") to "use force in intercourse" or to "kill a bear with one's bare hands"—we need not try to cite the English slang equivalents of these Chippewa terms, but if we recall macho terms for dealing sexually with women we know there are such equivalents.

I have not paired Frost and Erdrich to put down one or the other, but I do think that alongside Erdrich's Honkytonk Horror-Babes we may see Frost's Edenic portrait of Woman—her voice so "soft" that only when she is calling out or laughing does it reach the birds in the treetops—as offering a few too many sweets to the sweet. But it is perhaps also true that Erdrich's Life-on-the-Rez portrait of Macho Man Unmanned is less a poem of healing than a celebration of power, and power used to capture and control – a reversal rather than finding a good way. Still, I like the way each poem does its thing, and the thing each poem does.

Old English, New English: Unriddling America

I want now to do something immodest: to show that it is possible for a contemporary poet —in this case, myself—to use the "classical" forms of English poetry to "say things" about this world, now, and yet (I hope) be readable. It happens that my Irish and Scotch-Irish mother's father, shortly before he died, told me to go to college (he himself had got only into the third grade when he had to drop out and work on his father's farm in the Ozarks). I admired and loved my grandfather greatly—he was always good to me, good to work alongside, good to go on walks with, a man who never lied, and though he could act a fool when he drank too much, a man whose judgment was trusted by everybody most of the time and whose heart was trusted at all times. So when Aleck Camp told me to go to college, they would have had to kill me to prevent it; and of course nobody tried to stop me, everybody did what was possible to help me. But we had no money, nobody in the family had been to college, and getting there was no sure or easy thing.

Still, I made it. That is, a lot of people lifted me up to that dazzling window and cheered me for climbing through it. And once I got to college and jumped through the necessary hoops to clothe myself in a sheepskin, the great teachers at the University of Tulsa put me up for a Rhodes Scholarship and that was given me and so I got over to Oxford University, and to get the B.A. in English Literature there I had to study Old English language and literature, had to learn how the Old English alliterative meter works, had to memorize accidence and morphology and phonology and all that, so we could read *Beowulf* and *Dream of the Rood* and other poems. Later, in Yale Graduate School, I wrote a dissertation on Middle English alliterative poetry, and since then have taught History of the English Language and medieval literature a lot.

And one semester—you probably wondered where all this was going, and here I hope you will see it is getting to the point—I had to fill in for a younger teacher, Tom Goodman, who is much better at Old English than I am, when he was called out of town that day, and the class that day happened to be considering some of the Old English poems called Riddles. With these I had a nodding acquaintance, had worked through some of the less tough ones. But now suddenly I had to face a group of students and not disgrace myself while talking with them about the "Book" and "Swan," and others of the Riddles in which whatever creature the poet taps must tell the listener/reader in enigmatic ways its life story. Here, for instance, is the magnificent "Swan," who speaks to us from the *Exeter Book* (written around A.D. 950–1000), as I translate its chant:

The Swan's Song

Garbed in silence	I go on earth,
dwell among men	or move on the waters.
Yet far over halls	of heroes in time
my robes and the high	air may raise
and bear me up	in heaven's power
over all nations.	My ornaments then
are singing glories	and I go in song
bright as a star	unstaying above
the world's wide waters,	a wayfaring soul.

It would be a grave mistake to think one had "solved" the riddle of this poem by saying, "Swan!" The Old English poet surely meant us not just to listen to each clue as the poem unfolds, and gradually deduce who is speaking to us here. We certainly are meant to go through that process, to observe that this creature telling its life story lives in silence among human beings or on the water; but then it takes to the air, rises far above human habitations and looks down from that height on those, even the most heroic of them, dwelling below; and when it moves at that height its ornaments (which the Old English original implies are the same as its "robes") "sing" and "shine," so that in flight it moves in glory that is beyond the mortal heroes on earth. And we are surely meant to see with astonishment in the poem's last few words that this earth-mute, heaven-musical traveler is a pilgrim soul. That is, everything in the poem comes together in those last few words, and we see this "swan" is an emblem of the immortal soul which in its flesh is relatively mute and slow and likely to be held of little account, but when it rises to its heavenly destination makes part of the angelic choir, going in glorious music toward the throne of God, its wayfaring at last reaching that place of power and beauty far beyond the palaces and thrones of human monarchs and heroes.

In translating, I have pretty much kept Old English alliterative meter: each line has two half-lines, each half-line has two strong stresses. So every line will have at least four stresses, and at least two of these must alliterate. It is the number three stress—that is, the first stress of the second half-line—which is the key to any line: stress 3 *must* alliterate with either 1 or 2, or with both of them. In "The Swan," for instance, line 1 alliterates on the /g/ of stresses 1 and 3: GARBED *in Silence I GO on earth*. In line 8, the alliterative stresses are 2 and 3 (*bright as a*

STAR unSTAYing above), although there is extra alliteration also between stresses 1 and 4 (*BRIGHT, ABOVE*), an effect I like more than did Old English poets, probably.

But now comes the immodest part: I want to show you this old Anglo-Saxon poetic form is still alive, will still blossom and fruit if planted deep and watered from Indian springs. What has to be done is the same as with any ancient form: treat it with respect, not as entertainment but as revelation. I have said elsewhere that the Old English poems usually called "riddles" are meant to call before the reader certain astonishing created beings in this universe and let them speak their spiritual dimensions, cleanse the doors of perception and bare the witty ligatures by which things are put together, held together, pass into and out of human comprehension.[13] The Old English poet gives them their voices and lets them re-member themselves for us, coax us into re-cognizing them. If we want to write a "New English" Riddle, we need to try and give the creatures of our time such voices and dimensions, we have to realize that in our everyday life there are amazing and mysterious convergings of power and mystery: as Wordsworth said in his great Immortality Ode, we are "moving about in worlds not realized." If a house spoke its being, it would tell of its power to summon the dead Beethoven's majestic music, or the ghosts of dead movie stars to dance or machine-gun or sing us to sleep; any house could tell us how within it the great rivers rise to our lips in drinkable water, spray over our heads in cleansing coolness, flush away the grime and filth of our daily lives. Or we could ask a Television Set—say a Sony from Japan—to speak its mundane mysteries to us:

On this azure eyeball
its monstrous mushrooms,
as the holster hardened
from barrels of black
on floating steel
through a gate of gold,
to an iron horse
unpacked me and pinned
a long tail, tipped
A woman acquired me,
set me high on an altar
drove Dracula teeth
touched me until

where hell twice raised
my mind's eye opened
for its hot ghost-gun
dinosaur-blood; shortly,
men steered me eastward
gave me then
that hauled me here,
upon my backside
with metallic teeth.
carried me home,
for adoration,
into tight joyholes,
she turned me on –

I reached into heaven	and handed her down
from its ether Caruso's	heart in a clown-suit,
spread time at her toes	like a tiger's skin
until she yawned,	touched me again,
and I went blind.	I bless FAR-SEERS
who know my name	and now will speak it!

I have followed the Old English poets in using enigmatic metaphors ("kennings") like *azure eyeball* for Planet Earth, and *monstrous mushrooms* for the bomb-clouds over Hiroshima and Nagasaki. I "transfigured" the TV's cathode-ray tube as a "hot ghost-gun"—it "shoots" arrays of electrons at a "target" screen and evokes "ghosts"; in fact, since actors and historical figures on our TV screens often are long dead, their TV icons are ghosts as nearly "real" as we can live with. And since the TV case or frame is made of plastic from polymerized petroleum, I figure it as "holster" for a "ghost-gun," and call the oil "dinosaur-blood"—not much of a far-fetch, considering the old green dinosaur on the Sinclair signs: advertising people are more poetic than plenty of our poets.

The poem won't "work" unless readers have fun figuring it out—not only as a kind of game but as a way of getting into what marvelous magical things a TV set really is and does. Poems, like jokes, work best if they don't need explaining, but unlike jokes they can be effective more than once (though differently)—and even, I would claim, *after* being explained.[14] The old *Reader's Digest* pieces are not so far from the Old English Riddles: "I am Joe's Kidney," for instance. And the poem ought to do something else besides give a Nintendo-like play-pleasure; it ought to be informative, the reader ought to come away saying: Well, that's true, I see some things now better than before, and maybe some things I didn't see before—things look a little different, a little clearer and interlocking now. Teach and delight, as Horace said: that's what I sort of hoped would happen once the reader got through the more simple "floating steel" (the paradox of those huge steel ships, which we forget "ought" never to float) and Golden Gate and Iron Horse, and fetched up on that tail and its teeth. I hoped the teasing and fun of what the woman was doing was like what some of the Old English poets did with their double entendres, and I hoped those Dracula teeth in "joyholes" would be clear enough metaphors for the plug and socket. After all, we get a lot of joy—or we expect to—from those electric outlets in our living rooms.

Then I "reversed" the usual direction of the metaphoric shift when the TV says the woman "touched me until she turned me on"—to "turn on" somebody was to a cliché of Beats and Hippies, so I had fun letting a TV speak it literally of itself. And once "turned on" a TV does literally "reach into heaven" to collect its images, it "hands down" from the "ether" an old recording of, say, Caruso singing in *I Pagliacci*, so that a TV set "kills" time, makes a "trophy" of it like a tiger-skin. I thought that notion might justify the TV's saying it "spread time like a tiger's skin" at the feet of the woman viewing such old scenes. (Yes, the old rhyme about Elinor Glyn was running through my head at that point: "Would you rather sin / With Elinor Glyn / On a tiger skin . . . ?") And last, I had fun translating the Greek/Latin TELE- ("far") VISION ("seeing") into FAR-SEERS, telly-veiwers. The in-joke here is that an Old English poet might "give away" the solution to one of these "riddles" by writing its name in ancient runes instead of the Latin-derived alphabet used for most of the poem. So FAR-SEER in capital letters is a clue to this riddle's "solution"—*TV SET*.

But Old English poetic form will hold less technology-driven points. So let me end this essay with one short and one slightly longer example of how I have tired to use the alliterative Riddle genre, adapting WAS poetics for American Indian themes and purposes.[15] Here is the short piece, which I hope needs no commentary:

Birch Canoe

Red men embraced   my body's whiteness,
cutting into me   carved it free,
sewed it tight   with sinews taken
from lightfoot deer   who leaped this stream –
now in my ghost-skin   they glide over clouds
at home in the fish's   fallen heaven.

And finally, I have tried to compose one Riddle in gratitude for the gift of eagle feathers, given me by Bob and Evelyne Voelker when I was elected to the Board of Directors of the American Indian Center of Mid-America. I asked a friend, Dale Besse, to bead these into an Eagle Fan, which I carry when I dance; since the late 1970s I have been a Gourd Dancer. The poem tells how an eagle in flight pierces clouds just as a beadworker's needle goes through beads and the white buckskin of the fan's handle spiraling round sky and fan; and how the eagle flies from dawn to sunset, linking colors of day and night as they are linked on a Gourd Dancer's blanket (half crimson, half blue), and just as they are beaded onto the handle of the Eagle Fan. In the poem, ordinary things are given mysterious names: tree leaves are green light-dancers, wood is tree-heart or ash-heart, clouds are thrones of thunder-beings. Readers may like to name for themselves what I have called a "one-eyed serpent with silver-straight head."

What the Eagle Fan Says

For the Voelkers, the Besses, and all the Dancers

I strung dazzling thrones   of thunder beings
on a spiraling thread   of spinning flight,
beading dawn's blood   and blue of noon
to the gold and dark   of day's leaving,
circling with Sun   the soaring heaven
over turquoise eyes   of Earth below,
her silver veins,   her sable fur,
heard human relatives   hunting below
calling me down,   crying their need
that I bring them closer   to Wakonda's ways,
and I turned from heaven   to help them then.
When the bullet came,   it caught my heart,
the hunter's hands   gave earth its blood,
loosened light beings   and let us float
toward the sacred center   of song in the drum,
but fixed us first   firm in song-home
that green light-dancers   gave to men's knives,
ash-heart in hiding where   deer-heart had beat,
and a one-eyed serpent   with silver-straight head
strung tiny rattles   around white softness
in beaded harmonies   of blue and red –
lightly I move now   in a man's left hand,
above dancing feet   follow the sun
around old songs   soaring toward heaven
on human breath,   and I help them rise.

Herbs of Healing

Not all healing herbs are sweet, and I have had some bitter observations to make in the discussions above. But I hope that it will be with us as with Peter Rabbit and his siblings: the chamomile tea on the one hand, and the fresh blackberries and bread and milk on the other, are surely the right medicine in each case. I hope readers will have found the sweet and nourishing, the bitter and healing, in some measure in this essay. We are talking about a so far undiscovered country, five hundred years after Columbus mistook it for Japan or China or India or the Earthly Paradise. We are talking about some undiscovered writers whose work is good for this America. I wish you the joy of it.

Notes

1. I am thinking of Allen Bloom, George Will, Dinesh D'Souza and their sort, whose approach to literary and cultural matters reminds me of words put by clever Oxonians into the mouth of the great Plato scholar Benjamin Jowett: *Here am I, my name is Jowett: / There is no knowledge but I know it. / I am the Master of this College — / What I know is not knowledge.* Or, again, they are like Jim arguing with Huck Finn about whether French is a human language or not: "Is a Chicano—or Black, or American Indian—REALLY an American? Then why doesn't he SPEAK like an American?" By their standards, of course, Mark Twain had no business letting the narrator of his greatest book speak in the vulgar uneducated English of a grade-school dropout, which obviously cannot be used to communicate anything to such educated persons as our cultural guardians.

2. See, for instance, Frank Lentricchia's brilliant discussion in *Ariel and the Police: Michel Foucault, William James, Wallace Stevens* (University of Wisconsin Press, 1988), 3–27.

3. "Speaking" has been republished in Simon J. Ortiz, *Woven Stone* (University of Arizona Press, 1992).

4. Wallace Stevens, "Anecdote of the Jar" in *Wallace Stevens: The Collected Poems* (Alfred A. Knopf, 1954), 76.

5. What I said was, "I *had* noticed that culture stops at the Hudson, but I'm from Oklahoma—I'll bring some over to you, if Massachusetts Customs allow it."

6. Milton, it must be said, made no known protest against the slaughter by Oliver Cromwell's men of the Irish Catholic women, children, and men who surrendered the besieged towns of Drogheda and Wexford, not long before the massacre of Protestants in the Piedmont. What WE do is a military necessity; what THEY do is a massacre.

7. I have modernized spelling and punctuation of Milton's text. Though written in 1655, it was not published until 1673—a year before Milton died, by which time King Charles II was no longer trying to imprison or execute him for having helped, in 1649, to overthrow and execute Charles's father. In 1673, the sonnet would still wake echoes of the deadly Civil War of thirty years before, and its protest was highly relevant to the current political situation: Charles II was secretly Catholic and receiving illegal financial support from the French tyrant Louis XIV, while the English Parliament in 1673 would pass the Test Act by which both Catholics and Puritans were excluded from holding any civil or military office. Milton's protest against minority-bashing was thus published in a year when the restored English monarchy was conniving to make Catholicism the state religion

and the restored English parliament was excluding both Catholics and Puritans from power.

8. Wendy Rose, "I Expected My Blood and My Skin to Ripen" in *Lost Copper* (Malki Museum Press, 1980), 14–15.

9. Robert Frost, "Never Again Would Bird's Song Be the Same" in *A Witness Tree* (Henry Holt, 1942).

10. Louise Erdrich, "Jacklight" in *Jacklight* (Holt, Rinehart, and Winston, 1984), 1–2.

11. A colleague I respect has suggested that however Frost treats women in the poem, he does patronize the birds by suggesting that since Eve arrived all bird-music has taken on a human over-sound. It's a good point, worth raising with students in an American Indian Literature class—though in Indian stories the lines between bird and human run differently.

12. I used to associate this sonnet with Frost's lyric "Come In," in which he tells of passing along the edge of the woods at dusk, hearing from the woods a thrush's final song before dark, and of being tempted to go into the dark woods himself and "lament" — but he refuses the temptation saying "No, I was out for stars, / I would not come in. / I meant not, even if asked, / And I hadn't been." I thought that in the lyric, printed not long after the death of Frost's wife, the bird sounded like the spirit of Frost's wife calling him to join her, a call which Frost, independent and skeptic to the last, held back from, both because he wanted more of life, being "out for stars," and because he rejected the thrush-call as inviting self-pity.

Recently, however, Michael Cornett has printed a transcript of a 1955 broadcast by Frost in which Frost speaks of "Come In" as a political poem—the last kind of reading I would have given it. He presents it as a response to the despairing "America is finished" poetry that was being written in the 1930s. Could it make indirect reference to the poetry of Robinson Jeffers, say in such poems as "Shine, Perishing Republic"? Biographers might check dates and letters to look into the notion at least.

13. See "Two Riddles," *World Literature Today* 66, 2 (Spring 1992), 229.

14. Of course people used to treat jokes as more like poems, preferring old ones as best. But if I am wrong, if "explained" poems don't take effect, then why do we pay hundreds of thousands of teachers to explain poems to readers who supposedly can't figure them out? I wonder, though, if professionalizing poetry-teaching has herded poets toward sheer obscurity, driven ordinary readers away from poem-reading, and subsidized bad writing that needs explaining. Who knows, the same may be true of prose-writers—it certainly is true of legal statutes and lawyer-interpreters, and may be for novelists. The next step might be to mystify newspapers and require a degree in reading newspapers before the voting booth is made available. I bet George Will would like that—until he saw how the teachers were demystifying his columns.

15. "WAS poetics" of course means "White Anglo-Saxon poetics"—they would not be Protestant until Henry VIII wanted to kick Queen Catherine out of bed, at which time the poetics turned *WASP-ish*.

SIMON J. ORTIZ
ACOMA PUEBLO

"Indigenous literature is Indigenous knowledge; Indigenous writers and poets are the instigators of that knowledge. You better believe it."

Few writers are more prolific than Simon Ortiz (1941–). He has written poems, fiction, criticism, and essays, and is one of the most influential of living Indigenous authors. Many of Ortiz's writings are set in or start from his home in Acoma, New Mexico, and address the traditions and landscape of the Acoma Pueblo people along with the life of his own family. Though the lineation of his poems is often tautly vertical, they are distinctively narrative and can even be chatty, while carrying an undercurrent of rhythm akin to song, as though each phrase is a measure of music. One of Oritz's great themes is survival—how a person, a community, a nation, and a people finds strength and endurance. In poems such as "Survival this Way" and "A Story of How a Wall Stands," Ortiz is both poet and philosopher. He reminds us of our place in the universe, and what Native peoples have lost, but moreover what America and the world have gained through Indigenous artistic, cultural, and moral contributions. Ortiz is never afraid to be political, but he is rarely polemical. Whatever anger one might detect in the poems, there will be twice that much patient wisdom.

*See also page 9, for Carter Revard's discussion of Simon Ortiz's poem "Speaking."

Culture and the Universe

Two nights ago
in the canyon darkness,
only the half-moon and stars,
only mere men.
Prayer, faith, love,
existence.
                    We are measured
by vastness beyond ourselves.
Dark is light.
Stone is rising.

I don't know
if humankind understands
culture: the act
of being human
is not easy knowledge.

With painted wooden sticks
and feathers, we journey
into the canyon toward stone,
a massive presence
in midwinter.

We stop.
                    Lean into me.
                    The universe
sings in quiet meditation.

We are wordless:
                    I am in you.

Without knowing why
culture needs our knowledge,
we are one self in the canyon.

And the stone wall
I lean upon spins me
wordless and silent
to the reach of stars
and to the heavens within.

It's not humankind after all
nor is it culture
that limits us.
It is the vastness
we do not enter.
It is the stars
we do not let own us.

Survival This Way

Survival, I know how this way.
This way, I know.
It rains.
Mountains and canyons and plants
grow.
We traveled this way,
gauged our distance by stories
and loved our children.
We taught them
to love their births.
We told ourselves over and over
again,
"We shall survive this way."

A Story of How a Wall Stands

At Aacqu, there is a wall almost 400 years old
which supports hundreds of tons of dirt and bones—
it's a graveyard built on a steep incline—and
it looks like it's about to fall down the incline
but will not for a long time.

My father, who works with stone,
says, "That's just the part you see,
the stones which seem to be
just packed in on the outside,"
and with his hands puts the stone and mud
in place. "Underneath what looks like loose stone,
there is stone woven together."
He ties one hand over the other,
fitting like the bones of his hands
and fingers. "That's what is
holding it together."

"It is built that carefully,"
he says, "the mud mixed
to a certain texture," patiently
"with the fingers," worked
in the palm of his hand. "So that
placed between the stones, they hold
together for a long, long time."

He tells me those things,
the story of them worked
with his fingers, in the palm
of his hands, working the stone
and the mud until they become
the wall that stands a long, long time.

Our Eagerness Blooms

In the shadows beyond the creek,
now only patches of snow remain.
Greening growth is soft urgency.
Eagerly, we dug the soil yesterday.
We kept looking at the browning hills.

It doesn't matter if it snows again.
We're fearless as the coming spring.
It could never be the same as last month.
The moving earth tells us that.

The shadows are luminescent, eager
to receive the early spring light.
Trees, we can tell, are growing supple.
Last night, a sensual odor flew
through the window we didn't close.

What sure sign there is comes gradually.
We trust our eagerness is not foolish.
It's not, and although spring may disappoint,
always it is ready to receive us again.
Snow hides into shadow, and we bloom.

from Song, Poetry, and Language—Expression and Perception: A Statement on Poetics and Language

My father is a small man, in fact, almost tiny. I think it must be the way that the Pueblo people were built when they lived at Mesa Verde and Pueblo Bonito. That's a long time ago, around 800–1200 A.D. One thousand years ago—this man? He's very wiry, and his actions are wiry. Smooth, almost tight motions, but like currents in creek water or an oak branch in a mild mountain wind. His face is even formed like that. Rivulets from the sides of his forehead, squints of his eyes, down his angular face and under his jaw. He usually wears a dark blue wool cap. His hair is turning a bit gray, but it's still mostly black, the color of distant lava cliffs. He wears glasses sometimes if he's reading or looking closely at the grain swirls of wood he is working with.

My father carves, dancers usually. What he does is find the motion of Deer, Buffalo, Eagle dancing in the form and substance of wood. Cottonwood, pine, aspen, juniper which has the gentle strains of mild chartreuse in its central grains—and his sinewed hands tough the wood very surely and carefully, searching and knowing. He has been a welder for the ATSFRY railroad and is a good carpenter, and he sits down to work at a table which has an orderly clutter of carving tools, paints an ashtray, transistor radio, and a couple of Reader's Digests.

His movements are very deliberate. He holds the Buffalo Dancer in the piece of cottonwood poised on the edge of his knee, and he traces—almost caresses—the motion of the Dancer's crook of the right elbow, the way it is held just below midchest, and flicks a cut with the razor-edged carving knife. And he does it again. He knows exactly how it is at that point in a Buffalo Dance Song, the motion of elbow, arm, body and mind.

He clears his throat a bit and he sings, and the song comes from that motion of his carving, his sitting, the sinews in his hands and face and the song itself. His voice in full-tones and wealthy, all the variety and nuance of motion in the sounds and phrases of the words are active in it; there is just a bit of tremble from his thin chest.

I listen.

"Stah wah maiyanih, Muukai-tra Shahyaika,
duuwahsteh duumahsthee Dyahnie guuyyoutseh mah-ah.
Wahyuuhuunah wahyuuhuu huu nai ah."

Recently, I was talking with a friend who is enrolled in a Navajo language course. She is Navajo, but she does not know how to speak Navajo. That is the story at present with quite a number of Indian young people who use English as the language with which they express themselves. English is the main language in which they experience the meaning and the uses of language.

She made a comment about not being able easily to learn Navajo as a course of instruction. She said, "I can't seem to hear the parts of it," referring to inflections and nuances of spoken sentences and words.

I referred to a remark I made sometime before, "The way that language is spoken at home—Acu. The tribe people and community from whom I come,is with a sense of completeness. That is, when a word is spoken, it is spoken as a complete word. There are no separate parts or elements to it." And I meant that a word is not spoken in any separate parts, that is, with reference to linguistic structure, technique of diction, nuance of sound, tonal quality, inflection, etc. Words are spoken as complete words.

For example, when my father has said a word—in speech or song—and I ask him, "What does that work break down to? I mean breaking it down to the syllables of sound or phrases of sound, what do each of these parts mean?" And he has looked at me with exasperated—slightly pained—expression on his face, wondering what I mean. And he tells me, "It doesn't break down into anything."

For him, the word does not break down into any of the separate elements that I expect. The word he has said is complete.

The word is there, complete in its entity of meaning and usage. But I, with my years of formal American education and some linguistic training, having learned and experiences English as a language—having learned to recognize the parts of a sentence, speech, the etymology of words, that words are separable into letter and sounds and syllables of vowels and consonants—I have leaned to be aware that a word does break down into basic parts or elements. Like that Navajo friend who is taking the Navajo language course, I have on occasion come to expect—even demand—that I hear and perceive the separated elements of Indian spoken words.

But, as my father has said, a word does not break down into separate elements. A word is complete.

In the same way, a song really does not break down into separate elements. In the minds and views of the people singing it at my home or in a Navajo religious ceremony, for whatever purpose that a song is meant and used, whether it be for prayer, a dancing event, or as part of a story, the song does not break down. It is part of the complete voice of a person.

Language, when it is regarded not only as expression but is realized as experience as well, works in and is of that manner. Language is perception of experience as well as expression.

Technically, language can be disassembled according to linguistic function which mainly deals with the expression part of it. You can derive—subsequently define—how a language is formed, how and for what purpose it is used, and its development in a context. But when the totality is considered, language as experience and expression, it doesn't break down so easily and conveniently. And there is no need to break it down and define its parts.

Language as expression and perception—that is at the core of what a song is. It relates to how my father teaches and sings a song and how a poet teaches and speaks a poem. . . .

My father sings, and I listen.

Song at the very beginning was experience. There was no division between experience and expression. Even now, I don't think there is much of a division except arbitrary. Take a child, for example, when he makes a song at his play, especially when he is alone. I his song, he tells about the experience of the sensations he is feeling at the moment with his body and mind. And the song comes about as words and sounds—expression. But essentially, in those moments, that song that he is singing is what he is experiencing. That child's song is both perception of that experience and his expression of it.

The meaning that comes from the song as expression and perception comes out of and is what the song is.

> Stah wah maiyanih, Muukai-tra Shahyaika,
> duumahsteh suumahsthee Dyahnie guuhoutseh mah-ah.
> Wahyuuhuunah wahyuuhuu huu nai ah.

This is a hunting song which occurs to me because it is around deer hunting season. I look around the countryside here, the piñon and the mountains nearby, and feel that I might go hunting soon, in November. The meaning the song has for me is in the context of what I am thinking, of what I want and perhaps will do. The words are translatable into English and they are

> My helping guide, Mountain Lion Hunting Spirit Friend,
> In this direction, to this point bring the Deer to me.
> Wahyuuhuunah wahyuuhuu huu nai ah.

. . . A song is made substantial by its context—that is its reality, both that which is there and what is brought t about by the song. The context in which the song is sung or that a prayer song makes possible is what makes a song substantial, give it that quality of realness. The emotional, cultural, spiritual context in which we thrive—in that, the song is meaningful. The context has to do not only with your being physically present but it has to do also with the context of the mind, how receptive it is, and that usually means familiarity with the culture in which the song is sung.

The context of a song can be anything, or can focus through a specific event or act, but it includes all things. This is very important to realize when you are trying to understand and learn more than just the words or the technical facility of words in a song or poem. That means that you have to recognize that language is more than just a group of words and more than just the technical relationship between sounds and words. Language is more than just a functional mechanism. It is a spiritual energy that is available to all. It includes all of us and is not exclusively in the power of human beings—we are part of that power as human beings.

Oftentimes, I think we become convinced of the efficiency of our use of language. We begin to regard language too casually, thereby taking it for granted, and we forget the sacredness of it. Losing this regard, we become quite careless with how we use and perceive with language. We forget that language beyond its mechanics is a spiritual force.

When you regard the sacred nature of language, then you realize that you are part of it and it is part of you, and you are not necessarily in control of it, and that if you do control some of it, it is not in your exclusive control. Upon this realization, I think there are all possibilities of expression and perception which become available. . . .

The song is basic to all vocal expression. The song as expression is an opening from inside of yourself to outside and from outside of yourself to inside but not in the sense that there are separate states of yourself. Instead, it is a joining and an opening together. Song is the experience of that opening or road if you prefer, and there are no separation of parts, no division between expression and perception.

I think that is what oftentimes happened with our use of English. We think of English as a very definitive language, useful in defining things—which means setting limits. But that's not supposed to be what language is. Language is not definition; language is all-expansive. We, thinking ourselves capable of the task, assign rules and roles to language unnecessarily. Therefore, we limit our words, our language, and we limit our perception, our understanding, our knowledge.
. . .

My father teaches that the song is part of the way you're supposed to recognize everything, that the singing of it is a way of recognizing this all-inclusiveness because it is a way of expressing yourself and perceiving. It is basically a way to understand and appreciate your relationship to all things. The song as language is a way of touching. This is the way that my father attempts to teach a song, and I try to listen, feel, known and learn that way.

When my father sings a song, he tried to instill a sense of awareness about us. Although he may remark upon the progressive steps in a song, he does not separate the steps or components of the song. The completeness of the song is the important thing, how a person comes to know and appreciate it, not to especially mark the separate parts of it but to know the whole experience of the song....

I listen carefully, but I listen for more than just the sound, listen for more than just the words and phrases, for more then the various parts of the song. I try to perceive the context, meaning, purpose—all of these items not in their separate parts but as a whole—and I think it comes completely like that.

A song, a poem, becomes real in that manner. You learn its completeness: you learn the various parts of it but not as separate parts. You learn a song in the way that you are supposed to learn a language, as expression and as experience.

I think it is possible to teach song and poetry in a classroom so that language is a real way of teaching and learning. The effort will have to be with conveying the importance and significance of not only the words and sounds but the realness of the song in terms of oneself, context, the particular language used, community, the totality of what it around....

My father tells me, "This song is a hunting song, listen." He sings and I listen. He may sing it again, and I hear it again. The feeling that I perceive is not only contained in the words but there is something surrounding those words, surrounding the song, and it includes us. It is the relationship that we share with each other and with everything else. And that's the feeling that makes the song real and meaningful and which makes his singing and my listening more than just a teaching and learning situation.

It is that experience—that perception of it—that I mention at the very beginning which makes it meaningful. You perceive by expressing yourself therefore. This is the way that my father teaches a song. And this is the way I try to learn a song. This is the way I try to teach poetry, and this is the way I try to have people learn from me.

One time my father was singing a song, and this is the instance in which this—perception by/expression of—became very apparent for me. He was singing this song, and I didn't catch the words offhand. I asked him, and he explained, "This song, I really like it for this old man." And he said, "This old man used to like to sing, and he dances like this," motioning like the old man's hands, arms, shoulders, and he repeated, "This song, I really like it for this old man."

That's what the song was about, I realized. It was both his explanation and the meaning of the song. It was about this old man who danced that way with whom my father had shared a good feeling. My father liked the old man, who was probably a mentor of some sort, and in my father's mind during the process of making the song when he sang it subsequent times afterward, he was reaffirming the affection he had for the old guy, the way "he danced like this."

My father was expressing to me the experience of that affection, the perceptions of the feeling he had. Indeed, the song was the road from outside of himself to inside—which is perception—and from inside of himself to outside—which is expression. That's the process and the product of the song, the experience and the vision that a song gives you.

The words, the language of my experience, come from how I understand, how I relate to the world around me, and how I know language as perception. That language allows me vision to see with and by which to know myself.

DIANE GLANCY

CHEROKEE

"Those voices always have been with me."

Just as poet, novelist, playwright, and essayist Diane Glancy (1941–) writes between genres, so too does she write between cultures. Her work is a heightened stirring together of old and new myths, present and age-old conflicts, and collisions between modes of belief. Known for her interest in both Christianity and Indigenous religions, Glancy asks difficult questions about how we know what we know and why we believe what we believe, as in "Buffalo Medicine." Much of her fiction and poetry is grounded in the contested territory of the Plains, in particular Oklahoma, Missouri, and Minnesota, as she re-enacts losses caused by invasion and settlement (see "Without Title"). The roles of Biblical and Native women fascinate Glancy, especially the ways in which women's voices and presences may be remembered and forgotten simultaneously. Glancy is a virtuoso of the persona poem, where speakers are historical, familial, or invented figures that aren't the authobiographical poet and yet, in some alchemically poetic way, actually are. Her current work-in-progress is *Island of the Innocent*, a reconsideration of the Book of Job.

The Bat House

Those voices always have been with me. The belief I had minimal distance to the Cherokee heritage, but distance nonetheless.

Native heritage is not always in neat categories. Native heritage is not always documented. There are loose hairs and strays.

I have been a controversial non-fit in both worlds. "Tell my friends I am dead." I have wanted to give up trying to be. But I have the other travelers with me on the road. I think I have seen them. A portal in the dark as I wake. An image of some dim, dawn-light with figures looking from. I don't know how else to say it. I don't know that it should be said. But others are with me.

Some of it no more than chalk on the sidewalk as I drew a road where I was going to the places I went. I tell you of a long journey that is not yet over as it was not as yet for Lorca. Yet the blue cloth floating there. I have waited for the poplars to fall, but they have stayed awake.

Grandparents. Great-grandparents and back and back.

ADNA test was European but for 9% Iberian with some contact with northern Africa. Research in Cherokee DNA has identified the mid-eastern components. The sea-going Phoenicians who settled on the Iberian peninsula to be closer to the ocean.

A great-grandfather, Woods Lewis, who was born in Meigs County, Tennessee, where many of the Cherokee were from. Who later showed up in Indian Territory and later settled in northern Arkansas. A heritage researcher said, "The removal of the Cherokee from their lands east of the Mississippi River to Indian Territory did not include many Cherokee who had already had purchased land and were established as part of European American society. Over time these individuals and their descendants lost their identity as Native American. This can make documenting Cherokee heritage very difficult. So far, woods Lewis and his family member have been identified as white in every U.S. census. However, there was no incentive to distinguish themselves as Native American on the census."

The researcher also sent the Civil War records of Woods Lewis, which I had seen anyway. Company L of the 4th Tennessee Cavalry, Union. He was 5'8", had black hair, black eyes, dark complexion. Yet marked himself white. The only other choice was black.

There was otherness in my father's family. I have felt the others with me. I think I have seen them.

I like the Native American story of the bat that attended both councils of the birds and animals, and was looked at suspiciously by both. The bat is a mammal with wings. He was both and neither of both.

I speak for the many who are undocumented. The un-papered Indians. Not Indian. But Indian. A shadow-land. A marginal being. Not having a whole self but divided. With elisions. Lacuna.

Upside-down. The ceiling is the floor. The floor the ceiling. Pictures hang upside-down also. A bat dreams upside-down. A bat sleeps with his wings folded across its chest.

Without papers, one is a faux bat. French for fake. Bogus. Ersatz. A constructed narrative. There are tropes. Tromps. Trimps.

There was otherness in my father's family. I have felt the others with me. I think I have seen them.

I am Fauxian. Fauxesque. Indeterminate.

Using appropriation. I speak for the large tribe — the lost tribe of them. The poplars on my grandfather's farm by the creek beyond the edge of the field. Or was it pasture?

From here — the inconclusive evidence — as "I went to my star without bread."

Without Title

For my Father who lived without ceremony

It's hard you know without the buffalo,
the shaman, the arrow,
but my father went out each day to hunt
as though he had them.
He worked in the stockyards.
All his life he brought us meat.
No one marked his first kill,
no one sang his buffalo song.
Without a vision he had migrated to the city
and went to work in the packing house.
When he brought home his horns and hides
my mother said
get rid of them.
I remember the animal tracks of his car
backing out the drive in snow and mud,
the aerial on his old car waving
like a bow string.
I remember the silence of his lost power,
the red buffalo painted on his chest.
Oh, I couldn't see it
but it was there, and in the night I heard
his buffalo grunts like a snore.

Buffalo Medicine

I want to speak buffalo.

It was a day for honor. The herd walked the Great Plains. This way the herd
walked. That. The little band of Indians followed. How they depended upon
us. How we clothed their bodies. Fed their stomachs. Provided hides for their

teepees. We often spoke to them. Grunting in language they understood. There was nothing we didn't give. But now we take our grasslands. Our lawn chairs and yard goods. Stampede to the other world. From the council fires of heaven we are called. The Great Spirit speaks in soldiers' guns. From trains, they pass shooting.

Sure America was made for us. Remember how often we delighted them. Deciding how we would run through the prairie with the wind in our ears. Our large heads pure with mind. The Great Spirit great as he spoke. Yo. We were his. We grunted his praises. Snorted and roamed in his will. Our calves grew up in our strength. We were kings. We allowed death. We gave ourselves for the Indians.

We are called Grandmother buffalo. Senor buffalo. Mon duc buffle. Herr burgermeister buffel. Savior buffalo. Universal buffalo. Surely the Great Spirit was made in our image. Touch us an you see the face of God. Our heads are angels fallen to the prairies. Touch us and you hear the grunting God.

He Dressed Me for the Pretend Cold

from *Island of the Innocent*

The camels of Bildad, Zophar, Eliphaz in the pasture. It was empty after Job's camels were taken. They always had talked to. But now they picked up on the emptiness. They wedged against the fence as though to feel solid against the open. They stood with one another as they once stood together against the herd of another whose pasture they were in. The servants there. The camel herders to keep them from harm. With sticks they said you here. You there. But the camels had intermixed. Now there was nothing but air to mix with. If others were taken could they be taken too? Was that the feeling they felt? Where had 3000 camels gone? They ate the grass of camels who were not there. And ah! They had ownership when others weren't there. A breaking and entering of sorts. As when passing other camel trains in the desert. The knowing they were with men and they let them pass. Now it was left to them to stand in the pasture not knowing. Backed into their own unintelligence of all that passed. They only had to step into the wide pasture. The nothingness. It was slow in coming. The train you hear at night pass all the way through town. Its horn at every corner.

Until the times of restitution — Acts 3:21

from *Island of the Innocent*

Jung thought Indians thought trees talked, skies moved because of vacuousness. A primitive, as yet not conscious of the place of self in the world. As someone who didn't keep their doors locked. There was a time anyone could walk in. Even without knocking.

Knockers were used by Anishinabe to knock rice into the canoe. Everyone with their own version of knocking. I could be excluded. As if forthwith I was not a part of enduring. For Job, it was three men who knocked at his door.

Another way to say it. A man from Uz suffered the loss of children in a storm. Tribal in that the animals suffered with him. His herds—sheep, camel, ox, donkey taken. The others—goat, peacock, ostrich, hawk, horse, leviathan, behemoth. All of them found in his book. Ask the animals and they will teach you, the birds in the sky. Let fish declare—Job 12: 7–8.

Job sat with friends who were not friends. As loose threads on a tunic. A robe or whatever Job wore to cover boils and knots in his thoughts. To ponder his situation. A forerunner for the Indian who lost his place and was made to sit and receive tripe from his visitors.

INFLUENCE

Federico Garcia Lorca's "From Here" was the mooring not only for individual poems but for the whole manuscript on which I was working: *Yet Trouble Came*, a creative study of the Old Testament Book of Job. It was the associations of "From Here." The dash. The natural landscape of the land—and the land. The language that stretched like landscape before me. The indirect address. The repetitions. A long journey driving from Kansas to Pittsburgh and back. A two-day journey each way. The rough weather. A meat-locker-cold in the eastern half of the country. Caught on the road. Following large trucks. Their eighteen wheels in the snow. Several trucks overturned. Jack-knifed. I kept driving, 20–40 miles an hour where I could have done 70 on a clear road. The distance. The distance. The isolation in the car by myself though I was with other cars on the road. It was in an independent bookstore in Pittsburgh where I bought the complete works of Lorca in which one spare poem, "From Here," spoke to me as a road marker. A literary road marker—.

This was a manuscript-in-progress that haunted me for years. A decolonization of the book of Job. I wanted a contemporary understanding. I needed something stricken. "Tell my friends I have died." Certainly that was a cord with Native history. "I went to my star without bread." Reading "From Here" transferred onto Job a Native perspective. I saw how the study of Job could incorporate the Other. It was the voice of a Spanish poet in "From Here" that told me I could go There—.

*

From Here
by Federico Garcia Lorca, translated by Sarah Arvio

Tell my friends
I have died
Water always sings
under the trembling woods
Tell my friends
I have died
How the poplars
sway the silken sound—
Tell them my eyes
stayed open
that the immortal
blue handkerchief
covered my face
And ah!
that I went to my star
without bread

ERNESTINE HAYES

Tlingit

"Traditions are not confined to the past . . ."

Ernestine Hayes (1945–) writes from a threshold where awareness of contemporary and older traditions touch and blend. With a style that conjoins the lyrical and narrative, and pulling from myth, memory, and shared custom, Hayes keeps in play the stories of Alaska Natives. In her work and in that place, humans and other beings exist interdependently, never divided from one another, but mingling to create a more responsive awareness of both worlds. Hayes's poems look directly and personally at what settler culture has done and continues to do to Alaska Native people, and does not turn away from the emotional complexities of colonization and modernity. Merging Tlingit and English, Hayes writes across linguistic and geographical boundaries and offers readers a wisdom borne from ancient ways.

Shapeshifters

My grandmother told me that if I saw myself on the street, I should approach and embrace the familiar shape. Her exact instructions were "Saankalyek't, walk up and hug yourself." The beings we might see, she explained, can present themselves in the form of those who see them.

I spent childhood summers at Hawk Inlet on the island whose name is Xootsnoowoo. I explored the forest and the beach while my grandmother and other Tlingit women worked in the cannery increasing the wealth of white man colonizers. On late evenings, shadows crept along the boardwalk between two rows of dark red cabins. Worn-down women unwrapped bandanas that had protected their hair from the raw smell of wealth sucked from the ocean, the smell of profit now headed into the pockets of white men through tins of salmon that should rather have been smoked and dried and baked and boiled on Tlingit fires. Grandmothers and aunties unpinned their now-uncovered waist-length graying hair and sat around kerosene lamps, gossiping and laughing and reminding little girls to stay inside.

Beings could be heard just outside the walls. As soon as someone sensed their nameless movement, the beings began to whisper like willow branches, whimper like dogs that still walked on four legs, grumble like wandering bears beguiled by salmon-soaked scarves. Grandmothers warned little girls that these beings might look like cousins or uncles or even themselves. There would seem no reason to suspect those beings, grandmothers instructed, but anyone who walked away with them might never come back. Anyone who did come back would not come back right away. Anyone who came back would be avoided by their loved ones. Anyone who managed to return would receive from their loved ones no more than a cautious embrace.

All the truths my grandmother declared are as plain as the world.

Land otter people

It was once said that land otter people can make themselves look like any thing of beauty. It was once believed that a sharp bite on the hand of a land otter man will reveal his nature. But no one now remembers the sweet taste of his shifted skin – skin that is flavored like blueberry blossoms salted with a vagrant's tear. And few remain alive who thrill at a suggestion of his whereabouts. Few remain alive who are not fooled by the whisper of a willow branch. He knows he will die when no one is left to embrace him.

He fades
He fades
He walks past
Becomes invisible
He has not prevailed against those merciless gates

He prepares for death
Still longing for the sting of a bitten hand

All the truths my grandmother declared are as plain as the world.

The Spoken Forest

Brown bear dances in the dark in the dark forest in the night to the remembered melody of a happy song his mother once heard her grandmother hum— the nearly lost memory of a song meant for this time of the night, to take away our grief, to help us laugh again, to set the bear surely to spin beneath the darkly spinning stars.

He knows winter when he sees it when he smells snow making the air fat with promises of sleep he knows he can eat fat that will burn his fires in the night in the dark night and warm his cave of dreams where his breath steams the air that carries our unforgotten songs our unremembered dances our unsaved prayers.

Spruce and hemlock whisper one to another. Our history our histories our story our stories our memory our memories our life our lives who we are what we are how we are where we are spruce and hemlock watch as we hurry to places with no sun no rain no humans they tenderly fold us into their whispers knowing that in the next days in the next generations in the next worlds our stories will be the at.oow they bring out to display to us their opposites when they host memorials for our impeccable purpose.

Land otter man uses his cell phone on the bus

When I look at him I know: This kooshdakaa has wrapped himself as human.

Human, yes. But . . . different in some way. Different in some ways. In the way his black hair lies flat straight back from his flat wide forehead. In his strict posture, his barrel chest. His always-shined shoes. His surprising, high voice. In the way his lip remembers the adornments his grandmothers wore when they were still those innocent girls before dleitkaa came to tell them they were dirty.

THE SPOKEN FOREST

I was thinking about the forest one day
and it came to me —
our stories,
our songs,
our names,
our history,
our memories
are not lost.

All these riches are being kept for us
by our aunties, our uncles,
our grandparents, our relatives —
those namesakes who walk and dance
wearing robes that make them seem like bears
and wolves.

Our loved ones.

Those beings who live in the spoken forest.
They are holding everything for us.

All the truths my grandmother declared are as plain as the world.

With Elegant Craft: Nora Marks Dauenhauer's "How to Make Good Baked Salmon from the River"

Nora Marks Dauenhauer (1927–2017) begins her poem "How to Make Good Baked Salmon from the River" with these words:

> It's best made in dry-fish camp on a beach by a
> Fish stream on sticks over an open fire, or during
> Fishing, or during cannery season.
>
> In this case, we'll make it in the city baked in
> An electric oven on a black fry pan.

Next, Dauenhauer instructs readers on the proper way to prepare fresh salmon, presenting images that rise from our place—alder wood, skunk cabbage leaves, ravens, fresh berries—followed by contemporary images that continue the tradition—paper plates, plastic forks, coffee and beer. With elegant craft, Dauenhauer subtly teaches us that traditions are not confined to the past, but are living, breathing, alive. This lesson is true for baking salmon, for telling stories, and for all the beliefs we cautiously embrace.

All the truths my grandmother declared are as plain as the world.

*

How to Make Good Baked Salmon from the River
by Nora Marks Dauenhauer

It's best made in dry-fish camp on a beach by a
fish stream on sticks over an open fire, or during
fishing, or during cannery season.

In this case, we'll make it in the city baked in
an electric oven on a black fry pan.

INGREDIENTS

Barbecue sticks of alder wood.
In this case, the oven will do.
Salmon: River salmon, current supermarket cost
$4.99 a pound.
In this case, salmon poached from river.
Seal oil or olachen oil.
In this case, butter or Wesson oil, if available.

DIRECTIONS

To butcher, split head up the jaw. Cut through,
remove gills. Split from throat down the belly.
Gut, but make sure you toss all to the seagulls and
the ravens because they're your kin, and make sure
you speak to them while you're feeding them.
Then split down along the back bone and through
the skin. Enjoy how nice it looks when it's split.

Push stake through flesh and skin like pushing
a needle through cloth, so that it hangs on stakes
while cooking over fire made from alder wood.

Then sit around and watch the slime on the salmon
begin to dry out. Notice how red the flesh is,
and how silvery the skin looks. Watch and listen
to the grease crackle, and smell its delicious
aroma drifting around on a breeze.

Mash some fresh berries to go along for dessert.
Pour seal oil in with a little water. Set aside.

In this case, put the poached salmon in a fry pan.
Smell how good it smells while it's cooking,
because it's soooooooo important.

Cut up an onion. Put in a small dish. Notice how
nice this smells too and how good it will taste.
Cook a pot of rice to go along with salmon. Find
some soy sauce to put on rice, maybe borrow some.

In this case, think about how nice the berries would
have been after the salmon, but open a can of fruit
cocktail instead.

Then go out by the cool stream and get some skunk
cabbage, because it's biodegradable, to serve the
salmon from. Before you take back the skunk cabbage
you can make a cup out of one to drink from the
cool stream.

In this case, plastic forks paper plates and cups will do, and
drink cool water from the faucet.

TO SERVE
After smelling smoke and fish and watching the
cooking, smelling the skunk cabbage and the berries
mixed with seal oil, when the salmon is done, put
the salmon on stakes on the skunk cabbage and pour
some seal oil over it and watch the oil run into
the nice cooked flakey flesh which has now turned
pink.

Shoo mosquitoes off the salmon, and shoo the ravens
away, but don't insult them because the mosquitoes
are known to be the ashes of the cannibal giant,
and Raven is known to take off with just about
anything.

In this case, dish out on paper plates from fry pan.
Serve to all relatives and friends you have invited
to the barbecue and those who love it.

And think how good it is that we have good spirits
that still bring salmon and oil.

TO EAT

Everyone knows that you can eat just about every
part of the salmon, so I don't have to tell you
that you start with the head because it's everyone's
favorite. You take it apart bone by bone, but make
sure you don't miss the eyes, the cheeks, the nose,
and the very best part — the jawbone.

You start on the mandible with a glottalized
alveolar fricative action as expressed in the Tlingit
verb als'oos'.

Chew on the tasty, crispy skins before you start
on the bones. Eeeeeeeeeeeee!! How delicious.

Then you start on the body by sucking on the fins
with the same action. Include crispy skins, then
the meat with grease dripping all over it.

Have some cool water from the stream with the salmon.

In this case, water from the faucet will do.
Enjoy how the water tastes sweeter with salmon.

When done, toss the bones to the ravens and
seagulls and mosquitoes, but don't throw them in
the salmon stream because the salmon have spirits
and don't like to see the remains of their kin
among them in the stream.

In this case, put bones in plastic bag to put
in dumpster.

Now settle back to a story telling session, while
someone feeds the fire.

In this case, small talk and jokes with friends
will do while you drink beer. If you shouldn't
drink beer, tea or coffee will do nicely.

Gunalcheesh for coming to my barbecue.

ADRIAN C. LOUIS
Lovelock Paiute

"Poetry is art, period."

Reviewing the book *Wild Indians & Other Creatures* in the *New York Times Book Review*, David Bowman called the writing of Adrian C. Louis (1946–2018) "Wild, sometimes foolish, sometimes poignant, often cartoony," and praises the way a Louis story "starts off . . . sardonically, then surprises us with its (and his own) heartfelt grace." Likewise Louis's poetry juxtaposes contrary qualities so masterfully that one might at times forget this is "poetry." Each poem becomes a small world built of anger, amusement, pain, and tenderness, which Louis allows a visitor, if only for a moment, to undergo alongside him. Louis has a posture, tone, and manner that may seem harsh, but his ability to provoke emotion and alertness demonstrates a genius all his own. Blunt and truthful, Louis combines statements and reflections to depict reservation realities, historical happenstance, and the brutality of contemporary American life, while the imagery is anchored in icons, rituals, and artifacts from popular culture. Paralleling and accentuating throughout are rhythms, so that a poem can sound like a mongrel somewhere between song and war chant. Critics tend to foreground Louis's subject matter, but the qualities that transmute his poetry's rough surfaces are an elegant technique, dexterous line breaks, and musicality.

In Lieu of a Communion Wafer

More often than not
growing up in poverty
extinguishes any sense
of irony, but our humor
(often it's a cruel humor)
abounds & saves, yeah,
it abounds & saves us
like a big, fat frybread
saves a watery soup.

Prairie Madness

Box my bone ash. FedEx me to my high desert
home. Toss me high into the coyote air; let me
dust the sage & horny toads. I refuse to sleep
under this alien soil, this Minnesota moon-
scape, this cold cheese land devoid of sane
hills & trees. Fuck this flat world of poisonous
cornfields & ceaseless wind. This abominable
prairie wind. This divine wind of madness.
This rapist wind.

A brassy woman materialized last week one
block from me. She's made of bronze with
billowing skirt & windblown bonnet. She's a
pioneer woman, a settler woman, the kind of
woman who ran from her sod house & stink-
ing husband & ceaseless wind, ran to the In-
dians who always seemed calm. I walked by
her last night & tweaked her a la Trump. She
remained dead calm. I ran home & chopped
off my hand.

Skinology

Yellow roses, wild roses,
their decades of growth,
a fierce fence between
the drunkenness
of my neighbors
& me.

*

I have known
some badass Skins.
Clichéd bad-to-the-bone
Indians who were maybe
not bad but just broke,
& broken for sure.

*

Late winter, late night,
a gentle rapping, a tapping
on my chamber door . . .
some guy selling a block
of commodity cheese
for five bucks.

*

You climbed a tree,
sat there for hours
until some kind voice
called you back home.
You unfolded your wings,
took to the air & smashed
into earth. They hauled

you to ER, then Detox
where they laughed
at your broken wings.

*

Once, I thought
I saw eagles soar,
loop & do the crow hop
in the blue air while
the sun beat the earth
like a drum, but I was
disheveled & drinking
those years.

*

Indians & the internet.
Somewhere, sometime.
Whenever a Messiah
Chief is born, jealous
relatives will drag him
down like the old days
only instantly now.

*

In a brutal land
within a brutal land
with corrupt leaders
& children killing themselves
we know who is to blame.
But, we are on a train,
a runaway train & we
don't know what to do.

*

The good earth,
the sun blazing down,
us in our chones, butts
stuck in inner tubes,
floating down a mossy
green river, speechless,
stunned silent with joy
& sobriety & youth,
oh youth.

*

She smiled at me
& got off her horse.
She smelled of leather
& sweat & her kiss has
lasted me fifty years.

*

Bad Indians do
not go to hell.
They are marched
to the molten core
of the sun & then
beamed back to
their families,
purified, whole
& Holy as hell.

The Hermit's Diary

1.

Age has withered my rage. The roiling, molten core
of my youth has cooled into dull, cold metal. Nev-
ertheless, sometimes I grab a butter knife & dance
around the kitchen, threatening the sluggish Mr.
Coffee machine.

2.

I grew up in a shack. I lived in an 8x10 closet off
the front porch of an old railway house. Me, my
cot, some small shelves on one wall where my mom
stacked my clean clothes. I hid out there most days
to avoid the cruel, white demon that was my step-
father. I waited in the oppressive air of desert af-
ternoons for him to leave for the swing shift at the
copper mine.

Decades later, I rise in another shack of a house at
five in the morning, make coffee, putter around un-
til the early afternoon heat creeps up on me. Then
I turn on the air conditioning & go to bed. When
I am shivering from the cold, I pull the blankets up
& take a nap. I have worked my whole life for such
peace.

3.

Escaping the glare of the computer, I find myself
motoring past my former place of employment.
"Itchycoo Park" is playing on the oldies station. I
soak up the summertime college mist like an old,
dry sponge. Tan girls taking remedial courses are
lounging upon the lawns. Firm bottoms & bellies

& heads filled with helium. The good ole USA. The euphoric scent of sun Coppertone simmering on the skin of young women. I inhale the intoxicant as I slowly drive by.

Cruising past the hospital, I breathe in the hot tar a road crew is laying down. I love the aroma of tar. One desert summer, I worked as a flagman for a paving company. Then, I had a firm bottom & belly. My head was not filled with helium but small, smiling clouds of incinerated flora. 1966.

4.
What will we do there? — We'll get high.
What will we touch there? — We'll touch the sky.
       —Small Faces, 1967

Magpie in Margaritaville

A shimmer of green
floats off the glossy
black feathers as he
raises his sharp beak
to speak. "I piss on you
& your pithy depictions
of woe & woe unto you
who lack spirit guides.
You have made careers
on the backs of red folk.
Do not for an instant,
pretend you know me
when you cannot see
that my feathers are red."

Of Craft, Cub Scouts, Mayonnaise, and UFOs

So, the Adrian was asked to write a "craft" essay to accompany the poems that you've just read. You did read them didn't you? If you didn't then why are you reading this faux essay? Don't piss the Adrian off. Go back and read the poems, memorize them, and stroll about your homelands reciting them to your people. Your people will either smile broadly or punch you in the nose. And maybe you need a nose punch to bring you down to earth, make you more grass-roots. And in the process learn to improve your ninja skills. Life can be rugged out there on the island of turtles.

So, I don't like writing about craft. I don't like to read about it, don't like to hear people talk about it. I mean I understand objective correlative and all manner of poetic-wonky stuff, but the word "craft" sticks in my throat. Sounds too much like arts and crafts, crafts being the lesser of the two . . . like something any fool could learn. Poetry is art, period. I'm not saying you shouldn't learn good grammar and the elements, history, and mechanics of poetry, forms and all, but I have a hard time discussing the subject. And poets discussing their own work? Give me a damn break. I've said it before: poets should write their poems and should otherwise shut the fuck up. And don't get me started on the mayonnaise-skinned literary critics who discover the soul of the Indian by analyzing the writings of Indians and then writing about it. They perpetuate colonialism. And they make me twitch . . .

So, don't get me totally wrong. When I was young, I studied the hell out of literature, craft and all. These days, however, I'm better off talking about Kraft Mayonnaise which I will not eat. Get Hellman's Real Mayonnaise. It's so much better. It's gooder than good. It tastes like it's been crafted. Stay away from Miracle Whip. Too sickly sweet. Too fake, something Americans crave though. So many want a saccharine-coated reality like a television comedy show with a canned laugh-track. When you live in the dire, focus on the dire, or the dire will sneak up on you and slit your throat from behind. Become the dire and it will not harm you. Actually, one time I tried to craft mayonnaise. Olive oil, garlic, salt and pepper, and an egg into a blender. Truly dire. I can still taste the horror of it many years later. So hell yeah, Hellman's is the answer. BLTs with garden fresh tomatoes proves that God sometimes intervenes in the stumbling frailty of human existence.

So, craft is something you get a merit badge for in the Cub Scouts. Oh my god, yes, I was in the Cub Scouts for a few years learning to be a good American. How did that badge progression go? Was it wolf, bear, and then lion? I don't recall. What I do remember is one time we put on a scout circus. I was the designated tight-rope walker. I had to dress in my sister's shiny-green one-piece bathing suit and walk along a garden hose on the ground. People laughed at me. Another childhood psychic scar . . . among many too far worse to discuss in a relatively innocuous forum such as this.

So, to any young folks interested in writing poetry and getting your poetic merit badge, I would say this: come to an understanding of what poetry is and honestly evaluate your abilities with the art form. If you do not have a natural talent for it, then avoid it. Talent is not something you can learn. You can learn to improve your talent by reading other poets. This does not mean imitating them. Rely on your own unique vision. And read, read, read. Write about what you know and if your writing is horrid then give it up. Do something more useful. Build a canoe. That's a craft. Study the night skies. UFOs are crafts piloted by alien lizard folk. They are our relatives. Take care. Take two aspirins and call me in the morning.

CHRYSTOS
Menominee

"Poetry is loose, doesn't have to follow point a to b . . . and is, I think the closest form of colonizer culture to Native expression."

In a voice that ranges from furious to amorous, the poetry of Chrystos (1946–) is evocative, alluring, and powerful. Her art romps with language, twisting and morphing words from standard usage to her own meanings. Intense empathy for ostracized people never hides behind an intellectualized affect; what she cares about is stated boldly, as she reckons with the violence inflicted every day on Native and queer bodies. For Chrystos, poems are tools to demolish the colonial edifice, and weapons to defend the land, women, and alternative cultures long misinterpreted and misrepresented. And though her lines sound stark and strong, they're imbued with a beauty and gentleness that is never far from the surface. Listen to the audible sympathy in how she approaches nature, love, and intimacy—unyielding yet compassionate.

*See also page 330 for Chip Livingston's testimony to the influence of Chrystos's poem "Crazy Grandpa Whispers."

Sky Falls Away

Clouds tumble behind
old olive cedars
rich with rain
Blue memories of summer
wisp teasing
through piles of curly white wigs
who judge sodden gold corn stalks
bent for winter
in awkward skeletons
Ripe red leaves
spangle our path
where all of us
dozing
await Spring

Beauti Full Soft Black Tongues

of buffalo I fed in Golden Gate Park
through insecurity grid fences
touch my Spirit with flickering joy
Though they are imprisoned
they bear me no malice
Didn't bite as the race horses
whose stalls I mucked out for money
sometimes did
No one bets on buffalo
They haven't been able to run
for over four hundred years
Leaning into sheds of their reservations
scratching their sides on the savagilation
that has destroyed our lives
we stare at each other

across an abyss of near extinction
We don't even remember anymore
how to throw rocks
I carry my soul in their beauti full tongues
though now my hands are too big
to fit through their bars
    for Stormy Ogden

She Had to Go

to the Fort Steal Museum in BC
in order to see a portrait in oils
of her GreatGrandfather Chief Isadore
which is the property, technically
of the Queen of England
whom she'll never meet
She's not allowed
to reproduce or photograph this painting
We must ask permission
to have the pictures of our relatives
from white strangers
who want us to pay
I want to know how
they can claim rights
over those they've wronged
If they can own our ancestors
are we slaves
    for Sunny Birdstone

Palestinians & Indians Feel

her eternal arms
Earth embracing our dusty Spirits
in a slow curve of rocks rising
to kiss the sky
See small hills fragrant
with sage or olive groves
roll over our sorrows
Hear honeyed stones whisper
our stories of genocide
Smell clouds echoing landscape
in surprising swoops
No matter what
they do to us
kill us, kill our trees
kill our children
kill our culture
tear apart our homes
with cruel machines
take our food to claim as their own
Our place breathes in our lungs
Our place knows us
holds us
This place remembers us
This cannot be killed

I Still Have the Bullet

I loaded into my rifle when I was 13
planning to kill him accidentally
on a hunting trip
My life would have been so
much better if I'd had the courage

Some wind I can't name stopped me
perhaps knowing I could barely
carry my own weight
Dented, useless now I've no idea how
it is still with me
59 years later
through hundreds of moving vans
nut houses   breakups
I've lost so much I can barely
go to funerals
Yet here is this moment
when I was sure
I needed to murder him
when I felt I could be illuminated
by freedom
when I knew his rapes would go
on and on
I clearly remember leaning into
a live oak in the autumn light
I took the bullet out of the chamber
put it in my pocket
and reloaded
I felt I shouldn't kill a deer
with that hatred
which burns now on my desk
The wind was protecting me from becoming
him

The Earth Where I Live

has been contaminated with arsenic
from a smelting company called Asarco
now out of business
We were reassured by government agents

that all of the affected soil had been removed
This is a lie
& I know none of you are surprised
When I first came here, planted flowers
my bare hands cracked and bled
so I did not put in vegetables
10 years later the ground is still not safe to eat from
This soil not sweetened enough yet I grow my food
in pots from China
which are possibly also poisonous
with bags of dirt I've bought at Saar's
for $2.99 each
Who knows what's in that twiggy mix
though our air & water & wind come from Hanford & Chernobyl
This is the way of life
Pain becomes lakes becoming snow
Tonight we all share our breath
wedded by space
My cells are shedding with yours
we're one being of dirt & sludge
loon cries & river stones
We cannot buy freedom
from our joined fates
I water my gardens with rinsed dairy containers
as milk helps purify soil
This autumn I'll put in spinach
as I've heard it will pull out heavy metals
though it can't be eaten or composted
as it will be toxic

Which earth do I send these unholy leaves to
Which ocean   which Indian Reservation
which desert   which landfill poisoning someone's well
I also water my blooms with tears
Where I live there are no deer
no beaver no eagles
but you have a choice of eleven different

used car lots
We are warned not to let children or pets
play in the grass
or go barefoot
All of the fish & turtles in a nearby surviving lake
are dead & gone
There's a number you can call
on a yellow sign if you want to know more
The earth where I live is poison
when I touch her
my hands bleed

War Piece Craft

While I depend on various tools when I write, such as alliteration, internal rhymes, puns, end line manipulations, the senses (usual 5 + humor & "supernatural"), sound games (words which sound the same but have different meanings), metaphor & repetition, which are formally called craft, craft is not the focus of my work.

I enjoy playing with various forms, especially the sestina, and am aware of craft when editing, but I began speaking from the point of survival.

There remains a desperate quality in my writing which results from my deep fear that no one is listening. I literally was not heard in my family, who continue to posit that I'm crazy. Writing was, for many years, the only way I knew I existed. This is not a metaphor. I began writing to stay alive, to defend my existence and I am still driven by this project. So far I haven't published any fiction, though I've been fooling around with it during the last 15 years while I've taken a break from performing & publishing. I dropped out of being "Chrystos" for the most part because I don't like most of the aspects of "fame." I felt I was being used as a token, and being a token is a trap, a very small box in which to write. I'm deeply interested in writing in order to understand myself, others and the workings of colonizer culture. I'm not as driven now to share what I'm learning and have come to resent all the people who want to edit me or censor me or make me more "palatable." I never had privacy, as a sexually abused person from the time I was six months old, so I decided to retreat. I want to know what I think about my writing, not what others want to put on it. This is particularly true because

I've so often been misinterpreted as "angry" (does a lawyer presenting a case get put down for being angry?) or "brave" (an extremely contested word for First Nations people). There is no distance between myself and my words. Everything has happened in real time, not my imagination (although I do change details to obscure actual people). This is not to say that I don't "tart things up" (with craft) to make them more pleasing to read.

I am profoundly attached to the idea of freedom (and am very grateful to Alex WhiteCloud for his words on this subject) and craft often feels like a jail. I mostly write poetry because one doesn't need to understand grammar or paragraphs (neither of which I agree with, in any case). Poetry is loose, doesn't have to follow point a to b (which I can't do) and is, I think, the closest form of colonizer culture to Native expression. Poetry isn't pedantic. Normally one doesn't require a PhD to understand it. I am uninterested in being obscure or incomprehensible. I deliberately use simple words & phrases, in hope that my meaning will be clear (which distances me from academic poets). I think it is rude to position oneself as smarter than everyone else. The word hegemony is not poetic in any case.

Fame was also a jail. I began to feel I could no longer be honest because my reality could harm others. For example, I've been almost completely silent about my lifelong struggle with suicidal ideation and behavior. We already have enough of our youth killing themselves. Until this moment, I've hidden the period of my life about twenty years ago, when I was desperately fighting off a re-entry into heroin addiction. I have a reputation as being completely honest (which is also craft), which is, ironically, sometimes a lie. I conceal my agony because I don't want to "get it on anyone" and I don't trust the audience to support me. This lack of trust is my greatest enemy, as a writer. I have demurred being called an Elder because I know very well how idiotic I can be. Surviving is not wisdom, in and of itself. We have so little room to THINK nowadays that I doubt wisdom is even possible. Craft is not what helps me write. What drives me to write is trying to get my Spirit clear. I hope that my struggles help others to do the same, though I am adamant that I don't "speak for" First Nations people or even Native lesbians. Talking for someone is a colonizer trick I reject.

Each of us has a right and a duty to speak for ourselves (bearing in mind the people we belong to). Writing is my religious practice and my journey. I could not stop. I write to become a better person, not a "great writer." I hope to use my intelligence to dismantle colonizer thinking (which, by the way, does not demand that one is "white"). I work to tear off the masks of assumption, the lies, greed, ego. I know we are a special & beautiful people who have had to endure being kicked for over five hundred years. I hope to invent ways for us to dodge the boots. I believe that calling out the truth to dance is crucial in this very abusive world in which we live. While I would like to be thought of as a great writer, I worry that concentrating on form can be a way to avoid content or to repeat old ways of seeing (i.e. the soap opera novel or slam poetry—which assaults the listener as enemy, and so on). I continue to study craft, especially in the work of other writers I admire (a few are Elizabeth Woody, Joy Harjo, Luci Tapahonso, Denise Low, Janice Gould, N. Scott Momaday), but my primary goal is figuring out how to be a good person while writing about goodness.

I have to laugh here because I'm aware of various accusation that I'm violent, rude or using my ethnicity, etc. I write constantly (over two hundred and ninety journals) and so, to some extent, I'm unconscious of my own craft. I recognize certain of my tricks (liking to have titles merge as the first line of the poem; working to make the last line a strong punch; hiding rhymes & so on) but I'm not sure they qualify as craft—my writing seems to me to be more of a ripping apart of the concept of "what poetry is supposed to be." I'm a rebellious teenager—I continually drag topics onto the stage which others generally considered not poetic (or indeed, even acceptable for public discourse—I had to fight like hell with Press Gang to get "It Was a Saturday" printed in *Not Vanishing* and lost out on some other pieces which remain unpublished). I've been very amused by how many white women have tried to edit me, censor me, when they haven't sold over 20,000 copies of their first book of poetry. I share that feat with Dorothy Parker. I rarely brag but I'm not unaware of my influence. Often I'm uncomfortable with this state—I despise people fawning over me, which is probably where "rude" comes from.

When I do writing workshops, I usually run through craft pretty quickly and give the majority of time to concentrating on skills for revealing & listening to the individual Spirit which animates each of us and which unites us. Most writers are focused almost completely on craft, but I'm just trying to make sense of my life.

I often resist publishing what I write because the printed word is so final, so black and white, that it feels like a tombstone. As long as my writing is in my own hand, it can be changed & has life & gets to mean exactly what it wants to. Once words are published anyone can infuse them with a wrong meaning or make them a trap for me. The fluid is gone. My words are like the bird just outside my window now—twitching this way & that, hungry, unsure & ready to take off never to be seen again. The worst part of being published as having your words used against you—i.e. the notion that I'm angrier than others, or misinterpreted to say that "I hate white people." Sometimes I do, but it is not a fortress carved in stone. Since I have no power to control white culture, the issue is silly to me. I think that most whites are desperate to BE "white," in the sense of pure, chaste, innocent. They seem to need to be—forgiven? accepted?—I don't know—but it makes it very hard to communicate across the barriers which ARE there.

Writing is what one feels when writing. Feelings change—they're snow-flakes in respect to all being different and also, as quickly evaporating. Writing is, I think, a kind of obsession with declaring one's opinion. In a community where people talked to each other and cared for each other, I doubt there would be much writing. It is a kind of road out of loneliness & isolation, but I think I'd prefer a community who loved me despite all my many faults.

I'm grateful to my cat Bert, as she made a mighty effort to keep me from being a pompous brat by biting the paper, my fingers, laying across my neck so I can't see & jumping on the pen. I'm not sure she's been successful. I hope this has helped other writers. I'd write something completely different tomorrow.

A Litany for Survival

I was lucky to be taught to read by my father, from the Greek & Roman myths, when I was about five. By the time I arrived in first grade, I had no patience for "see dick run" and ignored the "doings" to read my father's books under the lid of my desk. When called upon, I had no idea where the class was and after not very long, was transferred into the special class for, as they said in those days, the re-tarded. I continued to secretly read until the fourth grade when someone decid-ed our IQs should be tested. My score was 160, which astounded the nuns. They told my mother they should go to a special school but she demurred. I continued to read from my father's library, which contained two books of the poet Walter Benton and several of e.e. cummings. I began reading them when I was nine and decided that I was going to be a poet. For a long time I wrote rhyming prayers to the virgin mary and so on. When I was introduced to public school, my English teacher was Mr. Brooks who had us read Edgar A. Poe. My next step was a book-store owned by Ferlinghetti (in San Francisco) where I read all the poets he car-ried, most of whom I didn't like. I did not "discover" Indigenous literature until I was about nineteen (N. Scott Momaday). I've been reading us since, though I do read others. My two favorite poems are Joy Harjo's "She Had Some Horses" (see page 267) and Audre Lorde's "Litany for Survival." I read them aloud often. I have no idea how these works have affected my writing.

A Litany for Survival

by Audre Lorde

For those of us who live at the shoreline
standing upon the constant edges of decision
crucial and alone
for those of us who cannot indulge
the passing dreams of choice
who love in doorways coming and going
in the hours between dawns
looking inward and outward
at once before and after
seeking a now that can breed
futures
like bread in our children's mouths
so their dreams will not reflect
the death of ours;

For those of us
who were imprinted with fear
like a faint line in the center of our foreheads
learning to be afraid with our mother's milk
for by this weapon
this illusion of some safety to be found
the heavy-footed hoped to silence us
For all of us
this instant and this triumph
We were never meant to survive.

And when the sun rises we are afraid
it might not remain
when the sun sets we are afraid
it might not rise in the morning
when our stomachs are full we are afraid
of indigestion
when our stomachs are empty we are afraid

we may never eat again
when we are loved we are afraid
love will vanish
when we are alone we are afraid
love will never return
and when we speak we are afraid
our words will not be heard
nor welcomed
but when we are silent
we are still afraid

So it is better to speak
remembering
we were never meant to survive.

LINDA HOGAN
CHICKASAW

"The poems are a part of giving back and of saving . . ."

It would be impossible to write an all-encompassing introduction to the works of poet, novelist, and essayist Linda Hogan (1946–) and to do justice to her contributions to the expanding canon of Indigenous literature. She has been writing and publishing poems and prose for over forty years and continues to reach ever more readers, Native and non-Native. Her writings, which she considers "traditionally centered," draw upon her own Chickasaw lineage while also carrying stories from other Native peoples and those of mixed origins, in order to help all readers perceive the natural world through traditional ways of knowing. Hogan's work is beautifully descriptive, but does not back away from the difficult matters of political injustice, environmental disaster, and historic tragedy. She writes with a muscular narrative authority and steady resistance to received "fact," continually questioning and repeatedly achieving a sense of discovery. Elegiac, prayer-like, and radiant, Linda Hogan's work is a vast study in the art of literary understanding. The new pieces featured here are from an unpublished collection, *A History of Kindness*.

*See also page 218 for Kimberly Blaeser's testimony to the influence of Linda Hogan's poem "Workday."

Bones at the River

When the river changed course
and washed land away,
each bend grew sharper.

Water takes what it wants.
This time it says, I will take
earth from where your people
are buried.

The river was far from our graveyard once,
this Washita that changed course,
stole earth and carried it
on the snaking back of its current.

Now it passes through
this place where my people were buried.

We are the ones
who came from the ones
who survived. They are buried there
after walking the death trail
from across the Mississippi.

We walked into this new territory
the lost and foreign place,
now having no homes
or even a body of peace
just the papers
with signatures
of those who made promises.

Now our bones are revealed like truth.
We've taken up two
from the once invisible lives

with newly lost names, lost horses,
our lost relations
who would have loved us.

From some other place they do.

And what they would feel knowing the force of water
once again, except that we always traveled by water.
It was our life. So go!

Creation

I am a warrior
wanting this world to survive
never forgotten, this earth
which gave birth to the bison, the scissortail,
the vultures of Tibet who consume the finally released
mystics like my own old ones
who taught that we are always a breath,
a breath away from bullets.

I am from a line of songs,
a piece of history told by our people,
with unseen boundary lines.
In every gulley lies the power of a forest song waiting to begin,
those the first ones sang when they crossed into this existence
and down to the canyon where I live.
I dreamed how they passed
to the creek-bed, each still canyon wall in place,
the stones I love, lichens already growing on them,
the route I know to the river where bear go to fish.

It is hard for some to know
the world is a living being.

Some live with forgotten truth
replaced with belief. Perhaps that's why
the books of the Mayans were burned,
written languages destroyed in the North.

You can weep over such things
as lost love, or the passing of loved ones,
but always remember those birds, the bison,
their grief, too, and how the land hurts
in more chambers than one small heart
may ever hold.

The Fingers, Writing

Not all fingers hold a nail
waiting for the hammer.
Not all take up white thread
and transform it to lace.
Even fewer pick up the pen
and offer words to a lover's
body where it is so beautifully dark
as we lay in the sunlit field of grasses,
wildflowers, olive trees,
a gathering of life.

The hands have their reasons
unknown to the heart,
a needed touch,
the kindness of another skin.

The fingers have their own aims,
to make beauty, to touch softly
something to live by.

But then I remember that sometimes they lie.
When from out of the dark corridors
of some mind
he signs a writ of death.

I remember the musician who had his fingers broken
for creating songs his country didn't want.
The same is true for other lands.

As for my people, a government of hands
entreat for their land, pen and ink like blood
wrote away each stand
of ancient forest, the waters
we drank gone with the grand larceny
of fingers holding nothing
but a pen and a bottle of ink,
our stolen indigo, dark as blood.

In the distance between hand and soul
lies the history of this continent.
So now I write this poem.
Some of us have to tell
what has been done,
what they will do
now, even tomorrow,
the truth of what happens.

About Myself

We come from a land once plenty.
We came out of caves to this world,
and tall grasses
where earth rises and falls
as the ribs of a body,

bones all in their hiding,
but also the waters,
their own breath with tides
following the moon.
The human signs are here
in this two-legged animal,
imperfectly woven
but twined well enough
to be a burden basket
filled with the gatherings
of a day's work,
returning home
with common hunger,
But about myself,
I am merely
one brief living shine.

Lost in the Milky Way

Some of us are like trees that grow with a spiral grain
as if prepared for the path of the spirit's journey
to the world of all souls.

It is not an easy path.
A dog stands at the opening constellation
before you can reach the great helping hand.

The dog wants to know,
did you ever harm an animal, hurt any creature
or did you take a life you didn't eat?

This is only the first of the map. There is another
my people made of what is farther
beyond this galaxy.

It is a world that can't be imagined by usual means.
After the first,
it could be a map of forever.

It could be a cartography
shining only at some times of the year
like a great web of finery

some spider pulled from herself
to help you recall your true following,
your first breath in the dark cold.

The next door opens and Old Woman
counts your scars. She is interested in how you have been
hurt and not in anything akin to sin.

From between stars are the words we now refuse;
loneliness, longing, whatever suffering
might follow your life into the sky.

Once those are gone, the life you had
against your own will, the hope, even the prayers
take you one more bend around that river of sky.

What I Keep

Once we had mountains
and they took them down.

It was enchanted before,
with the song of golden winds
of pollens from flowers also removed,
as if they were gold
they searched for. We gave our labor.

our food, our sleeping mats.
They slept a year before we sent them away
with burning arrows. Their fat ran across earth.

They took our plants on ships
away from our beautiful woods
from the ancient forest,
took them back to strange lands
already destroyed.
Then they needed our lands,
more labor,
and more
arriving until they took our homes
while we lived yet inside them.

They took the birds,
the rookeries of beautiful waters,
feathers for hats
made from the animals of this land
and all the time they were lost,
even so much
young woman had to lead the way
for their fame.

They need us now,
so I give
my knowledge, my mind,
and stone soup.
But to myself, for myself
I keep my soul,
our gods. These no others
will never take.

Poetry Is My First Language

My influences are numerous. In "The Rocks Took Charge," an article in the journal *Ecotone*, I spoke about Pablo Neruda and stones. Also, I look at many writers of my own generation, such as Pattiann Rogers, who adds science to the personal, creating a marriage of the two that works beautifully on many levels. Her work is an earth-bound, space-traveling daily life, more interested in content than in form. The new young Native writers are also influential to today's events. Layli Long Soldier's *Whereas* and one of her recent essays have influenced my thoughts on poetry, as she writes this long poem as if it were a legal treatise.

Here I've included one part of the whole, one section of a single long poem, but the entirety ends with something like a prayer, a hope, a yearning for home and for our future life: "the grassesgrassesgrasses."

from "Whereas"
by Layli Long Soldier

Whereas I drive down the road replaying the get-together how the man and his beer bottle stated their piece and I reel at what I could have said or done better;

Whereas I could've but didn't broach the subject of "genocide" the absence of this term from the Apology and its rephrasing as "conflict" for example;

Whereas since the moment had passed I accept what's done and the knife of my conscience pierces with bone-clean self-honesty;

Whereas in a stirred conflict between settlers and an Indian that night in a circle;

Whereas I struggle to confess that I didn't want to explain anything;

Whereas truthfully I wished most to kick the legs of that man's chair out from under him;

Whereas to watch him fall backward legs flailing beer stench across his chest;

Whereas I pictured it happening in cinematic slow-motion delightful;

Whereas the curled hand I raised to my mouth was a sign of indecision;

Whereas I could've done it but I didn't;

Whereas I can admit this also took place, yes, *at least*;

*

Craig Santos Perez is another writer I seriously watch. He includes a variety of environmentally important writing, seamlessly combined with history, politics, and the familial. I have found these combinations to be important in all the mentioned writers. Here is an excerpt from one of his long poems.

from understory
by Craig Santos Perez

for my pregnant wife, nālani, during her second trimester

nālani and
i walk

to our
small community

garden plot
in mānoa —

the seed
packets in

my pocket
sound like

a baby's

toy rattle —

when do
they spray

glyphosate along
the sidewalks?

from kunia
to waimea,

fifty thousand
acres of

gmo fields —
how will

open air
pesticide drift

affect our
unborn daughter,

whose nerve
endings are

just beginning
to root?—

Our generation had DDT and then, of course, the world-changing work of
Rachel Carson and a few other environmental writers, whose thoughts were
important to life in the future, and from life in the past. These were important
influences on poetry at the time. Poets able to integrate this kind of material in
their writing are important.

As for me, my main influences are my own tribal history from the Southeast,
an ignored and unknown group of nations who came from this earth, which is its
own poetry; and we had song.

I am deeply aware of the environment, the voice of the earth, and dismayed by what is happening politically. I try to search for ways to speak about these. The poems of my own that I've selected are all based on traditional history and truths not well known, but a part of my life and of a people's historical lineage. They consider the human body and what is happening in our time, even its derivation from the past.

For example, the bones of my ancestors really have been exposed. One of our few family cemeteries is locked because bones were exposed when the river changed course. But on the other hand, we were always river travelers, living up and down the Mississippi, and were said to have once ruled the great river. In truth, numerous nations traveled the river-ways and met one another for trade, information, and to learn from one another. Not any one people ruled. We were just strong fighters against the invaders from Europe. In truth, all our Southeastern peoples and those even from the North were dependent on one another. Our people had mutual gatherings not only along the river, but on numerous footpaths now visible in new kinds of mapping.

The poems are a part of giving back and of saving, as I hold within my own spirit a remembered knowledge of our life before Christianity. Religion was forced on those of us considered pagans, and now this has become the choice of many. Still others remain closer to the world of many gods and a more fluid concept of creation that is ongoing, always open and changing, one where the world, unlike so often in Biblical materials, does not ever come to an end.

We had, and have, our own knowledge of our part of earth. Knowing the ecosystems for millennia, knowing to care for them, and having our own astronomy—we had sky watchers, the astronomers who were most respected—this is all part of indigenous knowledge. Stories that went along with the sky are important to planting and other practical aspects of life. Much of this has been lost to tribal nations. But while we suffered many wars and thefts of our lands, I also come from the saved and protected line of songs, a love of this continent and waterways, all my heart can hold.

I am simply a human, part of a great weaving, a woman who now looks forward and back at the same time, with nothing but words to pass along what she knows, words based not on belief but on complex systems of knowledge. And I call poetry my first language. It allowed me to learn to speak, to be able to grow, and it opened this life to our world.

LESLIE MARMON SILKO

LAGUNA PUEBLO

When I use the term storytelling, *I'm talking about something much bigger . . .
something that comes out of an experience and an understanding of that original
view of Creation—that we are all part of a whole; we do not differentiate or frag-
ment stories and experiences.*

Known for her award-winning fiction, Leslie Marmon Silko (1948–) is also a
gifted poet; in fact, her first book, the small but powerful *Laguna Woman*, was
a collection of poetry, and appeared in 1974—three years before the novel *Cer-
emony*. And her fabulous and under-appreciated book, *Storyteller*, contains a
number of remarkable poems. Like her fiction, Silko's poems play with the old
and the new, the living and the dead. In "The Storyteller's Escape" and "When
Sun Came to Riverwoman," Silko converts traditional Pueblo stories into con-
temporary poems that problematize love, eroticism, and gender dynamics. Silko
also takes on gender and the connection between reproductive issues and colo-
nialism in "Poem for Myself and Mei: Concerning Abortion," which address the
controversial *Roe v. Wade* decision of 1973 by way of a series of poetic correspon-
dences between the human and natural worlds. One of Silko's great gifts is her
ability to write about complicated issues in a straightforward way. Amazingly
her poems, now over forty years old, feel both recent and timeless.

Poem for Myself and Mei: Concerning Abortion

Chinle to Fort Defiance, April 1973

1.
The morning sun
          coming unstuffed with yellow light
          butterflies tumbling loose
          and blowing across the Earth.
They fill the sky
          with shimmering yellow wind
          and I see them with the clarity of ice
          shattered in mountain streams
                    where each pebble is
                    speckled and marbled
                         alive beneath the water.

2.
All winter it snowed
mustard grass
and springtime rained it.

Wide fancy meadows
warm green
          and butterflies are yellow mustard flowers
                              spilling out of the mountain.

3.
There   were horses
     near the highway
     at Ganado.
And the white one
          scratching his ass on a tree.

4.
They die softly
against the windshield
and the iridescent wings
                    flutter and cling
                              all the way home.

Love Poem

Rain smell comes with the wind
out of the southwest.
Smell of sand dunes
tall grass glistening
in the rain.
Warm raindrops that fall easy
(this woman)
The summer is born.
Smell of her breathing new life
small gray toads on
damp sand.
(this woman)
whispering to dark wide leaves
white moon blossoms dripping
tracks in the
sand.
Rain smell
I am full of hunger
deep and longing to touch
wet tall grass, green and strong beneath.
This woman loved a man
and she breathed to him
her damp earth song.
I was haunted by this story
I remember it in cottonwood leaves
their fragrance in
the shade.
I remember it in the wide blue sky
when the rain smell comes with the wind.

The Storyteller's Escape

The storyteller keeps the stories
    all the escape stories

she says "With these stories of ours
    we can escape almost anything
    with these stories we will survive."

The old teller has been on every journey
and she knows all the escape stories

    even stories told before she was born.

She keeps the stories for those who return
    but more important
    for the dear ones who do not come back
    so that we may remember them
    and cry for them with the stories.

"In the way
    we hold them
    and keep them with us forever
    and in this way
    we continue."

The story is remembered
as her best story
it is the storyteller's own escape.

In those days
the people would leave the village
and hurry into the lava flows
where they waited until the enemy had gone.

"This time they were close behind us
and we could not stop to rest.
On the afternoon of the fourth day
I was wearing the sun
for a hat.

Always before
it was me

turning around
for the last look

at the pregnant woman
the crippled boy

old man Shio'see
    slowing up
    lying down
        never getting up again.

Always before
I was the one who looked back
before the humpback hills
rose between us
so I could tell where these dear ones stopped."

But sooner or later
even a storyteller knows it will happen.
    The only thing was

this time
she couldn't be sure
if there would be anyone
to look back
and later tell the others:

She stopped on the north side of Dough Mountain
    and she said:

"The sun is a shawl on my back
its heat makes tassels that
shimmer down my arms."

And then she sat down in the shade
and closed her eyes.

to see her face for the last time

and tell the others:

"The black hills rose between us
the shady rock was above her head
and she was thinking

There won't be any escape story this time
unless maybe someone tells

She was thinking
This was how she would want them
to remember her and cry for her
If only somebody had looked back

Someone who would know then

how the sweat spilled over the rock

making streams in hills
that had no water.

She was thinking

   I could die peacefully
   if there was just someone to tell
   how I finally stopped
   and where.

She believed

   in this kind of situation
   you have to do the best you can.

   So I just might as well think of a story
   while I'm waiting to die:

         A'moo'ooh, the child looked back.

               "Don't wait!
               Go on without me!
               Tell them I said that —
               Tell them I'm too old too 'tired

I'd rather just die here
in the shade
I'd rather just die
than climb these rocky hills
in the hot soon.

The child turned back for a last look at her
off in the distance leaning against a cool rock
the old teller waiting for the enemy to find her.
The child knew

how she had been on all the escape journeys
how she hated the enemy.

She knew

what she was thinking
what she was saying to herself:

"I'll fix them good!
I'll fool them!
I'll already be dead
when the enemies come."

She laughed out loud.

I'll die just to spite them!

She was resting close to the boulder
hoping the child would tell —
otherwise
how could they remember her
how could they cry for her
without this story?

About this time

the sun lifted off from her shoulders like a butterfly.

Let the enemy wear it now!
Let them see how they like the heat
wrapping them in its blanket!

She laughed sitting there
thinking to herself
until it got dark.

They would cry when they were told
the sun had been her hat

until she could walk no more
the sun had been a shawl
until she had to sit down in the shade.

This one's the best one yet—
too bad nobody may ever hear it.

She waited all night
but at dawn
there was still no sign of the enemy.
So she decided
to go back to the village.
What difference would it make
if she ran into an enemy?
She had already waited
all night
for them to come along
and finish her.

But she didn't see anyone
no enemy,
Maybe the sun got to be too much for them too

And it was the best escape story she had come up with yet

How four days later when the people came back
from their hide-outs in the lava flow
there she was

sitting in front of her house
waiting for them.

This is the story she told,
the child who looked back,
the old teller's escape —
the story she was thinking of
her getaway story

how they remembered her
and cried for her

Because she always had a way with stories
even on the last day
when she stopped in the shade
on the north side of Dough Mountain.

When Sun Came to Riverwoman

that time
  in the sun
   beside the Rio Grande.

voice of the mourning dove
  calls
       long ago   long ago

  remembering the lost one
  remembering the love.

Out of the dense green
      eternity of springtime
  willows rustle in the blue wind
     timeless
           the year unknown
             unnamed.
The muddy fast water
  warm around my feet
  you move into the current slowly
     brown skin   thighs
     deep   intensity
     flowing water.
Your warmth penetrates
         yellow sand and sky.
Endless eyes shining always
    for green river moss
    for tiny water spiders.
Crying out   the dove
         will not let me forget
    it is ordained
    in swirling brown water
          and it carries you away,
         my lost one,

                              my love,
                                        the mountain.

man of Sun
            came to riverwoman
            and in the sundown wind
        he left her
                to sing
                        for rainclouds swelling in the northwest sky
                        for rainsmell on pale blue winds
                                                from China.

from LANGUAGE AND LITERATURE FROM A PUEBLO INDIAN PERSPECTIVE

Where I come from, the words most highly valued are those spoken from the heart, unpremeditated and unrehearsed. Among the Pueblo people, a written speech or statement is highly suspect because the true feelings of the speaker remain hidden as she reads words that are detached from the occasion and the audience. . . . Pueblo expression resembles something like a spider's web—with many little threads radiating from the center, crisscrossing on another. As with the web, the structure emerges as it is made, and you must simply listen and trust, as the Pueblo people do, that meaning will be made. . . .

There are at least six, possibly seven, distinct languages about the twenty pueblos of the southwestern United States, for example, Zuñi and Hopi. And from mesa to mesa there are subtle differences in language. But the particular language being spoken isn't as important as what a speaker is trying to say, and this emphasis on the story itself stems, I believe, from a view of narrative particular to the Pueblo and other Native American peoples—that is, that language is story.

I will try to clarify this statement. At Laguna Pueblo, for example, many individual words have their own stories. So when one is telling a story and one is using words to tell the story, each word that one is speaking has a story of its own, too. Often the speakers, or tellers, will go into these word stories, creating an elaborate structure of stories within stories. This structure, which becomes very apparent in the actual telling of a story, informs contemporary Pueblo writing and storytelling as well as the traditional narratives. This perspective on narrative—of story within story, the idea that one story is only the beginning of many stories and the sense that stories never truly end—represents an important contribution of Native American cultures to the English language.

Many people think of storytelling as something that is done at bedtime, that it is something done for small children. But when I used the term *storytelling*, I'm talking about something much bigger than that. I'm talking about something that comes out of an experience and an understanding of that original view of Creation—that we are all part of a whole; we do not differentiate or fragment stories and experiences.

So in the telling . . . the storytelling always includes the audience, the listeners. In fact, a great deal of the story is believed to be inside the listeners. The storytelling continues from generation to generation. . . .

There are a great many parallels between Pueblo experiences and those of African and Caribbean peoples—one is that we have all had the conqueror's language imposed on us. But our experience with English has been somewhat different in that the Bureau of Indian Affairs schools were not interested in teaching us the canon of Western classics. For instance, we never heard of Shakespeare. We were given Dick and Jane, and I can remember reading that the robins were heading south for the winter. It took me a long time to figure out what was going on. I worried for a while about our robins at Laguna because they didn't leave in the winter, until I finally realized that the big textbook companies are up in Boston and *their* robins do go south in the winter. But in a way, the dreadful formal education freed us by encouraging us to maintain our narratives. Whatever literature we were exposed to at school (which was damn little), at home the storytelling, the special regard for telling and bringing together through the telling, was going on constantly.

And as the old people say, "If you can remember the stories, you will be all right. Just remember the stories." When I returned to Laguna Pueblo after attending college, I wondered how the storytelling was continuing (anthropologists say that Laguna Pueblo is one of the more acculturated pueblos), so I visited an English class at Laguna-Acoma High School. I knew the students had cassette tape recorders in their lockers and stereos at home, and that they listened to Kiss and Led Zeppelin and were well informed about culture in general. I had with me an anthology of short stories by Native American writers, *The Man to Send*

Rain Clouds. One story in the book is about the killing of a state policeman in New Mexico by three Acoma Pueblo men in the early 1950s. I asked the students how many had heard this story and steeled myself for the possibility that the anthropologists were right, that the old traditions were indeed dying out and the students would be ignorant of the story. But instead, all but one or two raised their hands—they had heard the story, just as I had heard it when I was young, some in English, some in Laguna.

One of the other advantages that we Pueblos have enjoyed is that we have always been able to stay with the land. Our stories cannot be separated from their geographical locations, from actual physical places on the land. We were not relocated like so many Native American groups who were torn away from their ancestral land. And our stories are so much a part of these places that it is almost impossible for future generations to lose them—there is a story connected with every place, every object in the landscape.

Dennis Brutus has talked about the "yet unborn" as well as "those from the past," and how we are still *all* in *this* place, and language—the storytelling—is our way of passing through or being with them, of being together again. When Aunt Susie told her stories, she would tell a younger child to go open the door so that our esteemed predecessors might bring their gifts to us. "They are out there," Aunt Susie would say. "Let them come in. They're here with us *within* the stories."

A few years ago, when Aunt Susie was 106, I paid her a visit, and while I was there she said, "Well, I'll be leaving here soon. I think I'll be leaving here next week, and I'll be going over to the Cliff House." She said, "It's going to be real good to get back over there." I was listening, and I was thinking that she must be talking about her house at Paguate village, just north of Laguna. And she went on, "Well, my mother's sister (and she gave her Indian name) will be there. She has been living there. She will be there and we will be over there, and I will get a chance to write down these stories I've been telling you." Now you must understand, of course, that Aunt Susie's mother's sister, a great storyteller herself, has long since passed over into the land of the dead. But then I realized, too, that Aunt Susie wasn't talking about death the way most of us do. She was talking about "going over" as a journey, a journey that perhaps we can only begin to understand through an appreciation for the boundless capacity of language that, through storytelling, brings us together, despite great distances between cultures, despite great distances in time.

From a letter to James Wright, September 12, 1979

Dear Jim,

The poems you sent with so filled with your special wonder and the sound of peace you find in evening light. . . . I don't think anyone—no American—has ever written like you do, has ever written this American language like you do. You are fearless of the language America speaks and you love it. Some I think did not or do not fear it, but they do not love it and so write an English we seldom hear outside of the university; and then there are many who love it but are afraid it isn't "poetic" or "literary." You bring such grace and delicacy from it, coax out the astonishing range of dissonances and harmonies it allows us, that with your poems behind me I can speak confidently now about a beauty which is purely from the American heart.

When I say "American" language I mean it in the widest sense—with the expansiveness of spirit which the great land and many peoples allow. No need ever to have limited it to so few sensibilities, so few visions of what there might be in this world. At the English Institute [annual conference based at Yale University] many of the members seemed so reluctant to acknowledge that Jamaican poets are using an English language which at once loves the music of the language so much as it loves the people and the life which speak the language. It seemed that the English Institute people have somehow "forgotten" what Shakespeare loved most and did best—created moments of powerful, overwhelming vision, but with he language the people spoke, not wrote. When I think of all the puns and jokes and political jibes Shakespeare worked into his plays—all because he was conscious of the "street" English used both by the common people and by the upper classes when they "went into the streets" either literally or figuratively— and then think of the English Institute growing uncomfortable with the idea that Native American English does exist—well, Jim, I think you get the point. I dislike even to label it "Native American" and would like to think that we could see language more flexible and inclusive, that we could begin to look for the passion and expression instead of language by rote. Television English in these past ten or fifteen—that hideous, empty, artificial language television speaks—is the result of the past fifty years of working to eradicate regional usages, regional pronunciations, i.e., regional and community expression from American English, always with the melting pot theory in mind. To have a "standardized" language, in a land as big and geographically diverse as this, certainly seems ridiculous to me. Pre-Columbian America had hundreds and hundreds—maybe thousands—of completely distinct language groups. Even with the Pueblo people who shared such similar views of the world and similar geographies there are/were tremendous differences.

That is what I love most in your writing, Jim, the gully and railroad track, the sumac and coal smoke—all could only be from the place you give us and that gives you to us, that Ohio country. That Ohio country gives us your voice in "Wherever Home Is" so that you can say "Good-bye to Leonardo, good riddance" and "I'm going home with the lizard"—because that's how it sounds in you from Ohio where you come from. . . .

Leslie

*

Wherever Home Is
by James Wright

Leonardo da Vinci, haggard in basalt stone,
Will soon be gone,
A frivolous face lost in wisteria flowers.
They are turning gray and dying
All over his body.
Subtlest of wanderers
Who live beautifully by living on other lives,
They cannot find a warm vein
In Leonardo, and Leonardo
Himself will soon
Be gone.

Good riddance a little while to the insane.
Although the wisteria gets nowhere
And the sea wind crumbles Leonardo down,
A new lizard frolics in the cold sunlight

Between Leonardo's thumb and his palette.
One brief lizard
Lavishes on Leonardo and on me
The whole spring.

Goodbye to Leonardo, good riddance
To decaying madmen who cannot keep alive
The wanderers among trees.
I am going home with the lizard,
Wherever home is,
And lie beside him unguarded
In the clear sunlight.
We will lift our faces even if it rains.
We will both turn green.

JANICE GOULD

KOYANGK'AUWI MAIDU (CONCOW)

"I began to see how poetry could convey a world I felt I understood."

Poet and scholar Janice Gould (1949–) has been a forerunner in Indigenous poetry for decades. Her important collection *Earthquake Weather* delves into distinct but interrelated issues—the history and suppression of the California tribes and the history and ostracism of lesbian desire. Oftentimes in Gould's poems the pleasures of love and sexuality are set in the contact zone of California's settlement era, since both states (California and the female body) have long been been battlegrounds. Among the remarkable traits of Gould's poetry is how she foregrounds the details of daily life. Her work abounds with specifics: clothes, rooms, food, beds, skin, cars, family, landscape, animals. Frequently a poem will begin in the kitchen or along a trail or in a pasture, then raise larger questions about disruption, oppression, and dislocation, reaffirming the degree to which for her the personal is always political and the political personal.

Indian Mascot, 1959

Now begins the festival and rivalry of late fall,
the weird debauch and daring debacle
of frat-boy parties as students parade foggy streets in mock
processions, bearing on shoulders scrawny effigies of dead
defeated Indians cut from trees, where,
in the twilight, they had earlier been hung.

"Just dummies," laughs our dad, "Red Indians hung
or burned — it's only in jest." Every fall
brings the Big Game against Stanford, where
young scholars let off steam before the debacle
they may face of failed exams. "You're dead
wrong," he says to Mom, "They don't mock

real, live Indians." Around U.C. campus mock
lynchings go on. Beneath porches we see hung
the scarecrow Natives with fake long braids, dead
from the merry-making. On Bancroft Way one has fallen
indecorously to a lawn, a symbol of the debacle
that happened three generations ago in California's hills, where

Native peoples were strung up. (A way of having fun? Where
did they go, those Indian ghosts?) "Their kids perform mock
war dances, whooping, re-enacting scenes of a debacle
white folks let loose," chides Mom. "Meanwhile we hang
portraits of Presidents on school walls and never let fall
the old red, white, and blue. My dear brother is dead

because he fought in a white man's war. How many dead
Indians do they need to feel okay? This whole thing wears
on my soul." In the dark car we go silent, and the fall
night gets chillier. In yards, blazing bonfires mock
the stars that glow palely somewhere above. A thin moon hangs
over the tule fogs. I've never heard the word "debacle"

before and wonder what it means. "What's a debacle, Mom?" I ask. "Oh, honey, it's a terrible and deadly collapse. Complete ruin." I've noticed how the hung Indians have their heads slumped forward. They wear old clothes, headbands with feathers, face paint, moccasins instead of boots. Little do we know this fall

living Indians at Feather Falls
leave tobacco to mark that, indeed,
we're still here, lungs full of indigenous air.

The Day of the Dead

I wish it were like this:
el día de los muertos comes
and we fill our baskets with bread,
apples, chicken, and beer,
and go out to the graveyard.

We bring flowers with significant colors —
yellow, crimson, and gold —
the strong hungry colors of life,
full of saliva and blood.

We sit on the sandy mounds
and I play my accordion.
It groans like the gates of hell.
The flames of the votives
flicker in the wind.

My music makes everything sway,
all the visible and invisible —
friends, candles, ants, the wind.
Because for me life ripens,

and for now it's on my side
though it's true I am often afraid.

I wear my boots when I play the old squeeze-box,
and stomp hard rhythms
till the headstones dance on their graves.

Kim

We sat on the stairs at our friend's house,
all of sixteen. Giddy with longing
and thick hesitation, I wanted
to touch her face. Had she
waited for that gesture?
What would she think?
I had gazed at her often,
wondering what to do,
how to be. She had listened
and nodded when I sang,
strumming my guitar.

At last, almost trembling,
I whispered, *Sometimes
I hate you*, and watched
as she recoiled from that slap.

She stood without a word,
and turned to look at me,
narrowing me with her eyes. Aghast,
I hardened myself,
stopped hot tears,
but felt myself falling,
like a rock hurled furiously,
through the arc of my shame,
my lie.

A Poem

A poem is about to flower
full force from my spleen,
my wrists, my ankles. I could feel
the pip of it in last night's dream
that kept threading its way
back to sacred land, where
I found myself in my twenties,
and where, later, you and I
were dream-happy. Our house,
the one that appears in all
the strange locales you and I
dream-inhabit, could be seen,
dimly, through the pines
on a dry hillside. Our landlady
was there, stooping over her garden.
We are always moving in or moving away
from that falling-down place made of stone,
or weathered wood, or adobe.
But just passing by our casita
as I did in last night's dream
made me feel excited — yes,
there it is! — and serene,
like seeing an old friend.
And when I woke, I longed
for that familiar dreamscape,
as if it is a real land, as if
that dark earth the landlady turns
with her trowel is scented
with loam, is mapped with leaves
and small roots, as if the wind
blowing dust down the mountain road
is an actual wind, as if a poem
could emerge from a seed.

Poor in Spirit

You, at midnight, suddenly awake,
blinking in the yellow light
of the single bulb
that hung from the ceiling.
You, in a disheveled nightgown,
pushing back your brown hair,
coughing, smiling shyly at me.
You, coming to my bed
not many nights later,
gazing into my eyes,
saying little, your finger tracing
my mouth. You leaning on
the shoulder of your boyfriend,
his arm around your waist. You
still watching me. You
with your nervous laugh,
your jumpiness, your
too-many-drugs.
You locked-down
in an overheated psych ward,
hunched over,
hugging yourself,
not looking at me,
while outside,
beyond wire-meshed windows,
Portland traffic stalled and started
along the old highway, a train
hooted at a nearby crossing,
guys in business suits spanked
young go-go girls in smoky clubs,
and a murder of crows mocked and scolded
among the downed leaves of winter trees.

INFLUENCES

Becoming a poet was an odd choice for me even though I had written a poem as early as first grade! It was about rain. At thirteen, I was inspired to write a verse about the ocean. My teacher was impressed. She had not even assigned us to write a poem.

I had a love-hate relationship with the poetry we read in high school. I remember one of my English teachers working privately with me to help me learn to "read" a poem by Siegfried Sassoon. I was frightened by my density and acutely embarrassed. I felt too stupid to understand the symbols and metaphors, how language was being shaped to convey a deeper, sharper meaning. But secretly poetry intrigued me because I understood that it could carry significance beyond literal words on the page.

A few years beyond high school, I found myself in Oregon. At the college bookstore, I found a translation of Rainer Maria Rilke's *Duino Elegies*. I had sat in on a class in which the First Elegy was discussed and was impressed by the professor's insight into this work. The language was gorgeous; it felt powerful. I did not understand Rilke, but I liked hearing the lines as I read them aloud to myself.

It was not until I took a class with poet Edith Jenkins at Merritt College a few years later that I really began to learn to read poetry. In her literature class we read the Romantic poets Wordsworth, Keats, Shelley, and the generation of English poets that included Rupert Brooke and Dylan Thomas. Knowing I liked to write, Edith suggested that I read Gary Snyder. I purchased *Earth House Hold* and struggled through it. Some of Rexroth's shorter poems were more to my taste, as were works by William Stafford. However, when I found Snyder's *Riprap and Cold Mountain Poems* and *The Back Country*, and Philip Levine's *Not This Pig*, I began to see how poetry could convey a world I felt I understood. For years I had hiked and backpacked in the high Sierra. I had worked in canneries, restaurants, factories, and on a ranch. I thought, "I can write like that." I meant that I could use my own diction, could write about work, travels, and my blossoming attraction to women.

In another class on women's poetry, we spent time with Sylvia Plath, Anne Sexton, Margaret Atwood, Marge Piercy, and Alice Walker. Probably I felt some kind of permission to understand my own shame and anger by looking at how women writers encountered these intense feelings, how they understood their place in the world. I began to look for other Native American writers. What were they saying and how were they saying it? An early anthology, Ken Rosen's *Voic-*

es of the Rainbow: Contemporary Poetry by Native Americans, introduced me to Leslie Marmon Silko, James Welch, Ray Young Bear, and others. I was particularly taken with the work of Colville poet Ramona Wilson because of how the land spoke to her, and how she brought it into focus and praised it through language.

Over time, these early influences told me I could write, and I have continued ever since to maintain and nurture a relationship with this strange and startling art.

*

Riprap
by Gary Snyder

Lay down these words

Before your mind like rocks.

      placed solid, by hands

In choice of place, set

Before the body of the mind

      in space and time:

Solidity of bark, leaf, or wall

      riprap of things:

Cobble of milky way,

      straying planets,

These poems, people,

      lost ponies with

Dragging saddles —

      and rocky sure-foot trails.

The worlds like an endless

four-dimensional

Game of *Go*.

ants and pebbles

In the thin loam, each rock a word

a creek-washed stone

Granite: ingrained

with torment of fire and weight

Crystal and sediment linked hot

all change, in thoughts,

As well as things.

RAY A. YOUNG BEAR
MESKWAKI

"English was a second language wherein poetry, the craft, required acceptance and then adaptation."

Ray A. Young Bear (1950–) has the ability to capture in words moments in life that seem incomprehensible. While working with situations of violence, confusion, and despair, with a beautiful command of language Young Bear creates artful poetic encounters. In poems loaded with metaphor and a lively surrealism, he sparks a strong emotional response and ensures that the complex spirituality of his people is visible and audible, entirely alive. In "The Bird of Aegis," for example, the poet locates Bear and Eagle clan deities alongside himself in order to enact personal and tribal loss. Young Bear's use of symbolic images recurs in many poems, for instance in "Four Hinterland Abstractions," as if the poems are questing for resonance in the indigenous mind rather than among European antecedents. Working along the intersections of Native and non-Native cultures, Young Bear renders incremental stories that when read together become an epic, historical and immediate, of the Meskwaki people and of his personal consciousness, which is constantly in the process of making and remaking itself.

To See as Far as the Grandfather World

The photograph. On this particular March day
in 1961, Theodore Facepaint, who was nine
years old, agreed to do a parody. With hand
balanced on hip and the left leg slightly
in front of the right, my newly found friend
positioned himself on Sand Hill before turning
to face the hazy afternoon sun. This was a pose
we had become familiar with:
                                    the caricature
of a proud American Indian, looking out
toward the vast prairie expanse, with one hand
shielding the bronze eyes. When I projected
the image of the color 35 mm slide onto
the wall last week I remembered the sense
of mirth in which it was taken. Yet somewhere
slightly north of where we were clowning around,
Grandmother was uprooting medicinal roots
                            from the sandy soil
and placing them inside her flower-patterned
apron pockets to thaw out.

Twenty-nine years later, if I look long enough,
existential symbols are almost detectable.
The direction of the fiery sun in descent, for example,
is considered the Black Eagle Child Hereafter.
Could I be seeing too much? Past the west
and into the Grandfather World? Twice
                        I've caught myself asking:
Was Ted's pose portentous? When I look
closely at the background of the Indian Dam
below—the horizontal line of water that runs
through the trees and behind Ted — I also know
that Liquid Lake with its boxcar-hopping
                            light is nearby.

For Ted and his Well-Off Man Church,
the comets landed on the crescent-shaped
beach and lined themselves up for a ritualistic
presentation. For Jane Ribbon, a mute healer,
a seal haunted this area. But further upriver
is where the ancient deer hunter was offered
immortality by three goddesses. While
the latter story of our geographic genesis
is fragmented, obscuring and revealing
itself as a verisimilitude, it is important.
Ted and I often debated what we would
have done had we been whisked through
a mystical doorway to a subterranean enclave.
Ted, unlike the ancient hunter who turned
down paradise, would have accepted —
and the tribe never would have flexed
its newborn spotted wings. In the hunter's
denial we were thus assigned as Keepers
of Importance. But the question being asked
today is, Have we kept anything?

Our history, like the earth with its
abundant medicines, Grandmother used
to say, is unfused with ethereality. Yet in
the same breath she'd openly exclaim
that with modernity comes a cultural toll.

In me, in Ted, and everyone.
          Stories then, like people, are subject to change.
More so under adverse conditions. They
are also indicators of our faithfulness. Since
the goddesses' doorway was sealed shut by
                    our own transgressions,
Grandmother espoused that unbounded
youth would render tribal language
and religion inept, that each lavish
novelty brought into our homes would

make us weaker until there was nothing.
                    No lexicon. No tenets.
Zero divine intervention. She was also
attuned to the fact that for generations
our grandparents had wept unexpectedly
for those of us caught in the blinding
stars of the future.

Mythology, in any tribal-oriented society,
is a crucial element. Without it, all else
is jeopardized with becoming untrue. While
the acreages beneath Ted's feet and mine
offered relative comfort back then,
we are probably more accountable now
                    to ourselves — and others.
Prophecy decrees it. Most fabled among
the warnings is the one that forecasts
the advent of our land-keeping failures.
Many felt this began last summer when
a whirlwind abruptly ended a tribal
celebration. From the north in the shape
of an angry seagull it swept up dust.
corn leaves, and assorted debris,
as it headed toward the audacious
"income-generating architecture,"
the gambling hall. At the last second
the whirlwind changed direction, going
toward the tribal recreation complex.
Imperiled, the people within the circus tent-
like structure could only watch as the panels
flapped crazily. A week later, my family said
the destruction was attributable to the gambling
hall, which was the actual point of weakness
of the tribe itself.

Which is to say the hill where a bronze-eyed
Ted once stood is under threat of impermanence.

By allowing people who were not created
by the Holy Grandfather to lead us we may
cease to own what Ted saw on the long-ago day.
From Rolling Head Valley to Runner's Bluff
                    and over the two rivers
our hold is gradually being unfastened by
false leaders. They have forgotten that their
own grandparents arrived here under a Sacred
Chieftain. This geography is theirs nonetheless.
and it shall be as long as the first gifts given
are intact. In spite of everything that we are
not, this crown of hills resembles lone islands
amid an ocean of corn, soybean fields,
and low-lying fog. Invisibly clustered on
the Black Eagle Child Settlement's slopes
are the remaining Earthlodge clans.
                    The western edge of this
woodland terrain overlooks the southern
lowlands of the Iowa and Swanroot Rivers,
while the eastern edge splits widely into several
valleys, where the Settlement's main road winds
through. It is on this road where Ted and I walked.
It is on this road where Ted met a pack
of predators.

Along the color slide's paper edge the year
1961 is imprinted. Ted and I were fourth
graders at Weeping Willow Elementary.
Nine years later, in 1970, a passenger train
took us to Southern California for college.
It proved to be a lonely place where winter
                    appeared high atop
the San Gabriel Mountains on clear days.
Spanish-influenced building styles, upper-middle-
class proclivities, and the arid climate had a subtle
asphyxiating effect. Instead of chopping firewood
        for father's nonexistent blizzard,

I began my evenings in Frary Dining Hall
where Orozco's giant mural with erased privates
called Prometheus loomed above. My supper
would consist of tamales and cold shrimp salad
instead of boiled squirrel with flour dumplings.
Through mountain forest fires the Santa Ana
winds showered the campus with sparks and ashes.
In a wide valley where a smoke- and smog-darkened
night came early, the family album possessed its
own shimmery light. Pages were turned. A visual
record of family and childhood friends. Time.
                    Ted and I transforming,
separating. During the first Christmas break
in which we headed back to the Black Eagle
Child Settlement, Ted froze me in celluloid:
against a backdrop of snow-laden pine trees
a former self wears a windswept topcoat
Levi bell-bottoms, cowboy boots, and tinted
glasses. Ted and I, like statues, are held
captive in photographic moments.
            As the earth spins, however,
the concrete mold disintegrates,
exposing the vulnerable wire
foundation of who we are not.

Our Bird Aegis

An immature black eagle walks assuredly
across a prairie meadow. He pauses in mid-step
with one talon over the wet snow to turn
around and see.

Imprinted in the tall grass behind him
are the shadows of his tracks,

claws instead of talons, the kind
that belongs to a massive bear.
And he goes by that name:
Ma kwi so ta.

And so this aegis looms against the last
spring blizzard. We discover he's concerned
and the white feathers of his spotted hat
flicker, signaling this.

With outstretched wings he tests the sutures.
Even he is subject to physical wounds and human
tragedy, he tells us.

The eyes of the Bear-King radiate through
the thick, falling snow. He meditates on the loss
of my younger brother — and by custom
suppresses his emotions.

John Whirlwind's Doublebeat Songs, 1956

I.

Menwi — yakwatoni — beskonewiani.
Kyebakewina — maneniaki
ketekattiki
ebemanemateki
ebemanemateki

*

Good-smelling are these flowers.
As it turned out, they were milkweeds
dance-standing
as the wind passes by,
as the wind passes by.

2.

Inike — ekatai — waseyaki
netena — wasesi.
Memettine
beskattenetisono.
Memettine.

*

It is now almost daylight,
I said to the firefly.
For the last time
illuminate yourself.
For the last time.

Four Hinterland Abstractions

1.
today a truck
carrying a Tomahawk
missile reportedly tipped
over on the interstate
                somewhere
labelled an "unarmed warhead"
its fabulous smoke had to be
placated with priestlike
words being murmured by
                yucca-wielding
authorities & while covering
the dormant but cross entity
with tarps that had paintings
of blue mountaintop lakes
                they affirmed
their presence with nudges
& reminders this valley

was sculpted by the once lovely
wings of a vulture & here
              is where
you will quietly attend to
the disorder we heard plainly
over the traffic's ubiquitous
din & before a smoldering
              star's song

2.
from one winter night
an inquisitive firefly has directed
itself toward my three children
& through its testament
              of cold light
floral patterns appear over
their snowy tracks replacing
shadows with light that's detailed
& compelling us to place ourselves
              beside the weeping
willow grandfather to ask him
please behold the witness
              witness

3.
previously as a winsome
ghost that's awash in green
& yellow pulsating colors
it taunted the blue heeler
              named
Simon simon ese who lunged
thereafter fishlike into the night
arcing its scaled torso in order
to bite the protoplasmic wings
              so make note
of this psychically attuned
defender i scratched on

the frosted car window
without looking around

4.
on a hot windy afternoon in
downtown why cheer he walked
across the street from where
the dime store used to be
                    pointing
to a remnant column he said
ke me kwe ne ta ayo a be i yo e te ki?
do you recall what used to be here?
having just arrived from
                    overseas
& wearing boots covered
with ochre grains of distant
battlefields he reached down
& crushed several into small
                    clouds
that sped over the sidewalk
as i nodded yes

The Summer of 1969: Children of Speakthunder

I.

While this long overdue narrative seeks to recount events and people from forty-eight years ago, some memories are in perpetuum fragmented. Since my early "word-collecting" days zipped by like shy meteors, I'm grateful for having recalled anything at all. For now, it isn't age-related forgetfulness. Basically, as a fledgling who was on the verge of weighing what to fence in or out, only so much could be processed. Moreover, English was a second language wherein poetry, the craft, required acceptance and then adaptation. Therefore, if there are chronologic or factual errors in this retrospective, then a rewrite or correction would be in order. Beyond that, this anthology has provided a door to finally contemplate the past. It's been challenging and wholly interesting. Inevitably, there were moments when more could've been said, but that would've taken more time, an element that has, at 67, become increasingly scarce.

> *Places:Meskwaki Settlement & Decorah, Iowa*
> *Bemidji, Minnesota & Claremont, California*
> *Vermillion, South Dakota & Cheney, Washington*
> *Missoula, Montana*

On a sunny, July 1969 day my family took me to Tama, Iowa. There, I boarded a Greyhound bus for Bemidji, Minnesota. Although I rarely ventured beyond the Meskwaki Settlement, a writers workshop, as proposed by Upward Bound staff, seemed worthwhile.

Only weeks earlier, I had dropped out of staff-recommended college preparatory classes. Basically, since college was scheduled for the following month, in California, a greater challenge was ahead. Moreover, since nothing could prepare me for what might be a tough academic year, my remaining time was better spent at home.

Several nights upon my return, I heard someone talking to my mother, in English, on the porch. I had just taken a shower.

Oh, there, he's done," my mother said, adding in a low voice that I wasn't doing anything anyway. Then, in Meskwaki she said, "Ke ki tti ta-wi na? Are you dressed yet?"

As I cautiously peered out the window, a staffer's face popped up, surprising me.

"Hey, Ray, there you are!" he said. "I came down to see if we can talk you into something: a writers workshop, in Minnesota."

When he explained real writers would serve as teachers, the idea quickly got my attention. I don't recall when I agreed to go, but a round-trip bus ticket soon arrived by mail.

2.

Up until then, two summers had been spent at Luther College, in Decorah, Iowa. That's where a writing assignment first piqued staff's attention. For whatever reason, as creativity or simply a short-cut, a poem resulted. Considering rock and roll lyrics and tribal songs were the closest forms of poetry I knew, the effort must've been raw. By the third summer, a poem had been published and James Dickey's Helmets was the only poetry book read. Granted, it wasn't much, but composing poems, in English, and then seeing them, in print, was fascinating. Without question, a writers' workshop would comport with my interests.

As this word-collecting journey began, a poem got me to Pomona College. In 1971, it was also featured in a student writing anthology Talkin' About Us. By then, roughly 60 first-draft poems were composed on campus, with several being published per Robert Bly's recommendations.

While Pomona didn't work out, its readings by Charles Bukowski, Diane Wakoski, Galway Kinnell, Seamus Heaney, and Simon Ortiz, to name a few, bolstered my aspirations. The books I bought at random by Conrad Aiken, May Swenson, Phillip Levine, Charles Reznikoff, and Rod McKuen were studied.

And akin to Robert Bly's editing lesson, highlighted hereunder, there was a belated impact from hearing Simon Ortiz speak Acoma in his poems. Similarly, N. Scott Momaday's song translation in House Made of Dawn, whether literary or traditional, became a spark for a future linguistic fire.

*

In the summer of 1969, David Bowie's "Space Oddity" was released and America's moonwalk made the news. But, like the bus ride to Minnesota, they're blurs. At Bemidji State College, however, I roomed with a college student named Merle Kessler (A/K/A Ian Shoals). The writing workshop instructors, at least the ones I recall, were Robert Bly, David Ignatow, David Ray, and Frederick Manfred.

At some workshop point, I was asked by Bly to meet him and Ray to discuss my work. Hearing my lines being read aloud and critiqued was remarkable. Occasionally, Bly would hover over my Haiku-type poems with a pen.

"Now, Young Bear," he asked, "do you see what we're doing?"

He was making strikethroughs that I had yet to learn about.

"We like 'Hail of Ice,' but some words aren't needed. Because what you've said here is adequate, if we make a few changes, like this."

3.

After being reduced, the poem looked and sounded better. Yet, since the poem dealt with climatic aberration, an event my grandmother referred to as naina - eakwikamikaki, when the world ends, was it appropriate? Could prophecy be reworded?

At twenty-one, the same questions prompted my exit of Donald Justice's class. Yes, I could learn from Iowa City, but could non-Indians edit Animism? Especially if they didn't believe in it?

Although Bly's editing lesson was significant, I believed the English words that flowed artistically from mind to pen and paper as gifts were untouchable. Thus, according to formative perceptions, they were exempt from edits. Today, in stark contrast, some poems--for the King of Revision--can take eight to ten years to finish. If fiction and nonfiction wasn't part of the regimen, perhaps there'd be less toil.

*

The next day, on a Bemidji campus sidewalk, Bly showed me a paperback called The New American Review.

"You can have it while you're here," he said. "Read it."

He then asked if I had ever heard of James Welch. When I said no, I learned Welch was a Blackfeet from Montana, with poems in the paperback. As Bly spoke in glowing terms, gesturing as if his hands could read, I scanned "In My Lifetime." Smitten by its structure and clarity, I became an instant fan. It was short of a divination. All of what I imagined, at 18, as being creatively possible in tribal-based poetry, if only I could mature quickly and write as well, had been done.

Interlacing the existential spectrum:1983 was the year I traded powwow songs with Floyd Rider, a Blackfeet from the Two Medicine Lake Singers. That's when my father said his father recounted a long ago visitor named Kipp. Apparently, he was Blackfeet who shared songs while passing through with a wild west-type show.

1987 took me to Eastern Washington University at the behest of Professor Elizabeth Lynn-Cook, a Sioux writer. One weekend, my wife, Stella, and I drove from Cheney to Browning, Montana to visit and sing with Two Medicine Lake. We eventually invited Floyd's drum group to a Meskwaki Music & Dance Symposium.

Also, in researching James Welch's novel, Fools Crow, in order to teach it, I learned the Blackfeet called medicine bundles with a name that sounded like my father's reference for same.

4.

At East Glacier Park, when Floyd spoke about Bigfoot brushing its body near the lower roof of his home, I translated the English name in Meskwaki, Memakikatata. He noted that it sounded like how they'd translate it, adding there were nights when the beings could be heard, calling one another from one mountaintop to the other.

1993 was underscored with an honorary degree from Luther College. In a
photograph taken by a former U.B. staffer, the one who pitched the Bemidji writers
workshop decades earlier, my cap and gown resemble floatation devices on a person
rescued from a lake. The following year, during a Poetry Society of America reading
tour, I met another former staffer and asked how the writers workshop idea came
to be. On the patio of the Chateau Marmont Hotel, the music professor reflect-
ed and then chimed, "Why, Ray, that's easy; we thought it'd be good for you."
Perhaps what no one expected was their encouragement for my interest turning into
a commitment. Occasionally, as with most things, there were questions regarding its
purpose. With time's passage, however, they vanished in a panoply of "word-collecting"
manifestations.

By 2003, as tribute to Blackfeet singers, two of our children received Kipp and
Rider as their middle names.

On the last night of the Bemidji writers workshop, we read from our work.
In a photograph from this event, with my hands clutching the podium, I look
like a person climbing back into a canoe.

It was emotionally difficult reading "Hail of Ice," the one Bly edited.

The next day, with no chance to return the New American Review to Bly,
I went home. By the second week in August, as I sat on the forest's edge beside
the Iowa River, I knew a decision that would change me forever had been made.
A train ticket for Claremont, California was waiting on my desk.

Within a year, Bemidji State College invited me for a poetry reading. At 19,
it was my first gig and a chance for redemption, to read without freaking out. It
might've been spring break when I flew from California to Minnesota. There was
snow in Bemidji and it was cold. Afterwards, in a state of bliss, I re-routed the ticket
for Iowa.

*

In 1971, an editor of the South Dakota Review invited me and other Indi-
an poets to read in Vermillion. We were part of his American Indian II issue.
In the introduction, the editor notes Bemidji as a place where I first came to
his attention.

Upon deplaning in Sioux City, the editor asked if I knew James Welch.

5.
""Yes, I know his poems and I've seen his photograph."

The editor smiled and pointed to a man in a suit coat next to him.

"Well, Bear, meet James Welch."

James grinned and began chuckling as we eagerly shook hands. In disbelief, before joining his laughter, I had to look twice at the grandfather of American Indian poetry.

The next night, we were at a renown Sioux painter's home, Oscar Howe. On the wall was a cubist-like painting of a sitting flute player that I admired. When Howe stood next to me, I told him so. After supper and drinks, a Navaho poet, Jay Ralph Johnson, and I took turns singing songs. I hope James appreciated them, including Duane Niatum, Simon Ortiz, and our hosts. By then, with a chapter from his novel featured in *American Indian II*, James was writing fiction. And there he remained, becoming a legacy and carving stories from the rugged landscape of American literature.

Meskwaki songs, like words, came early. By that virtue, like birds who magically usher in dawn's light, they are first. My love for tribal music hasn't waned since that night in Vermillion. In the 1980s, tribal songs were documented and translated. Eventually, compositions like "John Whirlwind's Doublebeat Songs, 1956," "Micah Rider's Song," and "The One I Live With" were made. Between now and the moment I cease to see daylight, more tunes are envisioned. After a half century of writing poetry in English, Meskwaki takes precedence. With linguistic atrophy near our doorsteps, it'd be good, if new and emerging tribal poets and writers, at some point, focused on their languages. The sooner the better. Here, the teachings are stringent: "The Creator doesn't speak English, so how will you speak to Him?" Could that question, paraphrased from my late grandmother, extend to others? Realistically, whether one is monolingual or bilingual, there's an advantage. Because empowerment dwells in the choices we make. Ideally, in my opinion, first language, culture, religion, and history should take priority. But upholding traditions isn't easy. Which is why I humbly stand in the shadows of those who bear great responsibilities. In an ever-changing world, where some succeed and others succumb, survival is hard fought. Fortunately, by a preponderance of our grandparents tenacity to face mad-

nesse and its machinations, there's assurance we can do the same. Because this, as we were told, is our land.

*

On August 3, 2003, James Welch left for the Grandfather World. He was sixty-two. On or about the same time, my wife Stella said that someone's hand, the back part, touched her temple during the night.

6.

We believe it was James visiting as a kind-hearted spirit.

Although I had the honor of meeting him just three times—in South Dakota 1971, Iowa 1978, and Montana 1987, I considered him a friend. We shared a penchant, to write creatively.

The last time I saw James was at his home in Missoula. My reading at the university had concluded. That's when Stella gave Lois, his companion, a necklace with a beaded medallion. A photograph was taken of James and myself that I have yet to see. I can still hear him chuckling as a mountain stream flowed wondrously nearby. The literary influence James instilled in my early poetic wanderings is monumental.

If I have a chance to meet James Welch in the Afterlife, I plan on asking him what I wanted to ask long ago: can we grab a six-pack and go fishing?

*

In My Lifetime
by James Welch

This day the children of Speakthunder
run the wrong man, a saint unable
to love a weasel way, able only to smile
and drink the wind that makes the others go.
Trees are ancient in his breath.
His bleeding feet tell a story of run
the sacred way, chase the antelope naked
till it drops, the odor of run
quiet in his blood. He watches cactus

jump against the moon. Moon is speaking
woman to the ancient fire. Always woman.
His sins were numerous, this wrong man.
Buttes were good to listen from. With thunder-
hands his father shaped the dust, circled
fire, tumbled up the wind to make a fool.
Now the fool is dead. His bones go back
so scarred in time, the buttes are young to look
for signs that say a man could love his fate,
that winter in the blood is one sad thing.

His sins — I don't explain. Desperate in my song,
I run these woman hills, translate wind
to mean a kind of life, the children of Speakthunder
are never wrong and I am rhythm to strong medicine.

JOY HARJO
MVSKOKE

"In the time between birth and speech, I lived primarily somewhere between the natural world and the dream world. I would travel to other times where I was not a child. And it was not Oklahoma. I knew the earth as a living being."

Joy Harjo (1951–) may be the most influential living Indigenous American poet. She has recently captured the 2015 Wallace Stevens Prize from the Academy of American Poets and the 2017 Ruth Lilly Poetry Prize from the Poetry Foundation, among the most prestigious awards in American letters, underscoring Harjo's place as one of a America's most important writers. She is also a celebrated musician, and musicality is bountiful in her poems. Lyrically and rhythmically, her work often utilizes refrains, and these poems feel like a mix of text, chant, and song. Her subjects range from individual people, often women, to the present state and potential future of Indigenous reality. As in "She Had Some Horses," Harjo often moves back and forth between unreal and real, ugly and lovely; and while her poems often pivot upon moments of anguish, anger, and fear, they always seek wholeness. Indeed, many of Harjo's poems summon us to liminal states—borders, portals, and nodes of contact—where as individuals and communities we can aspire to inhabit distinct realms.

*See also page 267 for Elise Paschen's testimony to the influence of Joy Harjo's "She Had Some Horses," and page 409 for Jennifer Elise Foerster's testimony to the influence of Joy Harjo's "Speaking Tree."

The Woman Hanging From the Thirteenth Floor Window

She is the woman hanging from the 13th floor
window. Her hands are pressed white against the
concrete moulding of the tenement building. She
hangs from the 13th floor window in east Chicago,
with a swirl of birds over her head. They could
be a halo, or a storm of glass waiting to crush her.

She thinks she will be set free.

The woman hanging from the 13th floor window
on the east side of Chicago is not alone.
She is a woman of children, of the baby, Carlos,
and of Margaret, and of Jimmy who is the oldest.
She is her mother's daughter and her father's son.
She is several pieces between the two husbands
she has had. She is all the women of the apartment
building who stand watching her, watching themselves.

When she was young she ate wild rice on scraped down
plates in warm wood rooms. It was in the farther
north and she was the baby then. They rocked her.

She sees Lake Michigan lapping at the shores of
herself. It is a dizzy hole of water and the rich
live in tall glass houses at the edge of it. In some
places Lake Michigan speaks softly, here, it just sputters
and butts itself against the asphalt. She sees
other buildings just like hers. She sees other
women hanging from many-floored windows
counting their lives in the palms of their hands
and in the palms of their children's hands.

She is the woman hanging from the 13th floor window

on the Indian side of town. Her belly is soft from
her children's births, her worn levis swing down below
her waist, and then her feet, and then her heart.
She is dangling.

The woman hanging from the 13th floor hears voices.
They come to her in the night when the lights have gone
dim. Sometimes they are little cats mewing and scratching
at the door, sometimes they are her grandmother's voice,
and sometimes they are gigantic men of light whispering
to her to get up, to get up, to get up. That's when she wants
to have another child to hold onto in the night, to be able
to fall back into dreams.

And the woman hanging from the 13th floor window
hears other voices. Some of them scream out from below
for her to jump, they would push her over. Others cry softly
from the sidewalks, pull their children up like flowers and gather
them into their arms. They would help her, like themselves.

But she is the woman hanging from the 13th floor window,
and she knows she is hanging by her own fingers, her
own skin, her own thread of indecision.

She thinks of Carlos, of Margaret, of Jimmy.
She thinks of her father, and of her mother.
She thinks of all the women she has been, of all
the men. She thinks of the color of her skin, and
of Chicago streets, and of waterfalls and pines.
She thinks of moonlight nights, and of cool spring storms.
Her mind chatters like neon and northside bars.
She thinks of the 4 a.m. lonelinesses that have folded
her up like death, discordant, without logical and
beautiful conclusion. Her teeth break off at the edges.
She would speak.

The woman hangs from the 13th floor window crying for

the lost beauty of her own life. She sees the
sun falling west over the grey plane of Chicago.
She thinks she remembers listening to her own life
break loose, as she falls from the 13th floor
window on the east side of Chicago, or as she
climbs back up to claim herself again.

A Postcolonial Tale

Every day is a reenactment of the creation story. We emerge from dense unspeak-
able material, through the shimmering power of dreaming stuff.

This is the first world, and the last.

One we abandoned ourselves for television, the box that separates the dreamer
from the dreaming. It was as if we were stolen, put into a bag carried on the back
of a white man who pretends to own the earth and the sky. In the sack were all
the people of the world. We fought until there was a hole in the bag.

When we fell we were not aware of falling. We were driving to work, or to the
mall. The children were in school learning subtraction with guns.

We found ourselves somewhere near the diminishing point of civilization, not
far from the trickster's bag of tricks. Everything was as we imagined it. The earth
and stars, every creature and leaf imagined with us.

When we fell we were not aware of falling. We were driving to work or to the
mall. The children were in school learning subtraction with guns.

The imagining needs praise as does any living thing.
We are evidence of this praise.
And when we laugh, we're indestructible.
No story or song will translate
the full impact of falling,

or the inverse power of rising up.
Of rising up.

Our children put down their guns when we did to imagine with us.
We imagined the shining link between the heart and the sun.
We imagined tables of food for everyone.
We imagined the songs.

The imagination conversely illumines us, speaks with us, sings with us, loves us.

Eagle Poem

To pray you open your whole self
To sky, to earth, to sun, to moon
To one whole voice that is you.
And know there is more
That you can't see, can't hear;
Can't know except in moments
Steadily growing, and in languages
That aren't always sound but other
Circles of motion.
Like eagle that Sunday morning
Over Salt River. Circled in blue sky
In wind, swept our hearts clean
With sacred wings.
We see you, see ourselves and know
That we must take the utmost care
And kindness in all things.
Breathe in, knowing we are made of
All this, and breathe, knowing
We are truly blessed because we
Were born, and die soon within a
True circle of motion,
Like eagle rounding out the morning

Inside us.
We pray that it will be done
In beauty.
In beauty.

Adapted from "One Song"

The first place to start is with the land, for context. That's what I've been taught by every indigenous culture that I have come into contact with, including my Mvskoke people. Though we were removed from our homelands in the southeast, I have come to believe that the earth lives within us: we essentially are the earth. I've considered this connection and our losses frequently as someone from a tribe forcibly removed from home. I come from those who were part of the resistance against the move, including my grandfather Monahwee and a great-uncle Osceola. Most of the citizenry fought the move, and most names we do not know because they would not fit into English words. I've traveled back to the southeast and recently lived there for a few years to directly witness our lands, to see what had happened. When you start with Native literature written in English, you start with the American holocaust. When I lived there recently, we were not there, we were written out of the story and appeared only in place names. Confederate flags were flown by the descendants of those who stole the land and would block Native peoples migrating up from the south in what is now known as Mexico, even though it's old knowledge that the currently political boundaries are nonexistent in other ways of seeing and knowing. The lands in the south, from Knoxville down into Georgia, Alabama and Florida are beautiful and rich and when we were on them we needed nothing else. It is heartbreaking to be there and my forthcoming book of poetry from Norton, An *American Sunrise*, is about this return, and what I learned there.

I would say that the first poems that inspired me were not in English or human languages. I was an outside girl, and I liked to be alone. I learned much that way—as I was always being spoken to—Sunrise was my favorite time, and it still is—many of my poems begin there. It was the plants who made their presences known then, the creatures of the earth, the sky elements, the stones... There, the world made sense when it often didn't in my growing up years in Tulsa, which is the northern border of the Muscogee Creek Nation west of the Mississippi. I loved the music that wrapped my ears when I was in this space. There was no confusion. We all go to the natural world to remember who we truly are as we walk through challenging personal and collective history.

I didn't speak the Mvskoke language growing up. My father's mother died when he was relatively young. My mother's mother grew up speaking some Cherokee, but that too was discouraged. It was difficult for people to maintain their language when it was forbidden, and the educational systems demanded English only.

I am learning the Mvskoke language now, song by song.

I am learning the language through singing, by writing songs in Mvskoke and learning them in Mvskoke. My album, *Red Dream, A Trail Beyond Tears*, includes many of them. Each new word, phrase, or concept opens up to a different reality. When I hear the word *vnvketckv* I see dignity, I see survivors of a several-hundred-mile walk, I hear the sun being acknowledged as a person, I feel kindness.

What is most resonant is that sense of connection between all beings. All beings have their own dignity, their own humanness. And the philosophy of *vnvketckv* remains at the center of what it means to be a Mvskoke person—that is, always keep your path in the direction of kindness.

*

My mother is the one who gave me poetry. And for her, poetry and music were the same creature. She wrote beautiful ballads to be sung by broken-hearted women. William Blake was one of her favorite poets. She loved voices like Patsy Cline, Nat King Cole and Hank Williams songs. These have influenced me. I can hear them in my poems like "The Woman Hanging From the Thirteenth Floor Window."

My father loved music but was not much of a word man. He was a great dancer, as was my mother. He never got over losing his mother when he was very young, and grew up as a Creek Indian man in Oklahoma during very racist years. Oklahoma prides itself on its Indian heritage, but it remains quite racist in policy and treatment when it comes to indigenous tribal nations. My father died when he was fifty-three. He had asbestosis from doing sheet metal work and working on brake linings. His lungs carried unbearable grief.

When we write, perform, heal, or are otherwise in that creative space, we can find ourselves beyond time. N. Scott Momaday has a beautiful passage about his grandmother Ko-san appearing to him in that space where he speaks about the power of words, about the calling into being. My earliest memories were in the time between birth and speech, I lived primarily somewhere between the natural world and the dream world.

Often I feel beyond any of the definitions ascribed to me as a person who is political, a feminist, indigenous, and so on. It is my spirit who is writing, speaking, singing, playing saxophone, and acting. My spirit is acting through a time and a place, a skin and a history. And I am identified with the time, place, skin, and history even as these feel small and far away. I am absolutely in the world — the struggle, the concerns, the celebration, and the mourning. I am entranced by the diversity of experience on earth, even as I feel—how do I say this?—beyond all that, when I am in the dreaming/visionary place....

*

I started going to a Bible church on my own when I was around seven. I was lured by the church people who stood outside of the school and gave us candy and invited us to vacation Bible school. Church was a refuge from my what my home had become after my father left us. I loved the songs, poetry, and thinking about God, but from early on I was not in agreement with many of the doctrines and beliefs espoused by the church. The Bible was used to prove racist beliefs, to justify misogyny, and to pronounce judgement on others. We were not to question, and I had many questions.

When I was in high school, my stepfather came up with a plan to send me to a fundamentalist Christian school. Neither my mother nor my stepfather were fundamentalist Christians. He was suggesting this as a punishment and I decided I would not go, even if it meant running away. I had seen notices of Bureau of Indian Affairs schools for Indian students and told my mother that's where I wanted to go. My mother took me to the Bureau of Indian Affairs office and signed me up for the Institute of American Indian Arts (IAIA) in New Mexico. We were told it was a new school that emphasized arts, and I was accepted when I applied with a stack of my drawings. I constantly drew and kept notebooks at that time in my life. There was nothing in my plan to be a poet or to write poetry. I wanted to be an artist, a painter, like my grandmother Naomi Harjo and my great-aunt Lois Harjo.

Going to IAIA saved my life. It was the first time in my education that I felt at home in the classroom, because all the students were Native. And our primary curriculum was the arts. The place itself, the land of mountains and desert in New Mexico was for me a place of refuge and inspiration. The roots of cultural creative synthesis found a place to grow there. We were indigenous students from communities all over the country, from Alaska to Florida, who came to that school and were asking important questions about cultural regeneration and making art that reflected our identities as indigenous peoples and as a generation. For instance, in my art, how could Jimi Hendrix, the stomp dance, Thomas Hardy, and the *Bhagavad Gita* all fit together?

It was the place—the mountains, desert, and light—that coalesced idea and image and inspired.

I remember saying to a friend of mine that I would "never get on a stage," and then I became a member of an innovative drama and dance troupe. Our teacher, Rolland Meinholtz, had a great interest in Greek drama and saw many correlations between Greek drama and what would become the principles of American Indian drama. We took several hours of dance a week, learned stagecraft, and rehearsed hours into the night. We incorporated dance into the plays. The process and outcome was quite thrilling and to be part of it was a dream. José Limón came out from New York City to see what we were doing, and we had support from the actor/comedian Jonathan Winters, who we learned had Native ancestry. We took the show on tour and performed in the theater under the Space Needle in Seattle. We read Edward Albee, the Greek classics, and American play classics. These have all been inspirational.

I loved the stage, though I was told that I was the shyest kid at Indian school. It's a kind of liminal space where magic can happen, after lots of hard work, crafting and revisioning. My recent one-woman show is now being published as a book by Wesleyan, *Wings of Night Sky, Wings of Morning Light: a Play by Joy Harjo and a Circle of Responses*, with my co-editor Priscilla Page. And I am at work on a musical play that will revise the story of American music to include southeastern Native peoples.

*

New Mexico is where I first claimed myself within a place. I was there as what became known as the "American Indian literary renaissance" became a moving force, beginning with N. Scott Momaday's Pulitzer Prize-winning *House Made of Dawn*. I was a student at the University of New Mexico in the early 1970s when the multicultural arts movements swept the country. I was in the presence of major Chicano/Chicana, indigenous, working class, feminist, African American, Asian American poets, artists, and musicians. I'm convinced that the spiritual presence of the land was behind the emergence of the movement(s). We are of the earth, the flowers, and the desert — the forces and spirits who move within, above, about, and around it even if we locate in the cities, or the cities locate in our lands. In New Mexico, where the population of the state is relatively small (close to two million), the land and sky are an obvious presence.

I met Simon Ortiz, the Acoma Pueblo poet, at the beginning of my time at UNM. We had a daughter together, Rainy Ortiz, and she is a very gifted poet, and is making a place as an artist. Through Simon I met Leslie Marmon Silko. I didn't start writing poetry until I was in my mid-twenties, around the time Rainy was born, which is also around the time I started learning the Navajo language for my university language requirement.

I had always loved poetry and read it on my own. At Indian school, I noticed there was a natural love of language and poetry among the students. After I met Simon Ortiz, the first "real" poet I had known, and the first native poet, and after meeting Leslie Silko, I decided to take poetry workshops. I changed my major from pre-med with a minor in dance, to studio art the second semester of my first year at the university. I loved painting and photography, and went about beginning work on a series of paintings of warriors, which would include women. My last year of classes I decided to declare my major as creative writing. I had begun to see myself as a poet by my senior year.

We were all part of a political awareness that emerged with our art in the midst of the indigenous rights movements. As native people, we basically had been disappeared by America and the American story, and we were writing ourselves back in, in the "enemy's language."

When I was a high school student at IAIA, Vincent Price, the great horror actor, was a great supporter of Native poetry. Every year an anthology was created of student poems. I did not take writing classes, or write (except for some lame acid-rock songs, or punchy limericks about situations we were finding ourselves in as students). I loved reading the student poems. I noticed that the language of poetry in these poems often took me someplace that I only knew in those moments of childhood when I found peace outside of the house, with the trees, the small animals and insects for whom the earth was their intimate universe. And I could hear my spirit speaking here. It was similar to the first time I read Emily Dickinson's "I'm Nobody, Who are You"—and I was being spoken to out of time and with time.

Then when I heard the poetry of Simon Ortiz a blazing door opened in my mind with works. Before this, poetry, though practiced by some iaia students, until then, had primarily been the province of people from the northeastern part of the U.S. or England. His poetry brought poetry, for me, to the lands on which I stood, the lands were my people made a stand and were making a stand. I began to understand how poems could hold time, many kinds of time in one place, which is how we exist anyway. During that time Geary Hobson, who was teaching at UNM introduced the poet Pablo Neruda to me with his book Captain's Verses. I loved how Neruda's poems turned on stunning, earthy images. It was during this time I heard the poets Ai, Anne Waldman, and Galway Kinnell perform. I could hear how poetry was a bridge between speaking and singing. Ai read from her book *Cruelty*. I had a job with Indian studies on campus (it wasn't called that), and I was researching indigenous arts. I started thinking about our root poetics, orality, which lead me to Africa and African writers. One of my favorite collections was by the Ugandan writer Okot p'Bitek. He was the first writer who directly expressed similar times that my relatives of a few generations back had experienced with the early onslaughts of European settlement and colonization, with his book *Song of Lawino*. I got to meet him some years ago, and that was a highlight.

Hearing Jayne Cortez perform in New York City in the late seventies when Ishmael Reed produced one of the first multicultural poetic events in the country. She heavily influenced me when it came to performing poetry with music. We became friends and I always saw her when I went to New York. The last time I saw her was at the Village Vanguard sometime in the very, very early nineties. We met there to hear my friend the Mvskoke/Kaw saxophonist Jim Pepper perform. I miss them. Both were influences.

In the early 1990's I was invited to the University of Hawaii–Manoa campus to peform with Haunani-Kay Trask and Dana Naone Hall. A chant was composed and chanted for us and in honor of the event. I was embraced by the poetry of it, and it changed the way I thought of poetry. It was similar to how I felt when I realized that most poetry in the world was not written down, not in books, but was oral. The poetry of the Mvskoke Nation is carried in the songs.

I wanted my poems to be like that—to eloquently weave between earth and sky.

Incantation and chant call something into being. They make a ceremonial field of meaning. Much of world poetry is incantation and chant. The poem that first made me truly want to become a poet was sung and performed by a healer in Southeast Asia. He appeared in a documentary I found on television. As he sang and performed the poem he became what he was singing/speaking, and even as he sang and spoke, his words healed his client.

*

When I first added music to poetry, I encountered much opposition. I grew up in educational institutions in which "literary" meant solely written work. Books meant education. But for much of world history, most literature existed (and exists) before books. And music and poetry have gone arm in arm.

The saxophone always sounded to me like a human voice, a voice of tears and laughter, of falling in love, of singing while on the edge of danger. My grandmother Naomi Harjo was a painter, and a saxophone player, and to take it up when you're running hard into forty goes against convention of what's possible. I've always had to struggle with what's expected and what I hear is my path, whether it's in my personal life or my art, and as the poet Audre Lorde reminded me, there is no separation.

I've always heard music when I've written. It could be a rhythm track, patterns, or singing. It just took me awhile to put it together. As my mother often reminded me, I am a late bloomer. I picked up a tenor sax and had someone write me out the G blues scale. And then I gathered a kind of dub poetry band of all Native musicians in the early 1990's, which became, Joy Harjo and Poetic Justice. I continue developing and am working on a new album to go with the musical play—which is about going back to the American roots of music, which will include Mvskoke tribal music. We are part of the story. And there is always: poetry.

I've come to understand that music is pure spirit. Words are a little clumsier because they carry the weight of history and laws, and have been so misused.

*

Some moments I sense that I am in alignment with those who have perfected their art when they were living. I am working alongside them. And some days I feel utterly alone and back in the muck. That is the human condition. No matter where we are in the process, it's important to keep going in the best possible manner, and bump up against the edge of unknowing.

Our most beloved teachers are those who have been tested the most in this world. Many suffered debilitating health problems, alcoholism or other addictions, or severe accidents or events which they navigated to survive and inspire. If we omit judgment or shame from any experience and use the experience to gain insight and assist others, then it can turn what appears to be absolutely destructive and disastrous to an experience that is healing and regenerative. I had to walk myself through this lesson so I could turn what wanted to destroy me, my family, our peoples, this earth, into something creative and life giving.

I've always kept my spiritual practice private and close to myself but everything we do, including writing poetry and music is that practice. We enter into it when we take our first breath.

And always I go back to what was given to me, what I saw so clearly without words in those very early years of my journey. And I return to my teachers, which can be other writers. (We have poetry ancestors.) The ocean has been one of my teachers. The sun is a teacher, is a person. We either ignore the sun, or we acknowledge the sun and make our own personal relationship with the sun. We owe gratitude, can turn the mind of our poetry in that direction. As a child I didn't need words to understand this. The relationship with the sun as a being is essential to human understanding in my tribal philosophy, as it is in ways of being all over the globe. Colonization and globalized religions cut our connection. The sun became a set of equations, an energy source, or a distant star. When you know the sun as a being, the dynamic changes. There can be a conversation. We need to honor the sun for the gifts.

What is common to all indigenous peoples is a belief that we are all relatives, all being. All is sacred. I have been given glimpses of what some call the "everlasting." I have seen this place in a newborn's eyes, in sunrise, in dusk, the darkest night, and the face of a flower — here and in dreaming. The everlasting is who we truly are, where we truly belong. It is the stuff of poetry, music, and dance, of all arts. In this place, we are one person, one poem, one story, and one song.

LEANNE HOWE
CHOCTAW

"I write about issues and events that have taken place in the past but resonate with the present."

LeAnne Howe (1951–) has emerged as a master of the persona poem. In almost all of her poetry, the speaker is a historical or invented figure, for example Mary Todd Lincoln (see "Now I Lay Me Down,") the Noble Savage, or even a rope. Frequently, her poems are conversations, as in "Gatorland," allowing Howe to play out a philosophical/cultural drama without imposition of an "authorial" voice. Irreverent, edgy, and often mordantly comical, Howe's creations dance upon the line between script and poem, and indeed often read like mini-screen-plays. As she takes advantage of the pages's blank spaces and plays with typography, graphic symbols, and the shorthand of social media, her clever formatting and proclivity for characters and conversation give her poetry an experimental feel, but these features also make the work recognizable and relatable. As she interrogates the ways in which pop culture and conventional history relegate "Indians" to caricatures or mascots, Howe's ability to simultaneously express high outrage and high comedy is unmatched.

Gatorland

I have Herpetophobia.

! Fear of alligators roaming the streets once Trump drains the swamp

? *How to recognize these wild beasts*

! There's her, that foul-mouthed sexter, a hard drinking blonde who learned to breathe heavily just so people in the next room could hear. A friend.

And Him, horsetail hair, orange body paint. His family, settlers in eveningwear, they constitute a high-heeled army in service to the super-rich. Straight shooters.

! See her #2,
The sleek suited hedge-fund type, she tells me
She carries a Glock 9 mm. Fears everything
Complains her swan furniture flirts with strangers,
It's the meds

There goes another creature in a black cocktail dress
Without a handgun

Well-heeled propriety
Won't last long

!

Not as chichi as the
Bald woman wearing chandelier earrings striking a pose in the white fur coat
She says she shot the foxes herself. She fears hair. Shoots at it in the dark.
Needs meds.

): I have Herpetophobia

?!   Don't be a moron, who ever heard of an American Indian Herpetophobic

Maybe I'll sign up for an alligator wrestling class
Carry a gun
Turn killer with a song in my heart
    As did the drunks and vagrants posing as settlers,

Nattering across our homelands like a proverb, singing "Holy, Holy, Holy"
Or maybe I'll forget who I am, party with alligators,
    Dine on the dead, breath reeking of poison

?.   You're making me horny, can you tell me more

⊙ Settlers carried a little bit of heaven into battle, the Hawken rifle
Sang "Just As I Am" with a Colt 45 in their hands
Killing Indians face-to-face was a blast

:)   Don't stop, I'm getting off, oh . . . oh

For long-range slaughter they dragged Big Fifty onto the field
A big girl rifle weighing 17 pounds, she fired .50/120 rounds
⊙ ⊙ ⊙ ⊙

Big Fifty was used at the battle of Adobe Walls. Felled Indians 1,500 yards away

Settlers, cavalrymen, sheriffs, deputies, peacekeepers used
Spencers, the .56-50 caliber
Henry Repeating Arms
Winchester '66
Winchester '73s

!   Thanks, I needed that

): *Maybe we're all Indians these days*

:)   Now you're talking

I have Herpetophobia

!   Nonsense, buy a gun and kill it

Noble Savage Learns to Tweet

Noblesavage Noble Savage I walk alone
11 seconds ago

Noblesavage Noble Savage I walk alone @ai.com
10 seconds ago

Noblesavage Noble Savage Please RT @ai.com
9 seconds ago

Noblesavage Noble Savage Contact Indian Agent @ai.com
8 seconds ago

Noblesavage Noble Savage Sample photos, comedy 2 horror @ai.com
7 seconds ago

Noblesavage Noble Savage On first-name basis with Wall street culture
@ai.com
6 seconds ago

Noblesavage Noble Savage Body paint assignments @ai.com
5 seconds ago

Noblesavage Noble Savage Wall Street bound . . . @ai.com
20 hours ago

Noblesavage Noble Savage Auteur theory & me from Ford to Cameron on
Wall Street @ai.com
1 hour ago

Noblesavage Noble Savage No idea too strange or too far outside the box
@ai.com
3 hours ago

Noblesavage Noble Savage Learning to cha-cha with Lady Gaga on Wall Street @ai.com
1 hour, thirty minutes ago

Noblesavage Noble Savage Nudity, a sign of the healthy Skin on Wall Street @ai.com
10 minutes ago

Noblesavage Noble Savage Tobacco clients welcome on Wall Street @ai.com
2 minutes ago

Noblesavage Noble Savage Hear on Wall Street, cool females wanted with that "suicide girl look!" Read more at @ai.com
1 second ago

The Rope[3] Speaks

At last free of Fort Snelling's coffin
I return to the past,
Swing like a fool on holiday
Unfinished business, here I come.

3 A single noose from the December 26, 1862, Dakota hangings has been preserved in the collections of Fort Snelling, Minnesota. In 2011 representatives from the Dakota Nation visited the collection to see the noose. Prayers were offered. For additional readings see The Thirteenth Turn: A History of the Noose by Jack Shuler.

Now I Lay Me Down

June 1875
Bellevue Place Sanitarium 333 S. Jefferson Street, Batavia, Illinois

4 a.m. MARY TODD LINCOLN *sits in a chair in her bedroom. A small candle blooms on the bureau.*

MARY TODD LINCOLN
Tattoos adorn his arms and hands.
Like night-blooming cereus they prick the skin, slash my will
The Savage says nit picking takes time and patience, but can be very enjoyable for both parties.

SAVAGE INDIAN *combs her oily hair.*
Immerse any nits or lice in kerosene water. Pull them from the hair; drop in bowl
Pin cleaned sections of the hair aside,
Scissor divided segments close to the scalp. Wait.

MARY TODD LINCOLN
These many days after dear Abraham, I have come to this, Hairless with a deformed cheek,
Those of us with eyes sewn open Perceive nothing to fear
Not
Gunpowder, walls afire, A Wild Dakota Indian
The Presidential Box at Ford's Theatre, A hangman's noose

SAVAGE INDIAN
Silence, Gar woman!

Ever so gently he takes two sharp flints from his leather pouch and examines them and chooses the smallest. He approaches her face with determination.

MARY TODD LINCOLN *picks up the mirror and studies her face. Her thin upper lip curling into a smile.*

I faint from the ecstasy.

Apocrypha

June 1875
Bellevue Place Sanitarium 333 S. Jefferson Street, Batavia, Illinoi

MARY TODD LINCOLN's *suite at Bellevue Place. Although there is only a small bed and a bureau in her bedroom, Mary believes her residence sprawls over three large sitting rooms, one containing a piano. Her residence is chocked full of trunks, six carpetbags filled with footstools, silk curtains, jewelry, fifteen pairs of kit gloves, and a few vials of laudanum hidden among her things.*

SAVAGE INDIAN *sits in a dark corner of the room. He wears a black Vigilante Town Coat, the one he was hanged in. The coat droops open because the hangman's wife cut off the buttons to use on her new frock.*

MARY TODD LINCOLN
Before you can think, you forget and then remember
A dress of blood, gloves I refuse to wash.
Ever.

What is it to a wild Indian? *The president is shot.*
Fool, I was his all-in-all, his Molly, his Child Wife and Mother, his Puss.

SAVAGE INDIAN *Thoughtfully*
Well, . . . he called me Puss, too.

Inner Conflicts

All my life I've been trying to outrun a barrage of bullets from weapons that seem to reload themselves.

"Hasn't everyone," asks the writer in my head? "Maybe this essay should be about electrocution."

I type on.

"American Indians have a genetic predisposition when it comes to dodging bullets triggered by h.S.1876+1, the so-called sanctified terror—or Holy Shit gene. One Native researcher[1] has theorized the h.S.1876+1 increases awareness of an impending slaughter by gunfire."

The other me, chuckles. The writer in my head doesn't.

"Be serious," I type.

"*Serious*?!" sneers the other me. "Your own mother was a carrier of the sanctified terror gene. Our ancestors carried h.S.1876+1. They passed it down, down, down in the stories until it got to you. Then you passed it like a football to your children. How can you say serious?"

The writer in my head continues typing. "Okay, okay, calm down. Fingers crossed our Choctaw blood has not been so diluted that it cancels h.S.1876+1 effectiveness.

"Test it," says the other me.

    *

Here, imagine an epic tracking shot of nineteenth-century Gatling guns firing on unsuspecting American Indians while they eat dinner in front of their teepees. Then watch the rather dreadful 2017 movie, *Hostiles*.

"Holy shit, children, look out for a hail of bullets. They're using trees as human shields."

The other me suddenly stops typing, runs out the office door but soon returns slightly red-faced, but scared witless. Types, "Test complete."

Jacked Conflicts

"Conflict," writes Canadian author and literary critic Douglas Glover "is any relationship of opposition."[2] Here, the writer in my head types, "No shit, Kimosabe, whites and Indians are deadlocked in opposition." The other me agrees, but tries a more diplomatic approach. "American Indians have had a long and difficult relationship with non-Indians because of land theft, removal, and genocide carried out at the point of a gun. It should come as no surprise that my fiction, creative non-fiction, and poetry are filled with episodes of murders, warfare, and rape; punctuated by rapid gunfire." Am I a writer with a violent agenda, or just telling the truth as I know it?

Ever After Conflicts

As early as age five I began running from an imagined volley of bullets. My first episode: I see my body falling, blood oozes out of my blue and green taffeta dress, the one my mother has made for me to wear on the first day of kindergarten. Ruined. Ruined when the sweet little gold chains my mother had sown around the bottom of the skirt for decoration got caught at the top of the playground slide. When I'd jumped feeling the wind in my long black hair as I sailed smoothly down to the bottom of the slide, the chain had gotten caught on the side rail and ripped the taffeta skirt to pieces. *I had to tell my mom something.* "They were shooting at me and my skirt got caught."

Of course I was never shot (you know that) but my mother took me out of kindergarten in Bethany because the teachers were frequently locking me in the closet. *Sounds worse than it was.* I learned to fight back, kick my teachers' shins once they let me out.

"This is petty tyranny," I screamed. (I never said that.) Alone in the closet I vowed to bludgeon my enemies. (I didn't know the word bludgeon but it's such a cool word here.) In truth, I must have been a hellion. Today, I would be brand-ed a "risk," in public schools, back then I was just a wild Indian. Decades later when I first began writing poetry in a walk-in closet converted for a quiet place to think, I scribbled my poetry by hand enumerating the petty injustices of my youth. Later, I graduated to typing petty injustices. (Hellion energy helps when you're becoming a writer.) Sometime in the 1980s, I graduated to a computer and kept writing. Always writing. Over the years I've branched out from poetry and fiction into cross genre writing. I like to think I've mostly stopped writing about myself. (Mostly.) But while crafting the essay on why I wrote "Gatorland," I realized how much of my work is influenced by the feeling I'm dodging bullets.

"Bloody hell," says the writer in my head, "Not this again."

The other me types, "Hold on, there's good reasons for this, keep reading."

Ada is a small town in south central Oklahoma with a violent history. I spent most of the early life there. Today I return every holiday and summer and live in my grandmother's renovated house. According to an August 8, 1907 report by the Office of Deputy United States Marshal T. Ed Brents, a staggering number of violent crimes were committed in Ada, Sulphur, and Roff (south central Okla-homa) during July 1907.

> Thirty murder cases.
>
> Fifty-two cases of assault to kill.
>
> Three cases of rape. Three young men while intoxicated commit-ted the horrible crime near Franks, I.T. (This is a famous case in Indian Territory; think Jack the Ripper x 3.)
>
> Four cases of assault to kill. "The defendants were intoxicated,"

wrote Brents.

One case of murder. "The same old story, the defendant was intoxicated."[3]

Could the reasons for the two different listings for "assault to kill" be that fifty-two persons were sober when they committed their heinous acts, as opposed to the latter four assailants who were drunk while firing at their intended human targets. Most likely. Here, I'm suggesting that warfare over land, and violence on the land creates an "ever after" affect within the people who live there. They or we carry it like a blood disease.

Indian Territory might be likened to one giant reservation[4] with all the Indians in the world squeezed into one place. Perhaps the thinking was that Natives from different tribes would kill one another because they were wild Indians and traumatized from walking 10,000 miles. (It wasn't 10,000 miles.)

Oklahoma as a landscape is stitched together like Frankenstein's monster, created out of Oklahoma Territory (mostly whites), Indian Territory (mostly American Indians), and the unassigned lands (again mostly white settlers.) I'm oversimplifying, I know. Today there are thirty-eight federally recognized tribal nations within Oklahoma's borders. Yet conflict and violence continue unabated as before. Ada was an Indian town long before statehood, and all my relatives were hunters with rifles. My grandfather owned a pistol, as he was once a sheriff's deputy. We still have his badge and gun. Ada is currently the seat of the Chickasaw Nation. Rampant violence still exists even with the patrols of the tribal police, Pontotoc County sheriff's department, and a strong city police department. (Note to President Trump: Everyone owns a gun in my hometown and it hasn't curbed gun violence yet.) As of July 1, 2017, with a population of 16,522, approximately 20 percent are American Indians; Ada authorities reported seventy-one homicides, down from 2016's high of seventy-eight homicides.

Violent conflicts grow like a virus and morph into many forms: random gunshots, rape, molestation, murder, and hangings. On April 19, 1909 sometime between two and three a.m. four men were hanged in a livery stable in Ada by a mob of 200 men. It is the largest mass outlaw hanging in U.S. history. The four men had been charged in the ambush and murder of Gus Bobbitt, a former local sheriff. The four were awaiting trial, but townsfolk took matters into their own hands.

In 2008, nearly one hundred years after the four hangings, violence still prowls Ada's streets striking against human beings or property. My grandmother's home was shot up with a modern assault rifle. I'll return to this later, but check out the crime rates for property in Ada. "When it comes to property crimes, Ada, OK is shown to be 22% higher than the Oklahoma average and 49% higher than the national average."[5] Land again. Here I turned to French Marxist Henri Lefebvre and his seminal philosophical work *The Production of Space* (1991). Lefebvre writes that "sovereignty implies 'space' and what is more it implies a space against which violence, whether latent or overt, is directed—a space established and constituted by violence." Lefebvre is not talking about tribal sovereignty, per se, he's talking about dominion over and independence from lands that were won and held in deadly confrontations. "The spread of sovereign power was predicated on military domination, generally preceded by plunder,"[6] says Lefebvre.

That's certainly the history of America, and the history of Indian Country, and my hometown, Ada.

Oh dear, I can feel my h.S.1876+1 gene acting up again, as a Holy Shit moment comes over me. No one will want this essay unless I get back to the issue of craft, poetry, and the literary influences on my work. Quickly the writer in my head types conflict and poetry. Poet W. D. Snodgrass to the rescue. "Perfect," the other me, says. Conflict is a modus operandi in Snodgrass's *The Fuehrer Bunker: The Complete Cycle*. He writes about Hitler and the Third Reich, and he employs multiple voices in the work. While I'm not comparing myself to his genius, I've tried to follow his example when writing about violent warfare perpetrated on Natives by invading Europeans. Key ingredient to understanding his work, is reading history.

Onward.

Shell Shaker (2001) is a novel in which there are eleven murders. When Auda Billy, the novel's protagonist, is raped in the office of Choctaw Chief Redford McAlester she returns the next day, lures him into having another go at her, then shoots him with his pants down. Land tenure, greed, and mendacity, are all forces that pushed the eighteenth century Choctaws into a civil war with their own people. Similar forces overwhelmed the twentieth century Choctaws in later chapters of *Shell Shaker*. There isn't a promise to the end of violence in the novel, but peace is restored to the community at the story's end. My second novel, *Miko Kings: An Indian Baseball Story* (2007), set in Ada, is filled with violent episodes: a Prussian settler squatting on Indian land is hanged for having sex with a chicken; the central baseball character, Hope Little Leader has his hands cut off for betting against his own team; and many other Natives and non-natives come to violent ends. Yet, there is reprieve. Speaking midway through the novel by Choctaw Henri Day, Miko Kings' manager, says, "... only Choctaw words can soothe the land and put to rest violent abominations." In other words Henri believes only Indigenous ceremonies by Indigenous people, prayers, chants, songs, conducted and repeated often, can save Indian Country, and America. Perhaps I believe it too.

So now, "Gatorland." I suggest the poem is a warning against violence even though it ends with a suggestion of more violence.

Crazy Conflicts: "Gatorland"

In her response to "Gatorland" (see page 150), scholar Amanda Gailey[7] writes, "Guns are the tools of the otherwise untooled, and when the only tool you have is a gun, every answer to every problem is to shoot it." What I believe is that the first stanzas in the poem reveal a message about the ills of having no national gun control laws in America. Spoken in a casual conversation, three disembodied voices attempt to warn the masses about the political power of gun rights' advocates and the reckless power of President Trump. In my essay, I attempt to replicate the three voices in "Gatorland" with three narrators: the other me, the writer in my head, and "I."

> *I have Herpetophobia* [Voice 1]

> ! Fear of alligators roaming the streets once Trump drains the swamp

> *? How to recognize these wild beasts* [The other me: Voice 2]

> ! There's her, that foul-mouthed sexter, a hard drinking blonde who learned to breathe heavily just so people in the next room could hear. A friend. [The writer in my head: Voice 3]

Stanza number eight in a poem of only thirteen is pure stream of conscience and hopefully illustrates a sense of community; shared humor, joy, tragedy, and irony in a polyvocal structure. In this way "Gatorland," as poetry, is true to a Native aesthetic. The three voices tell about land grabs, gun violence, and at the end Voice 1 contemplates even more violence.

Conflicts Poetical: W. D. Snodgrass

W. D. Snodgrass is someone I learned from and continue to study many decades after encountering his work. I first read his poetry in the *American Poetry Review* in 1977, and Snodgrass's work opened my imagination to new possibilities. He was writing about one of history's truly evil men Adolf Hitler, his lover Eva Braun, and many others in the Third Reich.[8] Hitler's regime enacts centuries long processes of extermination of the Jews, the disabled, Gypsies, anyone of difference, coupled with military might and land plunder. I suggest that this is the narrative of settler colonialism is in the Western Hemisphere. (Note to self: must re-read Lefebvre.)

Snodgrass's poetry in *The Fuehrer Bunker* made visible to me how to juxtapose the beautiful with malevolent. "Eva Braun" the poem, is ridiculous, haunting, and sublime. Her frivolous song in "Tea For Two"[9] inspired the cycle of Noble Savage and Indian Mascot poems in my first book of poems *Evidence of Red* (2005), and in my new book *Savage Conversations* (2019) about Mary Todd Lincoln and the Savage Indian she imagined that tortured her in 1875.

I return again and again to *The Fuehrer Bunker, Snodgrass's tour de force*. As a younger writer and poet I missed that "He" or "Him" were always capitalized in "Eva Braun." Duh. But by using song lyrics from a popular Broadway musical Snodgrass gives Miss Braun a voice to sing with, and an inner life we could not perceive without his poetry. He splices Eva's innermost thoughts with the lighthearted merriment of "Tea for Two," ironically foreshadowing her death and Hitler's.

Eva Braun was a German model for a photographer when she met Adolf Hitler. She was seventeen; he was forty in 1929 when they met. She became his mistress and attempted to commit suicide twice during their sixteen years together. One wonders if her suicide attempts were to prove to Hitler that she would kill herself for him, if she had too. Eventually she does do just that. After her second attempt he rented Eva an apartment of her own in Munich. Later, when the Nazi forces were defeated, Hitler married Braun on April 29, 1945, the following day they committed suicide in the bunker. She bit into a cyanide capsule (that takes guts); he shot himself with his pistol. According to most biographers, Eva wielded no influence in Hitler's political decisions. Most believe he chose her because she would never question his authority. In other words, Hitler knew Eva was devoted to him. Sadly, he believed she was a little dumb. Hitler's photographer Heinrich Hoffmann, in his memoir *Hitler Was My Friend*

(1955), called Eva inconsequential and "feather-brained." Yet Snodgrass brings her back to life with an agenda. She has agency and power over the "god" she worships, Hitler.

In *The Fuehrer Bunker* Snodgrass gives each character a larger-than-life personality, revealing who they might have been. They're scary. And he allows them to exonerate their unspeakable acts. But the effect is just the opposite; we see their duplicity and judge them guilty of crimes against humanity.

Oh dear, I wish I could make the writer in my head chuckle again. The other me grows weary of the history of Hitler, Eva Braun, white settlers, and Indians in Indian Territory, and modern Oklahoma, a landscape that is politically exasperating, and heartbreaking. A walking regret.

As I mentioned earlier, my home in West Ada in 2008 was shot up by a group of teenage boys playing kill or be killed. One of their bullets went through the outside wall of the house and drilled into a book about Alaska Natives in the living room bookcase. (Figures, right?) Six years later we discovered that our foundling grey cat, Lord Greystoke, aka Tarzan, was shot on the mean streets of West Ada. Happened before we adopted him. We found out when the veterinary x-ray revealed that the poor little guy still carries the bullet in his chest. It's inoperable.

The Truth About Conflicts

There's no such thing as the end of conflicts, not in real life or in fiction or in poetry. As I said in the beginning, I feel as if I've been dodging bullets all my life. And then what, you may ask? Answer: I don't know. Do we keep our heads bent, observe but quickly forget what isn't supposed to be happening, respond with sobs of gratitude when we survive another hail of bullets?

In America, indigenous people were targeted for extinction with guns of the state, and a society that wanted us all to die. Period. We're still here. The poet Snodgrass tells us of the end of Hitler and the Third Reich, as seen through the eyes of witnesses and characters such as Eva Braun, Albert Speer, Goebbels, and Goering and their hatred of Jews, and each other. Their stories end in 1945. I find comfort knowing they're finished. The voices in my own poems and stories of America do not die. We endure.

Maybe we are all Indians these days, and maybe, just maybe, that is a good place to begin.

Notes

1. Me.

2. Douglas Glover, *Attack of the Copula Spiders and Other Essays on Writing* (Biblioasis, 2012).

3. http://www.lhaasdav.com/law_order/adanews08.html

4. "The country's 310 Indian reservations have violent crime rates that are more than two and a half times higher than the national average, according to data compiled by the Justice Department." From "Higher Crime, Fewer Charges on Indian Land," by Timothy Williams. *New York Times*, February 20, 2012.

5. http://www.areavibes.com/ada-ok/crime/

6. Henri Lefebvre, *The Production of Space* (Basil Blackwell, 1991), 280.

7. Brian Clements, Alexandra Teague, and Dean Rader, editors. *Bullets to Bells, Poets and Citizens Respond to Gun Violence* (Beacon Press, 2017), 96.

8. W. D. Snodgrass, *The Fuehrer Bunker: The Complete Cycle* (BOA Editions, 1995), 117–120.

9. From the 1925 musical comedy *No, No, Nannette*. Irving Caesar and Otto Harbach, lyrics; Vincent Youmans, music.

*

Eva Braun
by W. D. Snodgrass

—22 April 1945.

*(Hitler's mistress received no public recognition
and often felt badly neglected. Her small revenge
included singing American songs, her favorite
being "Tea for Two." Having chose to die with
him in the bunker, she appeared quite serene
during the last days.)*

*Tea for two
And two for tea*

I ought to feel ashamed
Feeling such joy. Behaving like a spoiled child!
So fulfilled. This is a very serious matter.

All of them have come here to die. And they grieve,
I have come here to die. If this is dying,
Why else did I ever live?

                         Me for you
                     And you for me

        We ought to never flaunt our good luck
        In the face of anyone less fortunate —
        These live fools mourning already
        For their own deaths: these dead fools
        Who believe they can go on living . . .

And you for me
    Alone

        Who out of all of them, officers, ministers,
        These liars that despise me, these empty
        Women that envy me — so they hate me —
        Who else of them dares to disobey Him
        As I dared? I have defied Him to His face
        And He has honored me.

                     We will raise
                       A family

        They sneer at me — at my worrying about
        Frau Goebbels' children, that I make fairytales
        For them, that we play at war. Is our war
        More lost if I console these poor trapped rabbits?
        These children He would not give me . . .

A boy for you
A girl for me

            They sneer that I should bring
            Fine furniture down this dank hole. Speer
            Built this bed for me. Where I have slept

Beside our Chief. Who else should have it?
My furs, my best dress to my little sister —
They would sneer even at this; yet
What else can I give her?

Can't you see
How happy we would be?

Or to the baby
She will bear Fegelein? Lechering dolt?!
Well, I have given her her wedding
As if it was my own. And she will have
My diamonds, my watch. The little things you
Count on, things that see you through your
Missing life, the life that stood you up.

Nobody near us
To see us or hear us

I have it all. They are all gone, the others —
The Valkyrie; and the old rich bitch Bechstein;
Geli above all. No, the screaming mobs above all.
They are all gone now. He has left them all.
No one but me and the love-struck secretaries—
Traudl, Daran — who gave up years ago.

No friends and relations
On weekend vacations.

That I, above all, am chosen — even I
Must find that strange. I who was always
Disobedient, rebellious — smoked in the dining car,
Wore rouge when he said we mustn't.
When he ordered that poor Chancellor Schuschnigg
Was to starve, I sent in food.

We won't have it known, dear,

That we own a telephone, dear.

I who joined the Party, I who took Him
For my lover just to spite my old stiff father —
Den Alten Fritz! — and those stupid nuns.
I ran my teachers crazy, and my mother — I
Held out even when she stuck my head in water.
He shall have none but me.

Day will break
And you will wake

We cannot make it through another month;
We follow the battles now on a subway map.
Even if the Russians pulled back —
His hand trembles, the whole left side
Staggers. His marvelous eyes are failing.
We go out to the sunlight less each day. We live
Like flies sucked up in a sweeper bag.

And start to bake
 A sugar cake

He forbade me to leave Berchtesgaden,
Forbade me to come here. I tricked
My keepers, stole my own car, my driver Jung.
He tried to scold me; He was too
Proud of me. Today He ordered me to leave,
To go back to the mountain. I refused.
I have refused to save my own life and He,
In public, He kissed me on the mouth.

For me to take
For all the boys to see.

Once more I have won, won out over Him
Who spoke one word and whole populations vanished.
Until today, in public, we were good friends.

He is mine. No doubt
I did only what He wanted; no doubt
I should resent that. In the face
Of such fulfillment? In the face
Of so much joy?

> Picture you
> Upon my knee;
> Tea for two
> And two for tea . . .

LUCI TAPAHONSO

DINÉ (NAVAJO)

"The place of my birth is the source of the writing..."

Luci Tapahonso (1953–) grew up on a farm on the Navajo Reservation outside Shiprock, New Mexico. The importance of tribal culture was reinforced for Tapahonso at a young age as she learned to speak Diné Bizaad (Navajo) before English, a fact that allows her poetry to be truly bilingual and bicultural. Her most recent books, *Sáanii Dahataał: The Women are Singing* and *Blue Horses Rush In*, have confirmed her leading role among Indigenous voices as one of the few to write and publish in both English and a Native language. Demonstrating her ability to inhabit two seemingly divergent cultures, Tapahonso's poems move naturally between languages (and between verse and prose) with the clarity, elegance, and insight for which she has become widely admired. In work that turns on questions of autonomy and integration, exploring how one's identity is rooted in place, history, ritual, and family, Tapahonso's prose and poetry resemble a Navajo rug, as woven strands of everyday life are brightly transformed into startling points of convergence that weave the past into the present, the dead into the living, and the earth into memory.

See also page 343 for Esther G. Belin's testimony to the influence of Luci Tapahonso's "That American Flag."

Blue Horses Rush In

for Chamisa Bah Edmo, Shisóí 'aláąįį' naaghígíí

Before the birth, she moved and pushed inside her mother.
Her heart pounded quickly and we recognized
the sound of horse running:
> the thundering of hooves on the desert floor.

Her mother clenches her fists and gasps.
She moans ageless pain and pushes: This is it!

Chamisa slips out, glistening wet, and takes her first breath.
> The wind outside swirls small leaves
> and branches in the dark
Her father's eyes are wet with gratitude.
He prays and watches both mother and baby — stunned.

The baby arrived amid a herd of horses,
> horses of different colors.

White horses ride in on the breath of the wind.
White horses from the east
where plants of golden chamisa shimmer in the moonlight.

She arrived amid a herd of horses.

Blue horses enter from the south
bringing the scent of prairie grasses
from the small hills outside.

She arrived amid a herd of horses.

Yellow horses rush in, snorting from the desert to the south.
It is possible to see across the entire valley to Niist'áá from Tó.
Bah, from here your grandmothers went to war long ago.
She arrived amid a herd of horses.

Black horses come from the north.
They are the lush summers of Montana and still white winters of Idaho.

Chamisa, Chamisa Bah. It is all this that you are.
You will grow: laughing, crying,
and we will celebrate each change you live.

You will grow strong like the horses of your past.
You will grow storng like the horses of your birth.

The Motion of Songs Rising

The October night is warm and clear.
We are standing on a small hill and in all directions,
around us, the flat land listens to the songs rising.
The holy ones are here dancing.
The Yeis are here.

In the west, Shiprock looms above the desert.
Tsé bit'a'í, old bird-shaped rock. She watches us.
Tsé bit'a'í, our mother who brought the people here on her back.
Our refuge from the floods long ago. It was worlds and centuries ago,
yet she remains here. Nihimá, our mother.

This is the center of the night
and right in front of us, the holy ones dance.
They dance, surrounded by hundreds of Navajos.

Diné t'óó àhayóí.
Diné t'óó àhayóí.

We listen and watch the holy ones dance.

Yeibicheii.
Yeibicheii.
Grandfather of the holy ones.

They dance, moving back and forth.

Their bodies are covered with white clay
and they wave evergreen branches.
They wear hides of varying colors,
their coyote tails swinging as they sway back and forth.
All of them dancing ancient steps.
They dance precise steps, our own emergence onto this land.
They dance again, the formation of this world.
They dance for us now — one precise swaying motion.
They dance back and forth, back and forth.
As they are singing, we watch ourselves recreated.

Éí álts'íísígíí shił nizhóní. The little clown must be about six years
old. He skips lightly about waving his branches around. He teases
people in the audience, tickling their faces if they look too serious or
too sleepy. At the beginning of each dance, when the woman walks by to
bless the Yeis, he runs from her. Finally, after the third time, she
sprinkles him with corn pollen and he skips off happily, 'éí shił nizhóní.

The Yeis are dancing again, each step, our own strong bodies.
They are dancing the same dance, thousands of years old. They are here
for us now, grateful for another harvest and our own good health.
> The roasted corn I had this morning was fresh,
> cooked all night and taken out of the ground this
> morning. It was steamed and browned just right.

They are dancing and in the motion of songs rising,
our breathing becomes the morning moonlit air.
The first are burning below as always.
> We are restored.
> We are restored.

It Has Always Been This Way

for Lori and Willie Edmo

Being born is not the beginning.
Life begins months before the time of birth.

Inside the mother, the baby floats in warm fluid,
and she is careful not to go near noisy or evil places.
She will not cut meat or take part in the killing of food.
Navajo babies were always protected in these ways.

The baby is born and cries out loud,
and the mother murmurs and nurtures the baby.
A pinch of pollen on the baby's tongue
for strong lungs and steady growth.
The belly button dries and falls off.
It is buried near the house so the child
will always return home and help the mother.
It has been this way for centuries among us.

Much care is taken to shape the baby's head well
and to talk and sing to the baby softly in the right way.
It has been this way for centuries among us.

The baby laughs aloud and it is celebrated with rock salt,
lots of food, and relatives laughing.
Everyone passes the baby around.
This is so the child will always be generous,
     will always be surrounded by happiness,
and will always be surrounded by lots of relatives.
It has been this way for centuries among us.

The child starts school and leaves with a pinch of pollen
on top of her head and on her tongue.
This is done so the child will think clearly,
listen quietly, and learn well away from home.

The child leaves home with prayers and good thoughts.
It has been this way for centuries among us.

This is how we were raised.
We were raised with care and attention
because it has always been this way.
It has worked well for centuries.

> You are here.
> Your parents are here.
> Your relatives are here.
> We are all here together.

It is all this: the care, the prayers, songs,
and our own lives as Navajos we carry with us all the time.
It has been this way for centuries among us.
It has been this way for centuries among us.

Daané é Diné

In the midst of Phoenix,
the warm March sun is overhead.
Traffic rushes by, and every ten minutes or so
airplanes lift off or glide onto the black runways.
A train slithers by, our voices quiver from the vibrating air.
The ground beneath us shivers.

We are witnesses to the excavation
of the old Hohokamki homes
where archaeologists are working
at the Pueblo Grande site.
A cache of clay animals was unearthed this afternoon,
and a ripple of excitement swept through the work site.
This is the most significant find to date.

The archaeologists feel certain that the small figures
are ritual ceremonial images. The figures were in the center
of a pithouse alongside a huge pot that had been shattered
by centuries of dirt and layers of civilization.

A small dog stood upright; its neck had been broken,
then reattached, evidenced by a small crack line.
There were other dogs, sheep, and some goats.
The miniature clay bodies were chubby,
the surfaces uneven and bumpy. The fingertips
of whoever had made them were clearly embedded.
These small figures stood upright as if the children
had just left and would be returning to continue their play.

At the end of the day, I returned to my hotel room, several hundred yards from
the site, and tried to push the images of little clay animals from my mind. I ate,
tasting nothing, and watched TV a bit. Then I lay down, closed my eyes, and
dreamt of my childhood.

On a clear, warm day we played under the huge cottonwoods surrounding
the house. My mother came out and sat down with us, spreading her skirt out
around her. "Shúúh, look, I'll show you how to make some toy people," she
said, taking a small cloth square and putting a pile of sand in the center. "Díígi
'át'éego ádeiilyaa, shiyázhí, like this, my little ones, she murmured, turning the
cloth-covered ball right-side-up, forming the head. Then she put a stick into
the center of the ball so that the remaining cloth formed a skirt, and a small
crosswise stick made the arms of a woman. "Jó áko," she said, "daané'é asdzáán
iilyaah. We have made a doll woman." We drew in her face and daané'é asdzáán
stood ready to play.
    "K'ad hastiin sha'? How about making a toy man?" We tore more squares of
cloth, filled the centers with sand, tied them, and put in center sticks to make
them stand up. "There," my mother said. "K'ad iilyaah. We've made a toy fam-
ily." She got up, gathering her skirt, and went inside to make bread. We looked
at the little figures standing in the dirt—a mother, father, and five children of
varying sizes.
    "Ti', shiáłchini," my sister said, pretend-talking to the dolls, "Chi'yáán
'ásdįįd. Naalghhéhé bá hooghangóó deekai. Let's go, my children. There is no
more food. We are going to the store." We put the people and some little mud

animals on a flat piece of wood and pushed the imaginary car to a make-believe store under the next tree.

The next morning, the eastern sky glowed clean yellow. The sun had not yet risen. From the hotel window, I could see the Pueblo Grande site. Thin wisps of fire smoke rose from the camps of the homeless who stayed nearby. I wondered if they heard noises from the excavation site at night or if they saw the spirits of the Hohokamki, who were being unearthed, walking about. Maybe the wandering spirits of the Hohokamki gathered with the homeless, some of who are recent war veterans and feel similarly displaced in modern America.

And I wondered what had happened to the toys we had made as children. Had they been absorbed back into the soft dirt beside my parents' house? Had they been carried off by the wind, or by our children? Had they been buried by seasons of rain, leaves, and snow?

from *the Preface to Sáanii Dahataał: The Women Are Singing*

In the morning, we woke refreshed and happy. The morning air was clear and crisp with a harvest chill, and there across the blue valley stood Shiprock, a deep purple monolith. I drank coffee outside, watched the dogs act silly, and then I caught up on news of what had happened since my last trip. While we ate breakfast, my father watched news, the table radio played Navajo and English songs alternately, my mother told me a little story about when she was four or five years old, I braided my daughter's hair, and two of my sisters came over for a visit. This is the familiar comfort I felt as a child, and it is the same for my children. The songs the Yeibicheii sang, that the radio played, and that my mother hummed as she cooked are a part of our memories, of our names, and of our laughter. The stories I heard that weekend were not very different from the stories I heard as a child. They involved my family's memories, something that happened last week, and maybe news of high school friends. Sometimes they were told entirely in Navajo and other times in a mixture of Navajo and English.

There is such a love of stories among Navajo people that it seems each time a group of more than two gather, the dialogue eventually evolves into sharing stories and memories, laughing, and teasing. To be included in this is a distinct way of showing affection and appreciation for each other. So it is true that daily conversations strengthen us as do the old stories of our ancestors that have been told since the beginning of Navajo time. . . .

The combination of song, prayer, and poetry is a natural form of expression for many Navajo people. A person who is able to "talk beautifully" is well thought of and considered wealthy. To know stories, remember stories, and to retell them well is to have been "raised right"; the family of such an individual is also held in high esteem. The value of the spoken word is not diminished, even with the influences of television, radio, and video. Indeed, it seems to have enriched the verbal dexterity of colloquial language, as for instance, in the names given to objects for which a Navajo word does not exist, such as "béésh nitséskees" or "thinking metal" for computers and "chidí bejéí" or "the car's heart" for a car battery.

I feel fortunate to have access to two, sometimes three languages, to have been taught the "correct" ways to use these languages, and to have the support of my family and relatives. Like many Navajos, I was taught that the way one talks and conducts oneself is a direct reflection of the people who raised her or him. People are known by their use of language. . . .

RUBY HANSEN MURRAY
Osage

"We need to see the places where we come from, both lovingly held and skillfully interrogated."

Ruby Hansen Murray (1953–) is a poet of place. Bringing her Osage sensibilities and photographer's eye to the settings she travels, Murray focuses on the most potent of topics—political, social, and environmental—and the reader cannot look away. With a stern and reportorial exposition, using form with great flexibility and transparency, Murray's narrative style and long lines build up in layers, carrying multiple insights. Her work is exhaustive, fleshing out the smallest details to bring a complete picture to the page. This is particularly evident in fine poems such as "Nch'i-Wana" and "*The Little Osage Captive*, Elias Cornelius, 1824." And in "The Dark Mother," the poet refuses to back down—here and throughout Murray's work, the reader must continue to hold with the image, with the idea, to the point of feeling the speaker's own distress. Only in the end, when Murray delivers a final blow, is the reader free from that concentrated focus.

The Dark Mother

Say the Columbia River drains an area the size of France,
let the sibilance help get your arms around the 1,243-mile long snake you have
channeled.

With his sixty years along her bank, my husband speaks the language of her in-
sult Micah, Revelstoke, Grand Coulee, Bonneville, and McNary, for an Oregon
senator, John Day, for a woodsman lost from the Astor party in the winter of 1811.

I wonder if the engineers who stopped salmon from returning to the upper Nch'i-
Wana at the Chief Joseph Dam rest well, and whether building that life-stealing
dam made them sick.

Nch'i-Wana

She lies dreaming in the roar at Wyam,
salmon brushing rocks as they leap.

At her mouth, bare feet, the brush of cedar nets,
around those ankles, cotton skirts slosh water,
the heavy touch of salmon on sand.

Linen nets, horses' hooves.
Gillnetters putter an iridescent glow in the slack water of Blind Slough,
ferries make a slow beat from the Kathlamet's camp to the marshy island,
where chicken coops float with the tide.

Restless, her bed picked clean, stumps gone, the snag puller's cables coiled.
Dredges vacuum memories of sturgeon, ghost runs sweep past.

She hears oceangoing ships' horns along her rip-rapped banks, calls down the
cataclysm that will sweep her free.

Rest Assured

A radioactive rabbit caught at Hanford Nuclear Reservation just north of Richland[1] on Nov. 4th, 2010 has Washington State Department of Health workers looking for contaminated droppings.

There is no danger to the public.

Fox Urine Applied to Solve Nuke Problem

Workers have put up a chain-link fence to contain the rabbits. Department of Energy workers are spraying the scent of a predator animal.

Richland—Workers cleaning up the Hanford nuclear reservation are going after radioactive wasp nests.[2]

(There is) No public hazard.

The wasp nests, which could number in the thousands, are "fairly highly contaminated" with radioactive isotopes, such as cesium and cobalt. Mud dauber wasps built the nests in 2003, when workers finished covering cleaned-up waste sites with fresh topsoil, native plants and straw to help the plants grow.
Cleanup work provided a steady supply of mud, which the wasps used as building material.

Vegetative waste at Hanford nuclear reservation not safe

Gnats and flies ate a sugary coating used to fix radioactive contamination in soil, and spread the radioactivity to waste, such as banana peels and apple cores, that workers had left in offices in 1998.

No cause for alarm.

1. The 586-square mile Hanford site is located in the southeastern part of Washington state, north of Richland, Washington, and thirty miles north of the Oregon–Washington border. The Columbia River flows through the site for fifty miles.

2. Seattle Times, June 11, 2009.

Food Fight at Hanford, No Laughing Matter

A contaminated mouse crawled into a box of food collected by an employee food drive in central Hanford in 1996.

The mouse was trapped in an abandoned Hanford building previously used by the Tri-Cities Food Bank.

Stainless Steel Solutions

Tanks like giant stainless steel bowls were the first containers for high- level nuclear waste.

Storage tanks were built to last 20 years. Carbon steel corrodes in highly acidic environments like those in Hanford's tanks.[1]

The double-shell tanks, 28 of them, were built between 1977 and 1986. The double shell tanks are more robust, but are also made of carbon steel. To date, none of the double-shell tanks have leaked.

Common household items inspire engineers

The tanks use pulse jet mixers, which engineers describe as giant turkey basters, to keep the sludge stirred, preventing plutonium from concentrating at the bottom and starting a chain reaction or producing explosive hydrogen gas. The pulse jet mixers have never been used in the United States, and failed in tests to prevent material from building up at the bottom of tanks.

Successes sited by Oregon State NUCSAAF **include**
Workers have spent the past decade or so digging up **millions of tons** of

contaminated soil along the Columbia River and hauling it to a lined, engineered disposal site several miles from the river

Five [of Hanford's nine] plutonium production reactors were *cocooned* . . . where radiation within the reactor blocks can safely decay.

More than **530** truckloads of transuranic waste has been shipped to a disposal facility in New Mexico--predominantly protective clothing and building debris that is contaminated with small amounts of plutonium. Because it will be hazardous for **thousands of years**, it is buried deep underground to keep it away from people and the environment.

1. The tanks were never designed to permanently store high-level radioactive waste. Most of these tanks, 149 of them, are single-shelled and built between 1943 and 1964.

The Little Osage Captive, Elias Cornelius, 1824

May those who read her history, remember the means by which her last moments were rendered so peaceful and happy. It was through the instrumentality of CHRISTIAN MISSIONARIES, who were sent to the Indians, to teach them the Gospel, and to show them the way of salvation, that her mind was prepared for death.

Giving Voice to Place: Where You See Yourself

Finding your place in the writer's world is hard. I'm writing an essay about a poet of influence in my life in the weeks after award-winning writer and producer Sherman Alexie's predatory behavior is called out, his less than supportive responses to young indigenous writers detailed. Then, the acclaimed Dominican-American writer Junot Díaz publishes an essay about his rape as a child and his emotionally irresponsible behavior to women as he ran from his pain. He describes how the trauma intruded in his life and prevented him from writing; he writes about stolen time.

I was an early reader. In elementary school, I read the original bloody Grimm's Fairy Tales. As I got older I looked at each author's biography to see how they found space and time to write. What did these people do for work, I wondered, and who welcomed them along the way. Their lives sounded nothing like mine. I was working as a clerk in an emergency room writing on weekends, when a coworker told me how I could go to graduate school. I studied to become a family psychotherapist because I needed to earn a living. I worked fulltime and took classes and wrote around the edges.

Life is short: that's why I'm so angry with Alexie for throwing emotional roadblocks in front of indigenous women I know and admire. I've been in workshops with both Sherman Alexie and Junot Díaz. I sought them out, because I'm a citizen of the Osage Nation and my mother's family has been in St. Thomas for generations. I listen to my friends describe the painful legacies these men have left in their wake, personally or professionally, at the same time they created visibility for cultures we're part of.

In 2009, Osage writer and journalist Louis Gray held an Osage Writers Summit in Pawhuska, where I felt deeply grounded. That's also where I first heard poet Carter Revard read, the sonorous tones supporting Osage and Oklahoma detail, his rolling stories pantomimed.

Revard's poetry and essays in *Winning the Dust Bowl* offer a window into his early years climbing boulders at Buck Creek near my uncle's ranch and the Ware allotments. He describes bootleggers and Depression-poor farmers as well as Osage relatives. It's an intimate family history of eating watermelon from a truck in the creek bed in summer and his love for his adoptive Camp family, Ponca activist-fighters at Wounded Knee in the 1970s. He contextualizes Osage history back to Cahokia. He captures the lightheartedness of Native conversation, diving to the heart of family and community, as when he sees his Uncle Gus dancing after he'd passed. There's a generosity in his work I don't always match, but I'm grateful for his words, for seeing myself on the page. We need to see the places where we come from, both lovingly held and skillfully interrogated.

*

Wazhazhe Grandmother
by Carter Revard

> —I-ko-eh, tha-gthi a tho.
> *[Ho-e-ga, literally "bare spot": the center of the forehead of the mythical elk . . . a term for an enclosure in which all life takes on bodily form, nev-*

er to depart therefrom except by death . . . the earth which the mythical elk made to be habitable by separating it from the water . . . the camp of the tribe when ceremonially pitched . . . life as proceeding from the combined influences of the cosmic forces.]
—Francis La Flesche, A Dictionary of the Osage Language, 1932

They chose their allotted land
out west of the Agency
at the prairie's edge,
where the Osage Hills begin they built
their homestead, honeymooned there
near Timber Hill,
where Bird Creek meanders in
from the rolling grassy plains with their prairie chicken
           dancing in spring,
built in a timbered hollow where deer come down
at dusk with the stars
to drink from the deep pools
near Timber Hill
and below the
waterfall that seemed
so high to me the summer
when I was six and walked up near its clearness gliding
some five or six feet down from the flat
sandstone ledge to its pools:
she called it in Osage, *ni-xe,*
the dark water turning into
a spilling of light
was a curtain clear and flowing, under
the blue flash of a kingfisher's diving
into the pool above the falls
and his flying up
again to the dead white branch of his willow —
the whole place was so quiet,
the way Grandma was quiet,
it seemed a place to be still,
seemed waiting for us,

though no one lived there by then
since widowed during the war she'd moved
to the place south of Pawhuska,
and why we had driven down there from Timber Hill, now, I
can't quite remember —
was it a picnic, or some kind
of retreat or vacation time
out of the August heat of Pawhuska?
The pictures focus sharp-edged:
a curtain of dark green ivy ruffled
a bit by breeze and water beside
the waters falling there
and a dirt road winding red and rocky
across tree-roots, along which, carefully,
my mother eased our rumbling Buick Eight
in that Depression year when Osage oil
still gushed to float us on into
a happy future —
but whether I dreamed, or saw real things in time,
their road, their house, the waterfall back in the woods
are all
at the bottom of Lake Bluestem now,
because Bird Creek,
blessed with a dam,
is all Psyched out
of its snaggly, snaky self into a
windsparkling lake
whose deep blue waters are now
being piped into Pawhuska pure and drinkable,
filling with blue brilliance municipal pools
and sprinkling the lawns to green or pouring freshets
down asphalt gutters to cool the shimmering
cicada-droning fevers of August streets
even as
in Bird Creek's old channel under Lake Bluestem,
big catfish
grope slowly in darkness

up over the sandstone ledge of the drowned
waterfall, or
scavenge through the ooze of
the homestead and along the road where
an Osage bride and her man came riding one special day
and climbed down from the buggy in all their
best finery
to live in their first home.

LOUISE ERDRICH

Turtle Mountain Ojibwe

"My father taught me to learn poems by heart, and at one time I memorized all of Sylvia Plath's Ariel. *Her poems helped me get through a winter in Fargo–Moorhead, when I had no car and so waited in subzero weather for the bus . . . I suffered frostbite while muttering, 'Out of the ash / I rise with my red hair / And I eat men like air.'"*

Though she is best known for her fiction, the first book of Louise Erdrich (1954–) was a collection of poems, entitled *Jacklight* (1984), and contains poems that have become canonical texts in Indigenous American poetry. Erdrich's poems are often narrative—they tell stories, they have characters, and they contain plots. Frequently, an Erdrich poem uses a famous/infamous character (John Wayne, Mary Rowlandson) or policy (forced removal of Native children to boarding schools) as a kind of launch pad to ask larger questions about Indigenous identity in general and Ojibwe realities in particular. However, her poems also work as poems. They are masterfully crafted and exhibit rich, lyrical language and images. History and traditional stories often work their way into the poems, as does invented dialogue, making a poetic experience that is unlike any other.

Dear John Wayne

August and the drive-in picture is packed.
We lounge on the hood of the Pontiac
surrounded by the slow-burning spirals they sell
at the window, to vanquish the hordes of mosquitoes.
Nothing works. They break through the smoke screen for blood.

Always the lookout spots the Indians first,
spread north to south, barring progress.
The Sioux or some other Plains bunch
in spectacular columns, ICBM missiles,
feathers bristling in the meaningful sunset.

The drum breaks. There will be no parlance.
Only the arrows whining, a death-cloud of nerves
swarming down on the settlers
who die beautifully, tumbling like dust weeds
into the history that brought us all here
together: this wide screen beneath the sign of the bear.

The sky fills, acres of blue squint and eye
that the crowd cheers. His face moves over us,
a thick cloud of vengeance, pitted
like the land that was once flesh. Each rut,
each scar makes a promise: It is
not over, this fight, not as long as you resist.

Everything we see belongs to us.

A few laughing Indians fall over the hood
slipping in the hot spilled butter.
The eye sees a lot, John, but the heart is so blind.
Death makes us owners of nothing.
He smiles, a horizon of teeth
the credits reel over, and then the white fields

again blowing in the true-to-life dark.
The dark films over everything.
We get into the car
scratching our mosquito bites, speechless and small
as people are when the movie is done.
We are back in our skins.

How can we help but keep hearing his voice,
the flip side of the sound track, still playing:
Come on, boys, we got them
where we want them, drunk, running.
They'll give us what we want, what we need.
Even his disease was the idea of taking everything.
Those cells, burning, doubling, splitting out of their skins.

Indian Boarding School: The Runaways

Home's the place we head for in our sleep.
Boxcars stumbling north in dreams
don't wait for us. We catch them on the run.
The rails, old lacerations that we love,
shoot parallel across the face and break
just under Turtle Mountains. Riding scars
you can't get lost. Home is the place they cross.

The lame guard strikes a match and makes the dark
less tolerant. We watch through cracks in boards
as the land starts rolling, rolling till it hurts
to be here, cold in regulation clothes.
We know the sheriff's waiting at midrun
to take us back. His car is dumb and warm.
The highway doesn't rock, it only hums
like a wing of long insults. The worn-down welts
of ancient punishments lead back and forth.

All runaways wear dresses, long green ones,
the color you would think shame was. We scrub
the sidewalks down because it's shameful work.
Our brushes cut the stone in watered arcs
and in the soak frail outlines shiver clear
a moment, things us kids pressed on the dark
face before it hardened, pale, remembering
delicate old injuries, the spines of names and leaves.

Captivity

> *He (my captor) gave me a biscuit, which I put in my pocket, and not daring to eat it, buried it under a log, fearing he had put something in it to make me love him.*
>
>   —from the narrative of the captivity of Mrs. Mary Rowlandson, who was taken prisoner by the Wampanoag when Lancaster, Massachusetts, was destroyed in the year 1676

The stream was swift, and so cold
I thought I would be sliced in two.
But he dragged me from the flood
by the ends of my hair.
I had grown to recognize his face.
I could distinguish it from the others.
There were times I feared I understood
his language, which was not human,
and I knelt to pray for strength.

We were pursued! By God's agents
or pitch devils I did not know.
Only that we must march.
Their guns were loaded with swan shot.
I could not suckle and my child's wail
put them in danger.

He had a woman
with teeth black and glittering.
She fed the child milk of acorns.
The forest closed, the light deepened.

I told myself that I would starve
before I took food from his hands
but I did not starve.
One night
he killed a deer with a young one in her
and gave me to eat of the fawn.
It was so tender,
the bones like the stems of flowers,
that I followed where he took me.
The night was thick. He cut the cord
that bound me to the tree.

After that the birds mocked.
Shadows gaped and roared
and the trees flung down
their sharpened lashes.
He did not notice God's wrath.
God blasted fire from half-buried stumps.
I hid my face in my dress, fearing He would burn us all
but this, too, passed.

Rescued, I see no truth in things.
My husband drives a thick wedge
through the earth, still it shuts
to him year after year.
My child is fed of the first wheat.
I lay myself to sleep
on a Holland-laced pillowbeer.
I lay to sleep.
And in the dark I see myself
as I was outside their circle.

They knelt on deerskins, some with sticks,
and he led his company in the noise
until I could no longer bear
the thought of how I was.
I stripped a branch
and struck the earth,
in time, begging it to open
to admit me
as he was
and feed me honey from the rock.

Windigo

*The Windigo is a flesh-eating, wintry demon with a man buried deep in-
side of it. In some Chippewa stories, a young girl vanquishes this monster
by forcing boiling lard down its throat, thereby releasing the human at
the core of ice.*

You knew I was coming for you, little one,
when the kettle jumped into the fire.
Towels flapped on the hooks,
and the dog crept off, groaning,
to the deepest part of the woods.

In the hackles of dry brush a thin laughter started up.
Mother scolded the food warm and smooth in the pot
and called you to eat.
But I spoke in the cold trees:
New one, I have come for you, child hide and lie still.

The sumac pushed sour red cones through the air.
Copper burned in the raw wood.
You saw me drag toward you.
Oh touch me, I murmured, and licked the soles of your feet.

You dug your hands into my pale, melting fur.

I stole you off, a huge thing in my bristling armor.
Steam rolled from my wintry arms, each leaf shivered
from the bushes we passed
until they stood, naked, spread like the cleaned spines of fish.

Then your warm hands hummed over and shoveled themselves full
of the ice and the snow. I would darken and spill
all night running, until at last morning broke the cold earth
and I carried you home,
a river shaking in the sun.

Rez Litany

Let us now pray to those beatified
within the Holy Colonial church
beginning with Saint Assimilus,
patron of residential and of government
boarding schools, whose skin was dark
but who miraculously bled white milk
for all to drink.
To cure the gut aches that resulted
as ninety percent of Native children are
lactose intolerant, let us now pray to the
patron saint of the Indian Health Service,
who is also guardian of the slot machines,
Our Lady of Luck, she who carries
in one hand mistaken blood tests and botched
surgeries and in the other hand the heart
of a courageous doctor squeezed and dry.
Let us pray for the sacred hearts of all good doctors
and nurses, whose tasks are manifold and made more difficult
by the twin saints of commodity food,

Saint Bloatinus and Saint Cholestrus,
who were martyred at the stake of body fat
and who preside now in heaven
at the gates of the Grand Casino Buffet.
Saint Macaronia and Saint Diabeta, hear our prayer.
It is terrible to be diminished toe by toe.
Good Saint Pyromane,
Enemy of the BIA,
Deliver us from those who seek to bury us
in files and triplicate documents and directives.
Saint Quantum, Martyr of the Blood
and Holy Protector of the Tribal Rolls,
assist us in the final shredding which shall proceed
on the Day of Judgment so we may all rain down
in a blizzard of bum pull tabs
and unchosen lottery tickets, which represent
the souls of the faithfully departed
in your name.
Your name written in the original fire
we mistook so long ago for the trader's rum.
Pray for us, all you saints of white port
four roses old granddad and night train.
Good Saint Bingeous who fell asleep upside down on the cross
and rose on the third day without even knowing he had died.
Saint Odium of the hundred-proof blood
and Saint Tremens of the great pagan spiders
dripping from the light fixtures.
You powerful triumvirate, intercede for us
drunks stalled in the bars,
float our asses off the cracked stools
and over to the tribal college,
where the true saints are ready to sacrifice their brain cells
for our brain cells, in that holy exchange which is called learning.
Saint Microcephalia, patron of huffers and dusters,
you of the cooked brain and mean capacity, you
of the simian palm line and poor impulse control,
you of the Lysol-soaked bread, you sleeping with the dogs

underneath the house, hear our prayers
which we utter backwards and sideways
as nothing makes sense
least of all your Abstinence Campaign
from which Oh Lord Deliver Us.
Saints Primapara, Gravida, and Humpenenabackseat,
you patrons of unsafe teenage sex
and fourteen-year-old mothers,
pray for us now and at the hour of our birth,
amen.

Out of the Black Night

from Poetry

My father is known for being stubborn, for bicycling, and for his poetry. His name is Ralph Erdrich and he lives in a small town in North Dakota. One day, when he was eighty-eight years old, he decided to bicycle over to the next town where bananas were twenty-five cents cheaper. He was struck by a car. He flew up in the air and was sure he would not survive. But he was alive when he landed and seemingly unhurt. (Yes, it was miraculous, but that's how he is.) He continued on, bought the bananas, and bicycled home.

Three years later, he began to lose his memory. He reported that there were frightening gaps where his poems used to exist—"Ozymandias," "Invictus," "The Cremation of Sam McGee," "The Shooting of Dan McGrew," and "Provide, Provide"—the last line always recited with dark irony. There are many others, but those are his crowd pleasers. When the poems left, sucked away into black absence, he was distressed. He began to tremble uncontrollably, had trouble walking. He was diagnosed with vascular dementia.

None of his children felt that was accurate, but we also thought we might be in denial. He had refused to see a neurologist, but finally my brother Ralph, sister Lise, and mother Rita insisted that he have his head examined. The tests showed he had hydrocephalus, perhaps resulting from a fall, and once a shunt was placed in his brain the pressure that had stolen his poetry was relieved. He began to remember all sorts of things. New details cropped up in stories about his childhood. He remembered what had happened when he seemingly had no memory. He described the strangeness of his recovery, how into his mind long chunks of poems would float. How he was able to fit together word puzzles until he had an entire poem back. He is ninety-two, and still in the fell clutch of circumstance, old age, but his delight in these poems is infectious.

One way he likes to use poetry is to stymie politically motivated phone calls. He was horrified when Hillary Clinton was not elected. If the caller is espousing a right-wing cause, he recites "Invictus," which I would argue is the most Republican poem ever, but he has always used it as a cudgel. There is nothing you can do when a strong old man fixes his gray eye on you and recites "Invictus." You have to stand there and take it. Once, I saw him beat down a famous professor with that poem. Another time, while my father was enduring a painful repair on his ear, he used poetry as an anesthetic, hoarsely shouting "The Destruction of Sennacherib." As the young doctor made the first stitch, he roared, *The Assyrian came down like the wolf on the fold* . . .

"Stop," I told the doctor. "He needs more Lidocaine."

"Proceed," ordered Dad.

The doctor rallied. He had paled, but he placed the next stitch, endured the next line, and was there for the Angel of Death.

When Dad lost his poems, "Invictus" didn't quite disappear. He sometimes came up with lines, especially the last line, *I am the captain of my soul*, for "Invictus" is the poem of extremis. Famously, the poem helped Nelson Mandela survive his long imprisonment. "Invictus" was written with rat droppings on toilet paper and passed among US prisoners of war in North Vietnamese prisons. "Invictus" is also a CrossFit gym, Prince Harry's games for wounded service members, and a men's fragrance by Paco Rabanne. The perfume comes in a Winners' Cup-shaped flask and is accompanied by narrative phrases. *An epic hero facing the waves. A dive into the abyss. A god is rising above the ocean.* "Invictus" was also the final handwritten statement by Oklahoma City bomber Timothy McVeigh.

William Ernest Henley wrote "Invictus" in 1875, while recovering from the loss of one leg, and the near loss of another leg, to the ravages of tuberculosis. Radically for its time, it is a secular poem about going it alone without "whatever gods may be." So actually, I suppose the poem is probably less political than gendered. For it seems to me that "Invictus" resonates more with men than with women. It is a desperation brag. Each stanza contains despair or obstruction, then triumph. I thought the poem was masculine because men see themselves wrestling with monsters, or beset on all sides, or pushing boulders uphill. But then the poem started to creep into my own thoughts when I faced dreaded or seemingly insurmountable situations.

It crept into my thoughts, but I can't say it helped. We live in reductionist times and I kept thinking how easily the soul can be conquered by damage to the brain. I am much more comforted by "One Art" by Elizabeth Bishop. My sister Heid and I think it is a woman's "Invictus," for it too takes on loss but without the bombast. It too is about survival, but the soul in "One Art" is salvaged by flexibility, acceptance, and wondering irony.

My father taught me to learn poems by heart, and at one time I memorized all of Sylvia Plath's *Ariel*. Her poems helped me get through a winter in Fargo–Moorhead, when I had no car and so waited in subzero weather for the bus. Gripped by the kind of shattering cold I grew up with, wearing my deadly cool but uninsulated Spanish riding boots, I suffered frostbite while muttering, "Out of the ash / I rise with my red hair / And I eat men like air." For a while, after the invasion of Iraq, I would make friends uneasy by meandering into "Strange Meeting" by WWI poet Wilfred Owen: "Now men will go content with what we spoiled. / Or discontent, boil bloody, and be spilled." Then I realized how awkward it is to be recited to unexpectedly, and how I hated it when other people broke into poetry.

I can only bear to hear my father recite poems. Part of the pleasure is that I, the lady that's known as Lou, can stumble alongside those rocking-horse rhymes. He smiles at my mother when describing "The Face on the Barroom Floor." He fake pouts at *the picture pride of Hollywood*. And when he bites into "Invictus," I can't help it. There we are on the living room couch, in a town that has recently banned lap dancing, shouting *how charged with punishments the scroll*, while my mother, the soul of skeptical dignity, walks calmly through the room. Rita is the only one who can turn her back on "Invictus." She has been bludgeoned by chance as only a wife can be when it lands on her husband. But she's far too modest to talk about it.

*

One Art
by Elizabeth Bishop

The art of losing isn't hard to master;
so many things seem filled with the intent
to be lost that their loss is no disaster.

Lose something every day. Accept the fluster
of lost door keys, the hour badly spent.
The art of losing isn't hard to master.

Then practice losing farther, losing faster:
places, and names, and where it was you meant
to travel. None of these will bring disaster.

I lost my mother's watch. And look! my last, or
next-to-last, of three loved houses went.
The art of losing isn't hard to master.

I lost two cities, lovely ones. And, vaster,
some realms I owned, two rivers, a continent.
I miss them, but it wasn't a disaster.

—Even losing you (the joking voice, a gesture
I love) I shan't have lied. It's evident
the art of losing's not too hard to master
though it may look like (*Write* it!) like disaster.

GORDON HENRY JR.
Anishinabe (White Earth Chippewa)

". . . coming to rest where the noun lives in colonies and the poetry, singing singing singer, coming to rest, now and again, the verb singing breathing breather, breath, without even names for poetry, poem, poet. . . ."

Heid E. Erdrich describes the poems of Gordon Henry Jr. (1955–) as a "dreamscape charmed by powerful songs." Indeed, Henry's work harkens, in tone and pace and theme, to old Indigenous songs. Henry is interested in the tensions between traditional Ojibwe practices and contemporary American realities. A good example appears in the final stanza of "November Becomes the Sky with Suppers for the Dead: "The way home / fills with snow / our tracks / human and machine." That notion of person and inhabiting the same space is indicative of his perspective. Henry turns to music in order to link the concerns of jazz vocalists and musicians with the singers and drummers at powwows. Similarly, in "When Names Escaped Us," Henry uses aspects of traditional ceremony to pose larger questions about unity, identity, and aesthetic creation. Also an award-winning fiction writer, Henry brings a strong narrative drive to his poetry, and many of his poems are themselves stories in which characters keep on coming up against conflicts that dramatize many of the cultural hurdles Native people face, day in and day out.

When Names Escaped Us

The boy painted himself white and ran into the darkness.

We let the words "he may be dead, bury him,"
bury him.

We took his clothes to the rummage sale
in the basement of the mission
We put his photographs and drawings
in a birdcage and covered it with a starquilt.

For four nights voices carried clear to the river.

After winter so many storms moved in
strangers came among us
They danced
They shoveled in the shadows of trees

Then, somehow we all felt
all of us were of this one boy

November Becomes the Sky with Suppers for the Dead

I am standing outside
in Minnesota
ghost wind recalling
names in winter mist

The road smells
of dogs two days dead

White photographers talk in
the house of mainstream
media

I can't articulate
the agony of Eagle Singer's
children to them.

We celebrate the old
man while another
generation shoots
crushed and heated
prescriptions
sells baskets,
machinery,
the fixtures yet to be
installed in the house,
yet to be heated
by the tribal government,
for another night
stolen by the stupors
and the wondrous
pleasure of forget
everything medicines.

Back inside
Uncle Two Dogs rolls me
a smoke out of
organic American Spirit

I look to a last cup
of coffee.

The way home
fills with snow
our tracks
human and machine.

Jazz Tune for a Hiawatha Woman

You know where I'm coming
from
On the same street past the tracks
where last august
we drained a few predawn
quarts made promises against
a mural of imperial oppression
on the wall of the workers
of the world bookstore
(later closed up and reopened later
as a Hollywood Video.)
Now
a few tripped out
two-spirit women skins
verbally fuck with
a panhandling Devils Lake
wino in a Viking shirt
outside the currency exchange.
As I make my way toward
you over the bridge nicknamed
"Two Suicides" (with graffiti lightbulb
launch point on the railing
and sprayed fluorescent sketches
Of pornographic body parts, rubbing
up against dollar signs

on the concrete stanchions
underneath.)

Try not to blame me that
the pow wow windigo kahn got
your cell number from
the table at the city park
where I carved the digits

with a leatherman before I put
the last number down
in blood I drew with
broken glass and mixed
with a pinch of ash
from my menthol
camel.
(He wrote it all backwards
under his ANISHINABE name
on his fist)
Just tell him when he calls
you love it when he calls.
He'll go back to dancing
while reading the news in the
Circle just like he did
behind the middle-aged
jingle dress matrons,
dangling their moccasin
matching bags with limp wrists,
glaring under the beady flora
of woodland tiaras,
knowing and not liking
the clown mocking their
steps behind them
at the upper Midwest gathering.
I heard from Spotted Eagle
at the halfway   house
after he ticked off conditions for my
release from the freezing
moons of treatment:

(No drugs No pot No speed No black cadillacs No more shooting your
grandfather's HIS painkiller prescriptions No drinking No driving No
parties No bad influences AA twice a week ay You go to meetings at our
Lady of Whatyacall or you can go Tuesday at the Indian center just give
in to a higher power and keep up the sober interior monologues).

                    your Ma's still hanging on
to that Big Knife bricklayer
                              who ate the leftovers
        I brought from Hard Times Café
                              for you
                              the day I walked all the way
                back here
In clothes I found in a garbage
                bag in the back of a dodge
                              pickup parked in the drive
        at Uncle Salem's
                              only to find you'd gone north
                for a funeral.
Could it be more complicated?
                At 10 I tracked deer with my
                        Aunt and waited by a tree
                              in falling snow, shot
                                    my last round into the air
                        just to let her know
                where I was before it got
                              too late to search for me.

Nine years later, at the U
                        I took classes, studied philosophy,
                              European history and social
                                    linguistics, chemical tables
                        world religions and I still managed
        to remember my name and
                        the names of relatives and places.

I've lived and traveled
                        with no destination to speak of.
                I even stopped myself in the
                        middle of dreams just to wake up
        So I would remember faces
                              conversations, the speakers
And the voices, the mists and animals

                    the roads and enclosures,
            the running, the flying and
                        the fear dreaming of immobility brings.
Still,
        as I make my way back
                    to you, stand before another door
                            I know that inside there is
                No one, as your having left
                        remains the hand of another
door of my arrival.

LET US BE PAINTING PAINTING PAINTER SINGING SINGING SINGER: ON THE VERVE OF VERBS

for H. E. Ephemera

So, "this is poetry," is not poetry. We would rather be verb than noun or object even if the poem brings us to a final word as if settled on image or object image. A flat stone soaking water, a rainfall of women's voices, secret children of muses syncopating, in the weight of clouds running down roads in the passes of august memory. The noun lives in colonies, the verb escapes with a slice of bread taken from a table set, with fruit and a pistol, a shining watermelon glass of Kool-Aid, painting painting painter. Just as we would rather be singing singing singer, the echo coming from some filmy shore as we pass, paddling paddling paddler, gliding without enough names for water, over the surfaces named water, even as we believe this is poetry, even if we believe the event remains too limited, the extended, possibility of no context, no place, just the voice, in a small room, walls of books, rotting clothes, empty subjects, hanging jackets of winter, the voice alone, at a station, perhaps, singing, singing, singer, without enough names for lyric, for an uncertain longing, with sounds we call lyrical, even as the words end somewhere, in the extending impossibility of fixed context, stopping, coming to rest where the noun lives in colonies and the poetry, singing singing singer, coming to rest, now and again, the verb singing breathing breather, breath, without even names for poetry, poem, poet, coming to rest, as if we could be poet or anything other than breathing, breathing, breathing, breather, poet, breathing, breath, breathing, breather, poet, breathing, singing, sounding, singing, singer, sounding, poet, singing, the sound, sounding, song, poet, breathing, sound, breathing, song, breather, breath.

KIMBERLY BLAESER

ANISHINAABE

". . . miigwech for lush, defiant poetry that not only crosses boundaries, but works to erase them."

Known for her work as a naturalist, Kimberly Blaeser (1955–) has a poetic voice that seems to rise from the the rhythm of the streams, grasslands, trees, and earth that she writes about. Yet Blaeser's work cannot be seen as merely pastoral. Her poetry can also be timely and prescient, unafraid to to stand eye-to-eye with current issues both tribal and national. Steeped in fertile imagery and symbolism, and influenced by Northwoods oral tradition, in poems such as "Captivity" Blaeser shows a penetrating awareness of continued colonization in the U.S., and of the effects that settlement continues to have on the natural world and on Native communities. She can be explicitly political and meanwhile gently lyrical with a subtly veiled activism that is poignant, not didactic. This is especially visible in a poem like "Apprenticed to Justice," which links history, place, and people. Writing in hybrid forms that vary from extended narrative to haiku, Blaeser upends the expected with approaches that question the quotidian. In images that linger and an art that keeps on surprising and resisting, Blaeser's poetry is an immersion in the malleability of language.

See also page 305, for Heid E. Erdrich's testimony to the influence of Kimberly Blaeser's poem "Rewriting Your Life."

Captivity

I.

A mark across the body. The morning I watched my beloved uncle disappear down the alley. His car left sitting in our yard for 30 days. This tattoo we cover with shame. The stories my mother whispered as if *gitchi-manidoo* was a child who should not be told of the troubles of humans. All those taken. Visits made on dusty trains. Letters adorned like birch bark art with lines and tiny holes. My shriveled grandma "an accessory" hiding my cousin from the interchangeable uniforms of civil pursuit. Her white hair another flag of truce.

II.

This is how we look over our shoulder. This is how we smile carefully in public places. This is how we carry our cards, our identities. This is how we forget—and how you remind us.

III.

Mary Rowlandson made it big in the colonial tabloids. Indian captivity narrative a seeming misnomer. But ink makes strong cultural bars of bias. This is how we remain captured in print.

IV.

Now I harbor fugitive names. c sin came to my reading in ankle tether. Qu i chained herself before the R C building in protest. M cus who cannot receive email. The Ar t c at manager from Thi f ive ls. His whiskey-inspired stories tell of cicada existence—a cyclical shedding of "dangerous" identities.

V.

We molt. The shell of our past a transparent *chanhua*. Yes, we will eat it like medicine.

Apprenticed to Justice

The weight of ashes
from burned-out camps.
Lodges smoulder in fire,
animal hides wither
their mythic images shrinking
pulling in on themselves,
all incinerated
fragments
of breath bone and basket
rest heavy
sink deep
like wintering frogs.
And no dustbowl wind
can lift
this history
of loss.

Now fertilized by generations —
ashes upon ashes,
this old earth erupts.
Medicine voices rise like mists
white buffalo memories
teeth marks on birch bark
forgotten forms
tremble into wholeness.

And the grey weathered stumps,
trees and treaties
cut down
trampled for wealth.
Flat Potlatch plateaus
of ghost forests
raked by bears
soften rot inward

until tiny arrows of green
sprout
rise erect
rootfed
from each crumbling center.

Some will never laugh
as easily.
Will hide knives
silver as fish in their boots,
hoard names
as if they could be stolen
as easily as land,
will paper their walls
with maps and broken promises,
scar their flesh
with this badge
heavy as ashes.

And this is a poem
for those
apprenticed
from birth.
In the womb
of your mother nation
heartbeats
sound like drums
drums like thunder
thunder like twelve thousand
walking
then ten thousand
then eight
walking away
from stolen homes
from burned out camps
from relatives fallen
as they walked

then crawled
then fell.

This is the woodpecker sound
of an old retreat.
It becomes an echo
an accounting
to be reconciled.
This is the sound
of trees falling in the woods
when they are heard,
of red nations falling
when they are remembered.
This is the sound
we hear
when fist meets flesh
when bullets pop against chests
when memories rattle hollow in stomachs.

And we turn this sound
over and over again
until it becomes
fertile ground
from which we will build
new nations
upon the ashes of our ancestors.
Until it becomes
the rattle of a new revolution
these fingers
drumming on keys.

Goodbye to All That

1.

He could have taken you prisoner, of course
when our two tribes were at war
over whitefish and beaver territory
and the Anishinaabeg chased your Indian ancestors
from the woodlands he now brings you home to.
Or your Dakota relatives might have waged a war party
on their swift plains' ponies to avenge your taking
and bring you back from those uncivilized
they named in disgust the rabbit-chokers.
But those histories of dog-eaters and Chippewa crows
are just a backdrop now for other stories
told together by descendants of smallpox survivors
and French fur traders,
clan members of Wolf and of Water Spirit.
And now you gather,
trackers and scouts in new bloodless legal battles,
still watch for mark and sign —
for the flight of waterbirds.

2.

Old histories that name us enemies
don't own us; nor do our politics
grown so pow-wow liberal you seldom
point out the follies of White Earth tribal leaders.
(Except of course for the time our elected chair
mistakenly and under the influence of civilization
drove his pickup down the railroad tracks
and made the tri-state ten o'clock news.)
And Sundays behind the Tribune
he seldom even mentions the rabid casino bucks
or gets out his calculator and with lodge-pole eyebrows
methodically measures beaded distances,
results of territorial lines drawn in your homeland.

And even though I have seen him sniff, glance over
he really almost never checks the meat in your pot,
nor reconnoiters the place of your rendezvous
just to be sure.

Fantasies of Women

for Carol Marefka

They say:
there was an old woman
who lived in a shoe —
children, spanking, bed, no food
it's an old story,
one to rival the Peter tale
who kept his wife in a pumpkin shell,
or Jack Sprat who coveted
all the 90% lean cuts of meat,
while his ever-expanding
squat round wife
tumbles over the sides
of a tiny kitchen chair
over-filling the page
on which she is drawn.
We keep turning that page
but one caricature follows another.

Some claim:
women always were the delicate sex —
fainting, timid, helpless souls
you know that line
the length and breadth of those
whose names have scrambled
the letters of femininity
into unrecognizable derivations

Annie Oakley, Gloria Steinem
Wilma Mankiller
Rigoberta Menchu
Mother Teresa of Calcutta.
In pants or full veil
in every state of dress or undress
Cher's navel
the jewel on Cleopatra's forehead
burn like all beacons of dissent.

I heard:
A nation is never defeated
until the hearts of its women
are trampled upon the earth —
this one I believe
for I grew up among women
who could swallow a raw heart
whole or in infinitesimal pieces
deer heart, rabbit heart, turtle heart
and did swallow and chew
chew and swallow their own red hearts
beating *for survival*
            for survival
            for survival
            for survival.

And this is the single story
we write with our lives
women of travois, ox, or minivan,
of African brown barefoot toes
bound Chinese feet
or seventy-five dollars a pop Birkenstocks.
Together we walk on our houses of history
track true
the paths of indentured servants,
girl babies slain and buried,

this black dirt of bias exposed
overcome in
story cycles of scarlet fecundity
told through the fires of many tongues
and translated again
in the labor of women.

Now we sing:
There was a young woman
who lived in a shoe-obsessed
commercialized overstocked world
she had many children
and knew just what to do —
raise them to share the burdens
of all the people
to unearth the fantastic lies
they were taught to walk upon
to devour fear
chew and swallow
and to cast their hearts
for survival.

Of Fractals and Pink Flowering

after Eric and Heather ChanSchatz, "The Next Generation"

Imagine the geometry of flower
is hunger for balance,
is my child's hand on the gears of beauty
layering and interlocking color.
Picture me prone, a small center point —
one copper dot in the white Minnesota winter.
Picture my mother drying her hands
placing the compass and spinning
arcs and intersecting curves,

woodland flowers growing
into many-petaled mandalas
into limitlessness: a universe
of circles, of symmetry — sun,
stars, blooms and orange-hued fruits,
the berry, squash, ripe tomato wonder
of belonging.

       My own spirograph bursts
rush forth ornate like paisley, like fireworks
against dark summer sky. Spokes and wheels
and gears meshing — each pencil thrust
a tentative mark, a hopeful threading
of the cogs of longing. Imagine my fingers
holding tight to the friction,
watch the intricate flourishes appear
on white paper — the tabula rasa
transformed by oval,
just another language
another voice saying hello
to the spiraling bodies of self.

Imagine my psychedelic crayola
yearning, my January pining
after the purple florals
the cosmos, the daisy mix
(he loves me, he loves me not)
on Gurney's seed packs.
Now watch as we carve splendor:
my world is medicine wheel and hand drum,
is pow-wow bustle and beadwork in woodland design.
The sweep of nature tallied by curve,
by eye, assembled now as scarlet fractals,
as collage of vines, tassels, seed pods,
and a child's simple pink infinity.

"Air is Between These Words, Fanning the Flame"*: Poetry and Literary Inheritance

If I have gone AWOL from what might have been a careful partitioning of my "life" from my writing, or a separation of my literary work into neat categories like "spiritual" and "political," I blame Linda Hogan. Or I thank her. I say *miigwech* for lush, defiant poetry that not only crosses boundaries, but works to erase them. Linda's work gave me permission to speak my messy truth—to fold into my poems the varied voices that inhabit me, to trace my complicated unraveling of inherited dogmas.

Within the 2,500,000 gigabyte capacity that I am told make up my memory, I carry many lines from Hogan's oeuvre. Over the years, I've taught her work in the classroom, quoted her work in essays, given papers about her writing, and listened to her perform. My relationship with Linda's work awakened in me a new understanding of our role as writers—it became a key building block as I formed my own literary aesthetic. My awareness of the dual nature of poetry comes partly from two of her lines in the poem "Neighbors" where she writes both, "This is the truth, not just a poem" and "This is a poem and not just the truth." I use these lines when I remind myself and others that poetry is both "affective" and "effective"—beautiful as language, but does something in the world.

Among the many Hogan poems that simultaneously embody resistance and artistry is "Workday" from her 1988 collection *Savings*. Hogan fills that poem with truth and poetic beauty. It contains haunting, evocative images picturing, for example, "my sisters chained to prison beds" or "Victor Jara's mutilated hands." It invites an understanding of the unnamable longing that marks our humanity as when the speaker looks back to see "the woman are all alone / framed in the windows" or when the speaker uses the words "beautiful" and "perfect" to describe even the damaged bodies she observes. The poem also challenges the indifference with which we live our lives when Hogan pairs the speaker's preoccupation with everyday concerns with her awareness of "other" ongoing conditions of injustice: "I go to work / though there are those who were missing today / from their homes. / I ride the bus / and do not think of children without food." I embrace and have emulated Hogan's use of the lyric as poetry of witness.

For me, perhaps one the most important "teachings" of the poem comes through the following lines:

Now I go to the University
and out for lunch
and listen to the higher ups
tell me all they have read
about Indians
and how to analyze this poem.

As a poet and a Native women in academia, as someone bound by hierarchical rules and protocols while simultaneously filled with a rebelliousness and hunger for an-other tradition of learning, I understand viscerally the implications of this passage and the dissent it suggests. Early in my career, in a 1992 essay on issues of literacy written as a part of a special *World Literature Today* volume published near the time of the inaugural Returning the Gift Festival, I offered the following interpretation of the passage.

> Here the racism of Orientalism is again manifested in appropriation of identity, and the move to preserve power is manifested in the arrogant presumption of superior understanding. The Orientalist assumes the position of ultimate explicator. The Orientalism, the racism, lies not in the claim of the Orientalist to understand the identity and literature of another, but in the claim to understand it better than the spokesperson. Such a claim is a move to colonize both identity and literature. Of course, Hogan's poem itself is testimony not only of her comprehension of the subtle Orientalism, but of her resistance to this colonization. ("'Learning the Language the Presidents Speak': Images and Issues of Literacy in American Indian Literatures," 234).

As an historical document tracing the influence of Hogan's work on mine, this essay (which includes discussion of other of her writing as well) fills the bill well. In terms of literary legacy, the last claim I make in this quoted section is most notable. Clearly, I delighted in Hogan's ability to rise against the subtle racism indirectly through the vehicle of the poem. Literary acts of resistance have likewise often marked my own poetic work.

In 2013, I actually employed lines from Hogan's poem "Left Hand Canyon" as an epigraph when writing in response to the crackdown on protests and the literal silencing of dissenting voices within the capitol building in Madison. My poem, "This House of Words," which came out in the small regional publication

Turn Up the Volume: Poems about the States of Wisconsin (Little Bird Press, 2013), quotes these lines from Hogan's poem:

> You can't take a man's words.
> They are his even as the land
> is taken away
> where another man
> builds his house.

Looking at the poem I wrote, I am struck by the manner and tone of lines like these: "Still blue uniforms handcuff songs / in public spaces" and their similarity to Hogan's "my sisters chained to prison beds." The use of vivid image and the stark presentation of a harsh reality marks both.

Of course, I was undoubtedly influenced by many poets in regards to these qualities. But if, as I have come to believe, poetry is an act of attention, is an invitation to a re-seeing of the world, is ultimately gesture, then I have no qualms in attributing to Linda Hogan and her important poetic work an early schooling of my attention, of my re-seeing, and more importantly, of the poetic approach I might take toward subjects and situations toward which I would like to gesture, towards which I would like to direct the attention of my reader.

The toolkit of Hogan's poetic approach also includes multivocality and the use of allusions to other texts and agencies. For example, she frequently builds an ontological or metaphysical poetic critique through the juxtaposition of supposed truths with images of injustice, often including quotations from or allusions to Biblical texts. (I think of a poem like "Blessing" with its invoking of The Beatitudes through the use of lines such as these: "Blessed are the rich / for they eat meat every night. / They have already inherited the earth.") An authoritative other or a dysfunctional hierarchical system sometimes lurks in the background of her poems. (In "Workday," the "higher-ups" or "the University" stand in, but in that poem there is a larger pall of systemic inequality over the world of the everyday people.) The demoralizing and faulty methods of this system she unmasks by implication (or sometimes as in The Beatitudes example, by an ironic rewriting). I think it likely that my own tendencies toward polyvocality, textual allusiveness, the inclusion and undercutting of authoritative texts come partly from her exemplary use of these techniques.

In my own work, I also sometimes move into the territory of documentary poetry or toward the blending of witness and documentation. A poem like

"'Housing Conditions of One Hundred and Fifty Chippewa Families,'" for example, incorporates material quoted from Sister Mary Inez Hilger's *Chippewa Families: A Social Study of White Earth Reservation*, 1938 (Minnesota Historical Society, 1998). In order to unmask the inherent presumptions and the colonizing impulse behind such a study, in order to challenge its perspective and its findings, I strive to let the language of Hilger's book indict itself while still providing an-other cultural context for understanding. My poem alternates between the incessant and evaluative listing methodology of the Hilger text—"23 with broken windows / 99 without foundations, buildings / resting on the ground; / 98 with stove pipes for chimneys;" and the storying of the narrative voice—"June to November / the year my mother turned five, / Mary Inez you walked these lands."

Similar to this undermining of literal documents and their authority in my work, is the undercutting of inherited "truths." My poem, "Fantasies of Women," investigates the things "they say" about women and offers alternate truth, finally rewriting and replacing an old text with a new story: "Now we sing: / There was a young woman / who lived in a shoe-obsessed / commercialized overstocked world." Likewise, "Of Eons and Epics" strives to invite a certain kind of relationship to story and place partly by unseating some existing stories, by challenging "the way they tell it." In this instance, just as Biblical language became a subtext in Hogan's "Blessing," the Genesis account of eviction from the Garden of Eden (while never named) lurks in the background of my poem: "humanity a paradise of aloneness: / a solved mystery, a locked garden / a departure— / that story the walking away."

I suspect other aspects of Hogan's work have inflected mine as well. In both "Fantasies of Women" and "Of Eons and Epics," for example, I notice a Hogan-like movement to create a new ontology or to cleave to an Indigenous mythopoeic understanding of human place and relatedness. My poem "Afterwards" makes a fairly bold leap to give voice to this understanding in a way similar to many of Hogan's poems in *The Book of Medicines*. The opening line—"Because the smallness of our being is our only greatness"—contains a declaration akin in tenor to Hogan's "Skin is the closest thing to god" which opens her poem "Skin Dreaming." Is this the poet or poem as truth-teller?

In "Apprenticed to Justice," I recognize both the impetus to re-tell our history and to claim a certain kind of triumph. In this, too, I might discover literary genealogy at work as Linda Hogan often re-historicizes Native experience and her poems frequently extend themselves in a gesture of survivance. Part of that re-historicizing becomes a new mythologizing of personal, familial, or tribal stories. In "Workday" the small reference to "my own family's grief over the lost children" is blended into the larger milieu of her poem. But this pattern of personal myth-making is more apparent in Hogan's book *Calling Myself Home*. A poem like "Man in the Moon" from that collection satisfyingly collapses fantasy and reality to create a new story. Although my own need or tendency to write about family and tribal stories is innate, the freedom to trip between the various ways of "knowing" these stories likely has part of its origin in the delightful liberated crossings Linda makes throughout her own poetic "calling of herself home." In "Apprenticed to Justice" my re-telling the "history of loss" inevitably employs images of the land since the identity and welfare of Native people arise in relationship with earth places. When I gave voice to a sense of legacy in "Family Tree" and later in a more playful fashion in "Of Fractals and Pink Flowering," the impetus of place figures into these stories as well. This latter poem, for example, suggests that our aesthetic, our sense of the beautiful, also has genealogy in place and culture:

> woodland flowers growing
> into many-petaled mandalas
> into limitlessness: a universe
> of circles, of symmetry — sun,
> stars, blooms and orange-hued fruits,
> the berry, squash, ripe tomato wonder
> of belonging.

The focus here on aesthetic genealogy is, of course, apropos to this discussion. Today as Native writers, many of us undergo largely the same formal education as other Americans. Often times that formal academic training threatens to undermine our tribal sense of ourselves. When aimed at eliminating difference, it works to erase unique cultural understandings. Then, awash in a capitalistic system, we may find the traditional value we place on stories, or balance, or relatedness being eroded. The very ideas of what constitutes beauty, of why or how we employ song or poems, of what the rewards or responsibilities of artistic engagement may be can begin to be overwritten. We need literary voices that can help sustain an Indigenous sense of intergenerational groundings for contemporary work.

Linda's has been among those important voices for me. The final poetic aspect I will mention (but certainly not the final influence of her work on mine) is my overarching preoccupation with the natural world, the spirit and stories embedded there, and the "natural" reality of humanness. In a poem like "Refractions," I work to erase the distances a certain kind of science and logic creates, to invite an untethering from previous assumptions. Again, the inclination toward these subjects was likely inevitable for me, but the liberty with I approach them I likely owe partially to Hogan's own poetic fearlessness in writing across supposed barriers between the realms of spiritual, scientific, and mythic knowing. This plurality of understanding that marks her work marks mine.

What we inherit inhabits us. Finally, we are no longer ourselves without it. The idea of influence troubles some writers. I have always understood it as a Native value—to carry literary traditions. Do we write differently from our forebears? Yes. Can we, should we? Yes, yes. But that does not negate a literary genealogy. No. I align myself with Linda Hogan's vision of a poetic weaving aspiring to both beauty and truth partly because I understand it as a Native vision, as the way our tribal literatures have always functioned in our communities. Let them continue in me. How we manifest that vision and tradition may change as conditions change. Ledger artists adapted to new physical materials, to new spiritual conditions. Now we may adapt their artistic manifestations of traditions to our circumstances. Each artistic performance can still maintain a through line of Indigenous aesthetic understandings. To be a Native literary artist today means to continue to feed the heartbeat of both resistance and continuance.

I specifically mention ledger artists, because among my new work are ekphrastic pieces and a form I have named picto-poems—layers of text and image creating a kind of palimpsest (just as their work created palimpsest). My picto-poems continue the allusive referential interaction that characterizes poems like "Housing Conditions" or "Of Eons and Epics," but now involve not only polyvocality, but visual and verbal intersections. The ekphrastic piece "Captivity" includes a visual representation of redacted text in the body of the poem which, in concert with the photograph of the head and neck of a crane behind a blurry cross-hatched fence, add another aesthetic experience to the language-based elements of the poem. In this new strain of work, I am working across visual/verbal boundaries. This blurring of forms seems a natural way of seeing the world to me. Blame Linda Hogan—or thank her.

*This essay's title is drawn from Linda Hogan's "The History of Fire," from Dark. Sweet.: New & Selected Poems (2014).

*

Workday

by Linda Hogan

I go to work
though there are those who were missing today
from their homes.
I ride the bus
and I do not think of children without food
or how my sisters are chained to prison beds.
Now I go to the University
and out for lunch
and listen to the higher-ups
tell me all they have read
about Indians
and how to analyze this poem.

I ride the bus home
and sit behind the driver.
We talk about the weather and not enough exercise.
I don't mention Victor Jara's mutilated hands
or men next door
in exile from life
or my own family's grief over the lost children.

When I get off the bus
I look back at the light in the windows
and the heads bent
and how the women are all alone
framed in the windows
and the men are coming home.
Then I see them walking on the avenue,
the beautiful feet,
the perfect legs,
even with their spider veins,
the broken knees
with pins in them,

the thighs with their cravings,
the pelvis
and small back with its soft down,
the shoulders
which bend forward and forward
and forward
to protect the heart from pain.

C. R. RESETARITS
CHEROKEE-CREEK

"Storytelling begins in listening."

The poetry of C. R. Resetarits (1956–) embodies a practiced lifetime of seeking, questioning, and forgiving identity. Bound in tight phrasing, concise lines, and clean language, Resetarits's poems investigate loss and solace and the nature of things. Ranging through narratives ("Hovenweep") to laments ("Elegy"), Resetarits relies on repetition to assert a sense of enormous loss, and she creates a chant-like texture that resounds with the open, often windswept landscapes she depicts and celebrates. Her narrators remain somewhat in the background, revealing themselves in the quietest moments, which allows the poems' images and statements to reverberate. C. R. Resetarits searches for that which is hidden or misunderstood with a vigilant attention that accentuates the power of her reserved style.

Elegy

for Wilma Washam Rogers

Whoever is gone
was Loveland born
onyx eyes
ebony hair
Ava Gardner at twenty-eight.

Whoever is gone
fed her papoose
night bottle
in red velvet
and oceans of tuille.

Whoever is gone
was eaten by wolves
inside out
filched by white
shit-faced shamans.

Whoever is gone
left reservation child:
alphabet writing,
real ones reflecting,
shoe boxes of art.

Whoever is gone
is recaptured here
in green corn poem
by whoever once feared
leaving and losing most.

Arroyo

Not clean but splattered
from rain that hits these Western roads
from head to toe the season's
wind and rain mock this place, this time,
      ·   this dirty game.
Ash to ash, like alchemist twins
blackened hearth and cleansing lies
the gravity of me and man
the thing that follows foot to ground
to let go all that goes to ground
when days are done
        but, sometimes, I go now
in search of proofs arroyos lend.

So no, not clean but most obscenely drenched
in sweat and dirt and dew
from morning slides down wrinkling land
      listen
vesper, lark, or sparrow hawk —
their fine thin songs stitch pinyon trees
to pellucid skies. Marvel, trace,
hair full of twigs from rushing
headfirst chokecherry shrubs.
Not clean, but bramble burred,
next not to heaven and what's more
      glad, not next,
but dead on in the gulch
dirt smearing forehead, lips, and breast.

Hovenweep

The towers espy two small girls and
a woman gathering ground
cherry, beeweed, wolfberry, sedge
caught up in the folds of black tier skirts
caught up in the folds of high snow hearts.
They feast and dance and weave a dream,
a bent braid to offer gaping kiva.

A dusty land of loss.
One is lost to heaven,
one to ground,
one remains in shagbark bough.

Far away she spies the three:
bent braid whirling
through night's sky bowl
in larkspur blue the three glow stars
in larkspur blue they retake towers.
Braid unfurls and flows, a salve
to those cast back of back beyond
one bough, one sky, one sipapu.

Lost Tribes, Rain C. Goméz, and the Shadow Arts

My mother was Native American on her father's side—his mother Creek and his
father Cherokee—and Celtic, Scots-Irish on her mother's side. She looked like
Ava Gardner, only with a slightly softer cast to her eyes. She was very close with
her father, and until she died, I spent a lot of time with him and the extended
family. My grandfather was a storyteller, although of an oral rather than writerly
variety, as was his son, my uncle Harold. They could talk for days and months, or
at least make any stories feel that way by the end. I once wrote a poem about my
uncle's storytelling style. I said he "chain-told," like chain-smoking without the
tar and nicotine, the butt of one story lighting the start of the next.

That I like stories is partly their due. That I like them short and tight is also partly their due. My grandfather, William Sherman Washam, had many stories that revolved around growing up in the Indian Territories of Oklahoma, working with Will Rogers on a cattle drive at thirteen, and his mother's ways versus his father's. He would say his father was a cowboy and his mother was an Indian. I simply accepted this as a child, but it was actually a little more complicated. My grandfather's father moved in both Native American and White worlds. Sherm's mother, Mary, kept more with Native ways. Sherm's father was buried in some Protestant graveyard in Missouri, but his mother Mary was buried in the Creek graveyard in Creek Territory.

I didn't learn any of this until a couple years after my grandfather died and my uncle Harold came for a visit and talked about Sherm and Mathias and Mary and Oklahoma for what seemed like years but was actually only three days.

Stories are not bound by the same time realities as life. Stories have their own time, as do some Indigenous traditions and families and uncles. This is why I never know how long a story or poem will be until it is finished and why it never concerns me. It is what it is. I also never know what a story or a poem is leaving out until it drops it in later. I only work and wait.

Working at writing is essential. Waiting is essential. Time . . . is more relative.

*

The November that John F. Kennedy died, my mother died of cancer. She was only twenty-nine. In January her side of the family, the Washam clan—my Washam grandparents, uncle Harold, wife Jean, and their three kids and my mother's sister, Aunt Betty, her husband, and their five kids, moved to California. Except for a few visits—during which my grandfather and uncle talked and talked, talked enough to fill the gaps between their own histories and hearts and ears—the familial connection with my mother's family went silent. They simply disappeared, like many a tribe before them, like my mother, like words on air.

Storytelling begins in listening. Because I know this, I am a better storyteller than either my uncle or grandfather. I also understand that gaps and blank spaces are hints and doors and paths. Silence is a storyteller too.

*

Writers are readers. I read less today for influence or skill or technique but once upon a time I read compulsively for all those things and so much more. Today I often read for courage and belonging and inspiration. I read because writing is an alone business but reading is always, at a minimum, an act between two people, writer and reader, and often a whole room full of characters.

When I was putting together my first poetry collection, I had doubts about the poems referencing the loss of the maternal side of my past and present. Poems about losses, withdrawals, nullifications are not unusual, but I was finding them less than verifying. I was doubting my own validity. Mongrel Empire Press, who was publishing my collection, has always had a special relationship with Indigenous writers, but this only made me more unsure. I looked around the press catalog and decided to read Rain C. Goméz's *Smoked Mullet Cornbread Crawdad Memory* (Mongrel Empire Press, 2012). I half expected that reading a "connected" Indigenous writer would confirm my questionable status, that I would be found wanting. And part of me was fine with that. Instead of denying me, however, she sang to the missing half of me, offering food and words and other nourishments.

*

Rain C. Goméz (now L. Rain Prud'homme-Cranford) is from Louisiana. *Smoked Mullet Cornbread Crawdad Memory* won the First Book Award in Poetry from the Native Writers' Circle of the Americas. She has described herself as a "TriRacially Fluffy and Fabulous" poet. I could relate to the self-parody and multiple views. Her connections to her past were clear and ever-present, solidified by shared food, family, and traditions and might have felt the opposite of mine, but didn't. My heart recognized too much for that to be true. She still held her connections, while mine had packed up and moved away. But while her memories and stories of family and connection were wider and deeper than mine, they did not negate my experience. Rather the poems of Rain C. Goméz helped me calibrate the holes left by my mother's death and my own subsequent Washam abandonment. She might have her was-and-is but I had my was-and-is-not. It helped. She gave me courage. There was the whole of her collection that I found comforting and then there were individual poems, like "Mapping Shadow."

*

Mapping Shadow

by Rain C. Goméz

My veins, rivers, set upon traveled
interior of my body — explored, delved, claimed,
mapped, conquered — in name of you.
My cartographer.
My Lewis and Clark.
I, your dark lady.
My veins are prison cells
keeping blood hostage,
I long for shards of sharpened
obsidian to free whispering spirit
waters from your exploration.

        I have learned in minutes, in hours,
        in days, in nights, in weeks, in months —
        there are many forms of shadow.

Collected words like child
standing at shores dancing
waves two stepping aqua, silver.
I saved whispered fragments
of ancestors, like a child collecting
seashells I carried them as bits of promise,
remembrance, strung on sinew
dangling from my waist like father carried fish.
Strung one after the other tied and clipped
about his slim browned torso.
But I no longer find my way gulf sea.
So I collect words no more.

I hate my need and long for your claim.
In those moments I blame parts of me
that hail from places devoid of color.
I never dwelled in a world of white.

We are people of shadows.
Darkness is part of our narrative,
our song's history. We emerged
from darkness of earth through
gradient shadow rising like mudbug people,
like alligator people, from muddy bayou waters.

In months of your absence I wonder
in silence of empty bed, laid
upon pillows, cold north wind taunting
my soul longing for southern water.
In my lonely bed I long to drink myself back
into darkness like so many of mine before me.
You mapped all my secrets while I was sleeping.

There are reasons our wounds heal keloid,
that we have a topography all our own.
I want to shout at you, confront you:
What part of this land and her people
have you not documented?!
Drawing, mapping, wrapping
borders on all of us. Define me,
I will erase that finding.
Throwing net of woven palm fronds
out into estuary waters, tattooing spiral
symbols on flesh, cleaning mullet and catfish
under shade of cattail lean-tos.
There is more than one way to go home.
In time I will reclaim myself in absence of you,
despite longing for you.

>   I have learned in minutes, in hours,
>   in days, in nights, in weeks, in months —
>   there are many forms of shadow.

ALLISON ADELLE HEDGE COKE

Huron, Metis, French Canadian, Luso, and mixed
Southeastern Native

"The inescapable animal walks with me . . ."

Allison Adelle Hedge Coke (1958–) is poet of the senses. Reading her work, one cannot help but viscerally experience the words and images evoked. Hedge Coke writes with painstaking care for the sounds of words and the feelings they make in the mouth. Her poems fairly dance on the page and in the ear, as we respond to music layered in lines through alliteration, onomatopoeia, assonance, and a brilliant assemblage of varied languages. Her prosodic influences, as evident in "America, I Sing You Back," are manifested in precise rhythms that lay down a backbeat to her strong vocal lines. Hedge Coke's life experiences, ranging from day laborer to academic, have given her a vast capacity to question historical beliefs and the often misconstrued history of Native peoples. As expressed so poignantly in "Taxonomy," Hedge Coke skillfully creates poetry that explains what science cannot, and her words give voice to forgotten landscapes and missing persons, leaving the reader with music where silence had long reigned.

America, I Sing You Back

for Phil Young, my father Robert Hedge Coke,
for Whitman and Hughes

America, I sing back. Sing back what sung you in.
Sing back the moment you cherished breath.
Sing you home into yourself and back to reason.

Before America began to sing, I sung her to sleep,
held her cradleboard, wept her into day.
My song gave her creation, prepared her delivery,
held her severed cord beautifully beaded.

My song helped her stand, held her hand for first steps,
nourished her very being, fed her, placed her three sisters strong.
My song comforted her as she battled my reason
broke my long-held footing sure, as any child might do.

As she pushed herself away, forced me to remove myself,
as I cried this country, my song grew roses in each tear's fall.

My blood-veined rivers, painted pipestone quarries
circled canyons, while she made herself maiden fine.

But here I am, here I am, here I remain high on each and every peak,
carefully rumbling her great underbelly, prepared to pour forth singing —

and sing again I will, as I have always done.
Never silenced unless in the company of strangers, singing
the stoic face, polite repose, polite while dancing deep inside, polite
Mother of her world. Sister of myself.

When my song sings aloud again. When I call her back to cradle.
Call her to peer into waters, to behold herself in dark and light,
day and night, call her to sing along, call her to mature, to envision —
then, she will quake herself over. My song will make it so.

When she grows far past her self-considered purpose,
I will sing her back, sing her back. I will sing. Oh I will — I do.
America, I sing back. Sing back what sung you in.

Taxonomy

Mornings made delirious, scrambling into thread
out from dreaming, wrangling ways past delusion
into streets unpaved, unproven, unmet. It was hard-
over, no sunnyside — easy — and the only yolk — seated sky —
rose streaming over the lot of us quickened in some
strain no corona could bear resting, lean. Then
the mesa sat standing wayside, case some giants made
their way back into meantime, met us here, met us.

We were tabooed, shunned, mocked and on our mettle
most any pierce of day. Principal struck blows to show we
deserved no mercy. It was splintering. Holes bored blisters
each smacking wave. We were deserving. Wave after wave
first grade took the test out from me. Never did spill again,
no matter the syndrome. We were anything but beggars,
so we scraped by, held up. We flung ourselves into every
angle, withheld our curve. Split loose from whatever held on.

Motown made our mercy. Only soothe in western rooms
rounded in radio waves gleaning out the insides of maternal
mind. Unkind charge firing synapse beyond reasoning goals.
She moved through it like lightning, charging each wave
with serious challenge, but nothing made it bearable and
hands down was just a game call brag. Only hands down we
laid was on ball courts. Home front was daily challenge, there
was nothing certain other than each day just like the last.

Lest they moved you, sent you off to foster somewhere no

one warned might reckon. Sent you streaming. Gave you up
like paper. Tossed, crumpled, straightened up, and smoothed
out flat. That was that. It was nothing you'd remember, but
we do. Still taste that strangeness surrounding ones who go
between, move through other worlds while in this one. No
one lives like we do, least it seems so, always on the mind.
Why? Never time to question and still don't know. Only thing
we know we are different and not like you and even though
we try three times harder it never works out right. No,
nothing takes the sting of it, or scent either. We look off,
sound off, give off a presence everyone else knows stay away
and they do, so far from us we walk sideways vanishing
points return to horizons soaking us in, distinguishing us.
Mettle in our mouths as well, steely, and steal we did, still
do, no one's got more lift than us, no one's got more hunger.
How about the time they made us breakfast, real one, over
that pancake house off of 40, remember? Dad's Christmas
to us right before seeing her in The Pavilion, little dish of
butter looks like ice cream to kids like us. Made the eggs
slide over easy just like he did before the madness. *Man this
is rough country, get that straight. Mettle this!*

Radio Wave Mama

*for my mother Hazel who lost remembering,
and for those close who can't forget*

transistor radios
planted firmly
against ears
the children
smothered under
pillows over
their   heads   and
shoulders

escaping the sounds of "ssssss"
and vulgarities screamed
they didn't know the
true meaning of
and invented   replacement
definitions   from
expansive imaginations
when the vocal tensions   invaded
the safer   place
of refuge
under covers
over lumps   in
shared bed they composed
songs to   avoid
rhythms of madness
and poems to
describe hysteria   or
to rearrange
perspectives   of   life
their life
their metaphoric
existence
cropped by
delusions
when the wrath
dispensed   overflow
they crawled on
the floor
before school and
scrubbed the baseboards
with toothbrushes
and Babo
in accordance with
their mother's
instruction   from   thorax
or from the   radio
waves   that controlled

her mind,   her thought
processes and processed her individual dialect
and dialectic statements
intended specifically
to instill private belief
of the megalomania
knowledge factors
she alone had
privy to   in her
babies   those children
she bore   and   who
were expected to
bear witness   to
her testimonies
her "Electronic computer
PUP-PET-RY!
Comb your
hair   children!"   informing
those surrounding her
and surrounded by   her
voice
apart from   the crowd
a part of   their lives
they walked two
aisles over from her
in the Piggly Wiggly
listening to her
through the aisles and
hearing the comments
from strangers
from   pass-her-bys
in shock,   in awe,
in obliviation   to
her informative
speeches   and   semi-
silenced whispersssss
breaking silence

absolute with "sssss"
and vulgarities
"Get off my vulva.
You damn, dirty
pimps.   United States
government   prop-a-gan-da,"
she says and
grabs a box of
Kellogg's Corn Flakes   for
her husband.
"Quit raping me
with radio waves,"
she orders and
pushes the cart
with the broken
wheel skidding
slowly up the
row of   canned
goods and she
screams,   "Buggers,
PIMPS, IBM,
Esso, United States
Air Force,   you are
ALL in this together!"
and they say
"listen to that woman,
who is she?"
as if they didn't
know   and she
whispers,   "Sssssso,
you think you have
fooled me with thisssss
plot, thissss sssssscheme
to rule my mind.
Not thissss TIME!   Then
she wheels into the checkout and
exchanges pleasantries

with the checker
whom she calls
"Dear"   and gets upset
if she isn't addressed
by her last name
with formal prefix
the children try the
coin return   on all
vending   machines
within preschool   and
early elementary
grade reach of extremities
they run to the
Studebaker   as she
carries out   the
brown paper sacks
with nineteen-cent loaves of
bread and food for
five for a few
days   which in their
reality is supposed
to last them at least
a week or two,
and could very possibly as their
mother rants too
much to boil eggs
and they make the
cheese and macaroni
independently   by
three and try   when
they are younger toddlers
and due   to the
anorectic condition
of little sister   who
has the syndrome
at least a decade
before   the   word   is

coined for marketplace
they crawl over each
other   to the back
the very rear of
the wagon,   the middle
seat occupied by one
the oldest child
the other two in
the rear   and the
other three,   or four,
dead at birth or
shortly thereafter   as
the children have already
been informed by
their mother while
tucking them in at
night   when she thinks
it opportune   to
implant this knowledge
she alone walks with
she keys the ignition
rolling the engine past
sputters and knocks
the children appreciate
the pink, so pink, fin-tailed
Buick   next to them
and wish they had
a newer model like
that   it looks like
a spaceship to them
seven years before
the moon landing
where their mother
sometimes   resides now
applying foot to pedal
she squeals out   in
reverse   carts scattering

her path   and begins,
"Never, never, never,
before   here   were we
violated by these
computer puppets
these objects of technology!"
and the children fish
through sacks   for
animal crackers   they
threw into the cart
when she wasn't looking
knowing she wouldn't
know the difference
because she was "busy"
they pass by the
light   before   the train
crossing,   "Do you
see anything?"   the
lights flashing and boards, striped,
falling   in front of   the
grill,   "No, of course not,"
older sister says
and she proceeds
the train pouring on speed
as if there were no
time to s-l-o-w for
passenger cars
blowing its whistle
of Santa Fe and Atchison
Topeka and Ashland City
Tennessee   and they pass
the rear end tail pushed by
winds of the rail in
time, in time, with the
beat of the rail
da-nan-da-nan-da-nan-da-nan
the heartbeat of railroad

suddenly the wooden
bar goes through the back
   CHKCHKCHKCHKCHK
   PINGGGGGGPINGGGGGG
windshield on the far
side   and the children gasp
for breath and eat more
cookies   looking carefully
for witnesses   they tell
her, "go on, no one saw"
and she complies   it
has begun to sleet
and the ice rain is
falling on the streets
on cars   and on the
car of children   and
their mother   or
imposter   of mother
they're not really
sure yet   and it
freezes   patches of
the front   windshield
and sleets   through the
back   little sister
imagines the ice accumulations
windows   to another   place
she traces   in her   mind
and sings   "jimmy crack corn"
and "mama may have"   to
herself   her brother hits
and pulls her hair   and
sister sticks out her
tongue   she smiles
and sings louder   her
mother turning the
lyrics around, "Jimmy
Crack Corn the Master,

the Master, the Master,
the president of the
United States and the president
of the AMA"   and they
go down iced streets
the tobacco road
they follow   the girl
turns to Indian lullabies
her dad sings her to
sleep with   and the
mother says, "Don't you
make fun of your father!
He has a beautiful voice!"
and she is only trying
to sound   like him
to get away   from her
and the mother says,
"Buckle your seatbelts
the buggers are going
to make me wreck."
and the older sister
takes off her seatbelt
and dives headfirst into the floorboard
insuring complete concussion
she is unconscious now
the baby boy is
strapped into a belt
by   little sister   and
she glances out
to see a blur blurrr
of a car   through   the
iced windshield   and her
mother's concentration
on hitting this car
head on   and   she grasps
the back of the middle

seat and hangs on for
life, her life,   though
she doesn't really want
it saved   and by seven years of age
will be slitting her
wrists   and surviving that
anyway   because she
has the survival skills
the urgency to maintain
through anything   the
adaptability   of children
of the chronically
insane   parental influence
she grabs and holds   hard
and her mother slowly,
carefully, deliberately
drives into the innocent
car   steering   slammmming
into the car which
tears off the front fender,
driver's door, rear wheel and
breaks the glass
next to little sister's
cheeks   and careening off
the shoulder   trying
to steer away from
this mad woman
they assume   has lost
control of the wheel
when quite the opposite
is true   the control
is within   her, or the
voices she hears,   or the
place of their   origin
her mind
the mother is now
unconscious, liquid red eyes,

canyon gashed brow flowing   in   concussion
the older sister   is still   asleep
the baby is eating a
cookie   the other car's
passengers walking over
little sister pretends
to be knocked out
the police come
it is snowing   and a dark complexioned
man looks through
the broken rear windows
and sees the railroad
crossing bar
the little sister   waves to him
and he calls her
from the car
she sits in his police car
and calls her dad
on the two-way
"one adam twelve,
is this daddy?
one adam twelve
calling daddy
daddy are you in?"
the father asks
"Whose phone are you
on, who   dialed   for   you?"   "the copper's,
it's his"   and they   exchange
information of
insanity   of
split realities of
the mother   and
the children   the dad and the cop
little sister smiles
at all the people
gathering   and is proud
she could use a

police phone   and remember
the number   no one
ever taught her
she learned to memorize   by
teaching herself numbers and letters
she is three
she will always
remember this day
days   of   perspectives
that   other
people   will
never   be able   to
relate   to   without
an Artaud   in the
family   themselves
and when she grows
she will feed the
homeless   schizophrenics
she sees   wandering
streets   and   tobacco roads
and know that without her
father   her   mother
would have ended up
down the same path
of the pitiful   who
walk the other side
while they reside here
those that see   the   s p a c e
between second and third
dimensional arts   and speak it
the children witness
and play transistor radios

Streaming

for Sherwin & Travis

Ya,yan,e,tih
kettle
Yah,re,sah Yan,yan,quagh,ke
beans, cornfield
Yat,o,regh,shas,ta
I am hungry

Once, we walk long grass into weave
pacing stem wrappings
in concentric circling;
southwise sans temporal sway,
beat to counts, not ticks
in a dream where time poses as dust,
where echo-wrinkles reverberate
consciousness signals against
savannahs —

Sandhills overhead, their chortling
carries snow geese back to councils.
In this streaming, seasons shift
far past distressed unravelings,
where grasses seed sparseness
commingle alongside wrinkle, weavings, time,
signaling light shocks spreading fingerlike
across blue/white world —

Grass warp, weave, entwined, danced,
making mattress, woven mat
step crossing step, push/push,
making sure this place
brings matted dreamtime under
Dog Road, Darkening Land,
Cygnus, Swan, Northern Cross

echoing light/dark Albireo dreaming.

   Albeit night is with or without sun.

Circles align whether trampling
long stem beds over cracked earth,
into baited sun-whirled worlds,
whether north/cold, with or without light,
needling shafts through course indigos,
like velveteen, corded skeins, geese, yarn —

Somewhere woven; north of quipu hemp,
hemp laid moundwork blueprint, twined some
where north of periodical cicadas, mock locusts
now shivering night free with streaming song.

   Where light brings split shell husk, dry fly

appearances   under loosed locust ravished
leaf, 'neath not New Forest, but sweating
three-year Apache cicada who daylight
cannot swelter, no, cannot swelter nor
swing out across summer, cast into
swarming grasshoppers, winged, leaping
'neath cicada droning lovesongs, daylight
unimpeded desert caught in bleak receded
motion, overlapping, each trio member
keeping transparent winged vigilance.

Another cicada, here, north, now
prefers nightly monophony,
meatier female brings dreaming
tween utensil sticks we draw to tongue,
her veined wings set aside, soft burst
oral tradition, nourishment, medicine.

Three, thirteen, seventeen annuals

canopy contralto over unknown biomes,
under night waiting to break day
swallow it whole, lid shut, Leonids
rain over the closure, repeat passages,
stream, portal skipping, vortex threading,
weaving textural, lingual suffix, to stem/blade.

Some of us flew them, cicadas/Leonids,
    riding backbump, flying —

Some of us squirmed underworld with larvae, slick
retracing lives, Moon-Eyed passers, cavern travelers.

Some of us strictly scored trees,
edging along bark stream.
Some of called night/day
for union after splitting
our backs open, crawling out into light, flying —

But now it's winter,
first fire forms stone mouths,
whispers, *go in there we're with you*
alongside, trio here, trio women.

Wherein, the waking gives acumen
already over, somewhere
further along stream east/south,
perpetual echo-wrinkling,
cicada songlike field wave
light/dark wrinkle, weave, here
corded skirts, woven petticoats
'neath mulberry bark skirts —

Sending us back where women
stood spearing, yellow poplar canoes
mooring, mooring cold water,

moving upstream when hot houses
gave them up, hoisted,
sent them above ground,
back to waters, thirsty, hungry.

Waterskipping spider spinning
fire/firing clay, clay painted
on poplar trunks, fired,
top to bottom, released to sail waters.
Released to sail, placed in tutsi bowl,
slung upon her back,
lightning fired, sycamore clothed,
fire, furnishings for home:

      hot cicada, yellow jacket soup,
            strawberry jam/nectar.

Here, in the cylindrical and spherical,
in the curvilinear space
its echo-wrinkle reverbations,
discernments, definitive dissonance;
here, intuition/memory intersect,
prophesy source into beingness,
we in certain presence — being — at all times.

On a river of variable stream, channel flow,
confluence, departures give wellsprings,
condition broad throughways,
water comes, proper placement,
nourishes life, causes sustenance. Come fruition,

informed by being, by elemental colliding
intersections within these planes,
within swell of source throughout elements, earth,
animal, plant: animate, inanimate.
Swelling echoes moving in seven directions,
spherical in a sense of reverb actions and response

in waves of knowns we perceive, collide into,
multidimensional, the sense of time, space, place —
the experiential impressed by a familiar spiritual sense.

A girl eyes next turn,
                                        gives melody to droning.
Caught her lostness with hemp skirt,
traveled down mountain,
Bluest Ridge, like fire from leaf to root,

like ice now mooring 'neath glacial melt,
now impending, lest we continue
along this way, newly invoked,
along this burn, stream, somewhere
between hummingbird/sloth,
between here/now, when/then,
vibration strum fissure,
variable stream, channel flow —

until we all come tumbling, find melody, until
we drone nightly, thrum —

Impressions strummed   today
incite future impulsion,
                        create past prophecy.

Get it?

Along an echo-wrinkle in existence
        your presence permeates swaying.

Cries:

            Ya,yan,e,tih
                kettle
        Yah,re,sah Yan,yan,quagh,ke
            beans, cornfield

Yat,o,regh,shas,ta
I am hungry

Ya,yan,e,tih
kettle
Yah,re,sah Yan,yan,quagh,ke
beans, cornfield
Yat,o,regh,shas,ta
I am hungry

Ya,yan,e,tih
kettle
Yah,re,sah Yan,yan,quagh,ke
beans, cornfield
Yat,o,regh,shas,ta
I am hungry

Swaying permeates presence, your
        existence, in echo-wrinkle, along an
entry, chickadee messenger, cheeping
                this way, don't turn back.

Sloth carries hummingbird
alongside perpetual echo-wrinkling,
cicada songlike field wave
light/dark wrinkle, weave, here
corded skirts, woven petticoats
'neath mulberry bark skirts —

Clacking turtle hulls
shake world back into sequence.

Southwise turning
magnetic field migration.

Hummingbird fathoms navigation
along lekking glasswing routes,

sometimes monarchs, edge on milkweed
munch down Mississippi Valley
daisy fleabane, hackberry, willow.
                                        Like silkworms
ceiling coved, mulberry leaved, cocooned
then boiled away to entrap threadpoint, unravel,
ravel, spin, wind, capture beauty in cloth

woven way east, here cotton carries life,
its weevils ever after emanating loss,
now monarch opens case, cleaves, light
enters day, moving waters, streams
from pit to wingtip, extending — shaking.

Cicadas droning, girl singing,
magnetic reason   cranes
float thermals, far past reason,
high in orbit break away in eight points,
approach in fours, return, approach,
like horse dance, for innocence, mares there
airbound approach, approach, dance
in channels, pathways, roads,

far below moonlight shimmers
sends locust tree her dressings.
Wear them, Sister, now your beauty
petticoats, mulberry — open-backed cicada —

Some of us flew them, cicadas/Leonids,
        riding backbump, flying —

Once, we walk long grass into weave
pacing stem wrappings
in concentric circling
southwise sans temporal sway,
beat to counts, not ticks
in a dream where time poses as dust,

where echo-wrinkles reverberate
consciousness signals against —

a dream echoing light/dark, some of us flew them.
    Albireo dreaming —   streaming.

Ya,yan,e,tih
kettle
Yah,re,sah Yan,yan,quagh,ke
beans, cornfield
Yat,o,regh,shas,ta
I am hungry

Ya,yan,e,tih
Yah,re,sah Yan,yan,quagh,ke
Yat,o,regh,shas,ta

Ya,yan,e,tih
Yah,re,sah Yan,yan,quagh,ke
Yat,o,regh,shas,ta

I am hungry

Ya,yan,e,tih
kettle
Yah,re,sah Yan,yan,quagh,ke
beans, cornfield
Yat,o,regh,shas,ta

I am hungry

Beyond the Ballads

> *"That inescapable animal walks with me, has followed me since the black womb held, moves where I move, distorting my gesture, that secret life of belly and bone, stretches to embrace the very dear, dragging me with him in his mouthing care"*
>
> —cut-up excerpts from Delmore Schwartz's "The Heavy Bear Who Goes with Me"
>
> *"When embers from the sacred middle are climbing out the other side of stars, I'm talking about an early morning in Brooklyn, the streets the color of ashes"*
>
> —cut-up excerpts from Joy Harjo's "The Musician Who Became a Bear"

These are two of the poems that first spoke to me along with all the song lyrics ever before. Beyond the Edgar Allen Poe, beyond the ballads, these are two mad rushes into metaphoric measure, rhythm hinged, opening song stories welcoming audience to journey, and journey we do. I did. Still do.

*

The Heavy Bear Who Goes with Me
by Delmore Schwartz

> *"the withness of the body"*

The heavy bear who goes with me,
A manifold honey to smear his face,
Clumsy and lumbering here and there,
The central ton of every place,
The hungry beating brutish one
In love with candy, anger, and sleep,
Crazy factotum, dishevelling all,
Climbs the building, kicks the football,
Boxes his brother in the hate-ridden city.

Breathing at my side, that heavy animal,

That heavy bear who sleeps with me,
Howls in his sleep for a world of sugar,
A sweetness intimate as the water's clasp,
Howls in his sleep because the tight-rope
Trembles and shows the darkness beneath.
—The strutting show-off is terrified,
Dressed in his dress-suit, bulging his pants,
Trembles to think that his quivering meat
Must finally wince to nothing at all.

That inescapable animal walks with me,
Has followed me since the black womb held,
Moves where I move, distorting my gesture,
A caricature, a swollen shadow,
A stupid clown of the spirit's motive,
Perplexes and affronts with his own darkness,
The secret life of belly and bone,
Opaque, too near, my private, yet unknown,
Stretches to embrace the very dear
With whom I would walk without him near,
Touches her grossly, although a word
Would bare my heart and make me clear,
Stumbles, flounders, and strives to be fed
Dragging me with him in his mouthing care,
Amid the hundred million of his kind,
The scrimmage of appetite everywhere.

ELISE PASCHEN
Osage

". . . emotion should live at the core of a poem."

The poetry of Elise Paschen (1959–) is sensual, dreamlike, and lush. In a clear and forthright style, Paschen fashions rhythmical and emotionally charged lines that explore the past's imposition on the present. With dramatic contrasts and undercurrents of tension, much of what happens in Paschen's work happens just outside the firelight, as in "My Mother Descends" and "Parents at Rest." In "Oklahoma Home," familial absence is a powerful presence. Compositionally, Paschen is wide-ranging; attracted to shaped forms like the pantoum and the ghazal ("Under the Dome"), she can also be drawn to more volatile and fragmentary tactics, as in "Wí'-gi-e." Throughout her work, Paschen's approach is thoughtfully crafted and nuanced and rewards re-reading.

Oklahoma Home

There was a wood-pile fence
that kept your garden from schoolyard,
leaving open to sight the larkspur
and lavender-stretched boulevard

which skirted your house and the lattice-
work swing-set. Running parallel
to the street (on its other side)
a field bloomed full of asphodel.

Your window looked over the meadow.
The wind through grass like a seesaw
seemed to sound out the field and you
would repeat back *papaw, papaw*,

hushed as an owl. At times you'd note
the changes of the hour: the catch
and call of quails beyond the trees,
the pond shaded at four, a patch

of bluestem grass where Father's horses
grazed. From the outside of the house
it was your window upstairs where
white curtains, loose with air, would blouse

like sails. Evening was the time
when all the sounds had quieted.
Your father counted stars outside.
A coin would rise: an Indian head.

Under the Dome

for Agha Shahid Ali

At times they will fly under. The dome
contains jungles. Invent a sky under the dome.

Creatures awake, asleep, at play, aglow:
they float — unbottled genii — under the dome.

Southern Belle, a splash of black, dusted with gold,
dissembles, "assembling," acts shy under the dome.

Cattleheart, Giant Swallowtail, Clipper:
sail, navigate sky high under the dome.

Like confetti—a wedding—bits of Rice
Paper: sheer mimicry under the dome.

Magnificent Owl, in air, a pansy,
it feeds, wings up, eye to eye, under the dome.

Name them: Monarch, then Queen, last Viceroy.
What will scientists deify under the dome?

Basking against a leaf: a Banded Orange,
displayed like a bowtie under the dome.

A living museum. Exist to be observed:
never migrate, but live, then die, under the dome.

Lips, lashes, eyes. From the outside in,
do beings magnify under the dome?

Lepidoptera. From the Greek: scale-wing.
Chrysalis. Stay, butterfly, under the dome.

Wí'-gi-e*

Anna Kyle Brown. Osage. 1896–1921. Fairfax, Oklahoma.

Because she died where the ravine falls into water.

Because they dragged her down to the creek.

In death, she wore her blue broadcloth skirt.

Though frost blanketed the grass she cooled her feet in the spring.

Because I turned the log with my foot.

Her slippers floated downstream into the dam.

Because, after the thaw, the hunters discovered her body.

Because she lived without our mother.

Because she had inherited headrights for oil beneath the land.

She was carrying his offspring.

The sheriff disguised her death as whiskey poisoning.

Because, when he carved her body up, he saw the bullet hole in her skull.

Because, when she was murdered, the *leg clutchers* bloomed.

But then froze under the weight of frost.

During *Xtha-cka Zhi-ga Tse-the*, the Killer of the Flowers Moon.

I will wade across the river of the blackfish, the otter, the beaver.

I will climb the bank where the willow never dies.

*Spoken by Mollie Burkhart, whose sister Anna Kyle Brown was murdered during the Reign of Terror.

My Mother Descends

After he died, she slipped away,
visiting her husband, my father,
every night, in the underworld.

At dinner she hides spoons inside
her sleeves. After sunset she crosses
the River Styx, braving storm-torn waves.

Rehearsing death, she lies in bed
for twelve-hour stints. The skiff, so fragile,
shakes when she recovers her balance.

When she descends to bring him back,
clouds skim her eyes. She cannot see,
catching only glints of his silver hair.

There's never enough cutlery
for Charon. Cerberus snarls hot.
What she wouldn't give to convince Hades.

Awake at sunrise, her limbs, heavy,
ache from the labor. She is weary
and observes silence with the living.

Parents at Rest

Fairfax, Oklahoma

How, in the afternoon,
after performing chores
in sync — grocery shopping,
his cooking, her cleaning up —
they would lie on the angled couch,
toe-to-toe, his side, hers,
books in hand, his biographies,
her murder mysteries,
listening to Beethoven.
He'd nod off while she read
to the rhythm of his breath.
Outside the open windows
waves thumped on stony beach,
seagulls buffeting wind.

The houses of their birth,
both yellow brick, now crumbled:
one perched hilltop above
pasture, the other, Prairie-school
city house with sunken garden.
How he waited for her
these many years in the graveyard
below her childhood home
where now they sleep together
beneath the rhapsody
of meadowsweet.

Straddling Two Worlds

> *"She had horses who had no names. / She had horses who had books of names."* — Joy Harjo

I remember reading Duane Niatum's Harper's *Anthology of 20th Century Native American Poetry* while sitting at my desk in the Poetry Society of America offices on Gramercy Park. It was 1988, and I had been newly appointed executive director of the PSA. I looked to Niatum's anthology, among others, as a source of inspiration for programming poetry events, and now, I realize, as a source for my own writing. So many poems in that Harper's Anthology spoke to me, and, if I were to acknowledge one poem as a touchstone, it would be Joy Harjo's "She Had Some Horses."

I am an enrolled member of the Osage tribe, descended from my Osage grandfather, Alexander Tallchief. My mother, Maria Tallchief, was born on the Osage reservation but later moved with her family to Beverly Hills where she studied piano and classical ballet. She became known as America's first prima ballerina. Oklahoma and my mother's heritage have inspired my writing, and one of my first published poems called "Oklahoma Home" (written as a sophomore at Harvard while studying with Seamus Heaney) was an attempt to imagine my mother's childhood home in Fairfax, Oklahoma. When I think back on my high school and university education, though, I realize I had had little exposure to the writing of other Native American authors.

Before moving to New York City, I had been attending graduate school at Oxford University, immersed in studying the work of the Modernists and writing my doctoral dissertation on William Butler Yeats. I researched, for the most part, British male poets and my circle of poet friends at Magdalen College consisted mainly of British male poets. Once I moved back to the States, I hungered for new voices and for new means of expression outside the literary canon in which I had been educated. So now, at that desk in the National Arts Club, I listened to a mesmerizing Native woman's voice singing in my ear.

When I read Harjo's "She Had Some Horses" I viscerally encountered the incantatory power of poetry. I was drawn to her repetitions and to her surprising juxtapositions: "She had some horses. / She had horses who were bodies of sand. / She had horses who were maps drawn of blood. / She had horses who were skins of ocean water." Harjo lets her imagination run riot in this poem. She traverses treacherous ground and adventures passionately into uncharted territory.

I had always felt that emotion should live at the core of a poem, but this poem introduced me to new emotions—ecstasy, compassion, rage—and gave me license (later in my writing life) to tap into that anger: "She had horses who lied. / She had horses who told the truth, who were stripped / bare of their tongues. // She had some horses."

I was fascinated by the surreal nature of Harjo's writing and how, like the Metaphysical poets, she yoked disparate images together. She takes you on a journey—the horses seem literal, seem dream-like, seem metaphorical. Harjo writes about "She Had Some Horses": "I am aware of stepping into a force field or dream field of language, of sound. Each journey is different, just as the ocean or the sky is never the same from one day to another. I am engaged by the music, by the deep. And I go until the poem and I find each other. Sometimes I go by horseback."

We first met in person when Joy participated in a Native American Writers Festival we co-sponsored with Chris Merrill and Recursos de Santa Fe in June of 1990. We were celebrating the 80th anniversary of the PSA and establishing a southwest branch of PSA in Santa Fe. Other writers in that festival included Linda Hogan and N. Scott Momaday. Observing Joy teach a workshop and hearing her read aloud her poems floored me. Our friendship grew when Joy and Luci Tapahonso came with me, in the early 1990s, on a reading tour of England which the PSA sponsored thanks to an international grant from the NEA. Since that time, Joy and I have worked together over several decades.

Joy urged me to explore my Osage background and to go deeper into my self as a writer. When I was working on a poem called "Two Standards" for Joseph Bruchac's anthology, *Returning the Gift*, Joy pushed me to carve out the narrative of the speaker torn between the two worlds of her Osage ancestry in Fairfax, Oklahoma and her current life in New York City. As I look back on comments she made on a draft of the poem written in February 1993, she urged me to explore the notion of this division of the self and the search for identity. She said the key theme of the poem is the speaker's living in two worlds—being Indian and white. Joy's comments helped me tighten the poem and allowed me to plunge into the drama of the narrative. She said explore this double standard conflict and keep the focus on how this duality affects the speaker. Here are the opening lines of "Two Standards": "Joan's one eighth. I'm a quarter. / When we walk into Billy's / I want to look like her, / full Osage . . ."

In 2001, Joy encouraged me to apply to the Frances C. Allen Fellowship, which supports women of American Indian heritage, at the Newberry Library to research the Osage Reign of Terror. I had hoped to write a book of non-fiction about that horrific period of history (1921–1926) which took place on the Osage reservation when outsiders married Osage women and killed them for their headrights. My own Tallchief family lived in Fairfax during this time, my mother born there in 1925. I didn't write that prose book, but, several years later, I did write a poem called "Wí'-gi-e" which is spoken from the viewpoint of Mollie Burkhart whose sister, Anna Kyle Brown, had been murdered during the Reign of Terror. Giving voice to Mollie Burkhart, I could channel my own anger about this tragic annihilation of the Osage. Here are some lines from "Wí'-gi-e" which means "prayer" in Osage: "Because, when he carved her body up, he saw the bullet hole in her skull. // Because, when she was murdered, the leg clutchers bloomed. / But then froze under the weight of frost. / During *Xtha-cka Zhi-ga Tse-the, the Killer of the Flowers Moon* . . ." In that poem—which also uses an anaphoric structure—I can hear the music of "She had Some Horses" reverberating in the background.

*

She Had Some Horses
by Joy Harjo

She had some horses.

She had horses who were bodies of sand.
She had horses who were maps drawn of blood.
She had horses who were skins of ocean water.
She had horses who were the blue air of sky.
She had horses who were fur and teeth.
She had horses who were clay and would break.
She had horses who were splintered red cliff.

She had some horses.

She had horses with eyes of trains.
She had horses with full, brown thighs.
She had horses who laughed too much.

She had horses who threw rocks at glass houses.
She had horses who licked razor blades.

She had some horses.

She had horses who danced in their mothers' arms.
She had horses who thought they were the sun and their
bodies shone and burned like stars.
She had horses who waltzed nightly on the moon.
She had horses who were much too shy, and kept quiet
in stalls of their own making.

She had some horses.

She had horses who liked Creek Stomp Dance songs.
She had horses who cried in their beer.
She had horses who spit at male queens who made
them afraid of themselves.
She had horses who said they weren't afraid.
She had horses who lied.
She had horses who told the truth, who were stripped
bare of their tongues.

She had some horses.

She had horses who called themselves, "horse."
She had horses who called themselves, "spirit," and kept
their voices secret and to themselves.
She had horses who had no names.
She had horses who had books of names.

She had some horses.

She had horses who whispered in the dark, who were afraid to speak.
She had horses who screamed out of fear of the silence, who
carried knives to protect themselves from ghosts.
She had horses who waited for destruction.

She had horses who waited for resurrection.
She had some horses.

She had horses who got down on their knees for any saviour.
She had horses who thought their high price had saved them.
She had horses who tried to save her, who climbed in her
bed at night and prayed.

She had some horses.

She had some horses she loved.
She had some horses she hated.

These were the same horses.

SUZANNE S. RANCOURT

ABENAKI (BEAR CLAN) / HURON

"As artists, we have a foot in both worlds. We are bridges."

Adding to the abundant tradition of poetry by Natives of the Northeast, Suzanne Rancourt (1959–) brings dramatic voice, tension, and detail to an ancient but too often overlooked natural and cultural landscape. Through a marriage of exacting images and subtle rhythms, Rancourt's poetry scrutinizes what might be considered mundane, which she rearranges in ways that allow a reader to see anew. Rancourt asks big philosophical questions in her poems, but never undervalues the importance of everyday existence, whether now or long ago. "Fabric" and "The Smell of Blood" are fine examples of her ability to intertwine personal experience and communal history, as within her lines the poet layers different cultures and various traditions. Nothing seems to escape Rancourt's eye for specifics, each poem asking to be understoodd both sensually and intellectually.

Fabric

The weaver has become the pattern, plaid
full of angles and predictabilities
and the shuttling of husbands, children, lovers
wears her thin.

There are two movements: past and future.
The loose swatch of the present unravels,
always in ballet fashion,
dangles gracefully between flying and landing.

There is a texture in love that needs to be felt,
needs deft fingers to braid the over under of self.

Fingers that toe dance over warp and weft,
that understand the rhythm of the loom, the tapestry,
an arabesque of extended tones both subtle and vibrant.

With eyes closed, the clatter of shuttle and feet pumping the loom
like a grand pipe organ resonating across threads,
she remembers her last words to her first lover,
"like worn denim, love me like that."

Maccha*

I knew you when the tea was fresh
not yet steeped in bitterness and pale character. Before
spring water boiled and grew tepid as cordial greetings
no longer an exotic flavor taunting taste buds for words of kindness
love and simple acknowledgment.

I knew you when machismo was you and your carelessness
attracted desperate women Jonesin' for sex

because it was the only validation of beauty they could accept.
And when you became bored, your passion cold, I knew you then.

And when you fell in love for real and it threw you into isolation
like shattered cups against floors, walls, doors — I knew you then too.

When I was a child I fell down a flight of stairs.
I carried my treasured, hand painted tea set —
mauve pussy willows on cups, saucers, and teapot
the size of a hummingbird's nest —
My tailbone jack hammered each solid stair, from my hands
exploded Japanese porcelain, my childhood
shards of innocence, vaporized, all hope
an intermittent rumble of moans.

I saw a little boy in your eyes full of joy and love.
throw away books, pictures, gifts
like the boy who knew he had lied,
stole, killed, survived, knew himself
to be bad, unforgiving, undeserving.
Shame and guilt make a bitter brew
I knew you then too.

Tea.
I held you
when you brought flavor, comfort, warmth

*Finely ground green tea powder central to the Japanese Tea Ceremony.

The Smell of Blood

there is old plum blood clumped like grapes becoming raisins
dry and cracked on the edges, crystallizing like nano birdshot.

there is fresh blood vibrant as lips wearing lipstick
for the first time red with life and air
and knowing nothing but that moment in the gasping for more.

there is the in between blood that grows sticky with flies
like fruit juice spilt on clean linoleum that no one wants to talk about

as it has already been spilt and cleaning up the mess implies our guilt
so we sip quietly with downcast eyes onto table tops in outdoor cafes

or our mother's favorite butcher block and we pray
that dogs enter soon to lick up taboos now sticky with truth.

there is the pink frothy blood that effervesces into mist
alive with the last kiai — last words, last breath, last action,
beyond form and recognition.

there is the blood we suck from a paper cut, bright as words
we sliced with time. never
is blood alone but mingled with bitter gall, and bile, or the rank of gut
and brains.

there is the blood of unborn fetuses in glass vacuums
and plastic measuring cups in deep sinks
power washing the rot of vaginal infections

and there is the blood of life tainted with umbilical matter —
amniotic fluids, saline and protein enhanced with sweat
canaling through mergences, cavernous, cold, Salli Port pelvises.

there is the blood of death spattered with the last shit you'll ever take
and no one cares what your last meal was
but you and whoever made it.
Tabasco pizza, chocolate chip cookies melted into blobs from heat
while being shipped from runway to runway,
or sitting in back postal rooms in mail bags.

there is the blood of transfusions, transformations, transportation
into Warferin, Heparin, and morphine drips.

there is the blood of lies,
the blood of truth
the blood of consequences, conflicts, confusion that titrate
into the soil and dust of everyday living — the absence felt
when mowing the lawn
getting the mail
feeding the dog.

there is the blood of abstraction, nightmares, invaders
of songs, stories, horror metered by heart palpitations
tightening of chest and the constant neurotic obsessive unlocking
re-locking of doors, windows — load, fire, re-load.

there is the blood of love
that dries too quickly into a cacophony of smells that embrace
something someone somewhere describes as life.

Blood,
I smell you on flesh, in bathroom stalls, laundry baskets,
garbage cans, drain traps, band aids in locker rooms,
knee patches stiff with iron.

I smell you on the streets in the lives outside of reasoning.

So Glad You Asked

> "Sometimes, it is the illusion that moves the thing."
> —S. S. Rancourt

I am of Abenaki / Huron decent, born and raised in west-central Maine. I am
like many displaced peoples in that survival meant focusing on what one needs
to do to provide for families and to simply survive. I honor all of my ancestors

for without them I wouldn't be here doing what I feel I am intended to do. I did not grow up on a reservation. We were not financially wealthy people. We had knowledge and were / are strong people and work hard. We lived in the northern Appalachians which weren't much different from the southern Appalachians as far as humans go. The goal of the family was to focus on life and work. As my late father would say with a shrug of his shoulders, "Don't you know who you are?" then he'd scan the woods, meadow, or the mountain behind the house. For Dad, and his Dad, both renowned dowsers, some truths were simply innate. My life has and continues to be one of seeking. A GPS implosion of direction via inner roadmaps of discovery and mystery and wonder. And with that an appreciation for who I am: Identity.

My first recollection of being a writer is between three and four years old. I had "written" a two-page story in what language development studies refer to as emergent literacy i.e. scribbling. I distinctly recall blue ink scrawled across one sheet of paper—front and back—every line filled with my writing. The thing is, I knew that I had not yet learned to read. The concept of not being able to read equaling not being able to write simply did not exist in my psyche. Therefore, I had to take my story to an older sister and ask her to read it to me as I hadn't yet learned to read. I found my sister in our dormitory style, open floor upstairs where all us kids shared beds; modest bedframes set up on sawdust board floors. I recall my older sister looking at the pages of blue Bic ink deciding what to do: Hand the paper back stating that it's just scribble? Or, read a story? My sister read a story. In that moment, I called myself a writer.

My life challenges have been incredible fodder for writing. This essay for Tupelo's anthology of Indigenous poetry, a simple request, has also been a journey of realization that even among family in the mountains of Maine, there was isolation. We gardened, hunted, lived, worked, played, loved, and survived without question. We did as our ancestors had taught. And then, someone asked me, "What style of writer are you?" "Who do you read?" I've also had members of the academe, state to my face, "Native writing isn't writing and is not to be pursued." That last quote changed my life. Prejudice is non-discriminatory. One disrespectful kick to a boulder can dislodge a pebble or an avalanche. I am a writer.

I grew up in a rural sprawl of a village called Temple of which I write a little about in my poem "A Light Wind Beyond Temple" in *Billboard in the Clouds* (Curbstone Press). The town where we bought larger amounts of groceries and such, where the "big" schools and hospital were located, historically, was a Tory Town.

Although I was a voracious reader of all genres, it wasn't until I stumbled across Alain Robbe-Grillet and his New Novel style that I began to connect with a way of expressing in words the way I had been taught to observe through sight, sound, and "feeling." I would say that Robbe-Grillet's *The Voyeur* and its protagonist cycling a thematic shape piqued my interest, resonated with my cultural upbringing that emphasized observation, stillness, taking note of patterns, micro expressions—all the little things that our primitive senses record continually that our frontal lobes poo poo.

Robbe-Grillet's ability, via writing, to strip all culturally preconceived meanings, and definitions from the common, everyday item(s) and then reassign a new definition / meaning to said object, inspired me to explore further. For example: If I say "table" a *culturally specific* definition presents in our mind a picture of a table. But, what if, through narrative thematic discourse, I strip that object of its categorically and *culturally specific* description and reassign words to the "table" that are usually used to describe "chairs"? What if I also have my characters interacting with said object as though it were a "chair" as defined and envisioned per the cultural specifications of my, (the writer's) choice? *Et voila!* Have I not changed the table into a chair? And in so doing, possibly changed the reader's perspective or consciousness or belief in some way?

This Robbe-Grillet, I felt, was doing powerful stuff that employed the skills of my family. The skills that my family of rural hunters, lumberers, farmers, and dowsers lived by, and who taught me to live by. Nothing is as it seems. Always look below the surface. i.e. situational awareness equals survival.

Samuel Beckett's *Rockaby* fueled my inspiration to honor the sublime power of natural rhythms, timing and meter and in so doing, the understated power of nature expressed itself through characters, line breaks, phonemes, and space. I wanted to know, literally, what these linguistic clicks, and fricatives felt like in my body. Elongated *oos* and *aahhs* soothe and slow not just the tongue in one's mouth but one's body as well. Why? How? And, could I do the same with my writing? Could I write in a way that the reader could rock? How did one's language change linguistic rhythm and human movement? What did trauma feel like in my mouth as I spoke a story—a string of beaded sounds?

Eugene Ionesco's *Rhinoceros* swung open baffled gates of creative writing and the application of the power of the absurd as theme, plot, and character development. Again, dive below the surface: Writing as social change, as catalyst, and as vehicle for the marginalized, the voiceless, and the resonance of bearing witness, somehow further amplified the tectonic shift on a soul level, and deep human being level, a level of artistic expression and social responsibility . . . a metamorphosis (yes, I like Franz Kafka, too). Earthquake or avalanche: something was changing my writing and my art making process.

My artistic perspective reflects the rhythms, nuances, and language of the culture that I was raised in and am of. As a developing writer and human being throughout the 1960s, '70s, and '80s, I saw that the halls of academe supported antiwar (Vietnam) movements and the civil rights movement, and some were even aware of the American Indian Movement, however the halls of academe were not ready to welcome the unique perspectives, syntactic rhythms, and non-linear thematic threads or realities that dominant culture called absurd. ("Native writing isn't writing . . ." etc.) Many people were, and some still are, ignorant about the traumatic histories that generationally impacted Indigenous peoples and uniquely so depending on one's region, i.e. NW, SE, NE, etc. For example: the trauma history of people of the Plains circa late 1800s is not the same as the trauma history of the people of the north east which occurred several hundreds of years prior. A worthy book to read is Jack D. Forbes's *Columbus and Other Cannibals*.

I persevered, kept writing, and eventually found a few precious gems of humans, and Elders, that became mentors. They recognized stylistic qualities in my work, in my personhood, and guided me to the writings and work of Indigenous people. Joy Harjo's significant poem, "I Give You Back," calling out fear, facing fear, perpetrators of silencing and horror, and overcoming the oppressions of all that one carries as a trauma survivor, gave me permission to acknowledge my existence, voice and power as a survivor. Each discovery on this journey of becoming an artist becoming a human, exposed new facets of myself. Some were prettier than others.

"I am my own evidence." I have written extensively on those experiences using poetry, creative non-fiction, fiction, songwriting, photography, and dance choreography. To survive, one must employ all of their senses. I had also been told years ago, by a professor, that I could only use one modality. I was stunned. How could that be? From my cultural perspective, the Natural World is spherical, all encompassing, multi-dimensional, how could I, as an artist, be flat- one dimensional? Again, from my cultural perspective, I found this statement to be ludicrous. When I discovered the multi-modal artist/writer Michael Burkard's *My Secret Boat*, another significant piece of my artistic soul puzzle jigged into place. From "Lunar Night": "For Cree fell a far piece to the grass and the bees followed. They were an unknown guidance with their pain. And often these gifts must be bestowed in childhood, before one feels one knows what to make of them."

In Anna Halprin's stunning film *Returning Home*, she states that prior to her cancer "life informed her art," and after her cancer, "art informed her life."

Being true to nature, Anna states, is being true to one's own nature. My relationship with the natural world as a child running wild on the mountain behind our house, and my reconnecting with the natural world as an adult via Traditional Ceremonies and my art, is also a returning home.

"I am my own evidence" and all those years called life that my body so marvelously and miraculously compartmentalized my trauma memories in file folders inside of file folders via the synesthetic processing powers of smell, air displacement, sound, sight, touch, flesh on flesh pressure—art emerged in whatever modality "language" it spoke. And, I listened.

An implosion of black-hole proportions occurred in autumn of 2014. A cataclysmic event of trauma memory eruptions and process. They wanted to speak, to be heard, tell their stories, emerge as light. Academically speaking, they were not pretty in their tone, stories, or form. As Artist as vehicle, I kept writing, singing, creating art—finally, these once silenced characters were acknowledged, accepted, and honored. PTSD and its twisted thematic thread unraveled into a large manuscript of work, *murmurs at the gate* (forthcoming in 2019, from Unsolicited Press); murmurs at the gate, this is how it came to be: I stopped at a Barnes & Nobles on my way home from yet another heinously intense prolonged exposure therapy session at the local VA. (Blessings to Dr. S.) There was only one table available with one chair. On that table were two items. A significant work by Shawn Talbot, *The Cortisol Connection*, and the September 2014 issue of *The Writer's Chronicle*, opened to an article exploring the violence in the poetry of the multi-racial poet Ai. To quote Ai: *People whose concept of themselves is largely dependent on their racial identity and superiority feel threatened by a multiracial person. The insistence that one must align oneself with this or that race is basically racist. And the notion that without a racial identity a person can't have any identity perpetuates racism.*

What if the race you identify with is not, according to the dominant culture's specifically defined stereotypes, the race you look like? Because prejudice is non-discriminatory, identifying with a group or culture does not lead to immediate (if ever) acceptance to /of that group. As statistical outliers we become our own group—the in-betweeners, the mixed-race, the folks who have a foot in both worlds. As artists, we have a foot in both worlds. We are bridges. One Elder Grandmother often called us, "Connectoraters."

Regardless of popularity or academic acceptance, Ai gave me permission to tell the stories in the words of those who have born witness to the absurdity of trauma and violence. Meanings are manipulated and torqued into grotesque behaviors. As a human being being an artist, I have a responsibility to the future generations to tell the truth about trauma, war, moral dysregulation. I have a responsibility to tell the stories in the language modality the story and narrators dictate, not what I egotistically or ethno-centrically impose.

Being multi-modal is akin to being multilingual, multidimensional, or multicultural and perhaps, multiracial. I remember my Dad. We are of the Earth. We are of our Ancestors. We are of our culture, whatever that may be in its forthright natural beauty or its grotesque, unprecedented and absurd horror. We have a responsibility as artists to dive below the surface of our own prejudicial rhythms metered by the tempo of traumas, or privilege, or the rurality of existence. How we live, is who we are. Art making, regardless of modality, has the power to change that. And we must, as artists, as writers, keep writing.

*

Warrior
by Ai

You sharpen the tip of spear
with your teeth,
while your wife plows the ground
with jawbone of an ox.
She is a great, black fire.

The old blood is drifting up your throat
and the witch-men sing all night
of melon-breasted women in rival villages,
but the spear is wilting in your hands.

When you are standing in the river,
you grab a fish,
tear its flesh open with your teeth, and hold it,
until the bones in your fingers break up
and fly about you like moths.
The river, a fish, your fingers, moths,
the war song churning in your belly.

DEBORAH A. MIRANDA

ESSELEN / CHUMASH [OHLONE-COSTANOAN ESSELEN]

"It's not that you've found your voice through the pain of others. It's that their voices found you."

The poems of Deborah A. Miranda (1961–) move back and forth between the present and the past, and between the intimate and the worldly. Maps, history, spirituality, lesbian erotics, and family relations are the purview of her work. Miranda often sets her poems in California and the western United States, tracing the colonial legacies of westward expansion, as in "Juliana, 1803" and "Indian Cartography," where the poet makes provocative observations about the immediacy of times gone by, and about the ways place is inseparable from Indigenous identities. In "Erasurepoem" and "Novena to Bad Indians," she cunningly overlays native and Christian perspectives, and in the process manages to bridge huge gaps between truly different sensibilities and beliefs. This capacity for spanning distances is especially evident in Miranda's poems that explore queer or two-spirit aesthetics, where she has emerged as an essential voice.

Juliana, 1803

The iron lock turns at dusk, our parents on the other side in the mission village, us girls in this dark room. The priest carries the key in his robe, gives it back to the Madre at dawn so we can join him in prayers before receiving our work orders. I've hated night for as long as I can remember. When the Padre came to our hut, told my mother I was seven years old now, old enough to require the monjerio, she told me, "Remember the stars. Remember you'll see them again someday." But I've forgotten—are they silver, or gold? Which direction do they move? Where is the one my mother warned me was sly and mean-spirited? She told me once that blazing stars with long tails were souls on their way to the afterlife. I wonder if the sky burns all night now? Some of the younger girls still miss their mothers, cry half the night, wet themselves. They keep the rest of us awake. I don't feel sorry for them; I hiss the curses I learned from the soldados to frighten them, make them shut up. The pinche workday is long enough without losing sleep too. I don't remember being that weak. True, I had my two older sisters. For years they kept me tucked between them all night; if the door opened in the darkness, if soldiers picked the lock or stole the padre's key, or if the padre himself made one of his 'inspections,' Dolores pushed me behind her, Ines covered me with her blanket. Till they married those brothers and got out. Now I lie awake at night, tuck my back into this corner I've claimed and defend when I have to. Smelling some poor woman's shit as she crouches over the trench in the corner, moaning that the posole this morning must've had rotten meat. My own bowels twist and boil, but please God let me make it till morning, and the privacy of a bush or hillside. And I think about that soldier, Demetrio, the one who came with the San Blas Infantry from someplace called Mexico. The Spanish guards laugh at him, call him 'chulo,' which means, I think, halfbreed. They ask him which jail the military pulled him out of, what crime did he commit, has he learned how to shoot an escopeta. They make him sound like a little boy. I know he's not. Yesterday on the path returning from the lavanderia, I hung back, pretended my basket of wet clothes was too heavy. He slipped me a string of dark red beads, my favorite, and said he would speak to the Padre soon. Then he pressed against me, knocked my basket into the dirt, spilled all that hard work. He put his hairy mouth on mine. I couldn't move. Clara called my name, and he pushed me away, ducked back into the trees. Tonight I can still feel his hands clutching my breasts. I wonder. I wonder what it would be like, to see the stars again.

Indian Cartography

My father opens a map of California —
traces mountain ranges, rivers, county borders
like family bloodlines. Tuolumne,
Salinas, Los Angeles, Paso Robles,
Ventura, Santa Barbara, Saticoy,
Tehachapi. Places he was happy,
or where tragedy greeted him
like an old unpleasant relative.
A small blue spot marks
Lake Cachuma, created when they
dammed the Santa Ynez, flooded
a valley, divided
my father's boyhood: days
he learned to swim the hard way,
and days he walked across the silver scales,
swollen bellies of salmon coming back
to a river that wasn't there.
The government paid those Indians to move away,
he says; *I don't know where they went.*

In my father's dreams
after the solace of a six-pack,
he follows a longing, a deepness.
When he comes to the valley
drowned by a displaced river
he swims out, floats on his face
with eyes open, looks down into lands not drawn
on any map. Maybe he sees shadows
of a people who are fluid,
fluent in dark water, bodies
long and glinting with sharp-edged jewelry,
and mouths still opening, closing
on the stories of our home.

Novena to Bad Indians

"The only good Indians I ever knew were dead."
—General Philip Sheridan

In the Catholic Church, a novena is a nine-day period of private or public prayer to obtain special graces, to implore special favors, or to make special petitions. The novena has always had a sense of urgency and immediacy.

Day 1.
Indian outlaws, banditos, renegades, rebels, lazy Indians, sinful Indians, you gamblers who squatted out behind the church instead of assuming the missionary position behind the plow; oh, lusty Indians who tied bones to sheets thrown out of the women's monjerio, climbed up that swaying skeleton of salvation and made unsanctified love all night; oh, women who tossed down those sheets: hear my prayer.

Day 2.
Hail troublemakers, horse thieves, fornicators, I implore you, polygamists, Deer Dancers, idol worshippers, chasers of loose women, heathens who caroused in the hills, stole wine from the sacristy, graffiti'd Indian designs on the church wall, told Coyote stories instead of practicing catechism, torched mission wheat fields, set fire to tule roofs, ran away, were captured, flogged, put in stocks or irons, ran away again: help me, suffer me, in this hour of loss.

Day 3.
I ask for your grace, you dirty Indians, you stupid Indians who wouldn't learn Spanish or English, lazy bastards who mumbled "no quiero" when asked to load wagons with tons of stinking skins, who chased the bottle instead of cattle, who were late for Mass, confessed everything and regretted nothing, took the whip thick as a fist, laughing; you who loved soapstone charms, glass beads, eagle feathers but wouldn't learn proper usage of land or gold: have mercy on my weakness.

Day 4.

Queens of earth, you women who sold yourselves for a tortilla, a handful of beans, the dog's meat; sons of incorrigible cattle thieves like Juan Nepomuceno, who could no longer find elk or deer or salmon; cabecillas, ringleaders like Hilario, who endured the novenario for throwing a stone at a missionary— twenty-five lashes on nine separate days and then, on nine consecutive Sundays, forty more: oh my martyrs, grant me strength, grant me courage in my desperation.

Day 5.

Oh magnificent Aniceto, who refused to name thieves of money, chocolate, shoes, string, knives from the presidio—thirteen years old, you took a flogging in silence; oh renowned Yozcolo, alcalde from Mission Santa Clara who raided mission stores, freed two hundred women from the monjerio; dear Atanasio, found guilty of stealing from the comisario, shot dead by a firing squad at seventeen years of age, begging for your life as you knelt in the estuary at Monterey: guide me out of the stone walls of this cell.

Day 6.

Accept my praisesong, you women who aborted pregnancies conceived in rape by soldier or priest, attend me, barren Indian woman, stripped and prodded, who refused to let Father Ramon Olbes examine your genitals or test your fertility—you, who bit him, suffered fifty lashes, shackles, imprisonment, a shaven head, were forced to carry a wooden false baby for nine days; blessed Apolinaria, midwife, curandera, dancer, keeper of potent medicines: heal me.

Day 7.

Ever full of faith, Pomponio, who cut off your heel with your own knife to slip out of leg irons; terrible heart of Toypurina, shaman revolutionary who dared raise your gods against Spain's; blessed Chumash woman who heard the earth goddess Chupa tell you to rebaptize neophytes in the tears of the sun; Licquisamne, most merciless Estanislao, telling the padre, "We are rising in revolt . . . we have no fear of the soldiers": make me unrepentant.

Day 8.

Oh valiant Venancio, Julián, Donato, Antonio, Lino, Vicente, Miguel, Andrés, Emiliana, María Tata, who suffocated Father Andrés Quintana at Santa Cruz before he could test his new wire-tipped whip; oh Nazario, personal cook to Fr. Panto at San Diego, who slipped "yerba," powdered cuchasquelaai, into the padre's soup after enduring 124 lashes (you said, "I could find no other way to revenge myself"): I beseech your tenderness.

Day 9.
Oh unholy pagans who refused to convert, oh pagans who converted, oh pagans who recanted, oh converts who survived, hear our supplication: make us in your image, grant us your pride. Ancestors, illuminate the dark civilization we endure. Teach us to love untamed, inspire us to break rules, remind us of your brutal wisdom learned so dearly: Even dead Indians are never good enough.

Erasure poem

"The tract through which **we** passed is generally very good land, with plenty of water; and there, as well as **here**, the country is neither rocky nor overrun with brushwood. There are, however, many hills, but they **are** **composed of earth**. The road has been good in some places, but the greater part bad. About half-way, the **valleys and** banks of **rivulets** began to be delightful. We found **vines** of a large size, and in some cases quite **loaded with grapes**; we also found **an abundance of roses**, which appeared to be like those of Castile."

"**We** have seen **Indians** in immense numbers, and all those **on this coast** of the Pacific contrive to make a good subsistence on various seeds, and by fishing. The latter they **carry on** by means of rafts or canoes, made of tule (bullrush) with which they go a great way to sea. They are **very civil**. All the males, **old and young**, go naked; the women, however, and the female children, are **decent**ly covered from their breasts downward. We found **on our journey**, as well as in the place where **we** stopped, that they **treated us with** as much **confidence and good-will** as if they had known us **all** their **lives**. But when we offered them any of our victuals, they **always** refused them. All they **cared for** was cloth, and only for something of this sort would they exchange their fish or whatever else they had. During **the whole** march we found hares, rabbits, some deer, and a **multitude** of berendos (**a kind of a wild** goat)."

"I pray **God** may preserve your health and life many years."

"From this port and intended Mission of San Diego, in North California, third July, 1769."

"FRIAR MIGUEL JOSE JUNIPERO SERRA."

A Poem

We   here
are composed of earth
valleys and   rivulets
vines   loaded with grapes
an abundance of roses
We   Indians   on this coast
carry on
very civil   old and young
decent   on our journey
we treat with   confidence and
good-will
all lives
always care for
the whole
multitude
a kind of wild
God

s o n g   o f

I I ' U R*

[*one of the Kumeyaay words for
Juniperus californica

Tears of the Sun

The river is full of mica.
When we swim, our bodies

shimmer, wrapped in constellations
of stars. Our forearms swirl

and sparkle like the Milky Way,
legs glint with galaxies.

Our hands glitter gold as if dipped
in stardust. In July's white-hot

sun, sparks of the cosmos
bathe us in the dust of all

that has come before us.
See how we are embers

waiting to blaze and ignite.
See how the river dresses us —

lost, stolen, dispossessed, broken —
in living bones of granite,

in the light of our Ancestors.

The Bones Speak: Excavation and Reunion

"Our imperative is to resurrect, sometimes hundreds of years after the fact, a history that has been buried, lost, or ignored . . . This writing, I would say, amounts almost to an act of exhumation."
—Janice Gould*

My literary genealogy has so many brilliant branches, so many beloved writers. The danger here is not being able to name all of the stars whose words live in my bookshelves and heart; knowing this, I'm forcing myself to focus on just one author, an Indigenous poet, and just a single poem from that writer which came to me as a young writer at exactly the right moment. This poem's content, structure, and extraordinary use of English to tell an unspeakable Indigenous story, gave me deep insights into the risks, responsibilities, and craft of being an Indigenous writer.

I didn't grow up knowing that any Native writers existed. Born in Los Angeles, 1961, of an Esselen/Chumash father and white mother, I left California at the age of five. My father was in prison, my mother re-married; she, my step-father and I moved to rural Western Washington, about an hour south of Seattle. My tribal connections were cut, and although my mother told me I was Indian, she did not know the name of the tribe or anything but the fact that it had been declared extinct. No Native writers appeared in my school curriculum from first grade to my eventual graduation. The American Indian Renaissance, as the surge of writers in the 1960–1970s is sometimes called, remained invisible to me. Then, in my early thirties, I participated in a week-long poetry writing workshop. Janice Gould (Koyangk'auwi Maidu) was workshop leader; the first Native poet I had ever spoken with, the first California Indian I'd met outside of my family, and my first mentor of Indigenous literature. After that workshop with Gould, I immersed myself in an education that consisted not of syllabi and homework, but recommended-reading lists from Gould and writing sessions crammed into the wee hours, my children's afternoon naptime or (later) between housecleaning jobs. About this same time, through the efforts of both my mother and father (who had, soon after his release, moved up to Washington State as well), we reconnected with our California tribal community and became involved in efforts to reclaim culture, language, and make a bid for Federal Re-recognition as the reorganized Esselen/Ohlone Costanoan Nation of the Greater Monterey Bay area.

*In "American Indian Women's Poetry: Strategies of Rage and Hope"

It would be several years before I was courageous enough to apply to grad school, and still more years before I earned a doctorate in English, with a specialty in Native American literature. In those early days of my home-made education, I found very little literature by California Indians writing about the California "mission Indian" experience and inheritance, although that was exactly what I found myself writing. And don't we all look for ourselves in the poetry of others? Our younger selves, at least, need that validation. I was very young in 1994.

One day in the University Bookstore in Seattle, I found something extraordinary: a collection of Wendy Rose's work titled *Going to War with All My Relations*. In that collection I found Rose's poem, "Excavation at Santa Barbara Mission."

My initial encounter with this poem, this being, felt almost like meeting a person whose arrival I had been longing for, but did not know how to find. "Excavation" tore off the bandages from a wound I didn't even know my body bore. I had no idea it was possible to write *that* absence, *that* jagged rupture in history, *that* erasure, of my homeland's history: twenty-one missions founded and operated by Spain via the Catholic church from 1769–1822, followed by Mexican rule and closing down of the missions (along with what little safety-net they provided for the elderly and very young) 1822–1846, followed by the Gold Rush, and finally, United States governance in 1850. By the time my grandfather was born in 1903, the population of Indigenous Californians had gone from about one million to about twenty thousand. How could this kind of unthinkable, unspeakable trauma be captured in language?

"Excavation at Santa Barbara Mission" came into my life like a master teacher.

I remember the moment with my whole body: I can see where I stood in front of wooden bookshelves just the other side of the sole elevator, I see where among other books of poetry the slender book sat, I see the pages open in my hands, I see the words on the paper as I read this poem for the first time.

I remember thinking of my grandmother Marquesa, from the Santa Barbara and Santa Ynez area. I remember thinking, *I have ancestors who were in the Santa Barbara Mission.*

In that moment, I know, from Janice Gould's recommendations, that Rose is a Hopi/Miwok scholar and poet. I know that the Miwoks had also been missionized by the Spaniards, and I know that Rose holds a doctorate in Anthropology. Still, I am struck by the sense of complicity I feel as the poem opens with the speaker picking away at a mission adobe wall with her "pointed trowel" - an intrusion, a penetration, of what she learns is a hidden burial site, Indigenous bodies entombed in the mission walls.

The speaker's initial excitement is familiar to me: she says, "I want to count myself / among the ancient dead / as a faithful neophyte / resting there and in love / with the padres / and the Spanish hymns." Knowing she has Miwok lineage, this speaker wants to claim her small part in the larger Mission romance, beloved narrative of California's mission mythology: Franciscan missionaries, full of tenderness and kindness; eager Indians so good, so willing. Looking back now, I see that Rose's longing helped me recognize my own need to be part of history. Her confession of a desire to be seen, to count, to be represented, allowed me to admit my own vulnerability to accepting *any* representation, *anything* besides the erasure I had grown up with. In the moment, however, I am a mass of conflicted emotions.

Just a few lines in, this poem is already a painful crucible of identity.

And then it happens: "A feature juts out." This sharp point is where I see the speaker lose control. She no longer uncovers or discovers the bones; the agency here is in *the bone itself*, the way it penetrates *the anthropologist's* world. As if the bone is somehow still alive. I don't know it yet, but this is a kind of warning: once you start digging into an erased history, that erased history will dig into you.

Next, a series of similes pour out of the poem, much the way the adobe crumbles and reveals: the marrow is *like lace*, a piece of skull is *an upturned cup*, fingerbones scattered *like corn*, ribs *interlace like cholla*. I am transfixed as the body of an Ancestor reassembles itself before my eyes: manifestations of clothing, utensils, food, musculature.

The bones, like the speaker, have a complicated genealogy. Not just anonymous bones from a dead past, they are a vital part of transformation, the cycle which death allows. Standing there in the bookstore, I can't stop seeing those fingerbones "scattered like corn," in the earth: seeds, promises, waiting to sprout into new life.

The Anthropologist in this poem has made a discovery she did not expect; she seeks the past, the dead, the data, the measurable. What she finds is an entity, an energy, that has never died. What she has discovered is that there is no death, that the past "isn't dead, it isn't even past," to quote another writer deeply appreciative of complex genealogies.

In fact, Rose shows us those bones within that very moment of transformation as the speaker touches them: "How fragile / they have become/ to float and fall / with my touch / brittle white tips/ shivering into mist." Still in anthro-mode, the speaker at first sees the people buried here as weak, unable to adapt, disappearing before her eyes. It's as if the word "extinction" is on the tip of her tongue, and the inevitability of it allows her to speak of their remains in the most decrepit of terms.

But the bone dust mixes "with the blood of my own knuckles," and the poem quietly explodes.

At this point, I am holding my breath. Ancestral remains reach out to the speaker's hands, do the mixing. The Ancestors claim her by blood. The boundaries that the speaker once believed in—linear time, us and them, science and spirit—collapse in this intimate encounter. Or is it a reunion?

The speaker now acknowledges all that she does not know; she accepts the wounding that opens her skin to the Ancestors: "How helpless I am," she says, "... my hands empty themselves of old dreams"—both the romantic visions she had before the dig, and perhaps, the destroyed dreams of those whose bones she is uncovering. Hidden inside the mission walls, these remains have "survived" "the flags / of three invaders"—the relentless serial colonization of Spain, Mexico, and the United States—only to have their rest, such as it is, disturbed by her trowel. Now the speaker fully judges herself: "I am a hungry scientist / sustaining myself / with the bones of / men and women asleep in the wall"—raising the inescapable specter of cannibalism or vampirism that hovers over this section, an image of the ultimate colonizer—a "hungry scientist" who makes her living by feeding off genocided lives.

I recognize this raw place. Years later, in an essay titled "Voice," I will wrestle with what it means to find my voice as a writer through the pain and suffering of those I love most. *What do I do with that knowledge?*

It's a responsibility. It's a debt, this gift, and I must repay it by carrying the responsibility of giving voice to those who could not speak. Isn't that the answer? Isn't that the way to assuage my guilt at earning my living from the tortured cries of my beloved ancestors and relatives? To accept it as a charge, not a gift?

But I wasn't satisfied. It felt, not wrong, but incomplete. Too easy. And not enough. I know that often in those liminal moments between wakefulness and sleeping, revelation slips in, so I asked (myself, the Universe, the Ancestors): but what more is it? and ... the response came back almost as if it had been waiting for me to ask:

It's not that you've found your voice through the pain of others. It's that their voices found you.

But standing in that bookstore in 1994, Rose's book open in my hands, all I know is that those three "I am" statements—claims to identity—have taken an epic journey that I can hardly keep up with. First, "How excited I am," then

"How helpless I am," and finally, "I am a hungry scientist..."

What is the speaker's identity here? Who, or what, can she claim as her own? She has dug herself into her own grave ("crouching in the white dust"); put herself into her ancestor's experience. She is her Ancestors. Is she going to choose as her livelihood a future based on a mass murder in which she, herself, is a victim? Will she ignore what her blood tells her, and continue to dig for the benefit of Western science?

Rose's closing stanza answers all these questions.

> They built the mission with dead Indians.
> They built the mission with dead Indians.
> They built the mission with dead Indians.
> They built the mission with dead Indians.

This stanza stands on the page, in shape and intention, like an adobe brick. Seen against the sparse, lyric stanzas before it, the speaker and her reader literally run into a brick wall that does not allow for metaphor or erasure. Here is the fact that cannot be denied. Here are the bodies that lie in that gap history has mortared over, here are the voices that have been silenced, here is the ugly, gruesome truth that has been fabricated with the bones of the speaker's murdered Ancestors. The speaker must tell the story that cannot be told. But how?

In these last lines, is she speaking to the four directions, turning with each utterance so that her words are heard as an offering, a mourning song, a warning? Is she stunned into numb repetition? Do words fail her? I've returned to this poem again and again over the years, and I believe that Rose expresses all of these responses, falls back on sparse language that hammers out the blunt shape of truth: a terse stanza constructed in what I now read as a sequence of disbelief, followed by reluctant comprehension, chased by horrified grief, ending in the quiet rage that comes on the heels of genocide.

Wendy Rose says it: dead Indians are the foundation of the poem, of Mission Santa Barbara, of the entire mission system, and of this country.

I stand in the bookstore, re-read the poem again. Think about it. Mission Santa Barbara, known as "The Queen of the Missions," with "striking views of the Pacific, headquarters of all the missions," was built using Indian bones *as a kind of rebar*. The strength of the mission walls comes from the consumption of Indian bodies and souls. Mission Santa Barbara, described in pamphlets and websites as "one of only two missions continuously operated by the Franciscans since its founding, whose statues above the altar were brought to Santa Barbara from Mexico." Mission Santa Barbara, proudly bearing "unique twin towers of with six bells hanging within, each one dedicated to a saint and bearing the inscription of the cross." Mission Santa Barbara: not a monument to Franciscan triumph, not an architecturally beautiful remembrance of a glorious heritage, but a mass grave for her Indigenous Ancestors.

I took that book home with me. In the years to come, I would loan it out, lose it, replace it, purchase it as a gift for others. But "Excavation at Santa Barbara Mission" never really leaves me.

It's clear to me that in this poem, Rose resolves the identity issue that arises within its stanzas —is the speaker anthro or Indian?—and comes down firmly on the truth of the speaker's own Indigeneity. And yet, at the same time, the discovery of the bones—and all that they demand she face—is dependent on her work as an anthropologist; it is that quintessentially settler work which painfully skins her knuckles and exposes her blood to the powdered remains of her Ancestors, allows her to take in the Ancestors, on a physical and emotional level. Allowing the Ancestors to re-colonize—no, *decolonize*—her blood.

For many California mission Indian descendants, genocide goes so deep that knowledge regarding "bones in mission walls" (literal and figurative) has been lost to us. I know of no stories, oral or otherwise, that tell how Indian bones ended up in the walls of the Santa Barbara Mission, yet I believe that such a story existed at one point, and was silenced, erased, hidden by an oppressive settler society. Rose's job, as an anthropologist and Indigenous poet, is to reveal the horrible truths inside those walls. Ultimately, her choice is not one or the other; instead, she accepts that each identity informs the other. Poets Joy Harjo and Gloria Bird call this reinventing the enemy's language, taking it for our own purposes; Rose reinvents the enemy's science. The poem's speaker has not found her voice through anthropology; rather, the voices of the Ancestors are heard through an Indigenous anthropologist.

Indeed, the "Excavation at Santa Barbara Mission" is not just an excavation of Ancestral remains at the physical site of the mission, but of the living Indigenous identity of the speaker, hidden within her own body—buried, perhaps, by the same Eurocentric colonization that decimated California Indians at large. When the anthropologist walks away from that dig at Santa Barbara Mission, she is reawakened to her identity, and to her role as an Indigenous person. The bones speak to her. She carries that story away with her, puts it on the page, participates in the great transformational cycle that connects us in all ways, through all time, even across the chasm of genocide.

That is the most important work of this poem, and it is that inheritance that I trace from Wendy Rose in my own work: loss, excavation, and regeneration. I see those themes like recurring basket patterns in my poems about the missions, most obviously in my first book, *Indian Cartography*, and later in *Bad Indians: A Tribal Memoir*. Through my writing, the bones of my culture speak: and they are not dead bones, but bones like seeds, bursting with story, with that spiral of time that is past, present, future, an energy ripe with fertility and renewal.

I hear the themes of "Excavation," and the work it does, in my own poetry, even (perhaps because the journey is similar to for missionized peoples) poems written before I read Rose. "Indian Cartography," written at that long-ago workshop with Janice Gould, is a look at loss and continuance, a kind of map to a people and place that persists beneath grief and destruction. "Novena to Bad Indians," written much later, amplifies the voices of my Ancestors recovered through research, their yearning for love, for justice, for acknowledgment and honoring. A young Esselen woman, incarcerated in the monjerio much like Rose's bones themselves, speaks of her confinement and what parts of herself she would give up for freedom in "Juliana." Taking the reinvention of the enemy's language literally, "An Erasure Poem" re-visions the Franciscan missionary Junipero Serra's own words, turning it into an Indigenous credo. "Tears of the Sun" returns to Rose's imagery of bone dust, the embrace of Ancestors through their return as flecks of mica in a river.

I've carried "Excavation at Santa Barbara Mission" with me like a talisman through my journey as a writer. Maybe I would have written what I've written without ever seeing "Excavation." But it might also have taken me even longer than it has to hear the Ancestors. Without doubt, many other Indigenous writers have produced work that moves me, inspires me, teaches me; but it was this poem that weakened my knees in the University Bookstore, took me out of myself and towards myself. It is this poem that still scratches the skin on my knuckles, excavates me from the ruins.

Thank you, Wendy Rose. Nimasianexelpasaleki.

*

Excavation at Santa Barbara Mission
by Wendy Rose

> *When archaeologists excavated Santa Barbara Mission in California,*
> *they discovered human bones in the adobe walls.*

My pointed trowel
is the artist's brush
that will stroke and pry,
uncover and expose
the old mission wall.
How excited I am
for like a dream
I wanted to count myself
among the ancient dead
as a faithful neophyte
resting there and in love
with the padres
and the Spanish hymns.

A feature juts out. Marrow
like lace, piece of a skull,
upturned cup, fingerbones
scattered like corn
and ribs interlaced
like cholla.
So many bones
mixed with the blood
from my own knuckles
that dig and tug
in the yellow dust.
How fragile
they have become
to float and fall
with my touch,
brittle white tips

shivering into mist.
How helpless I am
for the deeper I go
the more I find
crouching in white dust,
listening to the whistle
of longbones breaking
apart like memories.
My hands empty themselves
of old dreams,
drain the future
into the moisture
of my boot prints.
Beneath the flags
of three invaders,
I am a hungry scientist
sustaining myself
with bones of
men and women asleep in the wall
who survived in their own way
Spanish swords, Franciscans
and their rosary whips,
who died among the reeds
to wait, communion wafers
upon the ground, too holy
for the priests to find.

They built the mission with dead Indians.
They built the mission with dead Indians.
They built the mission with dead Indians.
They built the mission with dead Indians.

HEID E. ERDRICH
TURTLE MOUNTAIN OJIBWE

"We do and we do not write of treaties, battles, and drums. We do and we do not write about, eagles, spirits, and canyons. Native poetry may be those things, but it is not only those things. It is also about grass and apologies, bones and joy, marching bands and genocide, skin and social work, and much more."

Heid E. Erdrich (1963–) dismantles (and re-mantles) literary forms; she merges science and Native histories, assembles poems from RSS feeds, plays with complicated interchanges of creation and translation, and ponders the indigenous skeletal remains in museums. Consider "Pre-Occupied," a mash-up of Superman cartoons, pop music, the Occupy movement, and the irony of America's continuing *occupation* by settler colonialists. In "National Monuments," she cross-examines what our society memorializes with monuments, and what nationhood is. While Erdrich often engages with canonical American literature, her writings embrace an Ojibwe worldview. She is a ceaseless literary experimenter, for instance in "Little Souvenirs from the DNA Trading Post," where she incorporates capitalized phrases that transmute into couplets in a regular typeface, which then shift into lower-case italicized lines that scatter across the page, punctuated by ellipses. Heid Erdrich is one of America's poetic innovators.

Little Souvenirs from the DNA Trading Post

A pregnancy lasts forever . . . because every woman who has been pregnant carries these little souvenirs of the pregnancy for the rest of her life.
—Dr. Diana W. Bianchi

BUT IT'S A DRY HEAT . . .

Touch me here and you touch her.
Cinnamon smell on the air—

I've never cared much for Time . . .
You mean the concept of time?

GREETINGS FROM SUNNY . . .

Touch me here and you touch what she left in me,
what ropes me to her—

Mountains made of Time, I like.
You interrupt me, darling.
You need not do so, you know.
You are with me always.

I AM FINE, WISHING YOU WERE HERE.

I hear you always, like Eiffel Tower earrings jingling in my ears,
like the silent snow in the globe,
vivid blue Seattle skyline behind—

You hear me in silence?

Yes. Most certainly. Do you hear me?

My healing hands—let me put them on you . . .

How do you know just where it hurts?

Touch you here and I touch me.

ODDEST KNOWN REVERSAL OF MATERNITY.

Cowgirl purse, leather-worked in miniature from Out West,
stone postcard labeled Artifacts of Ancient Inhabitants . . .

What did you bring me?

What did you bring me?

National Monuments

Low house of rough bark,
small enough for a fairy
delights my sight

until it's clear it covers a grave
and worse, it's stained deck-red
shingled with asphalt.

Some park official has kept up
what was meant to moss
and rot and fall.

Grave houses, clan-marked:
sturgeon scratched in pine,

simple lines of eagle and marten,

whiskered totems, some on crosses.
Other tribes carve headstones:
Six-Nations' eel flips its infinity of tail ∞

Bear tracks tell complex genealogy,
map land and tongue and history
to crane's stick legs and turtle's shell.

Doodem signs, national markers
the body makes by being born,
that speak your only, only name,

your last word etched, kept, engraved.

Kennewick Man Tells All

We didn't go digging for this man. He fell out—he was actually a volunteer.
I think it would be wrong to stick him back in the ground without waiting
to hear the story he has to tell.
> —forensic anthropologist James Chatters in the
> *New Yorker,* June 16, 1997

Ladies and gentleman of the press—

Kennewick Man will now make a brief statement
after which he will answer questions as time permits.

I am 9,20 years old

I am bone. I am alone.

Guidelines for the Treatment of Sacred Objects

If the objects emit music,
and are made of clay or turtle shell,
bathe them in mud at rainy season.
Allow to dry, then brush clean
using only red cloth or newspaper.
Play musical objects from time to time.
Avoid stereotypical tom-tom beat
and under no circumstances dance or sway.

If objects were worn as funerary ornament,
admire them verbally from time to time.
Brass bells should be called *shiny*
rather than *pretty*. Shell ear spools
should be remarked upon as *handsome*,
but beads of all kinds can be told,
simply, that they are *lookin' good*.

Guidelines for the treatment of sacred objects
composed of wood, hair (human or otherwise)
and/or horn, include: offering smoke,
water, pollen, cornmeal or, in some instances,
honey, chewing gum, tarpaper
and tax incentives.

If an object's use is obscure,
or of pleasing avian verisimilitude,
place rocks from its place of origin
within its display case. Blue-ish rocks
often bring about discovery, black rocks
soothe or mute, while white rocks irritate mildly.
All rocks must return to their place of origin
whenever they wish. Use only volunteer rocks,
or stones left by matri-descendant patri-tribalists.

Guidelines for the treatment of sacred objects
that appear or disappear at will
or that appear larger in rear view mirrors
include calling in spiritual leaders such as librarians,
wellness-circuit speakers and financial aid officers.

If an object calls for its mother,
boil water and immediately swaddle it.
If an object calls for other family members,
or calls collect after midnight, refer to tribally
specific guidelines. Reverse charges.

If objects appear to be human bone,
make certain to have all visitors stroke
or touch fingertips to all tibia, fibula
and pelvis fragments. In the case of skulls,
call low into the ear or eye holes, with words
lulling and kind.

If the bones seem to mock you
or if they vibrate or hiss,
make certain no mirrors hang nearby.
Never, at anytime, since Dem Bones.

Avoid using bones as drumsticks
or paperweights, no matter
the actions of previous Directors or Vice
Directors of your institution.

If bones complain for weeks at a time,
roll about moaning, or leave chalky outlines,
return them instantly to their place of origin,
no questions asked, c.o.d.

Pre-Occupied

River, river, river
I never, never, never
etched your spiral icon in limestone
or, for that matter, pitched a tent on cement
near your banks.
Banks of marble, stock still, all movement in the plaza,
river walking its message on an avenue
rallied in bitter wind.

Excuse my digression, my mind tends . . .
In reality, my screen is lit with invitations:
bake a casserole — send pizza — make soup for the 99%

Sorry, somehow I haven't time.
Flow, flow, flow both ways in time.
There's a river to consider after all.

No time, no hours, no decades, no millennia.
No, I cannot dump cans of creamed corn
and turkey on noodles and offer forth
sustenance again.

A bit pre-occupied, we original 100%
who are also 1%, more or less.
Simply distracted by sulfide emissions, tar sands, pipelines, foster care,
polar bears, hydro-fracking, and the playlist deeply intoning:
Super Man never made any money . . .

River, river, river. Our river.
Map of the Milky Way,
reflection of stars
from whence all life commenced.

100% of all life on our planet.
River in the middle, Mississippi,
not the East Coast Hudson where this all started,

waterway Max Fleischer's team lushly rendered
via the wonder of Technicolor.

Emerging from an underwater lair,
a Mad Scientist we comprehend as indigenous
has lost his signifiers (no braids, no blanket)
but we recognize him.
A snappy dresser who flashes a maniac grin,
he is not,
not your TV Indian.

Ignoble Savage: ". . . and I still say Manhattan
rightfully belongs to my people."
Superman: "Possibly, but just what
do you expect us to do about it?"

Occupy. Occupy. Worked for the 99.
Occupy, re-occupy: Alcatraz and Wounded Knee.

Sorry, somehow now I've too much time.
Flow, flow, flow both ways, story-history-story.
There's a river that considers us after all.
All time, all hours, all decades, all millennia.

River, river, river
I never, never, never —
but that is not to say that I won't ever

NOTES OF PRE-OCCUPIEID DIGRESSION: Descendants of the indigenous population of the US
remain just a tad less than 1% of the population according to the 2010 census. If you add Native
Hawaiians to the total we are 1.1% of the population. So, we are, more or less, the original 1% as well
as the original 100%. As the Occupy Movement took hold, indigenous groups continued struggles
to protect our homelands from imminent threats such as the tar sands in Canada and its Keystone
pipeline, copper mining in Minnesota and Wisconsin, and hydro-fracking elsewhere—everywhere,
it seems. This era of alternative energy has become the new land grab, the new water grab. Indige-
nous activists are thoroughly pre-occupied with the social and environmental issues I mention and
more. Activists can't be everywhere at once—not like Superman. I refer here, of course, to the Crash
Test Dummies' 1991"Superman's Song," that despairs the world will never see altruism like that of the
unpaid hero. In the 1942 cartoon Electric Earthquake, an indigenous (but not stereotypically "Indi-
an") Mad Scientist is thwarted, of course, by Superman. At one point Clark Kent admits indigenous
land claim as "possibly" valid, but says there's nothing the Daily Planet can do about it. A shrewd
Tesla wanna-be, our villain attempts to publish his demands first, then occupies Lois Lane while
toppling Manhattan skyscrapers. You can see this beauty all over the Internets.

Real to Me

The first time I read contemporary Native poets, around 1979 or 1980, it was in an issue of a magazine—likely *Spawning the Medicine River* from the Institute of American Indian Arts—that I was given by my eldest sister, Louise. I was a kid of fourteen. We grew up in a North Dakota town not too far from the Sisseton-Wahpeton reservation. The larger world was a mystery to me that I glimpsed from the white perspective on TV—a world mostly imagined. My naiveté was so dense that I did not even understand how magazine subscriptions worked, but the printed words of other Indian people were evidence that I and the world I knew were real. I clung to those poems.

How amazing it felt to read poets from places I had seen, to read poets who wrote a world that I knew! Before this, I had not known of any poetry written by Native people. I did not even know Louise was writing poetry. No one taught poetry in the public junior high in my home town, much less Native poetry.

That one issue became my lifeline at the East Coast boarding school I left home to attend on scholarship. I read poems from it at the school assembly because I wanted to introduce the mostly white community to the idea that American Indians were alive. Yes, my aim was this basic. When others there learned I was member of a tribe, the response I often heard was "I thought you were all dead."

At the boarding school English poetry was taught, and I struggled to get the layers of references, allusions, and images so different from my experience in North Dakota. The poems in the magazine full of Native writers, I got. That felt real and I wanted in. I wanted to write from home.

I wrote about jackrabbits and driving dusty roads. I wrote beloved tragic figures I knew growing up. Wildflowers stood in for me—for what I learned to call the self. I wrote memories of elders. I wrote about jackrabbits again, but with coyotes. No one knew what to make of my poems, but my high school English teachers encouraged me. It was not until my MFA that I was discouraged from writing my lived experience.

The poet I most recall from that magazine is Roberta Hill. In her images of plains and woodlands and familiar people, I saw home and was less alone. In her poetic voice, I heard a possibility that we could attend to a sense of loss with love and persistence, and that we could value the beauty of the natural world without being what even then I resisted, the human-in-nature stereotype that hippies loved, but that embarrassed me because it made us seem simple and primitive.

Much later, in the 1990s, I was awarded a rare opportunity to take workshops from Roberta Hill in a mentor program at The Loft Literary Center. Yes, I did feel what my kid would call "fan girl" giddiness. That mentorship meant more to me than my MFA years. In a workshop with all Native American peers, Anishinaabe and Dakota, we were not alone. We understood one another on a basic level and supported one another. We did not compete with each other, as my MFA teachers had urged, and we did not study writers who came before us with an eye toward eclipsing them, as my white male professors also taught. Instead Bobbi introduced poetic concepts, helped us interrogate aesthetics both new to us and familiar, guided us, and introduced us to Native writers we did not know. She grew a Native writer's community from that mentorship and it sustained and encouraged our work for decades.

Around 1995, several of us from The Loft group went to a Native writers conference at the Oneida Casino near Green Bay, Wisconsin. At some point we all piled into a blue muscle car that looked like it had seen three hundred thousand miles of rough road. In the dark, I plopped on top of someone's lap. I asked, Who is that down there? It's Jim, Heid—Jim Northrup said. We were in his infamous rez car and Kimberly Blaeser had the wheel. That car held, as far as I knew, 99% of the publishing Anishinaabe poets.

While the poems in that journal long ago opened possibilities for me, it was Kimberly Blaeser's poetry that most encouraged me. Her book *Trailing You* brought me home. It was her ability with detail that made it all so real for me. I remember reading her list poems, her lyrics, her narratives, and understanding for the first time that what was usual to me might be distinct to my readers. My poetic stance was right in front of me. It was the place, voices, meaningful moments in my life as an Ojibwe woman that I had to write, not the imitative, anxious stuff my MFA program encouraged or the overtly political work it discouraged.

By then, I had a manuscript that would become my first book. Over the next year, I revised and crafted new works to more sharply define my sense of origin, of place, and the mythic feel of stories we carry. Kimberly Blaeser's *Trailing You* liberated me from an argument I was taught to have: How to separate the poetic notion of *the self* from our (presumably pedestrian) lived experience? How to rise above our boring lives? My MFA training was with New Formalists and geared toward young white males from very similar backgrounds. Our teachers asked us to create a kind of poetic persona that viewed the world from a universal and (somehow?) distanced place. This approach asked the poet to rise above the body and reveal the complexity of the human mind. It told us to never use words like heart, soul, or self. And yet, it was right fond of the first person.

The first person was not for me, and I still struggle with it. After reading Kimberly Blaeser, I began to employ the third person where my first-person attempts had failed to produce a sensory world. I brought the poems back to earth and home. One of Kimberly Blaeser's poems, "Rewriting Your Life," an *ars poetica*, works as a craft lesson in how poetry can give those we've lost a voice, and carry them with us in poems. "Rewriting Your Life" told me to write to and for others, *across my pain*. It taught me to never write alone. This poem is written in the first person, yet it gave me the idea that I would be less self-conscious if I could approach the universal from outside myself, write in the third person, and be less alone in my poems. My poems became conversations with you, dear reader, and that has rewritten my life.

*

Rewriting Your Life
by Kimberly Blaeser

not just the past
that matters the most,

but those haunting scenes
that make anger and panic rise in your throat
at the domestic quarrels of strangers.
The same sort
that makes my pulse pound in my ears
to drown out that saccharine alcohol voice
of the women two booths away.

Erasing, replacing
the longings that arose from want
the causes
of your jacket fetish
the causes
of the bathtub in my parent's yard
the causes

of all old patterns stumbling on to renew themselves
of personal quirks
and other small tortures.

The children we were
we are.

I've added
a child with chink eyes
to those
bruised souls
whose lives
I rewrite
on my bluest days
and in the midst of my happiest moments
some part that seems physical
surges
with a longing
to repair
the past.

The aches in our bones are memories I'm told.
The tearing and stitching of our flesh
not the physical wear of age
really small but impossible hopes
dreamed endlessly
in smoke-filled pool halls
in one-room cold-water flats
dreams of grease splattered arms
taking shorthand
legs crossed at the ankles
just above a pair of black patent leather pumps.

The little tug in our voices
we wash down with complimentary water
at public podiums and in banquet halls
it is the pull of the small store of joy

of a people born poor
studying in school to be ashamed
it is the shiny marbles
our children shot across muddy school yards
and then washed and lined neatly to dry
it is fresh winter snow served with cream and sugar
nickel tent movies
and hurrah for the fourth of july!
It is your memories too now
that raise the flesh on my arms and legs.
And perhaps in time we can write across
that other life with this one,
but never enough to obscure it
just enough to make a new pattern
a new design
pitifully inadequate perhaps
for all that has happened —
but beautiful as only loved pain can be.

And so I write across your life that way
with mine
I write across your life with love
that comes from my own pain
and then, of course,
I write your face across my pain.

CELIA BLAND

CHEROKEE

"My poetry springs from a way of thinking about the living and dead…"

The poetry of Celia Bland (1963–) is known for its cinematic verve and vividness. Writing from within the panorama of her familial origins (as in "Cherokee 1974"), Bland's poems are dramatic and confrontational, never tentative in speaking of hard matters, now and in times past. Often delivered in sharp phrases that cut with a staccato tempo, Bland's poems stand up, stand out, and shout their truths, underscoring the urgency. "Car Crash" and "Lost Highway" deploy automobile and travel metaphors to interrogate the machinery and painful, poignant (im)mobilities of Native life. Celia Bland refuses to let readers ride passively; she insists we be drivers of our own consciousness.

Car Crash

There was the first crash when my cousin
crimped like a dog's ear the phone pole.
They cut him from Chevy's metal skull
with over-sized shears —
teen king Stanley, my man, cracked-up.

This was in Cullowhee, Valley of the Lilies in Cherokee,
an Acadia for Braves where they could suck
lily sweetness through ochre nostrils and
hunt the buck again.

Stanley's buckteeth gouged asphalt as he unstrung,
my pretty crew-cut redskin.
Chevy's radio tuning Grand Funk Railroad's
I'm Your Captain —
so cool this Injun Sunday School aide.
Broken.
A resident scotch-taped Stanley's backbone
to the buckboard, inflated his lungs with a
bicycle pump while we women — Bonnie, Sharon, my
mother, myself — keened by hospital bedpost,
hymn-singing, until his eyes bent like lilies
and we set him,
thighs set, ankles set, wrists set,
Adam's original rib set,
in Cullowhee again.

Jaw strung shut, pursed lips a bottle cap
about to pop, Stanley thought:
Memories are a way to hold on to time
but who holds on to me?
Who is brave enough to let me go?

He drunk those 13 beers through a Dixie straw.
The Impala crumpled like Kleenex
in the second crash.
Cullowhee! Cullowhee!
Crows scavenge his teeth for
brackish nests and the
new moon will not will not
will not set.

Cherokee Hogscape

> *We think of the key, each in his prison*
> *Thinking of the key, each confirms his prison.*
> —T. S. Eliot

Pops wd say, *these hogs'll knock you down and chaw yr eyeballs out of the socket.*

Pops collected slops from the poolroom café making you carry plastic buckets
— don't slop yr sneakers

w/ hamburger scraps, dollops of cream corn, loaf heels or cabbage cores, boy.
Tip 'em into that trough as the hogs shoulder like nimble church-goers to a
pew, jaws scooping pulp, tensile snouts like chestnut halves, snuffling. When
gravy slops your sneaks Pops hollers *Peel me a switch!* and flexes his arm. You
can read switches, calibrate heft to pain, welts testifying tensile swish to blood-
ied shins or mere blisters.

You like to choose wood that bled, flexing yr own arm to snap a limb from
some mud-spattered de-barked aspen in the hog pen, a bottom barren of grass,
leaf or bush.

Hogpack flanked you, 350 lbs of rippling sides, bristling eyes. You heard 'em
snuffling at night through the raw plywood walls of the room off the horse barn

where you and Pops under a chenille counterpane in the chill of 4 am pigeons
fluttering above yr plywood ceiling, coo-cooing.

It was in prison, it struck you:

it wasn't those hogs you hated but Pop's chickens. Those scores scratching sa
dust with spurred claws sequins pinned for eyes. Not the lash-lined & irised
hog-eyes watching as you shit between roots of oak, then waded into the creek
to sluice off chicken creosote.

Prison Mess — not cafeteria, Mess — is the scratch and caw of Pops' roosters at
the feeders. And here you are again, slopping potato goop into troughs.

They say a cock crowed when you denied our Savior, cockscomb like chawed
meat, a skull full of beans.

But even Jesus knew: chickens gotta doodle-doo.

Lost Highway

when his pops made him scrape that
chicken smush
from the barn's sawdust, he
caught a glimpse of a
blood bead on the bird's flattened beak
beautiful red as the opening he'd cut:
her mouth open
to a strangling language
slipping
like steam
into her silence.
The throat bone
bleached
as the plastic rings binding

a six-pack of beer
making him thirsty.
He felt
the uplift of flight.
Bird bone, where could he go?
And it was blood answered him.

Car Crashes, Shootings, and Ghosts

Minerva Price married a white man named Whitener. Her children were white-skinned, tall like the Cherokee, dark haired and eyed. Her white relatives demeaned her—they casually called her, "that N-r woman"—and yet she ruled the household and her large family, running everybody ragged; an implacable, ferocious matriarch intent upon frugality—using every last bit of the collards, the kale, the sow. Intent upon educating her children in how to live in a world where people are laid waste, lands stolen and wasted, she insisted that they fit in and yet remain apart. This is the disruptive, haunted expression of identity so common to the Carolina mountains.

Left hand vs. right hand. One does heavy lifting, one reaches, turns doorknobs and the other drifts into the air when I talk, keeping time, articulating emphasis, and communicating. Touching your shoulder. In dreams the left is paralyzed, the right can't get those knobs to turn. But the ghosts slip through all ten outspread fingers, as water through cupped palms.

Minerva's descendants, my aunts and cousins, still live outside the Cherokee Reservation in the Smokey Mountains of North Carolina, and the summers I spend there, driving up from foothills, are in a different world: a world of trees so massive two people holding hands couldn't circle them, of curling fiddlehead ferns, magnificent waterfalls, and, nearly every month, a car crash or a murder.

My poetry springs from a way of thinking about the living and dead, from the permeable universe of Minerva Price's stories and gossip that explains *why* and yet never says why. Stories of the Nantahala and of my family. Formally, these poems are inspired by the poems about ghosts in Cole Swensen's collection *Grave's End*, in which each line has a caesura, a gap where breath lives—*that* ghost. I think constantly about the temporality of the dead, their constancy when we mortals prove so inconstant. So many ghosts! In the Blue Ridge of my youth, there was a death every spring—some one from my high school who crashed on an icy mountain road, or, since ours was a dry county, on the way home from a wet county's liquor store. Car crashes, shootings, and Louise, a beautiful woman, killed by a man who was merely a ghost in waiting. Some of these poems are from the killer's perspective and others from hers. Many create a kind of ticker tape of her impressions before—and after—her death.

In Natalie Díaz's *When My Brother Was an Aztec*, her ghost-brother wounds her—she is Christ on the cross—and reaches into her to turn her on like a lamp. The way she is manipulated, used, abused, and sometimes amused, is told with such violent clarity that she is able to wrest a limited authority over uncontrollable life. The formal clarity to her language, and her exceptional facility with traditional poetic forms, gives a place to humor, to the warmth of emotion and of violence, to the injustice of love. She interprets her dreams even as she recounts them, even as the dead return, as they will, to pester the living. To mourn themselves. As her brother does.

Díaz does what I want my poems to do, too. To tell of people and places with the kind of particularity that refuses to say too much, to spell it all out or come to an easy conclusion. A poet, Philip Sidney affirmed, affirms nothing, and so never lies.

In the midst of the American casual, I must resist the urge to raise a curled hand to my mouth to hide the words, to keep a poker face. These poems, instead, speak in caesuras: they hold the breath, and the ghosts that exist between peaks of the mountains that are blue as a bird's wing.

*

When My Brother Was an Aztec
by Natalie Díaz

he lived in our basement and sacrificed my parents
    every morning. It was awful. Unforgivable. But they kept coming
        back for more. They loved him, was all they could say.

It started with him stumbling along *la Avenida de los Muertos*,
    my parents walking behind him like effigies in a procession

he might burn to the ground at any moment. They didn't know

what else to do except be there to pick him up when he died.
    They forgot who was dying, who was already dead. My brother
        quit wearing shirts when a carnival of dirty-breasted women

made him their leader, following him up and down the stairs—
    They were acrobats, moving, twitching like snakes—They fed him
        crushed diamonds and fire. He gobbled the gifts. My parents

begged him to pluck their eyes out. He thought he was
    Huitzilopochtli, a god, half-man half-hummingbird. My parents
        at his feet, wrecked honeysuckles, he lowered his swordlike mouth,

gorged on them, draining color until their eyebrows whitened.
    My brother shattered and quartered them before his basement festivals—
        waved their shaking hearts in his fists,

while flea-ridden dogs ran up and down the steps, licking their asses,
    turning tricks. Neighbors were amazed my parents' hearts kept
        growing back—It said a lot about my parents, or parents' hearts.
My brother flung them into *cenotes*, dropped them from cliffs,
    punched holes into their skulls like useless jars or vases,
        broke them to pieces and fed them to gods ruling

the ratty crotches of street fair whores with pocked faces
    spreading their thighs in flophouses with no electricity. He slept
        in filthy clothes smelling of rotten peaches and matches, fell in love

with sparkling spoonfuls the carnival dog-women fed him. My parents
    lost their appetites for food, for sons. Like all bad kings, my brother
        wore a crown, a green baseball cap turned backwards

with a Mexican flag embroidered on it. When he wore it
    in the front yard, which he treated like his personal *zócalo*,
        all his realm knew he had the power that day, had all the jewels

a king could eat or smoke or shoot. The slave girls came
　　　to the fence and ate out of his hands. He fed them *maíz*
　　　　　through the chain links. My parents watched from the window,

crying over their house turned zoo, their son who was
　　　now a rusted cage. The Aztec held court in a salt cedar grove
　　　　　across the street where peacocks lived. My parents crossed fingers

so he'd never come back, lit *novena* candles
　　　so he would. He always came home with turquoise and jade
　　　　　feathers and stinking of peacock shit. My parents gathered

what he'd left of their bodies, trying to stand without legs,
　　　trying to defend his blows with missing arms, searching for their fingers
　　　　　to pray, to climb out of whatever dark belly my brother, the Aztec,
　　　　　their son, had fed them to.

MARGARET NOODIN
ANISHINAABE

"Only by combining a poet's love of words and a linguist's passion for detail with many hours of Ojibwe conversation did I find my own voice . . ."

Scholar, linguist and poet Margaret Noodin (1965–) is one of the few people writing poetry in both English and Anishinaabemowin—the native language of the Anishinaabe. Her poems might sometimes feel to a reader as though they're coming from another era: they retain the cadences and motifs of oral tales or songs while carrying a quite contemporary expressive intensity. Noodin converges the ancient history and culture of the Anishinaabe with her particular personal or familial actualities. We see both vantages in "Daanisag / Daughters," a poem that also demonstrates her proclivity for portraying the natural world—otters, "pine seeds / and raspberry roots"—and the emotional spaces where human and beyond-human environments intersect, exemplified by the northern lights. Written first in Anishinaabemowin, Noodin then translates her poems into English as a kind of "lyric explanation" of the more complex, more musical original. Reading Noodin's poems in side-by-side bilingual form can be a disorienting but thrilling experience.

Daanisag

Apane gidaanikooshininim
   dibishkoo
nigiig niizhoninjiiniwaad
megwaa agwanjinwaad
enji-agwaamowaad gemaa enji-
   nibaawaad.

Miskweyaabiin gi gii
   maada'oonidimin
mii noongom ezhi-bimaadiziying
bizwaabiigisin miinawaa
   basangwaabiying
agwaabijigeying, boonakanjigeying.

Apii jagazigaade giizhigad
ishkode-bingwinan zhaabosaamang
zhingob-miinan wii mikamang
miinawaa misko-miin-ojiibikan.

Gi ga gikinoo'amawininim
ezhi-noondawangidwa maanidoog
ezhi-biizikamang waasnoode
ezhi-aanzinaagodizoying dibikong
ezhi-dabasendamoying boochigo
   dibishkoo
bezhig
manidoominens giizis agogwaazod
bakaanizid.

Daughters

Our connection is like
otters holding hands
floating together
on the sea and in sleep.

Once shared veins
became a way of life
tangled and blinking
casting nets and anchors.

And when your days burn down
I will sift ashes with you
to find the pine seeds
and raspberry roots.

I will teach you
to hear the spirits shake
to wear the northern lights
to shift shapes in the night
to believe in the beautiful humility
of one
bead sun   sewn
differently.

Nayendamowin Mitigwaaking

Apii dibikong gaashkendamoyaan miinawaa goshkoziyaan
endogwen waa ezhichigewaad bagwaji Anishinaabensag odenang,
mitigwaaking izhaayaan miinawaa anweshimoyaan.

Nimawadishaag zhingwaakwag miinawaa okikaandagoog.
Nimbizindawaag zhashagiwag miinawaa ajiijaakwag.
Niwiiji-ayaawaag zaagaa'iganing ogaawag miinawaa apakweshkwayag.
Nimaamakaadendaanan miikanan miinawaa asabikeshiwasabiig.

Apii biidaaban miidash niswi giiwosewag miinawaa
niizhwaaswi nimiseyag bwaawaabanjigaazowaad
baabimoseyaan nikeyaa naawakweng zoongide'eyaan.

Woodland Liberty

When in the night I am weary and wondering
what the wild young Anishinaabeg of the cities will do,
I go into the woods and rest.

I visit with the white pines and the jack pines.
I listen to the herons and the cranes.
I share the lake waters with the walleye and the cattails.
I marvel at the complexity of wild paths and webs woven.

Then when the dawn hides the three hunters
and seven sisters of the night sky
I walk bravely toward the noonday.

Apenimonodan / Trust

Apenimonodan gikendaman
Trust that you know

aanind bimaadizijig
some people

waa goshko'iwaad
who will surprise you

bamendamowaad akiing
with the way they care for the world

bamenimaawaad asabikeshiinan
and every small spider;

bamenimiwaad ge-giin
the way they care for you

bakiseyan mii gibaakwa'igeyan
as you open and shut

miidash bakiseyan miinawa
then open again.

waasikwa'agwaa ezhi-waaseziwaad
Polish the way they shine.

Nisidawinaadiyeg ojichaagobiishin
Recognize yourselves in shared water.

Like Sedimentary Stone

The poem "On leaving my children John and Jane, in the Atlantic states, and preparing to return to the interior," with its long descriptive name, was transcribed by Henry Rowe Schoolcraft after he insisted that their children Janee (age eleven) and Johnston (nine) attend an Atlantic coast boarding school for wealthy young Americans rather than the Indian Boarding School near their home in the Great Lakes. He wrote in his memoirs, "Mrs. Schoolcraft, having left her children at school, at Philadelphia and Princeton, remained pensive, and wrote the following lines in the Indian tongue, on parting from them, which I thought so just that I made a translation of them."

Like a sedimentary stone the verse contains bits of history and emotion pressed together: the removal of children, the erasure of language and culture through a system of boarding schools, the inevitable stretch of emotion required to survive the process of children growing older. I first encountered the poem when it appeared in Robert Dale Parker's collection of Jane Johnston Schoolcraft's work (*The Sound the Stars Make Rushing Through the Sky: The Writings of Jane Johnston Schoolcraft*, University of Pennsylvania Press, 2007). His volume proved to the world that she wrote eloquently, bilingually, at a time when "Indians" were not yet even allowed to be citizens of the United States. The poem appears with a "translation" of unclear provenance. Is it Henry's iambic interpretation of a language he did not speak? Is it Jane's proof she could write across cultures to draw a distinction between assimilation and acculturation? Both versions echo the pain of separation, but the Ojibwe version has only 18 lines and 24 words while the expansive English elegiac version has 36 lines and 340 words. As a teacher and speaker of Ojibwe I was fascinated by her ability to convey the ache of going home without her children beside her.

I also found the rhythm of repetition compelling and lyrical. She dares to repeat in ways that are discouraged in poetry workshops today. She uses sounds that have no direct meaning. Formally known as discourse markers, "nii'aa" and "iwe" add motion and emphasis without extraneous layers of meaning. Most beautiful of all are the final e's delicately set, just two of them, after the mention of each child, like trailing wails suppressed. These vowels were the reason I eventually re-imagined the poem as a song which is now found on the website Ojibwe.net,* where students of Ojibwe and mothers of children who are faraway can find the solace in her verse, which gives sound and shape to one of life's complex networks.

Jane Johnston Schoolcraft was also known as Baamewaawaagizhigokwe, and as a poet writing in Ojibwe and English she opened up the sky for me. I completed an MFA and honed my sense of poetry sometimes through practice and appreciation, sometimes by finding sharp contrast between what I wanted to write and what the world defined as readable. It seemed somehow not enough to know the mechanical and commercial aspects of poetry so I attempted to trace the structure of Ojibwe through a PhD in linguistics and literature. Only by combining a poet's love of words and a linguist's passion for detail with many hours of Ojibwe conversation did I find my own voice and begin to echo the writing of a woman whose Ojibwe name means "the sound that travels across the bright sky."

*http://ojibwe.net/songs/womens-traditional/nindinendam-thinking/

*

On leaving my children John and Jane, in the Atlantic states, and preparing to return to the interior
by Jane Johnston Schoolcraft, 1839

(original Ojibwe text)

Nyau nin de nain dum
May kow e yaun in
Ain dah nuk ki yaun
Waus sa wa kom eg
Ain dah nuk ki yaun

Ne dau nis ainse e
Ne gwis is ainse e
Ishe nau gun ug wau
Waus sa wa kom eg

She gwau go sha ween
Ba sho waud e we
Nin zhe ka we yea
Ishe ez hau jau yaun

Ain dah nuk ke yaun

 Ain dah nuk ke yaun
Nin zhe ke we yea
Ishe ke way aun e
Nyau ne gush kain dum

(modern Ojibwe)

Ni'aa nindinendam
Mekawiyaanin
Endanakiiyaan
Waasawakamig
Endanakiiyaan

Nindaanisens e
Ningwiwisens e
Ishe naganagwaa
Waasawakamig

Zhigwa gosha wiin
Beshowad iwe
Ninzhikeweyaan
Ezhi-izhaayaan
Endanakiiyaan

Endanakiiyaan
Ninzhikeweyaan
Izhi-giiweyaan
Ni'aa ingashkendaam

(English translation)

Oh I am thinking
I am reminded of
My homeland

Faraway
My homeland

My little daughter
My little son
I leave them behind
Faraway

Now always
It is near
I am alone
As I go to
My homeland

My homeland
I am alone
I am going home
I am sad about it

CHIP LIVINGSTON

Mvskoke (Creek)

"As a young, two-spirit writer, I was desperate to find images of other people like myself, specifically other queer Natives . . ."

The poetry of Chip Livingston (1967–)forays far into the nature of identity. More specifically, he makes a cross-examination of the cultural and societal expectations of maleness, of being Native, and of sexuality. Livingston's poetry roams widely in style and subject, reaching with both traditional and experimental means to touch the human core of two-spirit existence. In "Punta Del Este Pantoum," where the poet relies on parallel structures to accentuate sound and cadence, the result is melodic and incantatory. In "Stadium Mocs," the unifying form is just hinted at, as words and phrases dance across the page, as if coming to life. Suffused with Indigenous culture from ceremonial dance to echoes of oral tradition, Livingston braids familiar and strange.

Stadium Mocs

side   to   side
                    the moccasins slide-shuffle

left then right
                         in the round dance

the toe   and heel
                    of the chicken dance

these mocs   flex and   stretch
         to the   orange   rim
                         of the "don't get me started"
                                        on the hoop dance

my sneak-up shoes are the same as my stadium mocs

I don't hear the ref whistle to stop

                         just the emcee's call for another intertribal

Punta del Este Pantoum

Accept my need and let me call you brother,
Slate blue oyster, wet sand crustacean,
In your hurrying to burrow, wait. Hover.
Parse opening's disaster to creation's

Slate, to another blue-eyed monstrous sand crustacean,
Water-bearer. Hear the ocean behind me,
Pursued, asking to be opened, asking Creation

To heed the tides that uncover you nightly.

Water-bearer, wear the water beside me,
Hide your burying shadow from the shorebirds,
But heed the tides that uncover you nightly.
Gems in sandcastles, stick-written words,

Hidden from the shadows of shorebirds,
Washed over by water. Water's revelatory
Gems, sand, castles, sticks, words —
Assured of erasure, voluntary erosion.

Watched over with warrior resolution,
Crab armor, claws, and nautilus heart,
Assured of a savior, reconstruct your evolution,
Clamor to hear, water scarab, what the tampered heart hears.

A scarab's armor is light enough to fly.
In your hurry to burrow, wait. Hover.
Hear the clamor of the crustacean's heart.
Heed this call of creation. Call me brother.

52 Hawks

driving through muskogee, highway 62
is barbed wire. impossible not to mention
matthew shepard. not to mention orlando.

dusk silenced, we fuck in the vw
to prove something, we're alive at least,
and long enough to drain the car battery.

sleep then wake to a nightstick.
good luck, a cop's jumpstart west

from a dawn mourning too red. the hawk

must be a sign. you miss its flight, miss
the next one. there, i point. but you are reading
on your cell phone. obituaries. another raptor.

then a kind of rapture in the wish i make
aloud: a hawk to land on a fencepost. we begin
to count. one: you read stanley almodovar.

hawk two salutes: amanda alvear.
hawk three: oscar aracena-montero.
the hawks sentinel the road like honor

guards. 49 in six miles. they are something
we sing out names to. rudolfo. antonio.
darryl. angel. juan. luis. 49 hawks

and a morning full as a dance floor.
the 50th, a falcon, we call matthew
and quit our haunting inventory.

i metal the vw toward i-44
to flee the prairie purgatory. two birds on air,
there. you see and name us: not missing.

The Influence of Repetition in Chrystos's "Crazy Grandpa Whispers"

When I was first introduced to the poems of Chrystos, I was not yet writing poetry. I wasn't yet reading much poetry either, outside a few Native authors I was familiar with, but the directness of Chrystos's expression—as well as her language, the music she achieves through repetition and sequence, the way she seems to speak and listen with her whole body, and subject matter that deeply represented my own experiences and feelings—immediately caught my attention. I wanted to dance to her words. I wanted to chant her poems to the four directions. I heard rhythms from old traditions and new ones, put together in the same poems. I paid attention, knowing I had something to learn from this impressive Menominee poet.

Initially I was attracted to the subject matter, content often coming from the point of view of the two spirit-identifying author, and the seamless manner in which Chrystos seemed to blend her cultural and sexual identities. As a young, two-spirit writer, I was desperate to find images of other people like myself, specifically other queer Natives, and I found them in Chrystos's poetry.

Reading her work now for almost twenty years—a period during which I have completed an MFA in poetry, published two collections of my own poetry, and have become a poetry instructor—I return to Chrystos every semester and introduce her poetry and poetics to my current students, beginning each course with a similar question as posed by this anthology. I ask my students to identify a poem that made them want to be poets, and I share with them the poem that did the same for me, Chrystos's "Crazy Grandpa Whispers." I also end each semester with her giveaway poem, "Ceremony for Completing a Poetry Reading," and remind them that both poems can be found in Chrystos's collection *Not Vanishing*, published in 1989. This return to her book at least once a year, and to "Crazy Grandpa Whispers" specifically, has given me time to study and familiarize myself with Chrystos's words, and I now read them as a poet, as a poetry professor, and I see more clearly the elements that drew me—and continue to draw me—to this particular author's work and to this particular poem.

The first thing I notice in "Crazy Grandpa Whispers" is the repetition. The poetic anaphora (which according to the Academy of American Poets "refers to a type of parallelism created when successive phrases or lines begin with the same words") of the first four left-justified lines that open with "tells me:" followed by the delivery of the title's Grandpa's whispers. I receive the four repeating lines as an opening prayer and I appreciate, poetically, the rhythm created by the recursive phrase. That rhythm—compounded by the full-stop, plosive sounds in "take a pick ax to new car row   hack and clear the land"—echoes in my body like a powwow drum and sets up an expectation of pattern in the rest of poem.

The poem departs from its invocation with its first narrative turn, "Crazy grandpa supposed to be dead," where the situation of the poem deepens: the whispers aren't literal; and the almost immediate contrast to the idea, "Not dead I feel him . . . ," adds a complexity to the narrative that delights me as a puzzle solver.

The poem then moves to another type of refrain in its conclusion, return-ing to that pattern of four consecutive expressions, but this time in poetic apos-trophe, speaking directly to the grandfather, in phrases that begin: "Grandpa I hear you ...," "Grandpa if I obey you ...," "Grandpa it's such a fine / fine line," and "Grandpa I'm still learning...." The repetition of these opening and closing recursions, highlighted by the fact that they're spoken responses to the initial received whispers, balances the poem as a form of exchanged dialog.

There's also a fifth use of the repetition, giving intermediary attention to the anaphoric phrases—"tells me" and "Grandpa"—in the compounded sequence of "Grandpa tells me" that comes between the two voices in dialog and in al-most the middle of the poem (line 13 of twenty-four lines). I also appreciate that the poem isn't perfectly balanced, that the concluding recursions are marked by graduated indentions, suggesting pauses that distinguish the coming end-stop, softer steps toward the final beat. Again I'm reminded of a powwow song, a southern drum.

Those are the initial poetic elements I point out presenting the poem to my students, but I also share how the content personally resonates, how Chrystos relays an experience I identify with. "Crazy Grandpa Whispers" shows a speak-er caught between older and newer value systems, a speaker learning to listen "through the walls of (her) skin," but knowing that obeying those whispered di-rectives will likely get her locked up "again."

I grew up very close to my Creek grandfather, who is also now gone from this world, and his words are what influenced me most as a kid and what still carry me through current days. When I face a perplexing situation—as universal and recent, for example, as the last U.S. presidential election—I seek and listen, "imaginatively" perhaps, for what my PawPaw would advise. And like Chrystos writes in her poem, I hear my own grandfather counseling me "through the walls of my skin."

And like the speaker in Chrystos's poem, my own received advice and in-stincts are often contrary to the expected norms of polite or civilized behavior. I identify with that struggle of honoring the petitions and traditions of my an-cestors while, at the same time, attempting success or at least survival in a world of cell phone apps and mortgage payments. "Crazy Grandpa Whispers" reminds me, tells me, to put down my cell phone and make sure my neighbor also has enough food to eat.

Listening is an essential component of transferring information and experi-ence from one generation to the next for those of us descending from oral cultures, and "Crazy Grandpa Whispers" asks the reader to listen. Implied in the title, a whisper requires active listening for reception, or the softly spoken words will be missed. It also implies attention, not just hearing and harvesting words, but also sensing with your skin, noticing which direction the wind is coming from. I'm fascinated by the contrast of "whispering" such violent, law-breaking commands, and the poem's speaker's navigation of the world "without getting caught."

And while this particular poem doesn't present a specific gay and lesbian experience that much of Chrystos's, and my own, writing confronts, I still find the voice of that other "other" in this poem of resilience and resistance. I think "Crazy Grandpa Whispers" illustrates the queer perspective of nearly all of us from or living in the colonized continent of North America. To walk through life for many in the United States today is to tiptoe between contrasting and conflicting worlds; it's an ongoing negotiation between our "instincts & their sanity laws." "Crazy Grandpa Whispers" tells me I'm not alone in my confusion, and that's something I have always held as a goal to show in my own writing. I hope to also convey that sense of inclusion, relationship, and finding community to others. "Crazy Grandpa Whispers" tells me to listen with my whole body, and Chrystos reminds me how important it is that I also speak.

*

Crazy Grandpa Whispers
by Chrystos

tells me: take a pick ax to new car row   hack & clear the land
          plant Hopi corn down to the sea
tells me: break open that zoo buffalo corral
          chase them snorting through the streets
tells me: put up tipis in every vacant lot
          shelter the poor without rent
tells me: steal those dogs the pound suffocates
          cook them for Lakota stew
          feed the hungry without words
Crazy grandpa supposed to be dead   They locked him up
He withered   Not dead I feel him shrivel against my backbone
          when I see anybody behind bars

Grandpa tells me: take back these cities
       live as your ancestors   Sew up the mouths of the enemy
       with their damn beads
Grandpa I hear you through the walls of my skin
Grandpa if I obey you they'll lock me up again
         like they did you
           Grandpa it's such a fine

fine line
      between my instincts & their sanity laws
      I've no time to sew moccasins
         Grandpa I'm still learning how to walk in this world
          without getting caught

ESTHER G. BELIN
DINÉ

"The practice of poem making is the study of creating space."

A journey with the poetry of Esther G. Belin (1968–) is a jazzy, careening trip through textures, sounds, and storytelling, an adventure led by a guide who's sure-footed but not averse to risks. Pairing identity politics with Navajo philosophy ("Ruby and Me #1"), Belin writes with an artist's eye for detail, a musician's ear, and an activist's passion, and she writes writes bracingly about urban experience, as in "Blues-ing on the Brown Vibe." Sometimes sparse, other times crowding the page, Belin's poems take many forms: a receptive reader will enjoy the panoply of lists, columns, blank spaces, and typography that won't sit still, for example "_____ Child(ren) Left Behind" and "Public Record 1831," meant to challenge standard English and demonstrate for readers the new ways of writing about day-to-day Native experience.

This Is What I Mean

inspired by a poem of the same title by Simon Ortiz

As full as the clouds over Inscription House
As much as they seem dispersed and scattered — floating above the radio waves
　　of KUYI
The warm smile of smooth highway roads — beloved, glistening, glittering
　　glossy
The wideness of our memory
A permeating diaspora seeps into the cavernous English letters
Then the Flattening, of uniform accordance
The hollow curves of letters
The concave Vessel
With voices filling the bottom half of my alphabet
With voices holding the Indian-speak deep and wide in vast pockets
With voices stuttering fractured Diné bizaad
With voices carrying surgically removed pollen, exposed lacerations checker-
　　boarding the Land
With cell phone voices piercing Dzilth-na-o-dilth-hle, a new treaty language
　　bleeds out
With inaudible voices, a fracked up earth, Babylon-inspired diacritics inflame
The new Indian-speak is deconsecrated, an oil-slicked water hole — smooth
　　and smoothly and soothing
A never near peaceable stillness
Again, the ink in letters are replenished
Again, a darker pigment, a deeper deprivation, depletion

And this is what I mean
I mean
What I mean is — when I first read about _____
Reading about _____ placed me on the map
And this may not sound like a big deal but this is what I mean —
That I didn't talk much until I started to write
Until Saint Louis Bearheart showed me how to reverse the institutional dialysis
Until Saint Louis Bearheart showed me how to unlock the file cabinet of the

BIA superintendent

Exposing the praying Indians, bended knees and clasped fingers — this is what
  I mean

That my writing is like the praying Indians on bended knee, petitioning a savior to

Relocate me back to the inkwell that holds the letters, my alphabet cleaving to
  the page

Being absorbed into the orchestra of the flooding dark ink

Writing this theatre piece of myself as a linguistic formula

Urban + Indian = the lost sheep, with no clear markings

Only a slaughter, exposed neck, blood drained, the recorder hums between the
  drips, the hum

Recorded as breathing, the collected sounds catalogued and shelved

As full as the clouds over Inscription House

As much as they seem dispersed and scattered — floating above the radio waves
  of KUYI

The warm smile of smooth highway roads — beloved, glistening, glittering, glossy

The wideness of our memory

A breathing diaspora — a collection of ancestral winds — the form reforming

In uniform accordance — no longer a flattening surface

No hollow curves, no fallen syllables

Today, I stop conversing, start converting

Into the fullness of clouds

The inscriptions on my house

_____ Child(ren) Left Behind

Complete the following sentence then support your answer with evidence:

_____ saw Chief Joseph today while looking at _____.
*While crawling into the oxygen deprived space. I only had a second to look. I only
had time to . . .*

_____

_____

Here is my list:

1. The white hen.
2. Walking forward (*Soli Deo Gloria*).
3. The war we are playing is called _____.
4. The Issei woman, a trickster holding blossoms of broken English.
5. You say, "Tell me." I repeat the Declaration of Independence.
6. The barely visible target reveals/revels/wrestles with printed text.
7. My beach stretches a thousand miles and I can see the mating whales.
8. Chief _____ was laughing in between the photo shoot;
   he was sitting atop a horse.
9. That damn smile led to that amazing kiss . . .

Create a line graph, then breathe air into the blow-up person you create:

Sunset Beach	battlefield	white buffalo
199_	river	New Year's Eve
Crow Fair	dentalium shells	red chile
Oklahoma	Indian cornAbiqui	
beans and frybread196_	green curry	

Public Record 1831

1. Chief Justice John Marshall created our mythic image: "domestic dependent nations."
2. The basic principle of modern federal Indian Policy: small insertions of the "Doctrine of Discovery" serum, prescribed during each new fiscal year. Side effects from long term use: Genocide.
3. Indian Health Service: "How long has your Indian blood been killing you?"
4. The secretary took his words. They are now Public Record:
   the Eager wait to read and write in solaced tunnels, under covers, on the side of bridges
   the Hungry are eager to swallow, fluid, solid, both at the same time

they swallow
swill down
small packages like
a lover's tongue like
a stirring pot
like a long time after
death has occurred
the record
records

recordings like
stained linen parchment
a compilation in longhand
the rhythmic pulse of limbs
the nestling of the unborn
the tidal pull, saturating the tender lining
between
the scratchy turning of
histories

the mechanical swagger like
the latest trading post novel
post-
indian
postage
like a forever stamp
Aszdáán Tłogi nishłí
I am and I lick the corners
of the I am I am today
stuffed neatly into a medical bill
oh
we are out of _____ again
again
the prescribed medication
the pharmacist asks for my signature
as public record
again

Ruby and Me #1

middle child
smart child
$\frac{1}{4}$ Navajo

                $\frac{1}{4}$ Navajo

                                $\frac{1}{4}$ Navajo

                                              $\frac{1}{4}$ Navajo

four parts equal my whole
#311,990

enrolled = proof
50
80
100 if you can stand
it

veiled
minority status
alcohol
resemblance

Blues-ing on the Brown Vibe

I.
And Coyote struts down East 14th
feeling good
looking good
feeling the brown
melting into the brown that loiters
rapping with the brown in front of the Native American Health Center
talking that talk
of relocation from tribal nation
of recent immigration to the place some call the United States
home to many dislocated funky brown

ironic immigration

more accurate tribal nation to tribal nation

and Coyote sprinkles corn pollen in the four directions
to thank the tribal people
            indigenous to what some call the state of California
            the city of Oakland
for allowing use of their land.

II.
And Coyote travels by Greyhound from Albuquerque, New Mexico, USA thru
Dinétah
to Oakland, California, USA
laughing
Interstate 40 is cluttered with RVs from as far away as Maine
traveling and traveling
to perpetuate the myth
Coyote kicks back for most of the ride
amused by the constant herd of tourists
amazed by the mythic Indian they create

at a pit stop in Winslow
Coyote trades a worn beaded cigarette lighter for roasted corn
from a middle-aged Navajo woman squatting
in front of a store

and Coyote squats alongside the woman
talking that talk
of bordertown blues
of reservation discrimination

blues-ing on the brown vibe
a bilagáana snaps a photo
the Navajo woman stands
holding out her hand

requesting some of her soul back
instead
she replaces her soul with a worn picture of George Washington on a dollar bill

and Coyote starts on another ear of corn
climbing onto the Greyhound
the woman
still squatting
waiting
tired of learning not to want
waits there for the return of all her pieces.

III.
And Coyote wanders
right into a Ponca sitting at the Fruitvale Bart station
next to the Ponca is a Seminole
Coyote struts up to the two
"Where ya'all from?"

the Ponca replies
"Oooklahooma"
pause
the Seminole silent watches a rush of people climb in and out of the train
headed for Fremont
the Seminole stretches his arms up and back stiff from the wooden benches
pause
he pushes his lips out toward the Ponca slowly gesturing that he too is from
    Oklahoma
Coyote wanders
"where 'bouts?"
the Ponca replies
"Ponnca City"
pause
the Seminole replies
"Seminoole"

Coyote gestures to the Ponca
"You Ponca?"
the Ponca nods his head in affirmation
Coyote nods his head in content
to the Seminole
Coyote asks
"You Seminole?"
pause
the Seminole now watching some kids eating frozen fruit bars
nods his head

and Coyote shares his smokes with the two
and ten minutes later
they travel together on the Richmond train
headed for Wednesday night dinner at the Intertribal Friendship House.

IV.
And Coyote blues-ing on the urban brown funk vibe
wanders
in and out of existence
tasting the brown
rusty at times
worn bitter from relocation.

POEM MAKING AS MAKING SPACE

The practice of poem making is the study of creating space. Meaning (content). Placement (order). Aesthetic (Diné nishłį). What I mean is—the motion of making space— rearranges the sequential ebb and flow, ever so gradually creating beauty, before, behind, below, above.

One such poem with the ability to manifest beauty is "That American Flag" by Luci Tapahonso. The Diné poet masterfully weaves space; she enlarges it; she holds it with the balance of language order; she tenderly folds it creating intimate conversations told in corners of rooms.

Her poem addresses a controversial topic using a Diné rhetoric. I admire her method which creates a space for all audiences; inclusive. She challenges categories. Rather than dismiss and continue to divide with language, she engages her audience. She demonstrates the power of a cultural synthesis from a Diné origin. I appreciate her ability to craft space as large and massive, very close and deliberate, or sustaining—a kind of Diné esoterica with English language as a vehicle.

My favorite moments of the poem are in the second stanza: "But later that night, I wanted to call her and explain / about the American flag and us Navajos. / Let me tell you, I wanted to say . . ." The entire stanza weaves story: a placement that considers the nature of the universe, "five-fingered" beings, time, creation, growth, motion and order. The story is continuous, motioning a diaspora, creation; the visible is the action between humans and place; the method is language, sonical abstraction. There lies an incredible acknowledgement of Creator and creation which is central to Diné philosophy—the macro and micro constructs that humans craft to make sense of their world. I love how she then crafts awareness: "there's just something about me and the flag" and later positions that statement with: "we Navajos have many reasons not to honor the American flag, / but often it reminds us of our grandparents' enduring courage." Tapahonso fastens an esoterica to iconography. And it works because that fastening is a truly Diné cultural synthesis. In the case of the "ubiquitous" flag, a simple response could not suffice. The flag did not just suddenly appear in a department store; the flag is a place holder of memory. From recent memory. From historical memory, collective memory. A living memory exists between tribal peoples and the "ubiquitous" flag. Whether the appropriate non-response or inaction makes sense to the audience becomes an aside. And I love how Tapahonso suspends space for the reader; giving space for inaction allows a multifaceted response – so intimate and hidden.

The phrase: *I wanted to say . . .* is so potent for me since I frequently non-respond from that position. I love that position—for people who normally do not have access to power, that position is empowering, meditative, renewing. From a context of power, that non-response is where one exists (can truly exist). And this is where the conversation about audience becomes more apparent. As an indigenous being, why would I put forth more and energy to a system that lacks the ability or intention of listening—contribution, dialogue? How can such a person/people respond when a centuries-old construct acts as a created narrative suffocating a response? This is where much of the (re)vision(ing) occurs—the person, the poet, the persona, the politic, polemic, pedantic, prodigal. (En)vision, (in)vasion, (En)glish version verging -ing -ing -ing . . .

Tapahonso and other Diné writers make space for me; they change the depth and shape of my water, moisture, thirst; they tether the tangle of my wind as part of the main stalk rooted in hózho. Ahéhee' shikéí dóó shidine'é.

*

That American Flag
by Luci Tapahonso

"I wouldn't buy anything with the flag on it," my friend said
as I showed her a cute straw handbag at Mervyn's one summer night.
It had a small beaded flag in the corner.
"There's just something about me and the flag," she said. I didn't respond.
Yes, the American flag is ubiquitous these days,
and we had done our share of marches, protests, and sit-ins in the 1970s.

But later that night, I wanted to call her and explain
about the American flag and us Navajos.
Let me tell you, I wanted to say, that in the mid-1800s
that flag meant fear and untold turmoil.
Let me tell you, there was little we understood about those
who followed the American flag onto our land That thin rectangle of fabric
rippled in the dry gusts of wind as the troops approached Dinétah.
Though the men were five-fingered like us, their words
seemed loud and careless, and their mannerisms, dramatic.
Still, we watched for signs of compassion,
as these soldiers had been born of a mother somewhere.
Their mothers had been delighted to hear their first words,
just as some of these men must have talked to their firstborn soothingly.
Perhaps as they walked on Diné Bikéyah, they longed for their families.
These men walked upright, feet moving on the earth's surface, as we do.
From childhood they had grown upward toward the sun as the Diné do.
They breathed the air granted all of us by the Holy Ones.
They were like us in these ways, but their hearts were unyielding.
They were faithful to orders from afar.

They were faithful to voices they had not heard themselves.
They were bound by written orders and armed with deadly gear.
They were loyal to their flag of freedom.

The government had decreed that the Diné be moved to Fort Sumner
so that we could become Americans. We traveled hundreds of miles
to the south. The winters were cold;
our blankets became worn and frayed.
Though we were given jackets, wraps, and clothing,
the sick worsened, the elderly passed on, and often babies died at birth.
At times the children played as children do anywhere;
other times they were listless from hunger and fear.
The men remained resilient: they talked late into the night
and sang quietly so as not to disturb the soldiers. They prayed
for the strength and insight to lead our people home.

The women set up looms, though they were immersed in grief. "We have to
weave as we always have," they said.
"By weaving, we can make it through these waves of sorrow."
"Someday we'll go home," they said.
"We have to weave through this hunger, through the pain,
through the deaths that surround us. We have to keep up
our strength," they said. "We have to weave
to remember our land, our relatives, and our animals."

They unraveled the blue military jackets and red undergarments
and wound them into balls of crinkled wool.
They found bits of wool and cotton and sometimes sheep wool.
The military clothes became thin red and blue stripes in the rugs.
The stripes were laced, line by line—each weft tapped into place
by the weaving comb—its venerable echo a comfort in itself.
Sometimes they wove in strands of hair, feathers, bits of plants,
and knots of corn pollen to ensure strength and abundance.
These were offerings to the desolate land around them.
The rugs were prayers, with red, blue, black, and white stripes.

The rugs' white horizontal bands were for the early morning sky
and signaled new beginnings.
The background of the American flag is white,
as is our sacred mountain in the east.
Thus, the women knew we would survive.

The red stripes were for the dirt at home, the sandstone cliffs,
and for the sumac that turns brilliant red each fall.
The red stripes in the flag are for our blood and for our ancestors,
who tried to search for the good in everyone and everything.

By weaving blue into rugs, the women recalled the hooghans
they built when the men were gone. They recalled the graceful ease
with which their teenage sons chopped wood, built corrals,
and rode horses. In doing so, the women were reminded
of their own strength. The blue in the flag is for the promise
of each spring granted us since Fort Sumner. The blue stripes
honor the men and their strength, tenderness, and intellect.

Often, the women wove stars in the rug—its center is for our home,
Nihimá, the land that was given to us. We are told that
a specific star watches over us, this star knows everything.
The stars were prayers for the children, who held the future —
the ones who became our parents and grandparents.
The flag's stars signaled our eventual return to Diné Bikéyah.

When the clouds gather and darken over Dinétah,
the air becomes sweet with wet dirt, glistening sage, and creosote.
The black bands are like a woman's hair pulled back in a tsiiyééł,
which ensures clear thinking, guidance, and a wealth of songs and stories.

Sometimes the women wove crosses: a point
for each direction and each of the sacred mountains.
The four points signal the hope that the changing light of each day brings.

Late that summer night, I wanted to tell my friend that
we Navajos have many reasons not to honor the American flag,

but it often reminds us of our grandparents' enduring courage.
In the face of terrible odds, the stars and stripes came to mean
that we would return to our homeland. It taught us that our mother,
Nahasdzáán, cares for us as we care for ourselves and our children.

Let me tell you about the American flag and us Diné, my friend.
Let my grandparents: Shímásání dóó Shícheíí dóó Shinálike;
let them tell you about the American flag.

DG NANOUK OKPIK
INUPIAQ-INUIT

"The words are not my own: they are the ashes of all languages derived from all knowledge or intelligence."

The vivid vocabulary of dg nanouk okpik (1968–) flows into poems that speak in multiplicity, working with a surrealistic geography in the dimension of mytho-poeisis. Celebrated for her ecological compositional process, okpik draws on traditional Inupiaq and Inuit story. She can locate the landscape of her Alaskan upbringing in the political upheaval of the climate crisis, as seen in "Fossil Fuel Embers Haibun" and "Glacial Oil World." In language and forms that challenge the expected, okpik reaches into the past to bring forth artifacts as proof of the present. Her images are precise and her syntax razor sharp, while in tone and diction okpik's poems can resemble a natural oracle, chanting softly the words that map contemporary arctic indigeneity on ancient traditions.

Frightening Acid Flakes Haibun

If stars could bend
white-blue, copper, brass,
and sterling moonshine then,
caribou prancing onto moss floors;
wouldn't be at all encompassing.
Snowflakes fall and land in the cold
face of a monster, a split flamed-tongued-
beast, from the frigid, notched depths,
living on village ledges keep the people
in unsafe. They find peace in the fire,
lava-orange-red to the face of a Kaktovik
umiliak, Eddie Rexford.

> Feathers, fins and fur
> Frozen tundra bare night sky
> Here gone lies double deep

Fossil Fuel Embers Haibun

At Red Dog Mine boys and girls
(displaced) as trade dogs: *sit girl sit!*
for the Yankee Sailors slaves,
as large gul-guled wooden ships
started by taking coal. Black lungs
shiny in dead crawls. Each death,
I cut a notch on the driftwood
log, in my home; where I burn
because it makes embers.

> way in and one way out
> blackwood cooked slow over done
> skies whale gray-blue

Glacial Oil World

A gray-black storm lays low, above the sea.
A 78 mile per hour wind chill shatters any
water into icebergs, as I drown in my own element.
Rustling waves rolling me back to this massive
breakup outside and in. It glides past me blue-green,
blue-turquoise collisions of pinnacles and pressure
points which pinch. Volcano ash and radiation and
chemo ruins the physical. Old frozen cliffs, hoarfrost
lungs, clefts of monastic bergs adrift. I cough, cough,
up bowels of human limits of sanity, sounds of gale
winds rifting the clapboard house I call home, as my
lungs carry my brain; carries my heart, and innards,
hands and feet; I hand palm the distance of sky and light.

> Cut Yukon salmon
> In my eyes, the river flows
> The scent of burnt birch

Man and the Little People

The little people interacting
with man brought the east wind
dominating foul, uncertain
patterns of finbacks, through
seas of driftwood timbers, for
ribs of earth mounds slide
sea cliffs, whales quaver in
vexation of puzzle, through
koan dynamics, hex meddling
of heat/thaw.

mud and gravel no
land mass only mercury
earth's axis teeters

"The Owl": Thoughts on Word Choice

Arthur Sze's "The Owl," written in 1972, has specific verbs, tight multi-meanings,
compacted language, and knowledge of traditional and contemporary poetics.
One might say I refer to the use of strong verb choices in "perched" "stirred"
"quaver" and adverb use. I show two versions the poem inspired me to write. The
first two stanzas are Arthur Sze's, while the last two-and-one half lines are mine
by inspiration of his. "The Owl" helped me see my own self. The mirror effect of
change occurs naturally, as an awakening, from the interior to the exterior mind
of the poet, reader, the "I," in chromatics the light changes from purple to green,
in reflection of the climax to seeing each other, the owl, the poet, the owl, the
poet, the "I," and myself.

The Owl
by Arthur Sze

The path was purple in the dusk.
I saw an owl, perched,
on a branch.

And when the owl stirred, a fine dust
fell from its wings. I was
silent then. And felt

the owl quaver. And at dawn, waking,
the path was green in the
May light.

Perched: meaning roost, any place or object as a sill,
branch, or twig
for a bird animal or person
To alight or rest/settle upon
High or elevated position
A post up for a navigational aid (a tree)
Navigational Hazard

Stirred: meaning to set   to move briskly
tremulous   bestir
    the sound made by fluttering   stir oneself
      stirring   to rouse from quiet

contentment
moving slightly   indifference
irregular motion   to bring up/ to notice
to affect strongly   a mental impulse
excite   a sensation
instigate   a feeling
agitate   a jog or poke
dissolve   busy
to disturb
to rouse
    quickening impulse

Quaver: tremulous   shake
to sicken   quake
    peculiar   waver

Quavering: anxiously   apprehensively
  nervously   despondently
  despairingly   dismally
  dreadfully   agedly
  eager   weakly
  stammeringly
  quiver

My two versions:

The Owl

Sunlight in May,
the green path,
I'm waking at dawn.

I saw an owl quaver,
and felt silent,
from a fall of fine dust,

as the wings stirred.
Perched on a branch,
an owl saw me,
in the purple dusk
was the path.

The Owl

Sunlight in May
the green path —
I'm waking, at dawn.

I saw an owl quaver,
and felt silent,
from the fall of fine dust

as its wings stirred.
Perched on a branch quiet,
an owl saw me, in the purple dusk,
was the path.

SAMMIE BORDEAUX-SEEGER
SICANGU LAKOTA

"It is only an elder, a wise person, that the true meaning of the story will impact in the form of an epiphany."

Sammie Bordeaux-Seeger (1968–) stitches together the judiciously chosen ingredients of her poetry as carefully as she sews individual pieces of fabric into the star quilts she also creates. Working within a tradition that is ceremonial as well as pedagogical, she has joined with other artists and teachers to uncover a past that forever changed the Lakota people. Natalie Díaz has praised the ways Bordeaux-Seeger can "obliterate the structure of an American calendar or timeline." In "Blue Water," "No Water," and "1900" she explores reservation life and politics with stories that move forward and backward, breaking the narrative open and creating gaps where a quietly emotional vulnerability can reside. As Díaz has written, time in this poet's work is "a complicated knot of what has happened and what might happen, of tradition and modernity, of memorial and future, of our ancestors and our own lives. . . . A reader will not be able to come to these poems for a fast and healing dose of historical facts or nostalgia (yes, often America's griefs and outrages over its crimes against humanity can feel nostalgic)—instead, these poems require readers to face their own lives, memories, gestures, and ultimately their complicities."

Blue Water

That morning, men left for food.
women gathered the wash, found the blue water,
dipped pots in the stream, boiled dried papa.
Children came home with prairie chicken eggs.
Soup spilled on horse-trampled grass
when men returned with meat
found blood where blood should not be.

When we read about Blue Water,
there is always someone
named Little Thunder in my classroom.
The Spotted Tails, Iron Shells, Little Elks —
their names on my class roster,
on the treaty we are decoding,
make this story they never heard
bitter tasting.

In the early September memory of people
whose grandchildren sit in front of me,
this story is the one most never heard.

Why do we not hear this story before
we're twenty-one
in a college classroom
reading a book
that tells us about us?

Spotted Tail took the sword and fought back
then turned himself in, spent years in Fort Leavenworth
Today we have a brother or a cousin
still serving time for that act.
The butterfly effect of disarmament
put us here.
A classroom full of their descendants,
still descending.

No Water

Men in neon vests excavate outside the student center.
Campus emails flow across the screen,
always the same subject: No Water?

Re: No Water
No Water the name of the man who shot Crazy Horse.
Somehow this seems prophetic, a hundred and some years later,
as the campus dries out and restrooms are closed
and classes continue.

My students discuss No Water's jealous heart
and fickle women wearing elk-toothed armor
and what constitutes peace
when warrior hearts beat out of sync,
take an hour break, search for relief from
no water.

Standing Rock is still on our lips, drying out,
when oil bubbles up from marshfields across the state.
No one believed this would not happen.

No Water the sour faced assassin,
almost ended a nation. Could end a nation. could spell
the end of all nations.
All nations,
all related,
all spelled:
No Water.

Broken pipes, No Water, no water.

Men in neon vests have so much to answer for,
here where there is No Water and no water
and only oil to drink.

November

When that farmer told my people to eat grass
I could see my grandfather's eyes burn, then tear.
Not my grandmother. Her eyes were stones.
Aske Tiospaye, they say, is known for vengeful people.

Some of the people here on the Rosebud came from Santee,
following the forced march southwest from Mankato.

After the uprising, when they were exiled from their land,
still seeking food, my grandmother was separated
from her two-year old daughter, so she walked back,
across the flat golden fields to Mankato, and found her.
Who knows where a toddler might have hidden, among people
who didn't want trouble?

They pointed fingers at their own relations
let them take the blame, force marched away.

Today their grandchildren live in mansions, fed with another
kind of green from the white men. They do not recognize
their relatives who were sent away, who scattered from Santee
to Rosebud, Pine Ridge, Lower Brule.

We are Lower Sioux, outcasts.

My grandmother, 112, in the rocking chair in Aunt Barb's living room,
all us children gathered at her feet in front of the black and white TV,
she sits there behind us. Her eyes, stones, still walking
those cold miles south in November, alone with her mother,
still thinking about meals made out of grass.

1900

Great grandma as a little girl holds the quilt in which she is buried.
They had only had fabric for dresses and quilts a few years at that point,
only ten years past the 'Knee.
Little girls knew then any wildness could be punished with bullets,
the way we knew fear of spanking or The Big Owl,
who would come and take us in our sleep
to the top of the water tower, shove us off.
Grandma warned us every night before bed,
The Big Owl is going to come and take your bottles.
And five year old me would come home from Headstart,
make a double batch of chocolate milk for my little brother
in the cheap plastic bottles. Screw on the tops,
put ourselves down for a nap.
In 1900 there was only the breast, the milk,
the dead mother the child slipped next to for suckle.
That sigh.

Finding Resonance in Roberta Hill's "Star Quilt"

I was in my early twenties when I discovered the poem "Star Quilt" by Roberta Hill Whiteman (who now uses the name Roberta Hill). I read the poem in a class at Sinte Gleska University, where my instructor Beth Windsor brought the poem to the class to read. I admit I had no understanding of the poem in those days, was dazzled by the title and the image of a star quilt, an image that was embedded in my childhood and early adulthood as a member of the Lakota Oyate, known for their finely crafted star quilts used in giveaways, for the births of babies, the deaths of family members, the honoring of veterans. I was learning to make star quilts at the time I first read the poem.

After reading the collection *Star Quilt*, I discovered that Roberta had taught briefly at Sinte Gleska University (then Sinte Gleska College), where I received my bachelor's degree and where I now teach. Like Simon Ortiz, who also briefly taught at Sinte Gleska, she brought the land and weather at Rosebud to bear upon her poems. The book is filled with references to the landscape in which I grew up. I recognized those views in her poems. I knew those names. I knew the spirituality of those poems. They resonated across the decades from her pen to my imagination, and I knew that was what I wanted to do with my writing.

Years later in another class, presented with the same poem, it was pointed out that the protagonist in the poem had scratches and bruises, that the quilt covered abuse. The poem was blown wide open for me then, I saw it in a new way. My poems don't do that, I thought to myself. My poems are lacking any kind of subterfuge or subtlety. My poems just state what they want to say, blatantly and crudely, I sounded my barbaric yawp without anything like the grace of Whiteman (or Whitman). "Star Quilt" changed my poem worldview.

It sometimes feels as if I'm always writing to this poem because I've studied it for so many years. I keep coming back to it as if it were a homeland. The three-line stanzas are something I've tried in my poems. I've tried to take colors and make them mean something the way the "purple, yellow, red" in the poem suggest fading bruises on top of older bruises. I've attempted to introduce sensory metaphor the way that "candle locks / us in forest smells" brings that sensory experience to the poem. I don't know that I've succeeded in any of these attempts, but I attempted that kind of resonance of words and images and of saying something that was worth coming back to again and again.

The feeling I get from this poem is a memory from my childhood, the long winters when you were trapped in the house with the cold floors and the sound of wind on the outside walls, the power gone out, the candles burning up the darkness. I grew up in the 1970s, when Roberta was living on the Rosebud and teaching at Sinte Gleska and writing this poem.

Do we always return to our childhood in our poems, or is this something only people damaged in childhood might do? Do others understand the poem the way I understand it? How does the time period in the poem reach into my being and pull me back to that time? Is my understanding of this poem also damaged by my own memory? Am I too heavy for this poem? How do I create this kind of poem experience for people who might read my poems? And most importantly, who is my audience? Who am I writing these poems for? Is it for my own people, the way that I feel that Simon Ortiz's book *After and Before the Lightning* and Roberta's book *Star Quilt* were written for and about the Sicangu Lakota at Rosebud? And if it's for my own people, how does that audience change what I might write?

I ask all of these questions every time I read this poem, but answering these questions continues to involve me in the act of discovering what creates resonance; how can I bring that same sense of familiarity and relationship? I feel she was writing to me. That this poem was meant for my soul to understand, and yet my soul is still processing the understanding of this poem.

Years ago I took a class titled "Lakota Oral Literature." The instructor, Ron Goodman, told us that the Lakota have four essential understandings of a story. In the first understanding, when told to the very young, the story is an entertainment, something that might make them laugh. Hearing the same story as an adolescent, a listener might understand that the story is an allegory, a lesson to be learned. As an adult hearing the story, the meaning might have a more practical application to a larger world problem. It is only as an elder, a wise person, that the true meaning of the story will impact in the form of an epiphany.

This seems to me like our understanding of a poem. At first it is appreciated for its beauty, the lovely lines and the sound. Later, reading it again, it starts to suggest other things, perhaps the political intent or the underlying meaning of the words. A third listen to the same poem might bring some practical ideas about poetics, audience, the knowledge of the poet. Reading it again, a fourth time: epiphany.

Roberta's poem does this. It has that first dazzling image of the Lakota star quilt, a cacophony of color and aesthetics and comfort. Reading further you begin to understand the violence in the poem, the contrast between soft and hard in life. In the third meaning, I see practical applications that could be used for working with survivors or abuse. I have yet to reach the epiphanous moment with this poem, but I remain certain it awaits me. This is how I read poetry. This is how I slowly begin to understand the language of poetics. This is how I attempt the writing of poems.

*

Star Quilt

by Roberta Hill

These are notes to lightning in my bedroom.
A star forged from linen thread and patches.
purple, yellow, red like diamond suckers, children

of the star gleam on sweaty nights. The quilt unfolds
against sheets, moving, warm clouds of Chinook.
It covers my cuts, my red birch clusters under pine.

Under it your mouth begins a legend,
and wide as the plain, I hope Wisconsin marshes
promise your caress. The candle locks

us in forest smells, your cheek tattered
by shadow. Sweetened by winds, my mothlike heart
flies nightly among geraniums.

We know of land that looks lonely,
but isn't, of beef with hides of velveteen,
of sorrow, an eddy in blood.

Star quilt, sewn from dawn light by fingers
of flint, take away those touches
meant for noisier skins,

anoint us with grass and twilight air,
so we may embrace, two bitter roots
pushing back into the dust.

MOLLY MCGLENNEN
ANISHINAABE

"Poetry is connection; it's what allows us to travel to other people, to say hello, to honor."

Among the many modes of poetry in this anthology, none has a greater emotional directness than the writing of Molly McGlennen (1971–). Her poems are intimate without being overly confessional, domestic without being tame, and accessible without giving too much away. McGlennen frequently finds sources in Ojibwe traditions, including stories and recipes. Many of the poems in her first book, *Fried Fish and Flour Biscuits*, celebrate the ways food and family bring people together, as in "Living the Language." That notion of language's vital and continuing role in connecting generations is also at work in "Legend" and "Three Poems for Ellia"—the latter poem taking shape as three miniature letters to the poet's daughter. McGlennen has written of a "creative spirit that nourishes us all," and indeed her poems are wonderfully satisfying examples of poetry as sustenance.

Three Poems for Ellia

GRACE

For four days I snort and buckle in an East Oakland apartment. During nights of toil, I swim alongside myself. Four walls burn sage. I hang the medicine bundle he gave me. You are a small crescent moon turning on your head. We approach winter solstice together. A time to hear stories. I will tell you how you got your name. That December long ago, starving, they returned home with nothing they were promised. Unwavering. She teaches me this. The mis-handled allotment fees. Official rolls complete with her absence. That easily, we're erased. These tiny signatures we call names. Finally, you come — slick black hair, my relief — inscribing us with your long descent. Daughter, push these little words along. You, like her, determine our worth.

*

ALBUM

This poem is a box of photos. Names are photos refracted. Your hands spell our recipes. Biscuits flood morning kitchens and grandchildren's mouths. But what's in these names we've been given? What do they hold? We borrow and hate the dust that collects on bleeding tongues. What's better is smell: Blueberry pancakes. My baby-daughter's neck as she sleeps. What's better is memory: Her first kick like a cluster of ants inside my stomach. A smoothed crimson ribbon to hang. Arcs of light deviate from their path in pairs. Tear open these words. This poem is gratitude.

*

IN KEEPING

I keep lists of things for her. Lists become a mother's diary. Lilacs. Alleyways. Boulevards. Cherry blossoms. St. Francis Assisi statue. Overgrown rhubarb. Tangled tomato vines.

Lists become backyard ironies: Cutoff-shorts. Drop-lines and dug-up worms. Rusty hooks. The farmer's rock pile. Inner tubes on windy days bobbing in the lake. Raking seaweed. Picking carrots and beets for our cousins. Salting radishes.

Lists punctuate satire: Nuclear family visits Mount Rushmore. Grandmother goes to daily mass. Aluminum canoe. A Minneapolis duplex. 4th of July BBQ.

Lists mock memories: First basketball high-tops. Using a plant for a Christmas tree. Packing an old van. Leg-singeing vinyl seats. Catholic charities. Car crashes.

We will start new lists: Your days and nights mixed-up. Neighborhood fistfights. Oakland eucalyptus. A grandfather's song. Sunlight climbs into your cradle for the first time.

Each is your story.

Living the Language

She tells us the Ojibwe word for blueberry pie
is the recipe to make it:
miiniibashkimiinasigunbatagiingwesijiiganbiitooingwesijiiganibakwezhigan

as we pick the delicate fruit from each calyx
indigo bulb hanging from a perfect five-pointed star
a gift to relieve our hunger —
selecting each one, each star-berry staining our fingers purple-red.
We can't help but pop some in our mouths.

She had said the juice could cure a cough
and the leaves could be tea — would be good for our blood.
In the summers they'd dry them and store for long winters.

We trod through marshy ground searching for the next lowbush
can taste the pie already, baking slowly in her stove
can see her careful thumbs creating the wave that edges the crust
sliding the fork through the top in four directions
holes for breath

as we punch ours out now — blueberry hunting.
We are this language of progression, this recipe
renewed each time our pails are filled and
our fingers drip hard blood in gratitude at the end of days.

Legend

My body remembers
the time we rolled out dough
for two days.
Flour hands
salted heat
a kitchen like fire.
Careful not to pat it
too thin,
biscuits should fill
empty stomachs
you tell me.
No more school
after fourth grade —
what's a little girl to do
but listen
and follow the mark
of a hand,
hear a history
punctuated by story,
when your mother
would whisper hers
in between scaling
and gutting
the walleye,
ashamed to admit
how lakes
had always fed her family

how she had married
a pale Frenchman
moved away from the water.
So you
a daughter once removed
now stands next to me —
says history doesn't have to mean
coming over in a boat,
says this is how
you feed a family:
until your hands and arms ache
until your body remembers
the blood in its lines
like fried fish
and flour biscuits.

Preface to *Fried Fish and Flour Biscuits*

Our lives are made up of recipes. Poetry is a way to preserve and translate those recipes, those stories that we hear in bits and pieces and we never stop telling. Poems are what nourish us.

The best recipes are the ones we know by heart, the ones we fight to remember because when we follow them, we are drawing together many different elements from our life.

Lives-made-of-recipes. For me poetry is a way to process, to remember those stories I heard growing up and I continue to hear. Some stories I still haven't heard completely or never will. Still, they are there. Maybe, as Janice Gould says, they lie beneath our hearts. Or maybe, those guidelines-for-living are always out in front of us, placed there by our ancestors.

The voice in my poetry is many people and things at once. And because of this, poetry is best served aloud. One of my favorite things is to read poems to people. To see their faces. In those moments, I can give the poems away.

Voices from an array of people have lived in the poems even before they were written down. They are there, shaping the design of the poem and encoding their messages.

Though I'm sure this has been said before, these words are not mine alone. I do not think I'd have the courage to write poems if it weren't for family members (particularly a legacy of women) and a great many poets who have informed my creativity. Writers like Luci Tapahonso, Kimberly Blaeser, Elizabeth Woody, Diane Glancy, Simon Ortiz, Deborah Miranda, Gordon Henry, Chrystos, Gerald Vizenor, Joy Harjo, and Wendy Rose have articulated in one way or another that poetry is a form of community-building, a means to locate oneself in relationship to a network of people and places and memories.

This is why so many of my poems are dedicated to or written for other people. Poetry is connection; it's what allows us to travel to other people, to say hello, to honor. And, by those networks of connection, we find our paths of continuance . . . through urban streets and northern lakes, loneliness and companionship, through failure and balance, toward a creative spirit that nourishes us all.

M. L. SMOKER

Assiniboine–Sioux

"We are the places we inhabit."

M. L. Smoker (1975–) writes poetry to bear witness. Her themes weave personal struggle and identity with Native history. In a strong, natural voice and conversational manner, Smoker's poems peek into and beneath the quotidian concerns of family relations, aging, and enduring traditions. Her poems are coated in a sense of the familiar, easily relatable, while engaging in the inevitable, the everyday, and the sometimes comical. Smoker contemplates the limits of language, and she looks to Montana's writerly landscape (see "Letter to Richard Hugo") for answers to questions that range beyond reservation borders, finding symbols within contemporary culture and grounding in ritual. In "Mercy," for example, the way sentences and lines interact creates moments of sharp lyricism in a text that builds with both prose and verse. Aware of its materials and of the surroundings that generated it, Smoker's art provides another layer of geography for Big Sky Country, compelling her readers to take a long, good look in all directions.

The Feed

Several of my cousins lean up against the house, taking long drags
from the pack of Marlboros we share. We have always been this way
— addicted and generous. A pow wow tape plays from inside the open
garage where two old uncles are thinking to themselves in the safety
of its shadows. Our aunties are in the kitchen, preparing the boiled meat
and chokecherry soup and laughing about old jokes they still hang onto
because these things are a matter of survival. Outside, we ask about
who was driving around with who last night, where so-and-so got beat
up, whose girlfriend left him for someone else. (But she'll go back to
him, we all think to ourselves.) Aunties carry the full pots and pans to the
picnic table, an uncle prays over our food in Assiniboine. We all want to
forget that we don't understand this language, we spend lots of time
trying to forget in different ways. No one notices that the wild turnips
are still simmering in a pot on the stove.

Another Attempt at a Rescue

And to think I had just paid a cousin twenty dollars to shovel the walk.
He and two of his buddies, still smelling of an all-nighter,
arrived at 7 am to begin their work.
When I left them a while later I noticed their ungloved hands
and winter made me feel selfish and unsure.
This ground seems unsure of itself
                         for its own reasons.
Real spring is still distant
and no one is trying to make themselves believe
this might last, this last unreasonable half hour.
It is six-thirty in eastern Montana and the cold
         has finally given way.
The time is important not because this has been a long winter
or for the fact that it is my first here

since childhood, but because there is so much else
to be unsure of.
                     At a time like this
how is it that when I left only a week ago
there were three feet of snow on the ground,
and now there are none, not even a single patch
holding on in the shadow of the fence-line.
               We do not gauge enough of our lives
          by changes in temperature.
When I first began to write poems I was laying claim to battle.
It began with a death and I have tried to say it was unjust,
not because of the actual dying but because of what
was left. What time of year was that?
I have still not yet learned to write of war.
I have friends who speak out--as is necessary--with subtle
and unsubtle force. But I am from
this place and a great deal has been going wrong
                    for some time now.
The two young Indian boys who might have drowned
last night in the fast-rising creek near school
are casualties enough for me.
               There have been too many
just like them and I have no way to fix these things.
A friend from Boston wrote something to me last week
about not have the intelligence
to take as subject for his poems
anything other than his own life.
For a while now I have sensed this in my own mood:
this poem was never supposed to mention
itself, other writers, or me.
               But I will not regret the boys who made it home,
or the cousins who used the money at the bar.
Still, something is being lost here and there are no lights
on this street; enough mud remains on our feet
to carry with us into the house

Letter to Richard Hugo

1.

   Dick: The reservoir on my end of the state is great
for fishing. Some of the banks are tall and jagged, others
are more patient, taking their time as they slope into
rocky beaches. If you were the kind of fisherman I
imagine, then you might have considered it a great place
to cast from. My family has gone up there ever since the
water on the Mni Shoshe was dammed off. My
grandparents put on their moccasins and beadwork and
danced for FDR when he rode the train out to see the
finishing touches of this great industrial project. I haven't
yet decided if this is something I wish to be proud of.
Maybe this summer I'll spend more time up there, on the
edge of a lake that was never meant to be a lake, and form
an actual opinion. Maybe too I'll write you again. But
you have probably already figured as much. I almost
thought of not returning to finish the writing program
you began with your own severe desire for language. But I
did. And now I'm at the end. Already though, I'll admit
to you, I'm thinking of home. I have been this whole
time.

2.

   Dick: Once, in one of the small creeks that runs
from Fort Peck Lake I saw a catfish, swimming upstream,
trying to make it back to the shelter of a larger body of
water. It was late summer and there wasn't enough of the
creek to cover the top half of his fins. Still, he pushed
down into the mud and kept on. I did not envy him.
Nor did I devise some plan to help him make it back to
safety. I'll let you draw your own conclusions about what
type of person this makes me. And since we're on this
track: I have a sister I haven't spoken to in years. And
the language my relatives spoke while getting ready for

the dam's inaugural ceremonies is close to extinction, but
I have always made up something more important to do,
rather than take the risk of saving it. I am still angry at
times with my father because I long for the type of
mother mine could never have been. I go on mourning
her, even though a medicine person has told me it was
time to let her go to the other side. I wonder if she is
still close, or if years ago she ignored me and went on. I
certainly didn't know that today—when I'm a week away
from packing up, leaving Missoula for good, and making
my way east for home—I would sit here in the purplish
light of the first real snowfall of the year and write to
you. I could go on, tell you about my poetry, about how
much it's meant to spend time with Ripley, about the
influence Jim has been. (Thank you for telling him to
write what he knew. That allowed me to write what I
know, twenty-five years later, from another rez a little
farther down the road.) I'll just close by saying the
salmon are plentiful, even if they begin their lives in a
hatchery down below the dam. For the time being, I
don't mind this as much, and I have an idea you
wouldn't either. There's just something about the
remissable wave of a cast which feels like the biggest
commitment of all.

Mercy

And you begged and begged and begged — of the lifeless bottle,
of trees in winter, of the murmur of the small creek just beyond
the bedroom window. Please suspend this boned-in-misery,
bottomless, no room to even breathe. So the cacophony will pass
overhead and perhaps the grip of angst and sorrow can be let loose.

Drowning in loss is nothing compared to standing on its shore.
Purposeless. No one answers the stagnant call. It is late

and all your friends are gone. You wave wildly to the expanse of sky
asking for some small sign to — to what? You appear mad.
Yet, you know she is out there, looking on in wonderment at this tiny soul,
so catastrophic. Please. Understand what forgiveness means.
But the shadow voice is a mere vibration amongst the trees' thin leaves.

Stumbling along in disarray, yet from almost all appearances,
ordinary. And after a while, no one asks. Yet you remember, in some distant
  way: looking on, stranded as the water crests farther and farther from dry land.
Walking out on the bedrock, feet unsteady in the murky pool until
ankle deep, you can only sob there as the current breaks open and

an answer comes. Not that you recognize it at the time. Strange
memory, no longer a once vacant gift. You can feel the cool,
unnamable depth. No voice from the heavens or the water's lapping pulse,
just the impression of a gleaming, new heartbeat.
And the vast expanse of uncertainty is no longer something to fear,
but a careful vestige to be gathered up and guarded
late in the night of your protective arms.

HUGO

We all know that Richard Hugo fell in love with Montana—our waterways, our
barmaids, our dusty towns. His legacy remains one of a man who lived hard,
wrote even harder. And when he came to Montana in the early 1960s, he most
certainly changed a part of our state's cultural values forever. The '60s and '70s
were a very unique time, culturally and demographically speaking in Montana.
The state was still incredibly rural and remote as a landscape but also so far as
the collective mindset of a majority of the inhabitants. Montanans were con-
servative in nature, they were loyal to their families, their churches, their favor-
ite hunting spots, and their local basketball teams. Farming and ranching were
king. As Hugo entered MT and began traveling isolated gravel roads, exploring
our beautiful waterways, almost certainly he noticed all of these things. But as
he drove on and stopped at community after community, as he watched and
wrote—towns began dying out as more and more young people attended college

and made the decision to leave the family farm for other opportunities. Too, industries shut down, riverways became polluted and landscape was scarred. The state's first inhabitants, our twelve tribal nations, began their own journey of self determination, expanding sovereignty through better tribal government infrastructures, young Native families began returning home from big cities across the US after relocation efforts stalled and failed in large part. It was an incredible time to be an observer, a watcher, a detailer. And Hugo was *right* there, not only writing his own work, but influencing the poems about Montana during this era, including the writing of my literary hero James Welch, then also, continuing on over years and valleys, influencing me—an Assiniboine woman born in north-eastern Montana, traveling to the University of Montana as a graduate student as the Richard Hugo Fellow. Richard Hugo truly changed the cultural values of Montana forever.

What the Western world calls inanimate objects (stones, mountain ranges, streams), Hugo knew, as all tribal peoples do, that they are alive with a spirit that must be coaxed, respected, humored. And there are no irrelevant details when looking out across a vacant town that holds the contextual memory of the generations that have lived, loved, fought, fished, drank and dreamed there. Hugo could find himself, could recognize humanity in the bend of a river or the rust of an abandoned train track. We *are* the places we inhabit. Richard Hugo was a poet of the Pacific Northwest, yet his renown attests to a stature greater than that of most "regional" poets. He is noted for the tight, rhythmic control of his language and lines and for the sharp sense of place evoked in his poems. Hugo's images are urgent and compelling; he imbues the many minute or seemingly irrelevant details found in his poems with a subtle significance, thereby creating a tension between the particular and the universal. This tension is considered central to Hugo's most powerful poems.

In his poems Hugo reflected as much upon the internal region of the individual as on the external region of the natural world, and he considered these two deeply interconnected. According to Frederick Garber, "the landscape where things happen to Hugo goes as far into his mind as it goes outside of it"; Hugo's poetry "is about the meeting of these landscapes." The role of the past as a shaping force on the individual predominates. While "failed towns, isolated people and communities imprisoned in walls of boredom and rage," as Michael Allen notes, are often the subjects of Hugo's poems, there is also a pervading sense of optimism, of an uplifting hope, as Hugo puts it, "that humanity will always survive civilization."

I was trying to think of some sophisticated way to talk about Hugo's impact on me, but it is probably best said most simply: what he has meant to my writing is profound, but what is an even deeper and enduring connection is in his influence over the ways I interact and involve myself with the landscape of Montana. I might view and contemplate a graffiti-covered train moving across a mountain range in the winter, in the way I drive through a rural, tight-knit community and imagine the impacts of a mill being closed down. What we all now call Montana has been a geography in my blood, part of my DNA as an Assiniboine woman. But because of Hugo, I am more careful. I am more contemplative. We should never overlook what's right out our back doors, what's beyond the windshield. We all matter, we all have stories that are important—and through poetry and other forms of creative writing, I believe we are learning in MT that we have much more in common, more that connects us, than we could have ever imagined without it.

*

Degrees of Gray in Philipsburg
by Richard Hugo

You might come here Sunday on a whim.
Say your life broke down. The last good kiss
you had was years ago. You walk these streets
laid out by the insane, past hotels
that didn't last, bars that did, the tortured try
of local drivers to accelerate their lives.
Only churches are kept up. The jail
turned 70 this year. The only prisoner
is always in, not knowing what he's done.

The principal supporting business now
is rage. Hatred of the various grays
the mountain sends, hatred of the mill,
The Silver Bill repeal, the best liked girls
who leave each year for Butte. One good
restaurant and bars can't wipe the boredom out.
The 1907 boom, eight going silver mines,

a dance floor built on springs —
all memory resolves itself in gaze,
in panoramic green you know the cattle eat
or two stacks high above the town,
two dead kilns, the huge mill in collapse
for fifty years that won't fall finally down.

Isn't this your life? That ancient kiss
still burning out your eyes? Isn't this defeat
so accurate, the church bell simply seems
a pure announcement: ring and no one comes?
Don't empty houses ring? Are magnesium
and scorn sufficient to support a town,
not just Philipsburg, but towns
of towering blondes, good jazz and booze
the world will never let you have
until the town you came from dies inside?

Say no to yourself. The old man, twenty
when the jail was built, still laughs
although his lips collapse. Someday soon,
he says, I'll go to sleep and not wake up.
You tell him no. You're talking to yourself.
The car that brought you here still runs.
The money you buy lunch with,
no matter where it's mined, is silver
and the girl who serves your food
is slender and her red hair lights the wall.

SHERWIN BITSUI
Diné

"As a Diné, poetry was one way for me to speak to my experience—I was compelled to write into the silence that permeated every aspect of the relationship I had with these seemingly divergent worlds."

The poems of Sherwin Bitsui (1975–) are lyrical marvels. His work is dense and musical but also elliptical and philosophical. Bitsui's poems interrogate the ways that American/Western worldviews are at odds with *indigenous* perspectives, revealing how Western modes of living and behaving can seem very segmented, in contrast with Navajo practices. He is particularly interested in how the language we speak determines how we think and perceive. His work is often a series of questions that explore how and why experiences are different in Navajo than in English—and at times, English and its poetic tradition appear to be more like an enemy than a mode of connection. Bitsui's work seeks wholeness but often calls attention to disjunction and dislocation. His poems spring from the Dinetah landscape and language but also the legacies of Surrealism, as in the untitled poem "[stepping through the drum's vibration]." Surrealism's facility with juxtaposition enables Bitsui to make quick associative leaps that effect jarring distinctions between worldviews. However, woven into the harshness is a layered beauty that reveals this poet's deep love of language. Bitsui is a great poet of sounds, of breath. His lush images and smart line breaks make reading his poems an immersive experience.

Atlas

Tonight I draw raven's wing inside a circle
    measured a half second
        before it expands into a hand.
    I wrap its worn grip over our feet
        as we thrash against pine needles inside the earthen pot.

He sings an elegy for handcuffs,
    whispers its moment of silence
at the crunch of rush-hour traffic,
and speaks the dialect of a forklift,
    lifting like cedar smoke over the mesas
        acred to the furthest block.

Two headlights flare from blue dusk
    — the eyes of ravens peer at
Coyote biting his tail in the forklift,
    shaped like another reservation —
        another cancelled check.

One finger pointed at him,
that one — dishwasher,
he dies like this
    with emergency lights blinking through the creases of his ribbon shirt.

A light buzzed loud and snapped above the kitchen sink.
I didn't notice the sting of the warning:
    Coyote scattering headlights instead of stars;
howling dogs silenced by the thought of the moon;
constellations rattling from the atmosphere of the quivering gourd.

How many Indians have stepped onto train tracks,
    hearing the hoofbeats of horses
    in the bend above the river
        rushing at them like a cluster of veins

scrawled into words on the unmade bed?

In the cave on the backside of a lie
    soldiers eye the birth of a new atlas,

one more mile, they say,
                        one more mile.

Apparition

I.
I haven't _____
since smoke dried to salt in the lakebed,
    since crude oil dripped from his parting slogan,
        the milk's sky behind it,
            birds chirping from its wig.

Strange, how they burrowed into the side of this rock.
    Strange . . . to think,
                they "belonged"
and stepped through the flowering of a future apparent in the rearview mirror,
visible from its orbit
    around a cluster of knives in the galaxy closest to the argument.

Perhaps it was September
that did this to him,
    his hostility struck the match on handblown glass,
not him,
    he had nothing to do with their pulse,
when rocks swarmed over
    and blew as leaves along the knife's edge
into summer,
    without even a harvest between their lies
        they ignited a fire —
            it reached sunlight in a matter of seconds.

2.

It is quite possible
      it was the other guy
            clammed inside my fist
who torched the phone book
and watched blood seep from the light socket.

Two days into leaving,
      the river's outer frond flushes worms imagined in the fire
onto the embankment of rust,
      mud deep when imagination became an asterisk in the mind.

In this hue —
      earth swept to the center of the eye,
            pulses outward from the last acre
held to the match's blue flame.

Mention _____,
      and a thickening lump in the ozone layer
      will appear as a house with its lights turned off—
            radio waves tangled like antlers inside its oven,
because *somewhere*
      in the hallway nearest thirst,
            the water coursing through our clans
         begins to evaporate
            as it slides down our backseats—
      its wilderness boiled out of our bodies.

Drought

I.

More drought, says the old woman digging roots from the arroyo bottom as the
sun becomes a spiral trail marked on a sandstone cliff that is now
a memory to the Maya.

A gathering of birds decides paths and rearranges footsteps, forming the
scribble of branches
and electric wires emerging from a cloud of red dust.

Where am I when I follow the satellite east?
Does the sun know that a rock soaks in a bowl of rice somewhere on the other
side of my palm? Does the sky recognize its feet when it is covered with light
bulbs
instead of the eggs of red ants?

A child climbs the blue ladder that has just appeared in his dream;
his mother then wraps a clock with a white sheet and listens to its slowing
pulse.

Two moths shake their fist at a young boy who unplugged his father's reading
lamp,
a newspaper then makes the sound of autumn,
    a silver horse snorts—
the dark windows remind him of his master's eyes,

the shadows of crushed grapes.

2.

I place a jar of teeth in the sun
so we can watch leaves grow;
after all, isn't calcium the color of our books
when we think of a cat purring over a bowl of milk?

A pale-lipped thespian slows his breath, crosses his eyes,

and finds a melted coin in a bowl of rice.

Will the person in the car approaching at high speed
slow down long enough to see that the coin was made in 1979?

A dog in the approaching pick-up truck licks his paws,
     fleas bite into our umbrellas,
and we find lightning bolts held between lovers who share the same clan
in two paint strokes on unstretched canvas.

Cinder blocks throb under our feet when we swallow fishhooks.

A church empties, eels are discovered swimming underneath the floorboards.
     Train engines stutter to a stop.
A priest sleeps on a coat hanger
     and dreams of feathered feet wrapped in stirrups
     floating through the eye of a needle.

3.
The noose in my dream becomes a deer and shakes dust from its eyelids,
it wants to cry for rain,
but we are keeping the rain in Styrofoam boxes at the bus station.

The grandmother was out there shaking a stick at the coal miners.
     That night she cried black tears
     and wove her hair into the feathers of a visiting night owl.

Juniper roots surface in the dishwater.

When one dreams of a mouth covered in white chalk,
speaking only in English,
it is a voice that wants to be cut free from a country whose veins swim with axes
and scissors.

4.
Tonight
the beginning   ends.

I singe the nerves of a camera lens smooth
because it captures rain
    that does not enter from the east.

I dream of lizards and bulls and watch a silver moth penetrate the window screen.

How do we remove our thumbprints from fences,
    when axes are left to grow under the sun in a bucket of water?
When the corn roaster goes to town grinding his teeth,
    and his wife discovers a miniature railroad curling in and around her
    pelvis?
Will he then run his fingers down the length of his gun,
    imagining a cosmonaut brushing his teeth in zero gravity?

5.
Each day
    the city grows an inch taller,
the children in her streets draw stares from planes dipping into low altitude.
    Do the pilots see the buttons their teachers have sewn onto their ears?

Listen, the gravediggers unfold the earth's bandages
and remove vacuum cleaners filled with killed pottery and broken arrowheads.

A cyclone curls around my fist when I approach city limits.
A boat is released from land,
covered with snails licking rust and salt.

We anchor our cars to a bundle of prayer feathers.
A train slides underneath the parasol of a woman beading her skin cells to
curved asphalt,
    sensing that we have finally listened
and are now strolling our televisions out the front door,
past the recently divorced mailman
and into the supermarket,
    saying we want our teeth back;
our fingers smell of wet ash.

6.
I turn away.
I must not look at the sweat beads of the snorting horse
or I will dream of being a wingless bird
lapping at the reflection of clouds in a rain puddle
left in the summer sun,
     shaking my beak at the mercury rising in the thermometer.

A child swallows water and does not wake.
Mother then rubs a book over his moist back.

Read this,
understand their language,
or sleep in a bottle of broken nails for the rest of your life.

The night sinks from my eyes;
mud men wash the earth from their knees;
a gate key is lifted from the gatekeeper,
who then pulls the doormat
from the drought's gravitational pull.

We descend into our basements,
searching the dark fro the wet noses of our mothers and fathers,
but we find pencils and postage stamps instead—
no paper, no address book.
So we begin sifting through the ash of burnt hooves in a field of rust,
    but find only broken glass,
        coat hangers,
           and the shoes of a dying priest.

[Stepping through the drum's vibration,]

Stepping through the drum's vibration,
I hear gasoline
       trickle alongside the fenced-in panorama
of the reed we climb in from
and slide my hands into shoes of ocean water.

I step onto the gravel path of swans paved across lake scent,
wrap this blank page around the exclamation point slammed between us.

The storm lying outside its fetal shell
folds back its antelope ears
and hears its heart pounding through powdery earth
underneath dancers flecking dust from their ankles to thunder into rain.

from "The Motion of Poetic Landscape: An Interview with Sherwin Bitsui"
by Bianca Viñas

from Hunger Mountain

Navajo is thought in motion, a very verb driven language. Everything is tactile; everything is about moving within the world or having the world move within you. [The Navajo] also have this ability within the language, its philosophy and worldview, to make the metaphorical very real . . . to make it literal in a way. Perhaps because we live in a ritualized, ceremonial space, our culture exists in an inner relationship with all things. A lot of the houses face east, because the eastern doorway welcomes the rising sun. I think we live in a dimension of place and time that is also spiritually linked, a kind of mapping/topography that belongs to the people.

    We have a word, *Nizhóní*, which describes something beautiful or balanced . . . the philosophy that everything must return to *Nizhóní*; everything must return to this balance.

When you are out of balance, ceremony and ritual language balance the forces, harmonizing it. And that is the other kind of poetic I have access to, an ancient poetry that comes from the soil, comes from this land. This is brought to a kind of quality that resonates with language, somehow becoming the voice of the land. Language is another kind of landscape, an extension that goes away like the mist or the air that you breathe. Colonial language feels very segmenting, in a way, like it has a different function living within that function, an architecture of these places and these thoughts that enter organic, traditional spaces. For example, traditionally, [the Navajo] live in one space. There was never a sense of "do I need a room of my own, a segmented living space?" Once this thought [of segmentation] entered into our traditional tribal spaces, a kind of segmenting happened [and an evolution of relationship to space]. The Navajo word for "north" is *náhookǫs*. As a child we knew it as the Big Dipper, the North Star, Polaris, but when you read it three times, it enacts a motion . . . a turning of the skies, like a clock. That is what I want my poems to do. I want them to be engines that turn something.

CEDAR SIGO
SUQUAMISH

"Not all poetry is meant to be slowed down into writing, some forces need to keep traveling."

The writings of Cedar Sigo (1978–) are a deep delving in poetic aesthetics. He uses personae to focus his poems through the eyes of others or uses first-person narration to dramatize a lively self. Influenced by the caprices of Surrealism and the gregariousness of the New York School and the Beats, Sigo's poems are fast-moving and sometimes fragmentary ("The Studio"), laced with contralinear combinations ("First Love"). Often his associative momentum prevails over plain discursive "meaning." Fascinated by identity, love, place, and the American poetic canon, Sigo's work lopes across the emotional and psychic plains, brandishing vocal gestures that are barbed, candid, and bent on propelling themselves with a brilliance that may well leave a reader breathless.

First Love

for Kevin Opstedal

I've never lived in New York
but I died there once while
visiting. Those empty river bed, organ
      blues (whose chords I never knew)

if the poems are dated surely
she is charting a breakthrough, "large
      black butterflies like birds" and "the
sun is a star" a form of trust plus

reintroduction to the act, dead heat
and playing it off, killing time
      in Isle de Mujeres . . . of quickly
drawn and dispelled passage, the shadow

of the board behind the door
      I signed once as Miss Crane,
once as Miss Valdez, jerked awake
the Atlantic Ocean had died and
           folded headlong — disappeared

The Material Field

And here
I thought polishing
knives alone
in the dark
was enough

a man that is a stone
holding open a thick

lined book,
       Samurais
blown back
on their horses
forever

the one eye
pops
a single auburn
strand is found
and the fiddles weep
as dreamers often do

drop them down
one hundred stories
into pits of fire
for rumors of
love-making
and printing
their own queer book

pickling
end papers

       the inscription in
Love Poems,
cursive blurred
by bloody tissue

       highly sought after
house fires
puddled bronze
queerish, episodic
       locked in over
a rainy weekend
instances of exposure
that amounted to dreams

        I subjected dementia
To my forthright
willingness

        locked hands
showing out
to the spirit, still
on moving sidewalks

        can you
get back
in?

        I've already been
sucked back
exiled to empty halls
        where several
solid
signs emerge

        the phantom flings me
all around the ballroom
just beyond
and with longing
        we ride away
the stars pull out

        I'm almost
in your
arms

The Studio

Coyotes on a torn paper hilltop howling at the sun, a blaring red stamp

A circular pond with animals feeding in droves around it, brown, pink, yellow
cheetah, bare trees full of lime colored birds

A wooden ladder that swings down off its hinge

A huge room without bolts or nails, full of ghosts of friends (makers of poems)

Turquoise and black at battle in square shapes and ends of blades interlocked
off-screen

Reams of paper in boxes (perfect, blank) next to ladders leading out the roof

Rodin's sink crusted over with plaster, dry wrinkled hands resting on threshold

Seafoam green door, withered markings, golden deadbolt, depression glass tomb

Spilled green wine teased into gargoyle, his eyes are seething, his ears are burning

Return to Graffiti Land

for Lydia Sigo, 11-28-17

Some people call me a poet, others say I'm an activist. Some say my poetry and music is political, others say it's about the spirit of my people. I don't buy into any of those labels. I may be a little bit of all those things, but I'm more than any of them. We all are, that's what makes us human.

It is a bit unnerving to write in appreciation of John Trudell as his uncanny eloquence and emotional availability still feel unparalleled. For this reason, I thought it best to leave a lot of his words (in italics) surrounding mine. Discussing his work is somewhat like trying to describe the writings of a Zen meditation master. Why not just read the actual writings again and refocus upon your path?

Somewhere in there, as the evolution continues on, we are being historically placed in a position where we have to do something or we are the enemy of our future. Because apathy makes us the enemy of our descendants. That's reality and we can't blame the predator because we have minds and we have the ability to use those minds.

When you are inside of Trudell's words, each one seems to be given equal weight. This is true of both his lineated poetry as well as his lyrics set to music. Sometimes in his interviews his incisive answers have the feel of amulets, a rock worn down to a perfect bead. The body can form and carry poetry in a million ways if the impulse is kept active, restless. The sources of poetry become impossible to name as they spread to inform every other venture, editing, publishing, lecturing, teaching. The more I continue to travel around the country the more I am convinced that the germ of writing should never be allowed to crystalize. I think of a man sending the first radio waves over the Pacific Ocean or some other equally fragile action. Who can guarantee that the body of the poem will remain intact?

Sometimes they have to kill us. They have to kill us, because they can't break our spirit. We choose the right to be who we are. We know the difference between the reality of freedom and the illusion of freedom. There is a way to live with the earth and a way not to live with the earth. We choose the way of earth.

The question of craft is interesting to place over Trudell's work as it has never been addressed apart from the content of his poetry. So, the "best" of Trudell's poems become those that compel the reader to act. We are invited into enacting the aspirations of his words, and in a final (circular) step, the forms themselves are offered as strategies for change. Performing poetry live often feels like an attempt to explore the surface of the poem in actual time. To uncover the patterns that occur between words, these tend to build up night upon night. This is as close as I can reasonably come to a description of Trudell's uncanny flow and his charisma too, certainly—his instant registration upon our senses, why we want to listen . . .

Universally the Earth was regarded as the mother—historically speaking another idea appeared and the other idea said that God was number one and God was a male and God was removed from the earth—god was somewhere else and this is when all the predatory energy began and its evolution has been continuing since then. Once the dominant energy became a god removed from the earth then it became ok to attack and exploit the earth. As that attack began, fear became one of its main, main instruments.

Trudell's wife Tina Manning, her mother Leah, and their four children were killed in a suspicious house fire on February 12, 1979. The fire occurred hours after Trudell had burned an American flag in Washington, D.C. In order to truly engage with his life/work we must confront the presence of evil. Trudell himself offers the useful term "predator energy." How do you kill someone and leave their body living? In the past, this question had been answered by Josef Stalin with prolonged banishment of poets like Osip Mandelstam to Siberia, or the persecution of Marina Tsvetaeva that would only end with her suicide. In Trudell's case, it is a poet that emerges out from the darkness to walk between worlds. He has said he was given his first poetry, his "hanging on lines," only after the death of his family.

> *Welcome to graffiti land*
> *All the rides are in your head*
> *The ticket is what is thought*
> *And what is said*

In the Trudell poem I have selected, he speaks of the poet in solitude and of the several dimensions commonly available to that condition. In a sense, the poet is always alone, slightly out of time or then ahead of the game. Poetry becomes the perfect disguise for indestructability. I used to stress myself out over forgotten lines of poetry, racking my brain for hours later, and often in vain. I have since learned to let these lines wash over me. Not all poetry is meant to be slowed down into writing, some forces need to keep traveling. The mind and the heart shoot faster than language, faster than a poet waving from a train window.

*

Rant and Roll
by John Trudell

Welcome to grafitti land
All the rides are in your head
The ticket is what is thought
And what is said
Our attitudes are climbing
We don't have time for more mind wasting lies
Whatever it is you're doing we're not going to buy it
It's time to say something not a time to be quiet
Rant and roll heartspeak from the spirit
Say it loud so everyone can hear it
Say what you mean mean what you say
Rant and roll when you feel that way
Religions of men heavy with fear
Industrial war against the land
Every woman knows the fugitive
Rich men keep living off the poor
The soul is what's left after they eat your spirit
when every act is an act of self-defense
we have to do something or perish in the pretense
In this together and on our own
A reality of how we feel

Either we can dance with someone
Or we can dance alone
A plurality of sight and view
We and us are me and you
Predator views are way too tragic
Mother earth gives us power
Father sky makes us magic
Life doesn't have to be bitter
Even when it's not always sweet
Synchronicity is the rendezvous
When magic and power meet
Rant and roll heartspeak from the spirit
Say it loud so everyone can hear it
Say what you mean mean what you say
Rant and roll when you feel that way

JULIAN TALAMANTEZ BROLASKI

MESCALERO AND LIPAN APACHE, LATIN@, EUROPEAN

"I write in horse, but I see in athapaskan."

One of the most interesting and experimentally brilliant Indigenous poets, Julian Talamantez Brolaski (1978—) defies virtually all modes of description. A two-spirit and transgender poet and musician of mixed Mescalero and Lipan Apache, Latin@, and European heritages, Brolaski resists traditional gender classification. Brolaski identifies as "third gender," uses the pronoun "it," and has invented an ingenious system of gender neutral pronouns and possessives. Similarly, Brokaski's poems also elude easy classification. In "as the owl augurs," a poem for Brolaski's grandmother, the poet leaves out letters, uses backslashes, uses long, meandering lines next to short ones, and embraces a somewhat stream of consciousness aesthetic. Often Brolaski's poems invoke the urban energy of Bay Area poets like Jack Spicer and Robert Duncan, but they can just as often confront Indigenous issues as in "I had already shuttered an aspect of my vision." Skeptical of conventional syntax, grammar, and punctuation, Brolaski uses the poem as way of altering perspectives about the language that defines and confines us.

as the owl augurs
for Inés Talamantez

I have an hour to read marcabru and fall in love
to study the medicines and put a rock in each corner of the house
and pray over it with pollen as my elder advised
to test my unextraordinary knowledgeses
to briefly wonder whether I was actually under a spell
to write my poem about being a mongrel
I must love even the fox that impedes my path
n jettison my former ire n any gesture toward abstraction
n go to the dump finally w/ the disused bicycle tires and the broken antlers and
the cracked stained glass of a ship that formerly I wdve harbored because I did
not love myself
but the broken shelf
I want namore of it
the jangle-mongrel and the rose and the ndn cowboy that layall closeted
along w/ my availablility to my own mind and the killings of our familyes queer
and black and brown and ndn
slaughter at orlando symbol of our hermitude
massacre at aravaipa 'ashdla a cho o aa big sycamore standing there
bear river sand creek tulsa rosewood
n when I finally sussed them out
n laid the tequila in its proper trash
n attempted to corral the pony of my mind
they say the ohlone were here as if
there were no more ohlone
erected a fake shellmound called it shellmound avenue
my friends dont like that
my friends dont like that excrement
it's not like youd give away the algorithm, my bf pointed out,
to the one yr tryin to put a spell on
marcabru uses the word 'mestissa' to describe the shepherdess his dickish narra-
tor is poorly courting
which paden translates 'half-breed' and pound 'low-born' and snodgrass 'lassie'
but I want to say mongrel, mestiza, mixedbreed

melissima most honeyed most songful
what catullus called his boyfriend's eyes
honey the color of my dead dog's eyes the stomach of the bee
I'm going to gather pollen from the cattails in a week or two
to pray to the the plant tell it I'm only taking what I need
use a coathanger to hook the ones far from shore
filter it thru chiffon four times
what is love
but a constellation of significances
lyke-like magic
los cavecs noa aüra as the owl augurs
one gapes at a painting
the other waits for mahanna

in the cut
   for Cedar Sigo

his being punished / for talking Indian.
                    —*Cedar Sigo, 'Prince Valiant'*

person of clear salt water
warm clear deer

the mosquitoes I am
delicious to them
because of my fairy
or my indian blood

he is immune
to poison ivy
because indians dont
call it poison

utter unfaith in humanity

the leaves dont turn right
the leaves so that
they dont know how to turn right

when the guy at the bodega
complained about white ppl & gentrifications
you said me and my friend are native
I'm Suquamish, look it up

I vaporize the weed
we had for breakfast when
I come home from the poetry reading
thinking how low & how lively
we know of the cut

droppd my parasol in a ditch
pretend it didnt happen

I had already shuttered an aspect of my vision

after a string of broken treaties
each more humiliating than the last
geronimo was finally exhibited at the world's fair
alongside an african man
who could escape from the
tightly wound chains
but like geronimo was not his own person
and whose keeper took him to the moving pictures
fake images with real thunder
and the pinheads and the other freaks.
despite all the irreality I still clung
to my vision
a horse who could reckon land and water
and dance like a crow among the embers

never wondering why it didn't just fly off toward the sun
undulating like an otter
cracking shellfish on its chest and
just floating on its back, face to the sun
who never knew a saddle
who never knew nothing but sunshine
and this was a creature who could become other creatures
an eagle when it was lofty
a dog when it was lowly
when it began to dance
it led with the left leg, or flipper, or whatever limb or digit
it happened to embody
which is why humans
in imitation
start their dances
with the left leg
powow, twostep
tango, conga
we explain it to ourselves
that we're following the heart
my vision told me I did not know what I was
nor could I locate myself—
when I spoke the subject was obfuscated
so that I was even absent from grammar
the very medium in which I toiled
I said a certain person was doable
but I did not say by whom.
rocketed back to the place of my death,
I inhaled the stench of vomit, rotting fruit, exhaust
I understood what percentage of persons
were killed as they dove into the train
I had shuttered an aspect of my vision
in order to surf an already-ruined ocean
no life now to live
but an ever-retreating set of propositions
each more implausible than the last
a whale in the embrace of an octopus

Julian Talamantez Brolaski   401

the lifevest giving life
even as it moldered under the seat
—just a hand
fluttering in the ocean—
precipitated our rescue

JENNIFER ELISE FOERSTER
MVSKOKE

"Writing poems, for me, is about making imagery that is a kaleidoscope of motion."

Writing in a synthesis of tradition and modernity, Jennifer Elise Foerster (1979–) traverses the moving boundaries between real and surreal, her Native and European ancestries, and the reaches of time. Praised for their compression and precision, Foerster's poems create a sensory montage of glimpses. Drawing on geography and myth, she surveys the landscapes of Oklahoma ("Leaving Tulsa") and the wide American continent through lenses that rotate across the lush or barren, the epic or diminutive, as in the remarkable poem "Atlas." Building her unified sequences upon themes environmental as well as biblical and tribal, Foerster's poems court weirdness and estrangement, while securing a grounding in clear words and tactile images. Steadily fearless, her work searches to understand what it now means to be Native, to be female, and to be American.

from *Coosa*

I.
We were clamoring green out of the cane,
rainblowers calling to oncoming clouds.
We followed a path of winding white grass
to a river we found too wide to cross.
We had come to the edge of the visible —
blind, we weren't expecting to see
the bones of a lion, horns of a serpent.
None could cross the lake but two cranes singing
how floods would return to swallow the earth —
the children of thunder, red smoke and shells,
long ago, in one of many stories,
driven like snakes out of canebreaks, swamps.

II.
We were clamoring green out of the cane.
The surface beneath us rippled with time,
rainblowers calling for oncoming clouds,
our drowned towns' song, underwater thunder.
We followed the path of winding white grass,
sunned and dried our children on the shore
of a river we found too wide to cross.
We found a small blood clot, wrapped it in leaves
and came to the edge of the visible
to find our own people covered in fog.
Blind, we weren't expecting to see
trailing behind us a ribbon of water,
bones of a lion, horns of a serpent.
All the animals spoke the same language —
none could cross the lake but two cranes singing
a name to sound the town and its people.
When the flood returns to swallow the earth
those left behind will be lost together.
For thunder, red smoke, the children of shells,

we were named for the Town Lost in Water.
Long ago, in one of many stories
when the earth grew angry and ate up its children,
we were driven like snakes out of canebreaks, swamps
to travel the spiral road home.

III.
Clamoring green out of the cane
we came to the edge of the visible.
The surface beneath us rippled with time,
our own people covered in fog.
Where were the rainblowers, oncoming clouds?
We were blind and not expecting to see
our drowned towns' song, underwater thunder,
trailing behind us: a ribbon of water.
We followed a path of winding white grass
over bones of lions, serpent horns
to a shore where we sunned and dried our children.
We spoke the same language as animals.
But the river we found too wide to cross
and none could cross the lake but two cranes singing
to make a small blood clot and wrap in leaves
a name to sound the town and its people.

IV.
We came to the edge of the visible.
When the flood returned to swallow the earth
we found our own people covered in fog —
those left behind, we were lost together.
Blind, we weren't expecting to see
the thunder, red smoke, our children of shells
trailing behind us as ribbons of water.
We were named for the Town Lost in Water,
for bones of a lion, horns of a serpent.
Long ago, in one of many stories,
all the animals spoke the same language —
then the earth grew angry, ate up its children,

and none could cross the lake but two cranes singing.
Driven as a snake from the canebreak—a name
to sound the town and its people:

po somecekotos —

we travel the spiral road home.

Atlas

I have tried to erase you
but you are already blank.

I hang your dress
in the hot south wind.

Only a rustle
of crows in the trees

as far off, our atlas
curls over the ledge

like a little blue wave.

Leaving Tulsa

for Cosetta

Once there were coyotes, cardinals
in the cedar. You could cure amnesia
with the trees of our back-forty. Once
I drowned in a monsoon of frogs —
Grandma said it was a good thing, a promise
for a good crop. Grandma's perfect tomatoes.
Squash. She taught us to shuck corn, laughing,

never spoke about her childhood
or the faces in gingerbread tins
stacked in the closet.

She was covered in a quilt, the Creek way.
But I don't know this kind of burial:
vanishing toads, thinning pecan groves,
peach trees choked by palms.
New neighbors tossing clipped grass
over our fence line, griping to the city
of our overgrown fields.

Grandma fell in love with a truck driver,
grew watermelons by the pond
on our Indian allotment,
took us fishing for dragonflies.
When the bulldozers came
with their documents from the city
and a truckload of pipelines,
her shotgun was already loaded.

Under the bent chestnut, the well
where Cosetta's husband
hid his whiskey — buried beneath roots
her bundle of beads. *They tell
the story of our family*. Cosetta's land
flattened to a parking lot.

Grandma potted a cedar sapling
I could take on the road for luck.
She used the bark for heart lesions
doctors couldn't explain.
To her they were maps, traces of home,
the Milky Way, where she's going, she said.

After the funeral
I stowed her jewelry in the ground,

promised to return when the rivers rose.

On the grassy plain behind the house
one buffalo remains.

Along the highway's gravel pits
sunflowers stand in dense rows.
Telephone poles crook into the layered sky.
A crow's beak broken by a windmill's blade.
It is then I understand my grandmother:
When they see open land
they only know to take it.

I understand how to walk among hay bales
looking for turtle shells.
How to sing over the groan of the county road
widening to four lanes.
I understand how to keep from looking up:
small planes trail overhead
as I kneel in the Johnson grass
combing away footprints.

Up here, parallel to the median
with a vista of mesas' weavings,
the sky a belt of blue and white beadwork,
I see our hundred and sixty acres
stamped on God's forsaken country,
a roof blown off a shed,
beams bent like matchsticks,
a drove of white cows
making their home
in a derailed train car.

The Spiral: Circling Closer

I understand poetry as a paradox—a way of seeing what cannot be seen, a language for what has no language, a way, as Joy Harjo writes in "Speaking Tree" (see below), "To drink deep what is undrinkable." I cannot make an image for the undrinkable, but I can see, through the sounds and images of Harjo's poem, "the deepest-rooted dream of a tree"—the thirst, satiation, and longing, in the veins, in the earth, in memory.

The Italian poet Cesar Pavese explored the mysterious effect of images in poetry. In his journal writings published as *The Burning Brand*, Pavese contemplates what he calls the "image narrative" as a technique of poetry where "a glance through the window becomes the substance of the whole construction" (9 Oct 1935).[1] Pavese's idea of the image narrative is similar to Barbara Guest's proposition about the invisible architecture that develops and supports the poem. In her essay collection, *Forces of Imagination*, Guest calls the poem's invisible architecture "an architecture in the period before the poem finds an exact form and vocabulary—before the visible appearance of the poem on the page."[2] This invisible architecture is something that exists before and beneath the poem's consciousness. Once this architecture materializes, visually, on the page, it disappears. The architecture is not the written apparatus, but something like its shadow, elusive and changing with the light, or the dream that slips away the moment we attempt to translate it into language.

Pavese describes the image narrative as a combination "of the diverting image and the image-story" (9 Oct 1935), where the image-story is "the evocation of the various imaginative complexes" (20 Nov 1937). He questions whether—and how—it is the collection of images in a poem that, in their resonance and associations, can create a story beneath the surface of the story. He writes, "That the various images that merge and throw fresh light on one another may be the progressus of each poem is a matter of fact" (16 Dec 1935), but then asks if there is something else that actuates this "play of images." His writings explore this question, calling this "something else" the "moments of discovery and transition—the nuclei, in short" (15 Dec 1935). Nuclei are invisible to our perception yet generate the movement of all things. Perhaps poetry, in its revelation of "moments of discovery and transition" is the motion of nuclei made visible.

Writing poems, for me, is about making imagery that is a kaleidoscope of motion. Motion cannot be contained in a single image as referent, copy, or symbol; a symbolic image cannot be a key to a thing's essence, it can only link one thing to an idea of another thing. Cesar Pavese writes, "the surface is never anything more than a play of reflections of *other things*" (17 July 1944).

The poet Adonis writes that the image is significant not in its "visible surface," but as "a door that leads the spectator to what is behind it: the absent or the abstract, in its essence or nature."[3] I understand the absent as the image we glimpse only as it escapes us. The "absent" is not the "not-present," just as the "that" is neither nothing nor something, but is, as Michael Sells writes in *Mystical Languages of Unsaying*, "glimpsed in the interstices of the text, in the tension between saying and unsaying. It is . . . a mystery . . . a referential openness."[4] The absent is that which a spectator can only see when turning away from it. The poem's task is to activate this turning away.

Fanny Howe writes in her essay collection *The Wedding Dress*, "One definition of the lyric might be that it is a method of searching for something that can't be found. It is an air that blows and buoys and settles. It says, 'Not this, not this,' instead of, 'I have it.'"[5]

My first book, *Leaving Tulsa*, began as desire to find "it"—I endeavored to re-make a lost book by piecing together the fragments found in multiple landscapes. I imagined pages snagged in the straggly scrub oak on the side of Tulsa's turnpikes. Years later I read about a poet Ho-Pah-Moi, an Osage known as John Stink, who left poems scattered in trees around Pawhuska, Oklahoma in the early 1900s. It wasn't to Ho-Pah-Moi I wrote, but to a woman named Magdalena, who herself took multiple forms, who lived as fragments lifted from torn pages of history: she was a woman in a blue dress who appeared to me at the gas pump as I drove the highways west from Tulsa; she was America, before America was named, which was no-thing that could be in a single name defined; she was myself, once.

Poetry making, for me, was once about this: creating a semblance of continuity out of disparate pieces, fragments, snagged pages of some lost book. Robert Duncan wrote about his work as the making of a Grand Collage, an effort to create order of chaos. His vision was towards universalization: to realize the cosmic order, the grand design. He sought to follow networks of passages to achieve a wider field of vision. These passages took serial form. They threaded, submerging and surfacing through his works, with no beginnings and no closures. But this grand collage was ever haunted by the completion it could never attain, and Duncan, too, was haunted by failure.

It was the writing of *Leaving Tulsa* that taught me there was no lost book, no "it" to be puzzled together. I found no grand design or answer poetry could ever attain or make visible. Magdalena could not be grasped in the blur of passing landscapes out the window. Maybe if I had found her, or the sense of completion I thought she represented, I wouldn't still be writing poems. In poetry, and in life, perhaps the only possible completion is the absorption into a state of unknowing, something that seems like disorder, something like bewilderment.

Fanny Howe's essay "Bewilderment" speaks to the paradox that drives the visionary, lyric poet. Howe talks about poetry as bewilderment, which is also the way by which the Sufi whirling dervish touches God. "The whirling that is central to bewilderment is the natural way for the lyric poet . . . the belief that at the center of errant or circular movement is the empty but ultimate referent."[6] The poet knows the non-referent cannot be written yet writes—whirls—around this invisible center. Magdalena was my invisible center.

In H.D's *Flowering of the Rod*, the invisible center is a circle widening to infinity, an "out-of-time" space, a lost island around which snow geese hover and spiral.[7] The poet's drive is a spiral quest of these "actual or perhaps now / mythical birds—who seek but find no rest // till they drop from the highest point of the spiral / or fall from the innermost centre of the ever-narrowing circle // for they remember . . . what once was."[8] In the center of these infinitely opening circles is the vision of an origin.

But even the origin can only be glimpsed at the moment of its dispersal. "I am also, since I am again at my point of my departure, searching for my own place of origin," writes Paul Celan in his Meridian Speech.[9] Paradox is the beloved of poetry; it is the invisible center around which the poet spirals.

The first poet who woke me to poetry as a way of "seeing" in the world is the Mvskoke poet Joy Harjo, who has, from the beginning of her work, written with the spiral as her guiding form. As a fellow Mvskoke poet, I understand the spiral as a guiding form not just for poetry but also in life. Writes Harjo in "Heartshed": "Our bones are built of spirals."[10] For Mvskoke people, the spiral is a basis of our worldview; the spiraling dance is a path we follow, "sharing food, songs, and nights that made concentric circles of stories on the road to sunrise," writes Harjo.[11] The spiral form generates transformation by bringing us into the liminal, where paradox is embraced, where there is no *I* or *you*, no *this* or *that*, but a constant transformation, a whirling, among both.

> I could hear the light beings as they entered every cell . . . They were dancing as if they were here, and then another level of here, and then another, until the whole earth and sky was dancing.

We are dancing here, they said. There was no there.
There was no "I" or "you."
There was us; there was "we."

Poetic language, in its liminal suspension, embraces the dialectic; it allows the multiplicity or between-ness of things. To enact this liminal suspension, I work a lot with the sequence, or the serial poem. I believe sequencing is a form that generates transformation, which occurs in the liminal space of becoming/coming undone—being not this or that, but both and neither. The liminal is the paradox of the invisible center, and seriality is, I think, a compelling form to craft this motion.

Writes Howe: "The serial poem attempts to demonstrate this attention to what is cyclical, returning, but empty at its axis. To me, the serial poem is a spiral poem."[12] The poems in a sequence spiral out from the seeds they each contain, and from that bud, a blossom, and from that blossom, another seed—cyclically.

Sequences occupy a mysterious place between linear and non-linear narrative. While each section serves to take us somewhere new along a horizontal path, they can also unfold from and into all other sections in a circular, non-linear order. As each section of a sequence is essentially a microcosm of the macrocosm, the choreography may appear more like circles within circles. The order, then, is one that emerges internally. The true rhythmic design of the sequence is created from the deeply interlaid threads and embedded harmonic complexes. These are the centers of gravity that pull the reader not just along the sequence of poems, but into the larger poem. The poem as a whole exists in the accumulation of its parts; the macro-poem also exists whole within each of its microcosmic sections. The echoes among these multiple dimensions, along with devices such as repetition of sound and image to choreograph these echoes, are what create the spiral.

Joy Harjo commonly uses the devices of anaphora and repetition as a way of evoking the spiral. In an interview in 1990, she said that the poem "She Had Some Horses" (see page 226 in this anthology) was written out of a "ritualized acknowledgement" of ceremony, particularly through its use of repetition: "In any kind of ceremonial action, the repetition always backs up, enforces the power of what you've said."[13] She has spoken about repetition as ceremonial because of its transformative effect: repetition in a poem "becomes a litany, and gives you a way to enter into what is being said, and a way to emerge whole, but changed."[14]

Like Harjo's spiral, Fanny Howe's discussion of bewilderment as a poetics offers a way "to emerge whole, but changed" through circumnavigation. Howe writes: "to the spiral-walker there is no plain path . . . there are strange returns and recognitions and never a conclusion."[15] Celan similarly points toward the source as a *non-place* of no conclusion where arrival is impossible:

> here in the forevered Nowhere,
> in a memory of out-
> crying bells in — but where?[16]

Here, one spirals endlessly in the echo of the poem's sounds. The turning of poetry to sequences may be a way to honor what Barbara Guest calls "the unstableness of the poem." The poet desires both control and instability. The unstable poem is powerful because of its mutability, and because it is governed by an agency outside of our rational mind. The poet, writes Guest, desires to "wander freely, to nest in the invisible handwriting of composition."[17] The spacious loopholes allowed by a serial poem are passageways, wormholes for the unconscious, or whatever that invisible architect might call itself. But as conscious writers, we also want authority in our imagination. I often turn to long, serial forms because the writing of them requires attention and control, and satisfies my wish to be a craftsperson, to work tediously and methodically, to feel like I know what I'm doing, even when I don't.

The excerpt of *Coosa* featured here is from a serial project I'm currently working on. This four-part spiral poem is embedded in the third section of a sixty-four-part poem, and forms the directional posts to the section's sixteen poems. I designed this form to allow for a spiral of multiple voices, and the bewilderment of meaning that occurs when lines/voices shift relationships to one another. This excerpt is written for my fellow Mvskoke poet Joy Harjo, who reminds me, in *Conflict Resolution for Holy Beings*, "Don't forget that at the center is the Mvskoke ceremonial circles."[18] When I'm feeling lost in bewilderment, she reminds me to allow myself to be found there, too. "In music, we can become tragically and beautifully lost . . . and found again."[19]

Notes

1. Cesare Pavese, *The Burning Brand: Diaries 1935–1950*, trans. A. E. Murch (Walker & Company, 1961).

2. Barbara Guest, *Forces of Imagination* (Kelsey Street Press, 2009), 18.

3. Adonis, *Sufism & Surrealism*, trans. Judith Cumberbatch (Saqi Books, 2005), 171.

4. Michael Sells, *Mystical Languages of Unsaying* (University of Chicago Press, 1994), 8.

5. Fanny Howe, *The Wedding Dress: Meditations on Word and Life* (University of California Press, 2003), 21.

6. Howe, *The Wedding Dress*, 18, 20.

7. H.D., *Trilogy,* ed. Aliki Barnstone (New Directions, 1998), 153.

8. H.D., *Trilogy*, 119.

9. Paul Celan, *Collected Prose*, trans. Rosemary Waldrop (Routledge, 2003), 54.

10. Joy Harjo, *In Mad Love & War* (Wesleyan University Press, 1990), 62.

11. Joy Harjo, *Conflict Resolution for Holy Beings* (W.W. Norton, 2015), 52.

12. Howe, *The Wedding Dress*, 17.

13. Joy Harjo, *The Spiral of Memory: Interviews,* ed. Laura Coltelli (University of Michigan Press, 1996), 84.

14. Harjo, *The Spiral of Memory,* 17.

15. Howe, *The Wedding Dress*, 9.

16. Paul Celan, *Selected Poems and Prose of Paul Celan*, trans. John Felstiner (W. W. Norton, 2001), 263.

17. Guest, *Forces of Imagination*, 190.

18. Harjo, *Conflict Resolution for Holy Beings*, 81.

19. Harjo, *Conflict Resolution for Holy Beings*, 33.

*

Speaking Tree
by Joy Harjo

> *I had a beautiful dream I was dancing with a tree.*
> —Sandra Cisneros

Some things on this earth are unspeakable:
Genealogy of the broken —
A shy wind threading leaves after a massacre,
Or the smell of coffee and no one there —

Some humans say trees are not sentient beings,
But they do not understand poetry —
Nor can they hear the singing of trees when they are fed by

Wind, or water music —
Or hear their cries of anguish when they are broken and bereft—

Now I am a woman longing to be a tree, planted in a moist, dark earth
Between sunrise and sunset —

I cannot walk through all realms —
I carry a yearning I cannot bear alone in the dark —

What shall I do with all this heartache?

The deepest-rooted dream of a tree is to walk
Even just a little ways, from the place next to the doorway —
To the edge of the river of life, and drink —

I have heard trees talking, long after the sun has gone down:

Imagine what would it be like to dance close together
In this land of water and knowledge . . .

To drink deep what is undrinkable

LAURA DA'

EASTERN SHAWNEE TRIBE OF OKLAHOMA

"Land, language, people, all are measured and in the act of measurement, they elude easy capture . . ."

The charged, lyrical poetry of Laura Da' (1979–) is an interrogation of history, religion, family, and how these three entities shape identity. Known for her quick lines, surprising linebreaks, and startling imagery, Da' makes the poem a contested site for both writer and reader. In "Perspective," for example, a multi-part poem that ranges across two centuries and at least three generations, the speaker draws on both Indigenous and Christian symbols to get at who she is and was. What does it mean, after all, to survive? To have survived? Similarly, a poem like "Eye Turned Crow" relies on mythic, associative images that evoke rather than explain. Da' also uses spaces and stanza breaks ingeniously, which gives her poems a galloping sense of movement, as though they are themselves wild animals eluding easy capture.

Perspective

1.
Annunciation arrived
on lunar-pale slips of paper.

Rich stout linen pulp,
            a mannerly velum inventory

extolling home or in-center care.

Vignettes of survival
crowded to the margins.

Cessation of all interventions
was a sparse assertion —

painless void synchronicity

            of white space.

Thirty-five years;
edifices inside me,

Doric, Ionic, Corinthian:
I framed this memory
with marble columns

            to grasp at the exact

                        vanishing point.

2.
I woke up in a hospital bed
catechizing until sedated:

What do you remember

from when you were a child of five?

When my son was small
 he wanted to be an eagle dancer.

A nurse plotted
bleach-soaked bandages
on the side table,

        one after another.

3.
A smoky river-fog
diminution of selves
murmured off my skin.

Each direction
I swiveled my head —

mountain vistas and cedar-stacked
points of convergence.

On the chairs at my bedside
donors were hypothesized,
the miracles of 3D printers rhapsodized —

        brutally untouchable simplicity
        of a sophisticated filter.

My son's nighttime cries
tilted me awake.

I could not rise.

Necessary entropy
of the body swerving
into completion.

I watched in the porchlight.

He was in my husband's arms
wrapped in a blanket.

In the morning
he pronounced the moon

      both broken and his.

Pain was a slate-gray wolf inside me
whispering exile —

      sniffing at the timberline of my blood.

4.
I roved in a haze of barbiturates —

      a long line of stolen ease.

Members,
      citizens,
            descendants.

I ran a highlighter
over photocopied legal records from the last century:

      Turkey Ford, Oklahoma, 1904.

My great-grandmother disinherited
by a disinterested witness.

On the tribal message board:
two counsel members
groused in all caps.
 The Shawnee phrase of the day
was *Nethaawa Yaama* —
              Who is that?

My own slender hagiography:

W son of M,
last of the surname B,
son of L, my own father's father,
made citizen at age 14, died young.

5.
Occasion divides time by tense
in an exacting sapphire blaze —
sky door to the personal

              invention of perspective.

When my son was small

he watched eagle dancers.

              A small figure
              within the abiding ceremony.

San Ildefonso's ground-lapis sky
carried the Scrovigni Chapel
into my mind's eye.

Once, as a docent rambled
about angles of proportion,

I cast my arm against sunbeams
filtering through the tops of lancet windows

as if I were sheltering from a blow.
In the court of heaven,
                Mercy sat to the right.

To say I will remember

        to the end of my days

        begs numeration.

When my son was small
he watched eagle dancers —

        a small figure
        within the abiding ceremony
        moving his arms wide
        to mimic wingspan.

Eye Turned Crow

        We have no true
tragedy here —

the lecturer bemoans

American history's banality,

projects a glossy photograph
of Berlin's monument
to burned books.

Slipping out the side door,
                my eye turns crow.
 I've never seen book-burned violence —

charred edges of paper
            a murder of wings.
Running my hand
along moldering spines

is sometimes sufficient
to raven me

            into harried avarice.

Trace the indentions
of titles:
flood paths
in the Nisqually Basin,

paperback print
of the Dresden Codex.

The colophon of a sparrow
dimples the spine —
            a history of child labor.

Corvids in flight and repose
decorate the walls
spouting whimsical chains
            of Coast Salish.

When the workers
 were placing the last
creamy bricks

 along the crenels
of this library's
            gothic façade

anti-potlatch laws
allowed agents

to enter the ceremony

seize artifacts,
make arrests,
 cast narratives
upon the fire.

Crows follow wolves.

They break open carcasses

allowing them to feed — furtively,
I snatch a book from the cart

crack its spine;
             halved to marrow.

Leviathan

In Westport the small French cart
of the voyageurs earned the name mule-killer.

Once Shawnee was the lingua franca
up and down the Mississippi,

then *mollassi became molasses.*
For the bringing of the horse

it is said much can be forgiven: burn
of Missouri whiskey and aching molars,

lunatic fevers of cholera,
even those men

born astride. Rare beast to share
that weight on such fine and slender legs.

On James Thomas Stevens's *Tokinish*

Tokinish "wake him"—the initial epigraph of James Thomas Stevens's long poem commands an awakening. I remember reading this poem twenty years ago. I was a creative writing student at the Institute of American Indian Arts at a time when the writing classes were held in a doublewide portable that listed noticeably to the east. It gave the whole class a shipwrecked sway. I read the first galloping stanzas of this poem and my head snapped up.

In *Tokinish*, words, images, and concepts bend to the grasp of possession. The book itself held me in a kind of thrall for many years. In the pre-internet days of the late nineties, I searched for it with extreme avarice. Once I found a used copy in a bookstore in Boulder, I read it until the covers fell off.

Land, language, people, all are measured and in the act of measurement, they elude easy capture: "Island. / Look to a map to prove the concept mute. / All waters have a source and this connection renders earth island." I wrote the poems included in this anthology with this concept in mind.

*

from "Tokinish"

To walk the periphery of islands, as if knowing the border of body.
To mould the well-muscled
$\qquad\qquad\qquad$ curve of your back
modeled of river weeds hanging red on the scarp.
Water run down river rock,
the combe beneath your arm.
$\qquad\qquad$ Skin shining stone
$\qquad\qquad\qquad$ as the sun settles into its dumb orthodoxy.
Hemlock shoreline,
of trunks forced into silt's precision.

The vegetable earth on a mineral spine.

How to write island, the weighty peninsula of extremities.
The red of lichen on
a head of stone.

Weight is the catastrophe of what we don't know,
$\qquad\qquad\qquad$ the unsleeping gravity drawing boat to shore.

BOJAN LOUIS

Diné

"There is a balance in the tercet. Each stanza an encapsulation of image and lyric..."

The poetry of Bojan Louis (1980–) is alive with electricity. Louis's poetic voice sparks and vibrates with Spanish, Diné, and English, and with rhythms expertly reprised or broken, resulting in a characteristic music in a reader's mind. Coursing between literal and symbolic as they foray into myth, Indigenous culture, and individual history, in poems like "The Nature of Mortal Illness" and "Breach" the poet is unafraid to face serious dysfunction, whether his own, his family's, or his community's. Louis's writing exceeds the supposed expectations of a rural and reservation background while summoning an audience to understand the strength of word and faith. Formally, Louis's poems reflect an impressive aesthetic range: some are long-lined and narrative, others short-lined and song-like. In both modes, Bojan's poetry is a testament to the power of voice.

The Nature of Mortal Illness

As a kid skeptical of pollen plumes making my skin ash, mind migraine heavy,
and nasal cavity a sanctuary for deformed crustaceans seeking terrible refuge

in a false moisture   I wanted to believe *this* question:

are my brothers and sisters debris humming because they're what's left?

I'm no oceanic world, no fossilized imprint subject to excavation, but a man
sickness has left well enough. Common cold; chromosome infection; viral
                    ethnography; Southwestern desert lung fungus.

If there's safety within the earth then I'll go there. Otherwise, where do *I* find me?
Is it clear Gila Monsters border extinction? *You* endangered or enamored with this

                                                    development?

Flint, the sacred bolt of thunder, the syringe end of lightening can turn body to ribbons,
quilt it mosaic again. Can burn a thirsty land. Can armor one against the ill world and

suffocate today's protective notion of tomorrow.

In our history the Gila Monster might tell you, get your sickness away from me. But it's only to teach you to ask questions correctly, offer the necessary smoke, dispel phobia and the impatience for curmudgeons with wandering syntax.

Lesson: if it kills you spit at it for sure, kick dirt its way. If it reminds you of *your* ways, *your* doubts and regrets, and that shitty relative who molested you, curse it. Shake its hand,

which is the hue of your hand,   with black magic

ground fine from a loved one's bones. Remember? An agreement with death for Death? New tract home subdivisions explode from an imploded aquifer crusted with alkaline

                                        skeletons

shaped like a brontosaurus. We're headed there right? A studied, imagined subterranean being/thing explicated, sited as superfund. *That* earth great once like a marauder/murderer but more Billy Ray Cyrus than Prince.

When prospectors and pioneers sweated this tierra, this nahasdzáán they feared the toxic breath and bites of damn near every living thing, see? See, this now. The earth and its things:

medicinal/panacea/antipsychotic   whatever the fuck, labeled *illegal* unless pharmie.

As a kid, when I think of it now, I was stupid; Grunge trodden and late-blooming bony I wanted to breathe the confidence to say nice things, to experience keggers. However, I was opposite the

decorated locker and shower room. If I possessed venom I was built over and unable to relocate. But this isn't about high school, which doesn't matter.

                    It's burial. In tradition and home.

Beyond the urban-heat of this concrete desert on land as barren and at times hot, piles of yellow cake decorate Dinétah like the tempting skin of Dart Frogs. Nature's governance: protection.

When we fail our hearts the blame is inverted   like ice caps for summer

a crucifix for clean water and flowers. It can't end this way: the wind, exterminator, a great prop

          plane dusting the world. A heart so un-heart it forgets itself.

If Nothing, the Land

i. THE TOUGHEST SHERIFF IN THE WORLD

There is no other bad than what I say's bad.
It's tough-living on this land. Miles of desert,
undeveloped; the interstates, mostly unmanned,
are threads unspooled down broad hallways.
Beyond their edge the space is dead,
a rogue trailer or redskin reservation.
Backward problems
of methamphetamine and rape. Those doors

have their own police, their own dumb justice.
I concern my posse with invasion. Paperless
beaners. Rust that ruins a polish.
Inedible animals do no man any good
until buried to cease the flies and stink.

ii. FLOCK OF SEAGALS

If not thousands than millions of hours
I've played *bang-bang*; nabbed bad guy
brownies in kung fu-grip shoot-em-ups.
Who's better fit to patrol kids in tiny pants
than a convicted man? Limits,
like borders, stretch thin and tear. If anyone
can get a gun then shouldn't everyone
have one at the ready, like in the glory days:

a round up of savages, spics, and spooks out
to devalue our kids, good at killing their own.
I learned from watching birds nestled within
cacti: though there might be many, a single bird
more makes another cavity, an eventual collapse.

iii. COME MIERDA PARA EL DESAYUNO

Chickens dismantle, like pit crews can

a vehicle, scorpions quickly.
Urged forward by pickers the hens bob
and amble over fallen oranges, bruised grapefruit;
seek pincers, stingers, exoskeletons;
their work urgent and efficient.
Back at the coop, stubborn roosters fight;
bloody and unfeather each other

until the losers peck frail chicks from the clutch,
strew limp bodies beneath the florescent light.
The hens return, squawk and circle the carcasses,
until the migrants transfer them in sacks
meant for citrus to anonymous holes on the land.

Breach

Sitka, Alaska

I.
It's years I've been recovered.
Parents gone the way of worms
— mom alone, her own decision.

Dad, how he was always
asphyxiated until rolled over.
The frontier I'm abandoned to,

exposed root ribcages above ground,
rained on so much there's no dust,
no blow away — traceless surfaces.

     ---   ---   ---

With a single bag and one-way ticket
I rented the first found available:

three bedroom, living, kitchen, dining
— filled it with myself, every room
empty, except where I slept.
Girls I had over, fucked to the floor,

left sobered, mostly. Offered other
times at their places later. I accepted,
then abandoned, fixed at the clinic.

---   ---   ---

This high north, though not freezing,
an island settlement cut off the coast:
pines, spruce, and chaotic undergrowth

rise up along the crescent of mountains
open toward the ocean.
Rain more sky than the sky is sky.

I'm not home. Less
interested in finding it;
hours from the mainland.

II.
On an outlying island red deer
wait out hunters tracking
shit steam for rifle crack.

Otters cut away
supine through water,
to humans, hypothermic.

The turned-engine skiff
on sucking mud signals
the goddamned day's done.

---   ---   ---

Across the still, cobalt inlet,
cairns line the bald rim
of a sundowner volcano.

Glaciers imagined against
the sea/heaven horizon
melt when fog lifts

and missed shots echo,
fade into the tree line:
the casings mimic pebbles.

---   ---   ---

Anger defines me, here,
in what's seen in pictures
as pristine beauty, untouched

by man's dirty finger:
Dad's belched regrets,
Mom's frustrated, unspoken hurt.

I want recompense — solitude
and forgiveness' distance—nourishment
sought, sighted, and put down.

III.
Where welding fails
release hollers out the soon
to be empty space.

A continent,
a levee. What
rises, takes
— ice given heat,

like a child, spread
with hands telling, quiet.

      ---   ---   ---

Ocean hefted over stern
deflates
my ill posture

gone life drunk;
so drowned in drink
nobody wants to want me.

Rare are dads shouted
at by moms, Get — Don't feed
us — Sink, be eaten.

      ---   ---   ---

Jonah's a lucky fuck,
bowel-held
and undigested.

Dumb animal, him. Swallowed
entire, in warmer water.
I don't believe he escaped.

He's down in there still.
Hung from the beast's spine,
feet eaten, body untouched.

Between the Abyss and Here, Beauty

A basic electrical circuit consists of a hot, neutral, and ground wire. One wire powers an object or apparatus—what are we without light—one acts as a return path for live current, and the last is grounded to the earth and connected to any metal parts so as to prevent an arc flash, shock, or electrocution. We're all connected to the earth, or should be.

I used to work long days as an electrician doing residential and a bit of commercial wiring and troubleshooting. In order to ease the monotony of the work and the day I'd try to memorize a poem that I'd copied by hand the night before. Word by word, line by line throughout the day I'd recite it aloud. No one was watching, no one was listening. I was between the space of receiving directions and instructions from my boss and interacting with the client. I was repairing the balance of electrical power and my mind.

Residential electricity utilizes alternating current (AC). There are two busses in a service panel. With alternating current there is a millisecond or nanosecond where there is no current. This is liminal space, this is the abyss; the thread of dawn when we Diné offer pollen to the holy people and deities. Perhaps they listen and perhaps I don't say the correct things. Either way day brings the strength and power of the sun.

Whenever I work on a service panel, whether it be changing bad breakers or tightening loose connections I think of the tercet, of terza rima, though I don't often use end rhyme. There is balance in the tercet. Each stanza an encapsulation of image and lyric and this is what has brought me back, or what has been reignited in my memory, to the kinetic lyrical poems of Lynda Hull.

I first encountered the work of Lynda Hull during undergraduate poetry classes with both Barbara Anderson and Jim Simmerman, the later of whom, I believe, had been friends with Hull. I was given *Star Ledger* on lend and tore through the book's fierce lyricism and unflinching eye for the characters and images that Hull witnessed and envisioned between the spaces and cracks of society. I was hooked and one poem in particular kept me coming back.

"Studies from Life" is lyrical electricity composed of hanging-indent stanzas in tercet. Of course, during those lost and over-confident years I didn't realize that this poem would define much of my poetics, content, and themes. Marginalized voices set alongside religious imagery and contexts threaded through with street images both decadent and grotesque and coruscating alongside the beauty of art, ever reaching through and toward the beautiful.

Studies from Life

by Lynda Hull

Soot-blackened, marble angels freeze
        their serpentine ascent above scattered women
                in the pews, net shopping bags beside them as

the priest drones Mass before an altar carbonized
        with Madrid's incessant traffic fumes. In stone,
                the Virgin rests her foot upon the serpent

coiling a benighted world, and tarnished
        in their reliquary, the hermit's fingers play
                no instrument but incensed air. Such a meager

gathering, yet here is the visionary beggar riding
        tissued layers of soiled garments, notebook
                in her hands, transcribing helplessly

her transport in a code of suns and doves'
        entrails, crouched seraphim. Because he believed
                the mad inhabited zones of heaven, El Greco

painted in asylums — the saint's blue arms
        raised in rapture truly modeled from the madman's
                supplications. Cries and rough whispers,

nuns' habits sweeping across stone floors, disturbing
        the stacks of charcoal studies. He found derangement
                spiritual. The cathedral font is dry today,

stained glass rattling the passage of Vespas
        and taxicabs. The stairway tumbles, Baroque,
                to the boulevard twitching with heat, gypsied with

cripples, the sots and marvelous dancing goats.
          In the Prado, Greco's attenuated aristocrat
                    buys his way to grace beside a Virgin transfigured —

the Resurrection. What Calvary in the model's mind
          built that cathedraled radiance of her glance,
                    so matte and dense and holy? They're everywhere

in these vivid streets living parallel
          phantasmic cities that shimmer and burn among
                    swirling crowds along the esplanade — tangoing couples

dappled under trees, the fortune-tellers
          and summer girls like dropped chiffon scarves
                    sipping their turquoise infusions, planetary liqueurs

sticky with umbrellas. They chatter through
          a dwarf's frantic homily of curses. Simply
                    a ripple the crowd absorbs, but where is the saint

from the plains' walled city the tourists
          come to find? Oh, she is broken on the wheel,
                    milled into dust. She is atomized to history's

dry footnotes. Here is the sleek plane's vapor,
          the speed-blind train, and there the fragrant secrets
                    inside fine leather. Still, the painter shows the beggar's

empty bowl, irradiated shades, these gaseous figures
          writhing upward, hands knotting tremulous prayers.
                    And the mouths, the mouths . . . Such hollow caverns

that plumb what depths of human pain, or is it
          ecstasy's abandon? Past a twilight the color of sighs
                    on the street made numinous with restaurant lights,

he is there, the man kneeling before a shopfront's
        iron grille. Facing, rapt, a silk-swathed mannequin,
                he's chanting litanies in a perfumed tongue

of numerals, some unearthly lexicon. And if we could
        translate, we might hear how the saint dwells
                perpetual, the form of this hunger within.

CRAIG SANTOS PEREZ
CHAMORU

"I imagine that poems are song maps of my own journey to find Guam across historical and diasporic distances."

The Micronesian island of Guam is the westernmost territory of the United States. In 2010, as part of Resolution No. 315-30, Guam's legislature recognized Craig Santos Perez (1980–) as a "phenomenal ambassador for our island, eloquently conveying through his words, the beauty and love that is the Chamorro culture." Perez's poetry celebrates a culture and place often unknown and unmarked but very alive, and rich with customs (see "The Pacific Written Tradition"). Throughout Perez's work, especially in poems such as "Interwoven," a reader hears refrains of island music and folklore in lines charting Pacific life, native ancestry, the scourge of colonialism, and the diasporic presence. Perez lights up the ways in which Guam has been fetishized and marginalized, and his poems are marked by clarity—they are not hard to understand—and gravitas—they're often mournful in their honesty. Weaving personal narrative with his island home's history, Perez has created a series of books that are essentially one long poem, a revelation of Guam's complicated present.

See also page 88 for Linda Hogan's testimony to the influence of "understory" by Craig Santos Perez

Interwoven

1.

I come from an island
and you come from a continent,
yet we are both made of stories
that teach us to remember
our origins and genealogies,
to care for the land and waters,
and to respect the interconnected
sacredness of all things.

2.

I come from an island
and you come from a continent,
yet we both know invasion.
Magellan breached our reef
thirty years after Columbus raided
your shore. We were baptized
in disease, violence, and genocide.
We both carry the deep grief
of survival.

3.

I come from an island
and you come from a continent,
yet we both know the walls
of boarding schools. We were punished
for breathing our customs and
speaking our language. We learned
the Western curriculum
of fear and silence.

4.

I come from an island
and you come from a continent,

yet we both know desecration.
We witnessed minerals, trees, wildlife,
and food crops extracted for profit.
We mourn lands stolen and re-named,
waters diverted and dammed.
We inherit the intergenerational
loss of removal.

5.

I come from an island
and migrated to your continent.
Hundreds of thousands of us
have settled in your territories
for military service, education,
health care, and jobs.
We were so busy searching
for better lives, we didn't ask
your permission. We didn't even
recognize how our American dream
was your American nightmare.

6.

Native American cousins, I see you now
across this vast, scarred continent,
reviving your languages and cultures,
restoring native schools and tribal governments,
planting heritage seeds and decolonizing your diets,
blockading pipelines and protesting mining,
fighting for renewable energy
and a sustainable future.

Native cousins, I see you now
dancing, chanting, drumming,
rapping, writing, researching,
publishing, digitizing, animating,
filming, video gaming, and
revitalizing your ancestral stories.
I hear and honor your voices.

7.
I come from an island
and you come from a continent,
yet let us gather, today, and
share our stories of hurt,
our stories of healing.
I hope, seven generations from now,
our descendants will continue
interweaving our struggles.
I hope the stories we share today
and in the future will carry us
towards sovereign horizons.

Ode (Ending with a Confession) to the First Mango I Ate on Guam After Decades Away

All the mangoes I've tasted in
California were imported and
lost their true flavors in transit
from Mexico or Ecuador.

All the mangoes I've enjoyed
in Hawai'i were home grown
and ripened by island sun,
but they act too glamorous,
with their own annual festival
at a 5-star hotel, where local chefs
and mixologists dress them
in fancy pupus and cocktails.

But you, my love, are modest.
My godfather picked you from
his farm, and my godmother placed
you on a plate for my breakfast.

They're at mass this humid
morning, and we're finally alone.

So I fondle your skin, supple and cool
in the air-conditioned dining room.
I slowly undress you, nibbling
your tropical flesh until I reach the spot
where all your fibers tremble.

When I look up, I notice a large statue
of the Virgin Mary staring at us:
my fingers, lips, teeth, and tongue
sticky with the juice of our sin.

The Pacific Written Tradition

In 2010, I read aloud from my new book
to an English class at one of Guam's
public high schools. After the reading, I

notice a student crying. "What's wrong?"
I ask. She says, "I've never seen our culture
in a book before. I just thought we weren't

worthy of literature." I wonder how many
young islanders have dived into the depths
of a book, only to find bleached coral and

emptiness. *They* teach us that missionaries
were the first readers in the Pacific because
they could decipher the strange signs

of the Bible. *They* teach us that missionaries
were the first authors in the Pacific because

they possessed the authority of written words.
Today, studies show that islander students read
and write below grade level. "It's natural,"
they claim. "Your ancestors were an illiterate,

oral people." *Do not believe their claims.*
Our ancestors deciphered signs in nature,
interpreted star formations and sun positions,

cloud and wind patterns, wave currents and
ocean efflorescence. That's why master navigator
Papa Mau once said: "if you can *read* the ocean

you will never be lost." Now let me tell you
about the Pacific written tradition, about how
our ancestors tattooed their skin with defiant

scripts of intricately inked genealogy, stories
of plumage and pain. Or how our ancestors carved
epics into hard wood with a sharpened point,

their hands, and the pressure and responsibility
of memory. Or how our ancestors stenciled
petroglyphic lyrics on cave walls with clay, fire,

and smoke. So the next time someone tells you
islanders were illiterate, teach them about our visual
literacies, about how we are reclaiming

the skill to read and write the intertextual
sacredness of all things. And always remember: *if you
can write the ocean we will never be silenced.*

On Writing from the New Oceania and Cecilia Catherine Taitano Perez's "As I Turn the Pages"

~

When the tide
of silence

rises, say
"ocean" —

then, with
the paddle of

your tongue,
rearrange

the letters
to form

"canoe"

~

WRITING *from*

From indicates a particular time or place as a starting point; *from* refers to a specific location as the first of two limits; *from* imagines a cause, an agent, an instrument, a source, or an origin; *from* marks separation, removal, or exclusion; *from* differentiates borders. "Where are you from?" In the preface to my first book of poems, I wrote: "On some maps, Guam doesn't exist; I point to an empty space in the Western Pacific and say, 'I'm from here.' On some maps, Guam is a small, unnamed island; I say, 'I'm from this unnamed place.' On some maps, Guam is named 'Guam, USA.' I say, 'I'm from a territory of the United States.'"

From also indicates an excerpt or a passage quoted from a source. My own passage and migration *from* Guam to California often feels like living an excerpted existence; while my body lives here, my heart still lives in my homeland.

"Excerpt" comes from "excerptus," which means to "pluck out" *from* ex- "out" + carpere "gather" or "harvest. Poetry is a way for me to bring together these excerpted spaces via the transient, processional, and migratory cartographies of the page. Each of my poems, and each of my books, and seemingly every breath I take, carries the *from* and bears its weight and incompleteness.

I write *from* my native Chamoru culture. I write *from* a tradition of indigenous orality in which chants and stories are the vessels—or canoes—that carry our cultural knowledge, language, custom, history, genealogy, spirituality, morality, and ecological wisdom. I write *from* a tradition in which time—and narrative structures—are cyclical, spiral, and interwoven, as opposed to linear. Because the past and future exists in the present, and the present is shaped by the past and the future, my writing moves both forwards and backwards across pages and generations.

~

WRITING OCEANIC

The imagination is an ocean of possibilities. I imagine the blank page as an excerpt of the ocean. The ocean is storied and heavy with history, myth, rumor, genealogy, loss, war, money, the dead, life, and even plastic. The ocean is not "aqua nullius." The page, then, is never truly blank. The page consists of submerged volcanoes of story and unfathomable depths of meaning.

Each word is an island. The visible part of the word is its textual body; the invisible part of the word is the submerged mountain of meaning. Words emerging from the silence are islands forming. No word is an just an island, every word is part of a sentence, an archipelago. The space between is defined by referential waves and currents.

Oceanic stories are vessels for cultural beliefs, values, customs, histories, genealogies, politics, and memories. Stories weave generations and geographies. Stories protest and mourn the ravages of colonialism, articulate and promote cultural revitalization, and imagine and express decolonization.

~

Writing Archipelagic

An individual book is an island with a unique linguistic geography and ecology, as well as a unique poetic landscape and seascape. The book-island is inhabited by the living and the dead, the human and the non-human, multiple voices and silences. The book-island vibrates with the complexity of the present moment and the depths of history and genealogy, culture and politics, scars and bone and blood.

A book series is an archipelago, a birthing and formation of book-islands. Like an archipelago, the books in an ongoing series are related and woven to the other islands, yet unique and different. Reading the books in a series is akin to traveling and listening across the archipelago.

Because Guam is part of an archipelago, the geography inspired the form of my *from unincorporated territory* book series. Additionally, the unfolding nature of memory, learning, listening, sharing, and storytelling informed the serial nature of the work. To me, the complexity of the story of Guam and the Chamoru people—entangled in the complications of ongoing colonialism and militarism—inspired the ongoing serial form.

The first book of the series, *from unincorporated territory [hacha]* (2008), focused on my grandfather's life and experience on Guam when the island was occupied by Japan's military during World War Two. The second book, *from unincorporated territory [saina]* (2010), focused on my grandmother's contrasting experience during that same period. The third book, *from unincorporated territory [guma']* (2014), echoes and enlarges the earlier books through the themes of family, militarization, cultural identity, migration and colonialism. Furthermore, [*guma'*] focuses on my own return to my home island after living away (in California) for fifteen years. I explore how the island has changed and how my idea of home has changed. I also meditate upon the memories that I have carried with me, as well as all that I have forgotten and left behind.

The titles are meant to mark and name different books in the same series. Just as an archipelago has a name, such as the Marianas Archipelago, each island of the archipelago has its own unique name. The names can be translated as [one], [elder], and [home]. My first book was given the name *[hacha]*, to mark it as the first book, first island, first voice. While one might expect the second book to be named [second], I chose the name [elder] to resist that linearity and instead highlight genealogy, or the past. The third book, which means house or home, was an attempt to weave together time and space (the house or book as spatial and temporal). The fourth book, *from unincorporated territory [lukao]* (2017) includes themes of birth, creation, parenthood, money, climate, colonialism, militarization, migration, and extinction. The Chamoru name of the book, *[lukao]*, means procession.

My multi-book project also formed through my study of the "long poem": Ezra Pound's *The Cantos*, William Carlos Williams's *Paterson*, H.D.'s *Trilogy*, Louis Zukofsky's *"A"* and Charles Olson's *The Maximus Poems*. I loved how these books were able to attain a breadth and depth of vision and voice. One difference between my project and other "long poems" is that my long poem will always contain the "from," always eluding the closure of completion.

I also became intrigued by how certain poets write trans-book poems: such as Robert Duncan's "Passages" and Nathaniel Mackey's "Songs of the Andoumboulou." I employ this kind of trans-book threading in my own work as poems change and continue across books (for example, excerpts from the poems "from tidelands" and "from aerial roots" appear in both my first and second books). These threaded poems differ from Duncan's and Mackey's work because I resist the linearity of numbering that their work employs.

~

WRITING CARTOGRAPHIC

I use diagrams, maps, illustrations, and collage visual poetry as a way to foreground the relationship between storytelling, mapping, and navigation. Just as maps have used illustrations (sometimes visual, sometimes typographical), I believe poetry can both enhance and disrupt our visual literacy.

One incessant typographical presence throughout my work is the tilde (~). Besides resembling an ocean current and containing the word "tide" in its body, the tilde has many intriguing uses. In languages, the tilde is used to indicate a change of pronunciation. As you know, I use many different kinds of discourse in my work (historical, political, personal, etc.) and the tilde is meant to indicate a shift in the discursive poetic frame. In mathematics, the tilde is used to show equivalence (i.e. $x \sim y$). Throughout my work, I want to show that personal or familial narratives have an equivalent importance to official historical and political discourses.

Cartographic representations of the Pacific Ocean developed in Europe at the end of the fifteenth century, when the Americas were incorporated into maps: the Pacific became a wide empty space separating Asia and America. As imperialism progressed, every new voyage incorporated new data into new maps. In European world maps, Europe is placed at the center and "Oceania" is divided into two opposite halves on the margins.

As I mention in the preface to my first book, the invisibility of Guam on many maps—whether actual maps or the maps of history—has always haunted me. One hope for my poetry is to enact an emerging map of "Guam" both as a place and as a signifier.

The "actual maps" in my first book are, to me, both visual poems and illustrations of the rest of the work. In my imagination, they function in two ways: first, they center "Guam," a locating signifier often omitted from many maps. Second, the maps are meant to provide a counterpoint to the actual stories that are told throughout the book. While maps can locate, chart, and represent (and through this representation tell an abstracted story), they never show us the human voices of a place. I place this abstract, aerial view of "Guam" alongside the more embodied and rooted portraits of place and people.

"Song maps" refer to the songs, chants, and oral stories that were created to help seafarers navigate oceanic and archipelagic spaces. Pacific navigational techniques are often understood as a "visual literacy," in the sense that a navigator has to be able to "read" the natural world in order to make safe landfall. The key features include reading the stars, ocean efflorescence, wave currents, and fish and bird migrations.

Scholars and navigators describe this technique as "moving islands" because in these songs, the canoe is conceptualized as remaining still, while the stars, islands, birds, fish, and waves all move in concert. Islands not only move, but islands also expand and contract. For example, if you see an offshore bird associated with a certain island, then you know that island is nearby (thus, it has figuratively, expanded).

With this in mind, I imagine that poems are song maps of my own journey to find Guam across historical and diasporic distances. I imagine the reader is in a still canoe, reading the songs in order to navigate the archipelago of memory and story. In this way, books and words become moving islands, expanding and contracting, inhaling and exhaling.

~

My poetry be *from* Mongmong, Guåhan (Guam)
My poetry be insular & archipelagic, tidalectic & oceanic

My poetry be Pacific Islander cruising the Trans-Pacific highway on Pacific Rims
My poetry be Chamoru, native, & global indigenous
My poetry be migratory & diasporic, immigrant & citizen,
My poetry be California Dreaming & lucky we live Hawaii
My poetry be place-based & planetary
   Poetry be my aerial roots
My poetry feels homesick sometimes
My poetry be unincorporated, decolonial, & de-territorial
   Poetry be my DMZ
My poetry be documentary & ecological, compostable & post-consumer
My poetry be food porn, canned meats, & naked mixed-plate lunch
   Poetry be my family recipes
My most famous poem be about Spam
My poetry be organic, heirloom seeds, community gardens
My poetry be ex-Catholic, rosary beads, & litanies
My poetry be re-positioning the missionary
   Poetry be my history from below
My poetry be detours & returns, arrivals & departures,
My poetry be origins and destinations,
My poetry be subverting the tourist gaze
My poetry be hybrid, polyphonic, & multi-species
My poetry frgmntd, trenchant, & interwoven
My poetry be serial structures, spiral narratives, & cyclical time
Poetry be my terraqueous borderlands
My poetry be avant-garde af
My poetry got no fucks left to give
My poetry be talking story & talking shit
My poetry be trickster, be shapeshifting, be Juan Malo
My poetry be virtual & hashtag, meme & social media
My poetry be erasure, strike-through, & fade
My poetry be guerrilla archive & genealogical tattoos
   Poetry be my song maps & blood songs
My poetry be navigational chants & creation stories
   Poetry be my sovereign tongues

WRITING WAVES

My writing is deeply influenced by the older generation—or wave—of Pacific Islander poetry. The most influential poet on my work is also the first contemporary Chamoru poet that I have ever read: Cecilia Catherine Taitano Perez—also known as "Lee" Perez and "Hagan Ita" (meaning "Daughter of Ita" or "Blood of Ita"). She is a well-known poet on Guam, and was once considered the unofficial poet laureate of Guam. In 1997, she published a collection of creative writing as her master's thesis with the Center of Pacific Islands Studies at the University of Hawai'i. The thesis is titled *Signs of Being: A Chamoru Spiritual Journey*.

Comprised of poetry, prose, and commentary, Perez describes her cross-genre, multilingual collection as "a documentary in the form of creative writing, on the politics of cultural identity and historical memory in the process of decolonization of the Chamoru mind and senses. It is written from the self-reflexive view of an indigenous Chamoru woman writer from Guam, whose sense of physical sight is blurred." Her journey through a "Chamoru mindscape" travels across five chapters, or what Perez calls "passages": *Hinasso* (Reflection), *Finakmata* (Awakening), *I Fina'pos* (Familiar Surroundings), *Lala'chok* (Taking Root), and *I Senedda* (Finding Voice).

My favorite poem is "As I Turn the Pages" (see below), in which Perez depicts how Chamoru people are often invisible in western-authored histories of Guam. In the poem, the speaker is sitting in a lecture hall at the University of Guam, listening to a lecture by a history professor on "Romantic and Tragic" portrayals of Guam's history.

Perez asserts that our invisibility is a part of the colonially constructed narrative of our history, in which we, as Chamoru, were considered "passive props" in the struggle between various colonial powers (Spain, Japan, and the United States) to claim Guam. The poem continues with the speaker remembering how she has "turned those pages" of history, which often suggest a "fatal impact" thesis that Chamoru people ceased to exist after colonization.

The fact that the speaker herself is sitting in the classroom learning about our people's history is proof that we still exist despite four centuries of colonialism, despite the erasure of our continued existence in history books.

This theme of cultural survival is further articulated in a prose essay, "Signs of Being—A Chamoru Spiritual Journey," which appears in the second section ("Finakmata") of the collection. Perez writes:

I always come back to the idea of cultural survival. We are here. We are now. But what is it that brought us, as a people, to this point? Despite years of governance by colonial powers, our language and our ways persevere. We are not pickled, preserved, or frozen in time. We are not measurable or validated by blood quantum, ethnic breakdown, physical characteristics or DNA. We are vital, and vitalized by our tenacity and joined inner strength.

It is not in words spoken that we have been taught, but rather in the silent teachings of our *Saina*. What we learn is to open ourselves to the "collective memory" of our People who came before us and help us to move ahead—*I Taotaomo'na*. They show us how to remain in spiritual love and connectedness with each other and our homelands.

Where do we go from here? We are in uncharted waters, or maybe in familiar waters, unable to recognize the signs that show the way. Am I a navigator? Am I *the* navigator? Are we moving? Are the islands moving? Have we been following the navigator, so well-guided we don't even know the navigator is here?

With my diminishing eyesight, I try to expand my vision. I have stopped looking for signs and started feeling for signs. The islands are moving, and we are being guided. I felt my first wave, felt my first star and felt my first island here in recent memory. (24)

I was inspired by Perez's poem, as well as by her work as a whole, because it was, for me, a profound experience of reading the literary signs of Chamoru being, a reminder that my people are still here, still breathing, still writing ourselves into existence. How can we be erased if we are sitting here, reading and writing our once invisible stories?

Moreover, Perez's work inspired me to see, touch, smell, hear, feel, and remember our ancestors because, "Their pain is our legacy." I learned from her to let this pain guide us through the moving and changing islands. I learned from her to let our poems and stories guide us into *i hålom tano, the deep jungle*.

To me, Perez represents an older wave of Chamoru literary creation, and her work continues to guide me as I navigate my own path through our vast sea of stories.

*

As I Turn the Pages

by Cecilia Catherine Taitano Perez

Hungry fingers
feed
searching eyes
that rummage reams of text
between the lines
map the margins,
you'll never find
recordation
of Chamorro minds.

Translate
all you want,
archival
old Spanish
new English
some French, German, Russian, even
the rarely-talked-about Kanji.
You'll learn of flora and fauna
mountains
rivers
streams
and valleys,
that beche de mer
in Chamorro
is balati',
but,
you'll never
find recordation
of Chamorro thought.

In the drama
of what is called,
"The History of Guam,"
severed from

sister homeland,
Northern Marianas,
the stage is set:

sleepy
colonial
island,
Nanyo, extension of Nippon,
and
bastion of American democracy.

One of many scenes
is played:

Foreign actors walk in
float in   fly in   bomb in
inseminate into
the passive props.

Enter, the props:

docile
indolent indios
tawny-skinned
muscle-bound
robust
thieving
ignorant
natives,
but . . .
"they sail a great canoe!"

I've read that script,
I've scanned those books,
I've turned the pages
one by one
forward

backward,
I've turned those pages
looking
sensing,
"Now, if those scholars,
learned men and women,
wrote,
'And in the end . . .'

'in one final gasp for life . . .'
'the last Chamorro died,'
then,
who am I
who know
my self
to be
Chamoru,
and how is it
I sit here
thinking?"

ISHMAEL ANGALUUK HOPE

Inupiaq, Tlingit

*"The more centered I am in my Indigenous systems and ways of knowing
and being, the healthier I feel, and the more receptive to art, literature and wis-
dom I become."*

Invoking a cultural landscape as large as his native Alaska, Ishmael Angaluuk
Hope (1981–) creates poems suffused with Indigenous knowledge. Closely at-
tending to the breadth and also the limits of languages, Hope writes in both
English and Tlingit, and with a ferocity that compounds our comprehension.
His images, always grounded in a threatened landscape, emerge beautifully ren-
dered; and his philosophical meditations seem to promise that by emulating the
original storytellers, whose ways of knowing their home place can still be found
in words, there's basis for faith in the healing of the earth. Written in a flowing
narrative influenced by elders' stories, which address us directly from the land,
Hope's poetry is a gift and a balm.

Canoe Launching into the Gaslit Sea

Now, as much as ever, and as always,
we need to band together, form
a lost tribe, scatter as one, burst
through rifle barrels guided by
by the spider's crosshairs. We need
to knit wool sweaters for our brother
sleeping under the freeway,
hand him our wallets and bathe
his feet in holy water. We need
to find our lost sister, last seen
hitchhiking Highway 16
or panhandling on the streets of Anchorage,
couchsurfing with relatives in Victoria,
or kicking out her boyfriend
after a week of partying
in a trailer park in Salem, Oregon.

Now, as much as ever, and as always,
we need to register together,
lock arms at the front lines, brand
ourselves with mutant DNA strands,
atomic whirls and serial numbers
adding ourselves to the blacklist.
We need to speak in code, languages
the enemy can't break, slingshot
garlic cloves and tortilla crumbs,
wear armor of lily pads and sandstone
carved into the stately faces of bears
and the faraway look of whitetail deer.
We need to run uphill with rickshaws,
play frisbee with trash lids, hold up
portraits of soldiers who never
made it home, organize a peace-in
on the walls of the Grand Canyon.

We need to stage earnest satirical plays,
hold debate contests with farm animals
at midnight, fall asleep on hammocks
hanging from busy traffic lights.

Now, as much as ever, and as always,
we need to prank call our senators,
take selfies with the authorities
at fundraisers we weren't invited to,
kneel in prayer at burial grounds
crumbling under dynamite.
We need to rub salve on the belly
of our hearts, meditate on fault lines
as the earth quakes, dance in robes
with fringe that spits medicine, make
love on the eve of the disaster.

from Love Letter to the Future: A Book of the Land in Eight Acts

ACT 2, SCENE 1: *Sinew Ropes We All Slid Down From*

Pour, pour, pour, pour
pour a parabolic formula
down the Thorstein
      Veblen pipe of history. Reconnoiter
      at lunar tetrahedrons. Foxgloves
gasp at firecrackers
slouching off Mercury.

Ptarmigan yawps his entrance song, balances
      preciously betwixt a pair
      of watchmen, eyes glazed upon
      the wound that opens to mend itself.

Can you do math with music, curvature
          of the canoe's ribs, bind along
          polyphonic strands of warps? Develop me, coin
          for risings asunder glass-encased cormorants.
                    Mix with a trickster of mediastinum
delectation. Affixed for a term,
obedient ligaments which mention
the fate of five fully lived lives ahead
of us. More
appropriately,
it's the dime that skips
between two clapping heels.

Better step back, or the wolves
                    lining cliffs with their backs to the sun
                    will bespeak a fender abutting a ship
propelled by geese slapping wings
against Tide Master's
roiling brim, tears
whipped up to fog and foam.

Saltwater
sprayed
from killer
whale flippers
onto
hair,
eye-
lashes,
lips.

'Go with me.'
Mysterious future lover leads you into nighttime woods.

SCENE 2: *Into Nighttime Woods*

The axon of *what-is* resounds
  from cochlea, cottonwood buds,
  cabled pendulums in the neighborhood of
  telegrams beveled aside last evening's news.

Startled awake to find Kodiak bears
who don human masks, Buick pulled up to
their stick-covered den, mail clerk asserting
  how dire it is to leave messages in the mudroom.

Plasmic-speckled wings smeared
  on glaciers sprawled over rivers.
  Grandfathered in a flash, windblown Treadwell Mine
axe wound, soggy fronds parted in the shade.

The mighty shrew elucidates
  slight modifications to endeavor
  in the next go-round, dryfish under lip,
  glazed for days packing up winter fox pelts.

Brothers' faces powdered away
  at the grindstone, red snapper
  tunic arresting Cornerstone alumni
  as light rain stings the eyes of seagulls.

Spit chewed leaves at bones
  stuffed in Cannibal Giant's mother's
  bucket of leavings. Rubbed by a grass mat,
  mentored in the pied-bill grebe's sleet and marrow.

Massive water beetle's
intestines crammed with brothers' sludge pile,
ingrate, saturnine distinctions,
a puff of fog pawing at spider's legs,
scratches unattainable lover's

lake surface.
Moldering old summed up over a hill of iodine,
bombardment whisks and gusts, clubbed and brined.
Cannoneer sips, wet lips, arms lain exposed,
quiver tightened, atoms bent by leaves, token for the pyre.

Aim your arrow at the throat,
       the palm that extends to midday,
       a few stitches assembling tubes on each
       side, spun upward, buttressed against Foliage Moon.

Dive into the rich man's undersea
       town, ruffles like a robe, ether
       eclipsed simultaneously, trudges
above salmonberry stalks sprawled over streams.

*That spinal range you suppose no one else must glimpse, don't the elder birds pitter,
don't they patter?*

SCENE 3: *Don't They Patter?*

Lift a ladle to the lake monster's
       mouth. Moose hides clang the eight joints
of our last generation, a baker's mitten
       rubbed on the corner table edging the attic.

Ahead of steersmen mountain goat
whiskers joggle, amply
       abiding by the gunwale, a formline eye
       blinks, nostrils whisk in blueberry air.

That's not you, that's not you, this is
you,
       this is
you.
       This.

This
is you.

I greet the swiveling sun, says the husband who came from myriad argillite
ridges over.

And then, she
            said, "The ferns
            gifted me enough boxes of hooligan oil
            to reach ten stories.
            Come
            to my fireside."

The Woman of the Tides will comb beaches
            when a rainbow flips backward,
            water surface lunges for its turn at the sand
            contrary to eagle down drifting to fireweed hair.

SCENE 4: *Eagle Down Drifting To Fireweed Hair*

Gamely stray for the effect,
                        coddle night showers, rear-ending
            blight-addled pine mist, dressing nettle rashes,
            saturated dales rupture caked permafrost.

Inuit, I call for you. Your feet lick
            the roundness of the earth. Leather boots bitten
at the topsole, scrawny buck paws the Manslayer.
            The woman who married an albatross
            patches up Vitus Bering's
sealskin football.

Grams lighter than breath diffusing
            tendrils, a tree frog crept on rinsed out
stamens, bulbs,
torsos.

You shouted down the lightning rod,
  elbow-patched sportcoat dimming
  the winter chill, forget it's easy
  to forget the same they tell themselves.

You'll get me later and I was here before and I was in this movie that people saw.

Bricoleur confederation,
  the skies are Indigenous because of you,
  steel groaning at chasms by hands that tilled soil
  until the theater ore makes is polished by finger oils.

Will Rogers, carry a sack of beans
  so far you retrace your tracks, on par
  with glad-handlers prone to goose-stepping
  well beyond marshes where coals of salvation melt to shore.

Your father's father invites you in,
  water skin robe shimmers, flickers
  blink the torch-lit pathway to stormbound homes,
  makers forge antlers, microbeads, silkscreened posterboards.

A Story of Turtle Island

You know, I may be biased, but Indigenous is the best way to live. It's a whole worldview, a way of seeing things, and it is different than the constructs imposed on us. It's its own thing. The more centered I am in my Indigenous systems and ways of knowing and being, the healthier I feel, and the more receptive to art, literature and wisdom I become. That's what our Elders such as Angayuqaq Oscar Kawagley—who brilliantly articulated and popularized the idea of "Native ways of knowing"—teach us. (See A *Yupiaq Worldview: A Pathway to Ecology and Spirit*, Waveland Press, 2006). Native cultures are vast and diverse, yet they have some overall threads that connect each other. When it comes the oral literatures of our land that were mastered over thousands of years, one of the signs of a great story is its depth of visual acuity. Images are so crystal clear that it's like you're *there* as the story unfolds. As my Tlingit Elder David Katzeek said of his grandmother's stories, "You could smell the seaweed." The images are invoked so powerfully that it elicits the body's entire sensory system. While that feeling of being there is also present in Western literatures, perhaps it's not as focused on vision, as they may be looking for other things, such as psychological or linguistic complexity.

Sequoyah Guess, of the United Keetoowah Band of Cherokee Indians, is one of our world's great artists, a genius storyteller who I believe should receive the Nobel Prize in Literature, if only genuine appreciation for the oral tradition was much more widespread. I am grateful for Christopher B. Teuton, a scholar and member of the Cherokee Nation, for editing a book in which Guess and his Elder colleagues tell many beautiful stories, *Cherokee Stories of the Turtle Island Liars' Club* (University of North Carolina Press, 2016). Guess is also an accomplished writer who has published many works. Guess's laconic style and humility belie—or perhaps reinforce—his brilliance. He often ends his stories with "at least that's how Gramma told it," invoking his beloved grandmother, Maggie Turtle, who raised him, who told him most of his magnificent repertoire, and who lived to be ninety-eight years old. Every now and then Guess slips in a gloriously penetrating insight or a superbly crisp image, without fuss, without announcing its mastery. Lovers of Native stories recognize they are in the presence of greatness.

In just a few short pages, it can be quite challenging to demonstrate Sequoyah Guess's mastery, especially for those unaccustomed to what makes Native stories good. At some point there is a universal place where we all find common ground, yet it can get tangled up and the path can get blocked, so it takes some work, but only the kind of work it takes to appreciate a play by William Shakespeare or a novel by Leo Tolstoy. The literary excellence of those works, however, is taken for granted, and their aesthetic lexicon and scholarly upkeep are firmly in place. Also, I suppose I should justify using a Native story as a poem. We would have to expand our idea of poetry in order to include Sequoyah Guess's story of Turtle Island. Yet we call Homeric and Slavic epics poetry, so it's not a far stretch. Is the difference of meter really that important in an age when the use and recognition of meter, save for the internal analysis of sound patterns by practitioners and specialists, is practically extinct? Perhaps it is more about the unconscious bias against literary quality in Native oral literatures than it is about the definition of poetry.

I don't want to act like our literatures only began when White people introduced writing to us, or to merely treat our traditions and their bearers like vague sources to draw from. And we are not doing our ancient traditions any justice if we, like the rest of society, subjugate them to the anonymous folkloric corner, or strictly to the children's section. Our elders and ancestors are individuals, and they were often individuals of great beauty, complexity, mastery, intelligence and talent. The words of so many of them stand the test of time. It's a good time to learn just who some of these individuals are.

We've adapted where we've had to, like Cowichan knitters who learned the art of knitting from Europeans, yet they also firmly recognize the Indigenous nature of their knitting tradition, flowing from their own ancient weaving tradition and incorporating their own styles and innovations. Sequoyah Guess calls himself a "non-traditional traditionalist." He says, "As Gaduwas, we tend to be able to blend in with our surroundings. That is one of the things we have learned over the years, is to be a part of society but still be able to keep our own individual identities." (See Daniel C. Swann's interview with Sequoyah Guess on YouTube: "Native Peoples of Oklahoma: Literary Futures," retrieved online December 31, 2017.)

Guess's story of Turtle Island is one that's perhaps "well-known," yet it's the only telling of it that I've found from a Cherokee storyteller who speaks their language and is told in oral form. As a Native writer, I've learned not to get too caught up in ideas of authenticity, but I highly value the artistry of oral storytellers. The story reveals to us deep, fundamental properties of the "nature of nature," as my friend, poet, essayist, and translator Robert Bringhurst, observed when elucidating the meaning and function of mythology (see *Tree of Meaning: Language, Mind, and Ecology*, Counterpoint Press, 2008). As the late Elder Hastings Shade told Christopher Teuton, "We need to learn to listen to nature as our elders once did." Reading Guess's story, I locate in my psyche a place where everything intuitively clicks, where everything is connected, from the conscious teachings of the elders to the wellspring of insight of the stories to deeply internal, personal experiences and thoughts to the sensory and "extra"-sensory experience of nature. All the while, I recognize that there are likely deeper meanings that Cherokee people themselves know. While Native writers are rightfully countering and subverting stereotypes such as being "one with nature," I think there is something to the deep understanding of nature consciousness in our old stories and old teachings.

On the level of craft, I urge the reader to look through and perhaps savor, as I do, the delightfully idiosyncratic turns of phrase and word choices in this short story where not a single word is inessential, such as a "speck of mud," or "And that told the people that the mud was dry enough to step on now, so." The way Guess scaffolds and unwinds his stories evinces a vision where little is missed, and much joy comes from the image journey, apparently both for the storyteller and the listener. Still, this one short story isn't enough to successfully demonstrate Sequoyah Guess's artistry, just as we wouldn't know much of Shakespeare from reading a single monologue or sonnet. We've got to read, or better, listen to, many of his stories, for hours or hundreds of pages. And we've got to respect the work, perhaps *take for granted* its *literary merit*, and perhaps even its *literary mastery*, as we do works in the Western literary canon, and works propped up by elite literary institutions, both of which almost entirely exclude Native American oral literature, though Native writers of English sometimes get a pass.

I'd love it if more people enjoyed Guess's deeply complex Cherokee migration history, or could feel the chill of his grandmother's scary story about the ravenmocker, or basked in the whimsy of a short teaching story which always seems much more complex and open-ended than the moral it teaches. Hastings Shade, Sammy Still, and Woody Hansen also tell some incredibly fine stories.

We should bring to these texts the same serious consideration we give to writers of importance. What do we have to lose? Why is Native oral literature blotted out of the map, ignored, even, by many Native writers of English? Does it reopen old colonial wounds? Is it—as the missionaries expertly grasped when killing off our languages—a key into our sovereignty, self-realization, and empowerment? Again, what do we have to lose by simply giving this the time of day and extending it some courtesy and respect?

I have a sense of what we'd gain. Our minds and bodies would begin to absorb the clarity of vision the Elders have, that Sequoyah Guess has, from hearing so many stories as they unfold crystal-clear vision after vision, visions that emanate from the contours and consciousness of the land in all its history and transformation. We'd have a tighter community. And, perhaps as Hastings Shade suggested, we'd relearn to listen to nature as our Elders once did.

*

A Story of Turtle Island

told by Sequoyah Guess

A long time ago
the earth was covered with water.
And over this water
this giant turtle
flew.
And on the back of the turtle was us,
the people.
And, the people kept getting more and more,
until there was so many that they started falling off the sides.
Well, Uneltlvnv, the Creator,
saw that happening so he told
the water beetle to dive down
and bring up a speck of mud.
And so the water beetle dove down to the bottom,
brought up this little speck of mud.
But as soon as it hit air,
that speck of mud started spreading out.
And, the people, they sent out
the giant buzzard.
Suli.
To fly and find a dry spot.
And Suli flew all over the world.
And, as he started getting tired,
he kept getting lower and lower to the earth.
And, when he'd flap his wings whenever he'd go down,
that's where the valleys were formed.
whenever they'd come up,
that's where the mountains were formed.
And so finally, Suli got back to the turtle.
And he told 'em there was no dry land yet.
So the people waited a while again
and finally sent out a raven.
And it went out and it stayed out for a long time.
Finally, it came back and it had a

branch in its mouth.
And that told the people that the mud was dry enough to step on now, so.
So the turtle landed and the people walked off.
So that's how we got . . .

And I know that kind of sounds a bit like . . . Noah? With the birds and stuff.
But, that's a story that Gramma told me.

MICHAELSUN STONESWEAT KNAPP
Costanoan-Rumsen Carmel Band of Ohlone Indians

"I elected to resist breaking within the lines and stanzas where the violence of invalidation had been previously enacted upon us—I would break and self-determine validation."

In the poetry of Michaelsun Stonesweat Knapp (1989–) the self-generating insights are phenomenally keen, sceptical, and hip. Working with archival texts, the riff-raff of contemporary culture, and shrewdly chosen personal details, he creates chronicles of loves, fears, and hopes we share (despite so much else that's changed) with our predecessors. A poet exceedingly attentive to structure and lineation, Knapp's smart use of enjambment and his collisions in diction and lexicon may leave a reader breathless, asked to take difficult truths in heaping spoonfuls. Yet tonally, these poems often have a steadily measured gravitas, the weight of the past gathered into syntax. Knapp looks askance at history and the society around us, with a cock-eyed knack for making the known unknown or certainly less familiar.

Manwreck

Caillebote, Gustave. Jour De Pluie a Paris. 1877.
Miles, Nelson A. (Gen). Accepts the Surrender of the Nez Perce from
Chief Joseph after Years of Pursuit and War and Slaughter of the
Nez Perce. 1877.

so picture me reading from *The Eye of the World*
      in a Borders bookstore. Picture
       the book — the hand
    that slaps it from mine —

that dad's legs are mule deer legs
tattered by tatted mutts along shorelines
      cemented over. Picture

him standing like a chevron over me, shin and thigh disrobed —
thin beneath fetid shorn tendon cords, and tea
   colored calcaneus
      jutting naked in dead   air.
          Picture dad's

bullet-riddled black bear head, the antlers booming
    from his brackish eye
      sockets swept skyward
          then aft — hear

his brass steeple roar. Picture everyone silent, their eyes
    to pages in hand   secured — rather
         to my face it is
      which treble
   hooks have sunk into
  the gills of their memories: watching
    wet walleye choking on air. And picture
      as one, they all
        step and step out

of their bodies: shorter versions. Picture inches

                behind their now shrunken feet,
     their older
larger bodies lay deflated —

I picture them all crawling with silverfish — and ill-

           fitting on the carpet haphazardly
     piled so high no one can see
     the books. So picture
        dad swelled from the meat
               of my shoulder

                      — lips —
          deltas of blood, thin
        borders of sound

on a globe, dry and drowned. His demask hand held out
for mine — scented citrus, wood dust, exhaust, vanilla extract
                 "We're leaving."

    My wrist woven — wretched corvidae — cuffs
    of porcupine spines, petroleum-wrought and already
    sodden —   stays at his call and I

hear the clinking of copper and steel
     in the fog bank
       which raises
         sherbet   stains
           on every horizon

        after dark, to my eyes
under countless boar tusks, headlights.
Now picture my wrist

rising by fishing line   strung through bent and corroded dice,

around its radial artery,
                    to fall into the cup
                            of his palm as a door
slammed open
            and the floor before it.
                            Picture my mouth
            full of blood
from my cheek. Picture skin
pooling down the driveway,

        forming a formula for telling callused
                    and carotid materials
from each other. Picture the sun

            green as a bruise. Picture
        batwings of streetlight fluttering
    on my bedroom ceiling. Picture always
            will there be orphans
                and liars.

At What Number Are Numbers No Good?

Friedrich, Caspar David. The Abby in the Oakwood.
(Chief) Tecumseh. Address to (Indiana Governor) Harrison at Vin-
cennes, Indiana.

Father, today was not the first
ending of the world. I have lived

a thousand nights wept-through,
and built a house from a house.

I know blood does not stop

when begged. I do not know
what will be the consequences.

But, father, my ears are swelling

wombs of sound. From scoured whirls,
I knew you, and knew today

was not the first ending: Touch
the dirt on my neck, gathering in the oil

of the rifle and skin of our star as you

bring our foreheads together, our breath
together. Wading up our street

wreathed with havoc; if only for an hour, I will try

to end, again, this trouble between us,
but if alone —   —then alone.

On "At What Number Are Numbers No Good?" and *Tecumseh's Speech to the Osages*

Before I begin talking about the craft of any poem in this series, I first need to discuss some of the choices that make this series this series—as those requirements and choices will inform and make-less-arbitrary the craft choices of this particular poem, whose discussion begins with the fourth paragraph.

One of the guiding elements of the series that this poem is from was that the form of the poem should match the function of the poem—and each poem had several moving, functioning pieces in this series, and "At What Number are Numbers No Good?" is no exception. They are all triangulated from a notable event of American Indian history—Chief Tecumseh's (Shawnee) Address to Governor Harrison at Vincennes, Indiana—a piece of art completed within

12 months of the event on the Gregorian Calendar—Caspar David Friedrich's *Abby in the Oakwood*—and an emotionally germane piece of autobiography—my attempt to meaningfully bridge the conversation gap between my father and I without simply capitulating to his overbearing or dominance.

Once all three points were plotted, they created a plane or a lens; each point experienced a different amount of chiral motion which poured its images onto the lens so that the poem came into focus. Then, I would pull my hair out for weeks to months making as careful craft choices as I could, utilizing research I had done (whose depth was on an as-needed basis; some requiring quite a lot, some requiring hardly any) and stories I had been told; and consciously working within the limitations of my current threshold of experience and aesthetics—to then make what I 'see and hear' finally into poem.

The craft that went into "At What Number are Numbers No Good?" was heavily influenced from various recorded and reportedly-recorded speeches and exchanges between Tecumseh (Shawnee)—whose life's work became the unity of several tribal nations, following his brother's apotheosis as a prophet—to a then-Governor of the Indiana Territory, William Henry Harrison—who would later become President of the United States due to his life's work: killing Indians. Though President Harrison would be best remembered—not for his killings of the indigenous peoples of this land for the purposes of inexpensive American land acquisition sanctioned by the American State on the territories of otherwise sovereign indigenous nations', but instead—for the shortness of his presidency: dying in office like a dick after reading a two-hour inaugural address on a frigid and damp day in March without the necessary cold-weather accoutrement, like a jacket, to prove to his haters how tough he still was at sixty-eight years young.

Some of the language and intention of this poem most heavily draws from an exchange that Tecumseh reportedly had with Harrison in 1811 at a conference—which can be read with some salt that it is in its unaltered fullness in Edward Eggleston and L. E. Seelye's 1878 text, *Tecumseh and the Shawnee Prophet*—with a line even coming directly from the above text "... I do not know what will be the consequence ..." appearing in the poem. The poem's craft also takes inspiration from and against the form in what has been published as, *Tecumseh's Speech to the Osages*, as well as his use of repeated addresses to his audience as brothers, speaking to a gathering of male peers of the Osage nation; though, since the poem is to the speaker-of-the-poem's father—the speaker addresses his father.

Continuing the discussion of form, the poem takes inspiration again from

Tecumseh's Speech to the Osages in the brevity of what follows those addresses—which causes the speech, when published, to be in many short paragraphs—and so the poem's form follows this in that it is in couplets and single-line stanzas. However, I broke from the publication of Tecumseh's language translated into English when it came to my breaks, both of stanza and line. Since there are several instances where the published text makes better sense to have had several addresses in a single unified paragraph—form following function in prose regarding unity of tribal nations—and so to not have been split into different paragraphs.

This became my way of taking back or refusing to engage with the act that broke Tecumseh's language into said paragraphs by keeping with similarly simple breaks—which had been done by those who had recorded and published his oratory, which left those breaks as overly simple—and, as an indigenous person I become highly suspicious whenever I see indigenous people portrayed as simple, especially someone as complicated and talented as Tecumseh—and given that the verb break describes a violent action with permanent consequences, I elected to resist breaking within the lines and stanzas where the violence of invalidation had been previously enacted upon us—I would break and self-determine validation.

However, the poem does early on utilize endstopped breaks, which would seem to discount my above explained choices. The first sentence ends midline of the second line, "Father, today is not the first / ending of the world. I have lived // " . . . which keys in readers who are aware of Tecumseh that I am not making choices thoughtlessly.

And yet, this poem is not about Tecumseh. In enmity and diplomacy this relationship between the two men, Tecumseh and Harrison both convexly and macroscopically mirrors the relationship between the two figures in the poem, the speaker and his father. To say that there is a direct transplantation of one figure into another, I think is a question which both naturally springs from these juxtapositions, and also, to me, uninterestingly limits the complexity of the relationship: they are at times one, the other, both, and neither—and so they are always somehow like magnets: exactly similar and in complete opposition being shoved together across an ocean of tension and iron filings.

Discussing the content of this poem and its form somewhat, there is of a son plying for mutual respect and peace with his father (untrod ground in poetry if there ever was any), and so for the form to walk on these two different lines—it must show that the relationship is not just a father and son butting heads—the relationship is more complicated than only that—so at times the sentence ends protected with the beginning of a new sentence within a couplet of enjambed lines, very much the intended essence of a parent-child relationship. But this specific relationship has had something go wrong, and so there are endstopped lines, such as the third and fourth, "a thousand nights wept-through, / and built a house from a house. //"

The content of those lines meeting the form, right? Something about the relationship is ending or stopping where the lines are endstopped.

So, continuing this discussion of lineation, I should explain that part of my process involves the initial writing and editing of poems as prose-blocks whose lines are not broken until much later, and that I followed this process when writing this poem. When breaking the lines and stanzas in this poem, part of what influenced my choices of when and where was the advice given by M. Evelina Galang in response to someone else's question at an AWP panel in Minneapolis, and to paraphrase what she said, she said follow the sound, and it will take you to places no other guide will—or can, for that matter. So following the sound of this poem and its influences, the breaks began to appear and offered me small voltas in the text or offered me a moments of complication in understanding or syntax—all within a language partly mine and partly Tecumseh's which has evolved in a country that is everywhere always a graveyard.

MICHAEL WASSON
NIMÍIPUU

"I write because all of my storytellers are dead."

Bringing forth the stories of his ancestral land and the grandfather who raised him, Michael Wasson (1990–) writes poetry that originates in prodigious concentration. Joining fractured timelines with great tonal, phrasal, and typographical variation, Wasson's poems are laced with his native Nimiipuu language. His frequent shifts in diction and texture keep on registering the implications of preconceptions, exposing misguided factuality and mistaught narratives. Although some of his poems may seem as densely packed as prose, other poems are more free-form and spacious, utilizing open space to challenge the silences left by history, the gaps of suppressed story. With judicious formal choices and multilingual virtuosity, Wasson demonstrates how artistry can overleap the weight of historical trauma.

Aposiopesis [Or, the Field Between the Living & the Dead]

& forgive me
for I cannot

tell you how
to begin

but here
is the body

like the *urge*
to pray —

your mouth
already gone.

& we never
said *you*: a boy

woman
man — only

the animal made
with two hands

& lost
in the field

waiting
for human life

to reenter
as if through

a door
broken — &

yet the dead
who love

you — who
are still

remembering
the touch

of blood-
warmed skin —

abandon you
like every

yesterday —
like this

single paradise
of every-

body's silence
rusting day-

light into
the only dusk

we have
been made

to see.

I Say After-Rain, You Say Hahal̲x̲páawisa

I call out to you like a / You whose flesh is cleared out / from our ghosted
shadows to the cracked lips of / the horizon. There you are / at the cathedral

in my mouth. A garden: *tamsáasnim láatis. líickaw. tíms* bloomed / in
dirt & scattered. The doorway. Are you honest enough to say / You've ever

loved? To not forget tearing / down every door to beat Your image / into
your son's memory? You know / a boy's name but do you know mine? Say

ix̲tab with a cord slung / around your neck. Say *cannibal.* / *'ilcwéew'cix̲.* Or
tilípe' who leaps over / your deaths. Another dead / father is being brought

back to his son's thinning arms. / An ache that touches / the very wet end
of my tongue. Ignite me with this / blessing, Father. Give me this seventh

day to wash / You & your taste from my mouth. / Recall the ruined
entrance. The rust damaging / the architecture. Father, forgive me for / ever

asking. For a mother stands in your light / gone out. Screaming. Shattering
every last mirror in the house. To burn / the field & stand alone until the blood

of a forefather / rivers clean. Finally / motionless like the years / you've lived
You say: *the eighth day / I offer this eternal blessing.* Smelling of the dead

scorched grass: it starts to rain again.

Self-Portrait as 1879–1934

It has darkened here only because the light inside
the room. Now place your hand there. See. That —

no, this — this is your face & so: *what are you*

but a citizen of this nation you were born into

by no hands of your own. Like the architecture
of briefly lit chapels, you stand here so silent

you're already another century broken
in two. Your mouth looks just like your father's

when he was still alive, crying. Four white walls
in the dark. How his skin felt of scratched chalk-

board with each new written version of him
now so American: his name sparing his one blood-

red life. & see your mother kneeling at this quiet
cage of crushed windows that held the last image

of her black hair. Say you see nothing in this
language & everything inside *'iníise pewíski, ne'é.*

ne'é? This tongue of animals you give to the open
night. Like a lungful of gnashed syllables rusted

to the throat. Say *c'éewc'ew* like a promise made
of bone — because after the body, what's left

is bone. The jaw opened wide enough to say *your
name* like a wildfire spreading through your home-

land every summer when you are left to stand
in its pine forest. & god. The forest. Save me,

my lost savior. Save the boy who sees the blood
inside him. The forest. How it means: shadows

learning to breathe again — the disgraced light
here. It means all these branches are clotheslines

where nothing hangs anymore. It means you
touching the mirror is enough to crack apart

every America you've known since. It means no-
body is here. It means the ash in the dirt blown

to air was the braided hair of your ghosts longing
to welcome you back. Which is to say: yes, every-

one is here.

This Dusk in a Mouth Full of Prayer

When you came
                              into my mouth
                opened wide enough

to forget
                              how to swallow

light: this surrendering

                              the body is my skin

tracing starved beauty
                              in climax: *us*

lying in the dark
                              shadow of another
        lord: give me your dying

words like *father*
                              or my tongue

disappearing before
                    you: welík'ipckse
so tell me this

when you've forgotten
                    how to open

your lips into my name —

                    father: which is
another way to say *shadow*:

failed daylight
                    you say: *the sky*
touching the body: I
                    find myself entering

a night again wounded
          enough for the snow—

shined with moon
     — to reorder the stars with
our faces: broken

          through with so many

American mouths: like
                    ghosts singing

the very last bright word they

remember: *amen.*

Self-Portrait as Article 1 [1]. [Treaty with Nez Percés, 1855]: Cession of Lands to the United States

In the year of their lord, *this eleventh day of June*, I enter the boundaries of my body:

The said [centuries here dissolve & I re-ink *nimíipuu*] hereby cede, relinquish & convey—here,

I want to convey how my physical testament is written &, at a particular point, then erased into the land—

to the United States all their right, title, & interest in & to the country occupied or claimed by them,

bounded & described as follows, *to wit:*

in the year of their lord, in the boundaries of my body, *they* intend to clarify the divisions & say *to wit:*

& so I enter every name of the dead into each source of water, each river mouth, every flattened field:

& I cross out the cross of the divide & lie down on the crest of [every mountain has its name,

a place of, a place of where the animals & humans met, a place where the story began, a place where the blood was washed, a place at the heart named for our monster(s) & tim'néepe,

a place where the gray coldness looms like hiqúxqux̣cenki, where America names over the land [tąptłápt

wtetes], a place where the blue haze of warmth looms like hi'lap̓ãp̓x̣p̓ãpx̣canki, where the bodies lie

unburied]. I, a silhouette, a hereunto, am between the articles of the & a(n): indefinite, definite:

& it is here in the boundaries I have no choice but: to set [my] hands, on this eleventh day of June,

on behalf of the above-named, at the place, on the day & year hereinbefore written, to seal the body shut:

i.

[x] [an empty cross, fallen]

Sealed & signed in the presence of us—

I Am To Carry This History, This Body: "*Our Completion*: Oil on Wood: Tino Rodríguez: 1999"

In 1999, I was nine years old. Incomplete. I was a boy told that the world would be swallowed by a fatherly darkness. A night so black we could swear it was the sky's throat. My mother told us that three days of darkness would come. My brother said that the lights across the river would burn out. I prayed to myself, in the small corner of my year, asking somebody's Lord, "Why take us?" That night, when I remembered how my skeleton could ache when adults spoke about death like storytellers—no explanation, only events—my uncle said that all the bullets are being bought up to wipe us out. We didn't buy any bullets. We built a fire to keep warm.

i.

Before nourishment there must be obedience.

i.

I happened upon "All the Trees of the Field Shall Clap Their Hands" by Eduardo C. Corral. Something in his poem felt urgent, so I bought his book, *Slow Lightning*. I opened to the first poem and read.

The body grows into itself, the bones, the flesh. A human being. I, too, must kneel toward *some*thing.

I'm in the coffee shop down the street where I've been writing clunky, congested lines. Filled with terror and embarrassment, I try to find something to hold onto before every graduate level poetry workshop.

But I stare at the line "Before nourishment there must be obedience," and I feel a mouth whispering to my ear, so close the wet breath sticks to my eardrum like darkness. I stare until I lose myself, close my eyes, and remember how '*iceyéeye* could only bring back his beloved until he complied to the ghost figure who advised, "Do everything just so." And there, in the bright field between the living and the dead, '*iceyéeye* was in the field placing invisible, make-believe serviceberries to his tongue—nourishing his body with all that had vanished.

i.

In his hands I was a cup overflowing with thirst.

i.

In *his* hands. I was never a boy in his hands. My mother's hands shape my own. Ghosts miss their hands. I remember when my hands grew larger than my mother's. I put my palms to her palms, seeing how mine quietly edged over the border of hers. The first time I noticed how the body wants to reach past its creation, its creator. But then again, my ghosts are holding my body in place. I am the river water in their missing hands, cupped, motioning: *drink*. For it is this body that wants to swallow their language, swallow what they witnessed in those smeared centuries. I am this same cup, hollowed out. I am filled with something *felt*, no longer seen.

i.

Eighth ruler of my days, ninth lord of my nights:

i.

The eighth day is a day long forgotten. The final day, the seventh, is Sunday. *halxpáawit*: the day of becoming. There is an after-day in which nothing happens: *halxpawit'áasx*. There is a before-day in which we stand looking at the dusk, waiting for tomorrow, steady until we become again: *halxpawináqit*.

This line takes me back to a language I'm longing to remember, a tongue that insists a *before* and *after*, a day in which we are rebuilt, a day when the earth turning was the Lord and every animal walked toward us on two legs. Every small god knelt until we emerged from a violence of monstrous creation. We knelt beside their bodies and prayed for nourishment. *halxpáawit. k'uycú' hanyaw'áat*: nine creators. A perfect cycle of three before ten.

i.

he thrashed above me, like branches. Once,

i.

Every poem has its branches reaching back toward sources of light. Every poem has its roots tightening further inside the dark of a body—a history. Once, a ghost came to my window, but my brother said it was only the moonlight tangled in the curtains. When I remember thrashing, I see the deer's body still palpitating and its limp tongue. Its gnarled, panting lips. Steam rising. Somewhere its root, its throat glitching. Its mouth gasps like a newborn's as the hole in its head leaks around our feet. Crimson halos.

i.

after weeks of rain, he sliced a potato in half

i.

Weeks of rain. I hear my grandfather slicing potatoes in the kitchen. It's morning again, and the grease crackles in the pan. My grandfather's hands are gorgeous and brown—full of rage and heat. Always so oily, god-forsakenly dirty. When he touches my head, they're soft and dry like the sun-pressed undersides of fallen leaves. But his hand holds the knife. He slices potatoes as though clocks made for wider seconds.

i.

to remind me of the moon. The dark slept in the small

i.

The moon is another way to describe the luminary body that lights up the sky— no matter the sky. My grandfather says *hiisemtuks*. When I was a boy, I asked if *hiisemtuks* was the world. He was confused. I said that it looks like the world reflected in a mirror. I had imagined the sky a mirror. The earth a distant reflection of its face staring back. Later, I learned the verb *hitin'iikce*—the sun or moon performing its routine. In other words, it means the body of light moving across the sky. I am reminded of a dimmed figure, swallowed and, in its faint slow effort, ignited—burning alive.

i.

of his back. The back of his knees: pale music.

i.

Language is the mouth's first gesture towards music, toward prayer, addressing the body's need for incantation. For devotion. The body is a reservoir of all the music taken in. The touch of the hand will turn to heartbeats. The knees will knock together into butterfly wings, into *we'é, we'é, we'é*. The teeth will chatter like the *óxoxox* of bones clattering. The spine is a ladder I've been made to protect. It pins me with curved gravity.

Some days, I imagine the small of his back like a rain puddle. I reach in and pull out his hand I've longed to touch. The music of his body gone silent. Days and days of rain prattle the floorboards until we fall into the earth turned sky and hear only the wind of our descent.

i.

We'd crumble the Eucharist & feed it to the pigeons.

i.

I think about the last dinner I ever had with someone who is no longer here. I crumble before that person, that dearly beloved, that person's warm torso I placed my ear to. I heard the heart throbbing under the skin—deep in the body. Once, in the light of the living room, after preparing a meal for our relatives, after a full year of mourning, we leave some plates outside full of food. I never checked on the plates.

Michael Wasson 489

i.

Sin vergüenza. Escuintle. He Who Makes Things Sprout.

i.

kiceynúut. hacwaláam'yac. Without shame. Boy-child. *hikceyniw'úuce*, he goes to forget his shame. *tustimasáat'alpa*, the sun is high / we are about to gather roots in the higher grounds / this is the time when everything sprouts / June.

i.

In the margins in a book of poems by Emily Dickinson

i.

In high school, our textbooks were so old. The edges of pages, spines, their whole heavy structures tattered. In the margins, the people of my community wrote little messages from the '90s to *whoever* might be holding these books. The line I remember most is the line of black ink that ran through: ~~TREATY VS NON-TREATY.~~

What am I in the pages of a book? What divides me? What conquers me? I'm afraid to know.

i.

he scribbled: *she had a pocketful of horses/Trojan/*

i.

Now I'm lying down in the back of the truck. I'm told to stay low because we don't want to get stopped by the police before we make it up to the mountains. We always turn the volume up when Prince comes on the radio. My favorite line: *I guess I should've closed my eyes / when you drove me to the place / where your horses run free.* Someday I'll close my eyes, stand up inside all of this dragged wind and—like an appaloosa's silhouette about to slip away—crumble.

i.

& some of them used. Often I mistook him for a storyteller

i.

Does the poem always interact with the history of the body that stands in its own silence? Before I read some poems for the first time for a graduate school showcase, I tell the audience, I write because all of my storytellers are dead. I stare at the poem I'm holding in my hand. I feel like I've just torn the vessels in my wrists. I'm losing more than I'll ever be able to hold again.

i.

when he stood in the rain. *A su izquierda, huesos.*

i.

It's raining right now on this side of the world. How I want anyone with me right now. *'íinim cáky'axpkin'ika, pipíscim.* On my left side, only bones. Everyone whom this poem touches is gone. In a way, I'm gone too. In a way, I'm stepping outside into the rain, if only to stand. If only to raise the body up by the very bones I carry.

i.

A su derecha, mapas de cuero. When I'd yawn,

i.

wepsúuxpkin'ike, on the right side. But I don't know how to say *map*, so I write: *tíimenin' wéetes 'ipsúuski*—land written by the hand. To taste anything beyond the body, to survive, open your mouth.

i.

he'd pluck black petals out of my mouth.

Poems touch me like this.
So ignite the dark in my throat. Pull out any flicker of light I've long forgotten.
Reach into me, and make me remember. Please.

*

The preceding essay is composed as a line-by-line interaction of associative leaps between Eduardo C. Corral's poem "*Our Completion*: Oil on Wood: Tino Rodríguez: 1999" and my own writing development. Either via personal history, the sharpening or exploded view of metaphor, or even ruminations on how the text enters and transforms the body, Corral's poem is exemplary, potent, and an everlasting lighthouse. It provides an early instance of how I came to digest language and refract it through a new, blooming light (my own indigenous existence). At times, I return to childhood, isolate moments and sensations of touch, remember stories and fractures of *nimipuutímt* (in Nez Perce language), and consequently find myself reflecting on how poems find flesh in the body, often through coaxing from guidepost poems like Corral's was for me.

*

Our Completion: Oil on Wood: Tino Rodríguez: 1999
by Eduardo C. Corral

Before nourishment there must be obedience.
In his hands I was a cup overflowing with thirst.
Eighth ruler of my days, ninth lord of my nights:
he thrashed above me, like branches. Once,
after weeks of rain, he sliced a potato in half
to remind me of the moon. The dark slept in the small
of his back. The back of his knees: pale music.
We'd crumble the Eucharist & feed it to the pigeons.
Sin vergüenza. Escuintle. He Who Makes Things Sprout.
In the margins in a book of poems by Emily Dickinson
he scribbled: *she had a pocketful of horses/Trojan/*

& some of them used. Often I mistook him for a storyteller
when he stood in the rain. A su izquierda, huesos.
A su derecha, mapas de cuero. When I'd yawn,
he'd pluck black petals out of my mouth.

BENJAMÍN NAKA-HASEBE KINGSLEY
Onondaga

". . . truly I have set my compass to many of the poets here who are both honor-ed and honor-ing."

Benjamín Naka-Hasebe Kingsley (1990–) describes himself as "the Affrilachian son of two mixed-race wheelbarrow factory workers," and is a member of the indigenous Onondaga Nation in New York. He has lived all over the U.S., having grown up in Pennsylvania, gone to college in Los Angeles, earned advanced degrees at the University of Pennsylvania, and, after teaching in Florida, held fellowships in Massachusetts and now Baltimore. His first collection, Not Your Mama's Melting Pot, was published in 2018, and two more collections, Colonize Me and Dēmos, are forthcoming. He has said the aim of his work is to "lay bare mixed-race displacements: Indigenous Americans understood only as wax corpses in museums; the immigrant grind; anti-Latinx rhetoric still reverbing through our 21st century America; the quandary of Rust Belt poverty plaguing small Appalachian communities, its cycle of concrete ceilings, its left-hook-right-hook masculinity, its dirt-caked realities." His poems are tensile and combative, rife with anger but cannily structured, and with sudden turns to raw tenderness.

American Rust

Buried   palm to palm   beneath floorboards
trapped residue   of her forefather's will   small
cowhide gloves   burnt orange   well-battered

gloves so small   she knows   she could slip
inside them   how her hands will   reek
of sheet metal   the upriver   trout

for days   her fins   flail against a greasy fate below
the yellowed   rocks of her fingernails   oil squirms
reminding her   for years of   factory men

weekend walks   to the laundromat   tangled trash bags
bursting with work   clothes   the stained glint
of beer   in glasses clacked   with weekday husbands

caught in their sloshing   gait of hunger   patina of bootfall
each wade   slow   home in hammy down
pickups   loosened tool belts   each exhale then hard won

now left to her   mechanic's daughter   a better life
in her studio   the corner kiln fires   each day's work uneven
one armful of clay dried   to the bone   others wet

everlasting some of her   work   will never dry
a small rebellion   against the modern   mouth of automation
humanity whirring   on the primacy   of a future tense

her hands are wet   with the glaze   of decades
undying   memories overworked   so painstakingly
greased in American oil   they never truly   rust

just another horse poem

from the language of the Onondaga Nation in outer Appalachia

a filthy little indian   that's what she calls me
this stallkeep half woman   half corncob pipe
my ears smoke red   every time she huffs filthy
but I tamp down   my tongue quick
cause she lets me muck   stall after stall
better to smell like a horse   than an Indian
if I say *ain't that the truth*   she'll laugh and leave
she'll wade out   into blinding pasture
so far I can barely see   all the shadows
of what demons her   she'll stand scarecrow
for hours smoothing down   her own matted hair
while I dare to run   my fingers slick with spittle
through the base knot   after knot of one *sweet boy*
and his sticky mane   *if you touch him I will beat you*
redder than your Cherokee hide   I nod knowing
there are times to joke   and times to just nod
at night when I sneak in   *sweet boy* nods to me
between pipe bars   black stall after stall
lit by a pitcher of moonshine   and the shimmer
of his milky huff   my big toothed *agonze agonze*
I know where *agonze*   all the keys are hid
I sing him agonze   like a true name
he nods to me   nods and nods until my arms
are mottled in his hide   until he lies down
and I paint myself   across the musculature
of his back   and when he stands tall
I let my hands lie long   behind the pieces
of his shoulders and when I   hold the wet drum
of his heart   I am ne hochsàte I am
horsemen fullhearted   enormous I am
I am clean I am   bigger even than this

Run: 2nd Street Harrisburg PA Summertime '17

Bullshit   watch your sister   be arrested
for daring   to dance   her jay-stunting
across the street   be next   to her but say
nothing   because this ain't   Footloose
and you will   always be   a coward
instead just be   thankful   for the iphones
filming   for women   with stronger
forearms   for men   with bigger
voices   think instead about   your next
drink   don't be   thinking
about   every other   time
you were   not   brave
don't be   thinking   *I am a teacher*
sometimes   I even smile   at cops
I can win   this one over   with kind reason
he is bald   white   short
his uniform   has come   untucked
be close   enough   to see cliché
sweat   on his upper lip   be brave
be brave   you think   about anything but
boot scrape   baton clatter   police-grade
mace   your own knee's   crunch
against storefront   signpost   stumbling away
I could be   blind   what if I am
blind   forever   you think
why am I   mouthing   *Excuse me Sir?*

> *I ain't never ran from nothing but the police*
> —Summertime '06   Vince Staples

Our Work Is Never Over

"so much depends / upon / the red wheel / barrow . . .," and we know the rest by heart. For my mother, our daily bread depended upon a single wheelbarrow factory, thrown levers and thumbed switches, churning out True Temper farm equipment, hard-shelled and blue. Even though I was watered on the edge of a Pennsylvania Rust Belt trailer park—where rooting for the Pittsburgh Steelers felt more like religion than fanfare—my mother preached at the supper table pulpit that her side of the family was grown from nobler stock.

Because her father, my ojiisan, Naka Hasebe, was imprisoned in an iron cage for writing anti-WWII poetry, because my grandfather was repeatedly beaten within a few pages of his life in pursuit of peace, I grew up genuinely believing poetry was dangerous, political, affecting—a conduit for spiritual and social change. My ojiisan wrote: "See the warhorse cry / Japan setting in the sun / of her tear-stained eyes." Though years of public education would attempt to rob me of this conviction, convince me poetry was really a stale saltine, penned only by white men long buried, I kept that inked character of poetic beginnings inside my chest.

The first in my family to pursue higher education, I (like many English majors) thought I was destined for the assumed glamour of law school. When I mumbled the news to my mother that I instead wanted to be an English teacher, all the former talk about the nobility of poetry evaporated. She said I was now destined to become like my *other* grandfather, the one who fled a "free" government education and the security of boarding school (the Thomas Indian School); the grandfather who forever fled his Onondaga blood to ride the rails, only to return home an alcoholic. *Three college majors for nothing?* She said I would become yowamushi: good-for-nothing, a bum.

An unexpected crossroads tests the traveler's compass (or, perhaps more aptly in 21st-century America, their GPS app). The above was one such moment: one which tests the lynch pin that holds the compass hands steady. Mine had been set—and is surely still set—to so many of the poets honored in this anthology. As a very young man at the time of this writing (twenty-seven; Duane Niatum's *Harper's Anthology of 20th Century Native American Poetry* was born two years before me), truly I have set my compass to many of the poets here who are both honor-*ed* and honor-*ing*. And, when I have come to those many crossroads a writer stares down, it is my Onondaga sister Gail Tremblay's work that gives surest footing.

In my tribe, there is a famous clan mother, a peacemaker, Jigonsahseh: the cornerstone who united the Six Nations of the Iroquois Confederacy. Jigonsahseh was an intermediary who acted both as council and hearth-keeper for varying tribes, despite their disparities. When I am left-hook-right-hooked by life's many incongruities, Gail Tremblay's work has so often emboldened me, acted as an intermediary between me and the world, my work and what work I hope it's accomplishing in our small worlds.

At every one of the shitty apartments I've lived in, I keep my ethno-spiritual clan mother Gail's poem "Indian Singing in 20th Century America" printed out, up on the wall, just above my laptop, front and center. No doubt you will catch her influence in my poems—if you've made it this far with me, you're an incredibly generous reader. I've hidden the final lines kahséhtha' akweriákon. Deep, deep in my heart.

There is no period at the end of this poem. Our work is never over. Our remembering is never over. I am an Indian singing now at the dawn of 21st-century America, and as long as Earth breath eddies between my lungs, I will sing. I will sing.

Tremblay's song rattles itself into the poetic line now and perhaps even more resoundingly than ever. She speaks of the polarizing of our worlds, of one foot in and another out of time, and how truly this poem has forecasted not only the ending of a 20th-century America, but now the cry of a 21st. Here she sings, and with her we unite our voices. America, listen.

*

Indian Singing in 20th Century America
by Gail Tremblay

We wake: we wake the day,
the light rising in us like sun —
our breath a prayer brushing
against the feathers in our hands.
We stumble out into streets;
patterns of wires invented by strangers
are strung between eye and sky,
and we dance in two worlds,

inevitable as seasons in one,
exotic curiosities in the other
which rushes headlong down highways,
watches us from car windows, explains
us to its children in words
that no one could ever make
sense of. The image obscures
the vision, and we wonder
whether anyone will ever hear
our own names for the things
we do. Light dances in the body,
surrounds all living things —
even the stones sing
although their songs are infinitely
slower than the ones we learn
from trees. No human voice lasts
long enough to make such music sound.
Earth breath eddies between factories
and office buildings, caresses the surface
of our skin; we go to jobs, the boss
always watching the clock to see
that we're on time. He tries to shut
out magic and hopes we'll make
mistakes or disappear. We work
fast and steady and remember
each breath alters the composition
of the air. Change moves relentless,
the pattern unfolding despite their planning —
we're always there — singing round dance
songs, remembering what supports
our life — impossible to ignore.

ORLANDO WHITE

Diné of the Naaneesht'ézhi Tábaahí and born for
the Naakai Diné'e

"For me, the page in itself is a type of energy, an energy into which we enter. It balances the language."

No one is writing poems like those of Orlando White (1978–). No Indigenous poet is more micro, more focused on the power of an individual letter. All of his poems traffic in the semiotics of letters—their shapes, sounds, and symbolisms. And for this poet, letters are works of art, little people, signs and symbols of liberation and confinement. Consider a poem like "whit," which concedes and welcomes the text's relationship with white space. White likes to spread out his words, intermingling the darkness of print with the blankness of the page, which gives extra weight to each word in terms of how it looks and how it sounds. This way of composing is a continual act of resistance against colonizing by English and its linguistic and literary conventions. While White's poems may seem abstract or elusive, they are directly and immediately "about" how language tells us who we are—and what else might be possible.

Analogy

i
On the page, a man the size of a letter
wears a white necktie and a dark suit.

j
Next to him, a woman the size of a letter, too;
she wears a white scarf and a black gown.

-
Not a punctuation sign but a mark
of accentuation between two lovers.

ij
He says, "I am a single bone under the skin of a letter."
She says, "I too, am a letter, but I have a curved hipbone."

i-j
See them on the white bed of a page, how they hyphenate,
how they will create   language   together.

Sentence

Look:
                paper screen
                blank;
                the color white,
                        a zero,
                            hollow light bulb,
        the O   not yet typed.
This means
                    no imagination
                    without

                              its imagery.
Letters   can appear
                                        as bones
      (*Do not forget the image*)
            if you   write with   calcium.
      Because a subject
      can be half a skeleton,
        the verb, the other half
and the skull,
                        a period.

Writ

A man in a black suit with a zero
for a head follows me. He carries a gun
shaped like language; wants me written
and dead on the page. He can smell
my bleach-stained letters and can taste
what I have written; the inked bones of words.
But he cannot hear me breathe. Silence
is my refuge. I see the white door of paper;
I open it and enter. I was there forever it seems,
thinking of the origin and the end of poesis.
I thought I had lost him somewhere between
the point and line of *language*. But he finds me,
unwritten in the depths of the page. He lifts
the barrel of his pen, center on my forehead,
pulls the trigger. Through hair, skin, bone,
I feel the weight of ink enter my forehead.
The darkness takes up the white spaces
of my skull, I let him fill me with words.

Unwritten

Excavate what appears to be an *O*

remove its tiny white cranium.

Within text there is extinction,   bone-shaped artifacts.

Enough to reveal part of what covers a skull,   to scrape

out its ink   with a trowel: loop of an unfinished

alphabet,

    C bent in an incomplete circle.

_____ is not vacant only quiet and nameless,   an unswathed sound.

unwritten in the depths of the page,

See the skeleton of its head,   how it grins,

how its sentence teeth   clench

until it fractures a piece of a letter.

from layered page,

Dig the rest of its design

until bone exposes;

chip at its body

and feel it separate

fold paper in half

Chart its ink structure,

from its form.

just a body bag,

that framework of a word

that is where the calcium hardens.

Whit

There's a silence on paper that does not require ears only the reverberation

of a page turning—

She asks, so *how does it feel to be a letter?*

                    She is exclamation-like

She waits for him to notice her.

            but upended,   her feet tiptoeing,

            balletic   in her black tutu;

                    calligraphic, as if quill pen

scurrying dashes of ink

            on parchment   annotating solicitude.

He replies, "I think of it as a carapace, a place of solitude and cerebration —"

            She presses on to prance around him,

but he is ensconced,

his body catafalque as she divulges,

I like that you don't expire.

"— I will not lapse because we are equipoise,

we embody each other like iota,

we are obmutescent, you are verb, and I, noun;

when you locomote, your toes traipsing

I feel to urge from my exocarp

to accord my bones to tremble."

Orlando White 507

from Interview with Orlando White, by Veronica Golos

from Taos Journal of International Poetry & Art

I think if there's a poetics now, it's the poetics of one-word poems. I think of Aram Saroyan's and bpNichol's concrete poems, especially their one-word poems. What does it mean to experience a word visually, where a noun becomes, or is, a verb, concretely? In general, I feel that at the moment that's where I am in poetics. Also, thinking of how not to be routine in poetry . . . as poets we re-member lines, stanzas, imagery, sound, but for me I want to experience a word in the moment, *now*, and how a single word can create its own literary merit, status, experience outside of sentence, outside of traditional poetics, etc. . . . I tried to use and recreate some words like "ipseity," "communicatio," or "unwrit" in the poem "Block Cipher" to enable some sort of experience by either using an unconventional word or by misspelling or adding to a word . . .

Also, I think there is "compositional resistance" that allows the spaces between words to loosen up the authority of line break, of syntax. For me, the page in itself is a type of energy, an energy into which we enter. It balances the language. For me as an Indigenous person too, I see it as a type of resistance against English colonialism as well; that the spaces in-between are used to resist and release traditional rhythms and syntax. To see white space as a place of liberation, dissolving those boundaries between what is authoritative and what is not. And there are moments of silence as in the way we speak in Diné too, the use of apostrophes that enact brief pauses within the language, and I transpose all these with how I use the white space on the page.

"Compositional resistance" is using the white space, so when I read aloud I invoke silence and pause. Some people have a hard time with my live readings. So "How does your poem look on the page?" is a question I'm frequently asked. My answer is: What would happen if we read the way a poem is written on the page? To add the white spaces of the poem within a reading? To do things like, at a line beak, read the white space after it longer than usual! To break out of the standard use of language and page! Use the silence between letters, words, language to heighten the poetic experience! Because in some way when I read with pauses I feel like I'm resisting the authoritative poetics, and liberating myself as a poetry-writer!

LAYLI LONG SOLDIER
Oglala Lakota

"I have to sit, be patient, and allow the language to reveal itself."

Whereas, the first collection of poems by Layli Long Soldier (1972–), is among the most successful debuts ever by an Indigenous writer. *Whereas* was a finalist for the National Book Award and made nearly every "Best of the Year" list, including in the *Washington Post, San Francisco Chronicle,* and *Literary Hub. Whereas* was winner of the National Book Critics Circle Award in Poetry and the Griffin Prize, and Long Soldier appeared on the cover of *Poets & Writers Magazine* as one of Ten Writers Who Can Change the World. Innovative in overall structure and piece by piece, the book creates a fascinating intertextual dialogue with treaties between the United States Government and tribal nations. In the process, the poet not only undermines official discourse, she reinvents poetic form. Poems appear in squares, in columns, interspersed with blank spaces, in prose, in lyrical segments, lineated or oddly spaced, left-justified, with shifts in type size and face, cut across with thick or dotted lines, and in passages that can be read vertically and horizontally. Writing about thirty-eight Dakota men hanged in 1862 at the order of President Lincoln or about President Obama's 2009 official "apology" to Native Americans, Long Soldier's shines a probing light on injustices encoded in our poorly examined national history.

See also page 87 for Linda Hogan's testimony to the influence of "Whereas" by Layli Long Soldier

38

Here, the sentence will be respected.

I will compose each sentence with care, by minding what the rules of writing dictate.

For example, all sentences will begin with capital letters.

Likewise, the history of the sentence will be honored by ending each one with appropriate punctuation such as a period or question mark, thus bringing the idea to (momentary) completion.

You may like to know, I do not consider this a "creative piece."

I do not regard this as a poem of great imagination or a work of fiction.

Also, historicval events will not be dramatized for an "interesting" read.

Therefore, I feel most responsible to the orderly sentence; conveyor of thought.

That said, I will begin.

You may or may not have heard about the Dakota 38.

If this is the first time you've heard of it, you might wonder, "What is the Dakota 38?"

The Dakota 38 refers to thirty-eight Dakota men who were executed by hanging, under orders from President Abraham Lincoln.

To date, this is the largest "legal" mass execution in US history.

The hanging took place on December 26, 1862—the day after Christmas.

This was the *same week* that President Lincoln signed the Emancipation Proclamation.

In the preceding sentence, I italicize "same week" for emphasis.

There was a movie titled Lincoln about the presidency of Abraham Lincoln.

The signing of the Emancipation Proclamation was included in the film *Lincoln*; the hanging of the Dakota 38 was not.

In any case, you might be asking, "Why were thirty-eight Dakota men hung?"

As a side note, the past tense of hang is *hung*, but when referring to the capital punishment of hanging, the correct past tense is *hanged*.

So it's possible that you're asking, "Why were thirty-eight Dakota men hanged?"

They were hanged for the Sioux Uprising.

I want to tell you about the Sioux Uprising, but I don't know where to begin.

I may jump around and details will not unfold in chronological order.

Keep in mind, I am not a historian.

So I will recount facts as best I can, given limited resources and understanding.

Before Minnesota was a state, the Minnesota region, generally speaking, was the traditional homeland for Dakota, Anishinaabeg, and Ho-Chunk people.

During the 1800s, when the US expanded territory, they "purchased" land from the Dakota people as well as the other tribes.

But another way to understand that sort of "purchase" is: Dakota leaders ceded land to the US government in exchange for money or goods, but most importantly, the safety of their people.

Some say that Dakota leaders did not understand the terms they were entering, or they never would have agreed.

Even others call the entire negotiation "trickery."

But to make whatever-it-was official and binding, the US government drew up an initial treaty.

This treaty was laster replaced by another (more convenient) treaty, and then another.

I've had difficulty unraveling the terms of these treaties, given the legal speak and congressional language.

As treaties were abrogated (broken) and new treaties were drafted, one after another, the new treaties often referenced old defunct treaties, and it is a muddy, switchback trail to follow.

Although I often feel lost on this trail, I know I am not alone.

However, as best as I can put the facts together, in 1851, Dakota territory was contained to a twelve-mile by one-hundred-fifty-mile long strip along the Minnesota River.

But just seven years later, in 1858, the northern portion was ceded (taken) and the southern portion was (conveniently) alloted, which reduced Dakota land to a stark ten-mile tract.

These amended and broken treaties are often referred to as the Minnesota Treaties.

The word *Minnesota* come from *mni*, which means water; and *sota*, which means turbid.

Synonyms for turbid include muddy, unclear, cloudy, confused, and smoky.

Everything is in the language we use.

For example, a treaty is, essentially, a contract between two sovereign nations. The US treaties with the Dakota Nation were legal contracts that promised money.

It could be said, this money was payment for the land the Dakota ceded; for living within assigned boundaries (a reservation); and for relinquishing the rights to their vast hunting territory which, in turn, made Dakota people dependent on other means to survive: money.

The previous sentence is circular, akin to so many aspects of history.

As you may have guessed by now, the money promised in the turbid treaties did not make it into the hands of Dakota people.

In addition, local government traders would not offer credit to "Indians" to purchase food or goods.

Without money, store credit, or rights to hunt beyond their ten-mile tract of land, Dakota people began to starve.

The Dakota people were starving.

The Dakota people starved.

In the preceding sentence, the word "starved" does not need italics for emphasis.

One should read "The Dakota people starved" as a straightforward and plainly stated fact.

As a result—and without other options but to continue to starve—Dakota people retaliated.

Dakota warriors organized, struck out, and killed settlers and traders.

This revolt is called the Sioux Uprising.

Eventually, the US Cavalry came to Mnisota to confront the Uprising.

More than one thousand Dakota people were sent to prison.
As already mentioned, thirty-eight Dakota men were subsequently hanged.
After the hanging, those one thousand Dakota prisoners were released.

However, as further consequence, what remained of Dakota territory in Mnisota was dissolved (stolen).

The Dakota people had no land to return to.

This mean they were exiled.

Homeless, the Dakota people of Mnisota were relocated (forced) onto reservations in South Dakota and Nebraska.

Now, every year, a group called the Dakota *38 + 2* Riders conduct a memorial horse ride from Lower Brule, South Dakota, to Mankato, Mnisota.

The Memorial Riders travel 325 miles on horseback for eighteen days, sometimes through sub-zero blizzards.

They conclude their journey on December 26, the day of the hanging.

Memorials help focus our memory on particular people or events.

Often, memorials come in the forms of plaques, statues, or gravestones.

The memorial for the Dakota 38 is not an object inscribed with words but an act.

Yet, I started this piece because I was interested in writing about grasses.

So, there is one other event to include, although it's not in chronological order and we must backtrack a little.

When the Dakota people were starving, as you may remember, government traders would not extend store credit to "Indians."

One trader named Andrew Myrick is famous for his refusal to provide credit to Dakota people by saying, "If they are hungry, let them eat grass."
There are variations of Myrick's words, but they are all something to that effect.

When settlers and traders were killed during the Sioux Uprising, one of the first to be executed by the Dakota was Andrew Myrick.
When Myrick's body was found,

                                          his mouth was stuffed with grass.

I am inclined to call this act by the Dakota warriors a poem.

There's irony in their poem.

There was no text.

"Real" poems do not "really" require words.

I have italicized the previous sentence to indicate inner dialogue, a revealing moment.

But, on second thought, the words "Let them eat grass" click the gears of the poem into place.

So, we could also say, language and word choice are crucial to the poem's work.

Things are circling back again.

Sometimes, when in a circle, if I wish to exit, I must leap.

And let the body   swing.

From the platform.

                                      Out

                                            to the grasses.

from "Whereas Statements"

WHEREAS the word *whereas* means it being the case that, or considering that, or while on the contrary; is a qualifying or introductory statement, a conjunction, a connector. Whereas sets the table. The cloth. The saltshakers and plates. Whereas calls me to the table. Whereas precedes and invites. I have come now. I'm seated across from a Whereas smile. Under pressure of formalities, I fidget I shake my legs. I'm not one for these smiles, Whereas I have spent my life in unholding. *What do you mean by unholding?* Whereas asks and since Whereas rarely asks, I am moved to respond, Whereas, I have learned to exist and exist without your formality, saltshakers, plates, cloth. Without the slightest conjunctions to connect me. Without an exchange of questions, without courtesy of answers. It is mine, this unholding, so that with or without the setup, I can see the dish being served. Whereas let us bow our heads in prayer now, just enough to eat.

WHEREAS I sipped winter water cold-steeped in pine needles, I could taste it for days afterward, I taste it now. When I woke alone gray curtains burned in sunrise and down my throat to the pit, a tincture of those green needles changed me. When should I recount detail, when's it too much? My mother burrows herself for days at a time, so I listen to her. We speak about an envelope for receipts, dark roast coffee and the neighbor's staple gun I want to borrow. In the smallest things I watch the compass needle of conversation register her back to center. What has become of us, mother to her former self. Daughter to mother, present selves. Citizen to country, former and past to present or, is it a matter of *presence*? My daughter wouldn't do it when she was younger but this year she wanted to. For her birthday, an ear piercing. The needle gun hurts only for a moment, we assure her. In the old days Grandma held ice on my earlobes then punctured with a sewing needle. You'll have it easier, I affirm. She rushes through the mall to the needle chair, her smile. Eagerness, the emotion-mark of presence. I want to write something kind, as things of country and nation and nation-to-nation burn, have tattooed me. Red-enflamed-needle-marked me. Yet in the possibility of ink through a needle, the greater picture arrives through a thousand blood dots. Long ago bones were fashioned into needles. If I have my choosing I'd use this tool here, a bone needle to break the skin. To ink-inject the permanent reminder: *I'm here I'm not / numb to a single dot;*

WHEREAS my arm locked to aim on the ground I lay stretched flat deep in a game of marbles in a game of marbles inside a canvas pouch my garden of boulders cat eyes aggies peewees I played at recess as a fifth grader as a child I played in their shadows those bodies in cuffed jeans and sneakers three boys moved in stood over me heavy breathing I squinted upward my heart whirred loud as a card in the spokes of a wheel the big-boned blondie let out a piercing "warcry" three boys together whooped and played Indian circled and stomped hands fanning their mouths I lowered my aim rose to my knees gathered my marbles within a jeering circle pink faces sweat laughter the valley sun pounded my back my scalp my dark burning hair I toted my pouch across the playground walked alone as if climbing a descending escalator useless steps to safety I entered the classroom flip top desks with metal bellies glancing outward to classmates rows of post-recess chatter fluorescent lighting side glances no one spoke not one syllable to me I steadied my empty body at the desk stowed my marbles inside a metal belly never again to lie in the dirt on my stomach never again to call this a game in America;

And whereas in my bed in a doorway of dreaming I stood holding a stack of folded blue wool black metal eyelets buttons a wooden spool blue thread a pack of sewing needles as if a servant pliant and waiting my forearms upturned I held the makings there I felt a summons I turn to a black-and-white photo you're seated with a canumpa and cloth across your lap I trace a horizontal scar across the bridge of your nose in your eyes mottled irises a torn surface your life on your face this mirror of our family I note a plume in your top hat down both shoulders your hair wrapped in fur strong veins pump through wrists to a soldier's hands a choker above the top button of your wool coat I know how you got that coat I search for a place even marginal to share the story this thread in the seams of our family but what's on a page every stitch is up for ripping my dream never leaves me the laid blue wool shining buttons slim silver needles I recognize the elegance of materials just as they are untouched at the threshold of a room though I cannot see outward nor for whom I hold the materials I am ready;

WHEREAS *resolution*'s an act of analyzing and restructuring complex ideas into simpler ones so I place a black bracket on either side of an [idea] I cordon it to safety away from national resolution the threat of reductive[thinking]:

Whereas Native Peoples are [   ] people with a deep and abiding [   ] in the [   ], and for millennia Native Peoples have maintained a powerful [   ] connection to this land, as evidenced by their [   ] and legends;

*

Wheras the Federal Government condemned the [   ], [   ], and [   ] of Native Peoples and endeavored to assimilate them by such policies as the redistribution of land under the Act of February 8, 1887 (25 U.S.C. 331; 24 Stat.388, chapter 119) (commonly known as the "General Allotment Act"), and the forcible removal of Native [   ] from their [   ] to faraway boarding schools where their Native [   ] and [   ] were degraded and forbidden;

WHEREAS I read an article in the *New York Times* about the federal sequestration of funds from reservation programs, the cuts. In federal promises and treaties. The article details living conditions on reservations a suicide rate ten times higher than the rest of the country. Therein the story of a twelve-year-old girl whose mother died, she doesn't know her father, she bounces home to home to foster home, weary. I regard how plainly the writer imparts her repeated sexual abuse. For mental care, unavailable services. There's a clinic that doesn't have money after May, *don't get sick after May* is the important message. As I read I cry, I always cry, and here I must be clear my crying doesn't indicate sadness. Then I read a comment posted below the online article:

> *I am a fourteen-year-old girl who recently visited the _____*
> *Reservation in South Dakota, with my youth group. The conditions the*
> *Native American people were living in were shocking. When I arrived*
> *home, I wrote a petition on whitehouse.gov for the US to formally apol-*
> *ogize and pay reparations to the Native American people. This petition*
> *only stays up until July 23rd, so please sign and share!!! You signing it*
> *would really mean a lot to a lot of people. Thank you.*

Dear Fourteen-Year-Old Girl, I want to write. The government has already "formally apologized" to Native American people on behalf of the plural *you*, your youth group, your mother and father, your best friends and their families. *You*, as in all American citizens. *You* didn't know that. I know. Yet indeed, Dear Girl, the conditions on reservations have changed since the Apology. Meaning, the Apology has been followed by budget sequestration. In common terms sequestration is removal banishment or exile. In law-speak it means seizure for safe-keeping but changed in federal budgeting to mean subject to cuts, best as I can understand it. Dear Girl, I went to the Indian Health Services to fix a tooth, a complicated pain. Indian health care is guaranteed by treaty but at the clinic limited funds don't allow treatment beyond a filling. The solution offered: *Pull it*. Under pliers masks and clinical lights, a tooth that could've been saved was placed in my palm to hold after sequestration. Dear Girl, I honor your response and action, I do. Yet the root of reparation is repair. My tooth will not grow back. The root, gone.

[spiritual]
[belief]   [Creator]
[spiritual]
[customs]

[traditions]
[beliefs]   [customs]

[children]
[families]
[practices]
[languages]

from "Layli Long Soldier: interviewed by Kaveh Akbar"

from divedapper

[A] big part of my deliberation in writing "38" . . . I felt like that moment was so incredible that the language of re-telling could ruin it if I was not very careful. And because that was the heart of that piece, it took me a long time to think about how I wanted to encase that moment, to hold it up. That initial concern of not wanting to diffuse the moment, to be true to it and honor it, rippled out and determined so many other things in the way I handled the crafting. For example, I knew I did not want to embellish the moment, I felt like it spoke for itself. I desired simplicity. I wanted to be very careful with the account. So I felt like I did not need to enter into that account with my writerly fanciness.

I just wanted my telling to be very straightforward. Then I realized that anything that came before or after that moment must have a similar tone. I didn't want to make this "interesting historical account" for people to read. I say it in the beginning of the poem: "Historical events will not be dramatized for an interesting read."

The underlying values that I wanted to work with then helped me to determine the form of the poem. My determination not to dramatize nor make it an "interesting read" led me to the simple sentence. And, of course, the sentence has a double meaning in this piece. There's the death sentence working alongside the literary sentence.

Anyway, that led me to the sentence. And once I had the form, my wheels could start moving. Then what became most important was just working on each sentence. For the most part, every sentence holds its own space on the page. I did not want one to blur into another within a standard paragraph. Each needed a kind of integrity, a voice of its own. . . .

There's that principle proposed in Charles Olson's "Projective Verse," "Form is never more than an extension of content." That idea has always struck me because it is not something that I completely relate to. Sometimes form comes first. Sometimes a shape comes first. There is no content; the content is yet to come. I'll wake up and I'll see a shape or I'll feel a shape. I feel pulled toward a kind of form. I'll think, "Oh, this is something that I'd like to make on the page." I'll sit and work on it, and there's no language yet. I don't even know what I want to say. I'll tap out one word, then another, not quite sure if that's what needs to be written. But it's a process wherein I'm thinking in unison with the shape, know-ing that the visual speaks first, in many ways. So I'm watching the shape, asking it what it wants to say. . . .

It opens things up much more for me because of the way I work. I feel first and work with intuition. The shape is communicating something to me that I don't quite know yet. I reach toward that form and say, "Why are you tapping my shoulder right now? What do you want to tell me?" Then I have to sit, be patient, and allow the language to reveal itself.

Permissions

Tupelo Press is grateful to the following authors and publishers for permissions to use and incorporate the following texts:

Ai, "Warrior", Copyright © 1973, from *The Collected Poems of Ai* by *Ai*. Used by permission of W. W. Norton & Company, Inc.

Esther G. Belin, "Blues-ing on the Brown Vibe" and "Ruby in Me #1" from *The Belly of My Beauty* by Esther Belin © 1999 The Arizona Board of Regents. Reprinted with the permission of the University of Arizona Press.

Elizabeth Bishop, "One Art" from *The Complete Poems 1926-1979*. Copyright © 1979, 1983 by Alice Helen Methfessel. Reprinted with the permission of Farrar, Straus & Giroux, LLC.

Sherwin Bitsui, "Atlas," "Apparition," and "Drought" from *Shapeshift* by Sherwin Bitsui © 2003 Sherwin Bitsui. Reprinted with the permission of the University of Arizona Press.

Sherwin Bitsui, ["Stepping through the drum's vibration."] from *Flood Song* (Copper Canyon 2009). Copyright © 2009 by Sherwin Bitsui. Reprinted with the permission of The Permissions Company, Inc., on behalf of Copper Canyon Press, coppercanyonpress.org.

Sherwin Bitsui, Excerpt from "The Motion of Poetic Landscape: An Interview with Sherwin Bitsui," by Bianca Viñas, *Hunger Mountain: The VCFA Journal for the Arts*, December 1, 2017.

Kimberly Blaeser, "Captivity" previously appeared in *World Literature Today*, (May-August 2017), "Apprenticed to Justice," "Goodbye to All That," and "Fantasies of Women" appeared in *Apprenticed to Justice* (Salt Publishing, Copyright © 2007), "Rewriting Your Life" appeared in *Trailing You* (Greenfield Review Press, Copyright © 1994), and "Of Fractals and Pink Flowering" appeared in *Poetry Speaks* (Madison Museum of Contemporary Art, 2016). Reprinted by permission of the author.

Sammie Bordeaux-Seeger, "1900" previously appeared in *Connotation Press: An Online Artifact*, January 2017.

Chrystos, "Crazy Grandpa Whispers," from *Not Vanishing* (Press Gang Publishers, 1989). Copyright © 1989 Chrystos. Used by permission of the author.

Allison Adelle Hedge Coke, "Radio Wave" from *Dog Road Woman* (Coffee House Press, 1997); and "America, I Sing You Back," "Taxonomy," and "Streaming" from *Streaming* (Coffee House Press, 2014). Reprinted with the permission of The Permissions Company, Inc., on behalf of Coffee House Press, www.coffeehousepress.org

Eduardo C. Corral, "Our Completion: Oil on Wood: Tino Rodriguez: 1999" by Eduardo C. Corral from the book *Slow Lightning* (Yale University Press, 2012). Used by permission of the author.

Laura Da', "Leviathan" © 2015 Laura Da'. Originally published by the Academy of American Poets, www.poets.org. Used by permission of the author.

Nora Marks Dauenhauer, "How to Make Good Baked Salmon from the River" from *The Droning Shaman* (Black Current Press, 1989).

Natalie Díaz, "When My Brother Was an Aztec" from *When My Brother Was an Aztec* (Copper Canyon, 2012). Reprinted with the permission of The Permissions Company, Inc., on behalf of Copper Canyon Press, coppercanyonpress.org.

Heid E. Erdrich, "National Monuments", "Kennewick Man Tells All", and "Guidelines for the Treatment of Sacred Objects", from *National Monuments* (Michigan State University Press, 2008); and "Pre-Occupied," from *Curator of Ephemera at the New Museum for Archaic Media* (Michigan State University Press, 2017).

Heid E. Erdrich, "Little Souvenirs from the DNA Trading Post", from *Cell Traffic: New and Selected Poems* by Heid Erdrich © 2012 The Arizona Board of Regents. Reprinted with the permission of the University of Arizona Press..

Louise Erdrich, "Rez Litany", from *Original Fire: New and Selected Poems* (HarperCollins, 2003). Used by permission of HarperCollins.

Louise Erdrich, "Dear John Wayne", "Indian Boarding School: The Runaways", "Captivity", "Jacklight", and "Windigo" from *Jacklight* (Henry Holt, 1984). Permission requested from Henry Holt & Co.

Louise Erdrich, "Out of the Black Night" appeared in *Poetry Magazine*, June 2018.

Jennifer Elise Foerster, "Leaving Tulsa", from *Leaving Tulsa* by Jennifer Elise Foerster © 2013 The Arizona Board of Regents. Reprinted with the permission of the University of Arizona Press.

Robert Frost, "Never Again Would Birds' Song Be the Same" by Robert Frost, from *A Witness Tree* (Henry Holt, 1942).

Diane Glancy, "Buffalo Medicine," from *Asylum in the Grasslands* by Diane Glancy © 2007 The Arizona Board of

Norton & Company.

Bojan Louis, "Breach", previously published in *Black Renaissance Noire* (volume 13, issue 1: Spring/Summer 2013).

Molly McGlennen, "Three Poems for Ellia", "Living the Language", "Legend", and Preface from *Fried Fish and Flour Biscuits* (Salt, 2010). Permission requested from Salt Publishing.

Deborah A. Miranda, "Indian Cartography" from *Indian Cartography* (Greenfield Review Press, 1999). Used by permission of the author.

Simon Ortíz, "Culture and the Universe" from *Out There Somewhere* by Simon Ortíz © 2002 The Arizona Board of Regents. Reprinted with the permission of the University of Arizona Press.

Simon Ortíz, "Survival This Way" and "A Story of How a Wall Stands", from *Woven Stone* (University of Arizona Press, 1992); and "Our Eagerness Blooms" from *After and Before the Lightning* (University of Arizona Press, 1994). Permission requested from the University of Arizona Press.

Simon Ortíz, "Song/Poetry, and Language: Expression and Perception," from *Simon J. Ortiz: A Poetic Legacy of Continuance and Resistance*, edited by Berry Brill de Ramírez and Evelina Zuni Lucero (University of New Mexico Press, 2009). Permission requested from the University of New Mexico Press.

Elise Paschen, "Under the Dome" and "Wi'-gi-e", from Bestiary. Copyright © 2009 by Elise Paschen. "My Mother Descends" and "Parents at Rest", from *The Nightlife*. Copyright © 2017 by Elise Paschen. Reprinted by permission of Red Hen Press, Inc.

Elise Paschen, "Oklahoma Home", previously appeared in *Infidelities* (Story Line Press, 1996). Reprinted with permission of the poet.

Cecilia Catherine Taitano Perez, "As I Turn the Pages," from University of Hawai'i masters thesis, 1997. Used by permission of the author.

Craig Santos Perez, excerpt from "understory", appeared in *Poetry* (January 2016). Used by permission of the author.

C. R. Resetarits, "Hovenweep", from *Brood: Poems* (Norman, OK: Mongrel Empire Press, 2015). Reprinted by permission of Mongrel Empire Press.

C. R. Resetarits, "Arroyo" and "Elegy" appeared previously in *Talking Sticks: Native Arts Quarterly* 13.3 (2010).

Carter Revard, "Statement on Energy Policy", from *An Eagle Nation* (University of Arizona Press, 1993); "Herbs of Healing: American Values in American Indian Literature," from *Family Matters, Tribal Affairs* (University of Arizona Press, 1998). Reprinted by permission of the author.

Carter Revard, "Indians Demand Equal Time with God", from *Cowboys and Indians, Christmas Shopping* (Point Riders Press, 1992). Reprinted by permission of the author.

Carter Revard, "Driving in Oklahoma," "Wahzhazhe Grandmother," and "What the Eagle Fan Says," from   (Salt, 2005). Permission requested from Salt Publishing.

Wendy Rose, "Excavation at Santa Barbara Mission" and "I Expected My Skin and My Blood to Ripen" from *Bone Dance: New and Selected Poems, 1965–1993* (University of Arizona Press, 1994). Permission requested from University of Arizona Press.

Delmore Schwartz, "The Heavy Bear Who Goes With Me" from *Selected Poems (1938-1958): Summer Knowledge*. Copyright © 1967 by Delmore Schwartz. Reprinted with the permission of New Directions Publishing Corporation.

Leslie Marmon Silko, "Love Poem" and "When Sun Came to Riverwoman", from *Laguna Woman* (Flood Plain Press, 1993).

Leslie Marmon Silko, "From a letter to James Wright, September 12, 1979" excerpted from *The Delicacy and Strength of Lace* (Graywolf, 1985). Reprinted with the permission of The Permissions Company, Inc., on behalf of Graywolf Press, www.graywolfpress.org

Leslie Marmon Silko, "Poem for Myself and Mei Mei Concerning Abortion" and "Storyteller's Escape" from *Storyteller* by Leslie Marmon Silko, copyright © 1981, 2012 by Leslie Marmon Silko. Used by permission of Viking Books, an imprint of Penguin Publishing Group, a division of Penguin Random House LLC. All rights reserved.

Leslie Marmon Silko, excerpt from "Language and Literature from a Pueblo Indian Perspective", from *Yellow Woman and a Beauty of the Spirit* (Touchstone/Simon & Schuster, 1997). Permission requested from Simon & Schuster.

M. L. Smoker, "The Feed", "Another Attempt at a Rescue", "Letter to Richard Hugo", and "Mercy" reprinted from "Another Attempt at Rescue" © 2005 by M.L. Smoker, by permission of Hanging Loose Press.

W. D. Snodgrass, "Eva Braun" from *Not for Specialists: New and Selected Poems*. Copyright © 1977, 1995, 2006 by W. D. Snodgrass. Reprinted with the permission of The Permissions Company, Inc., on behalf of BOA Editions, Ltd., www.boaeditions.org

Acknowledgments

No work of this depth and range is ever completed alone. Thus, we the editors, are deeply grateful to the many hearts, minds, and hands that went into the conception, production, and completion of *Native Voices*. And, as always, we are most grateful to this land that holds all truths and the creator that watches over us.

Our deepest thanks go to the poets who contributed their voices to this anthology. Their lessons, stories, and poems serve as an example of the excellence and importance of Native literature. Thanks also to the ancestors whose texts appear herein. Let this work be always in conversation and a canon for the wisdom that each of these writer's, both Native and not, inherently carry.

Our first thanks go to Jeffrey Levine for providing the platform for this text. Without the help and support of allies, no healing would ever happen. So we extend that thanks to the entire team at Tupelo Press, including Kristina Marie Darling, Cassandra Cleghorn, and David Rossitter. Special thanks to Jim Schley whose knowledge, expertise, creativity, and friendship made this book beautiful and complete.

In the early stages of the inception of *Native Voices*, Tiffany Midge, provided excellent direction, guidance, and support for which we are deeply grateful.

Sincere thanks also to Diana Walczak of Harmless Little Bunny Productions for creating the brilliant video that helped raise the money to complete *Native Voices*. And thanks also to each contributor who responded to that campaign for bringing this collection to life, with particular thanks to William Prindle and D. G. Geis.

CMarie would like to thank her partner Caleb Zurstadt for his constant support, patience, and love. Without your belief in me, I would have little in myself. Also, I thank Kim Barnes, Brian Blanchfield, Mary Clearman Blew, Tobias Wray, Alexandra Teague, Michael McGriff and Luis Alberto Urrea for their words and their teaching. Heartfelt thanks to Adrian C Louis whose texts and emails and honesty assured me that I was doing the right thing at the right time. Thanks to the Kaag and Baillargeon families for giving me shelter and family while working on this anthology. I am so thankful for my mother and father, Dolores and Ron Fuhrman, and my sister, Janet Fuhrman. Also, to my IKEEP students and Dr. Vanessa Anthony-Stevens, for your inspiration and every little thing I have learned from each of you.

Dean wishes to thank his students at the University of San Francisco who have been eager readers of Indigenous American poetry for almost twenty years now. Big props to Jennifer Turpin, Marcelo Camperi, Eileen Fung, and my colleagues in the English Department and Honors College for supporting Native literature. I also want to give a shout out to my good friend LeAnne Howe who is, in every way, inspirational. Also, I feel infinite gratitude to my family near and far; they are always incredibly supportive. I want to dedicate this book to the memory of my father, Gary Rader, who passed away as CMarie and I were deep into the beginning stages of *Native Voices*.

Recent and Selected Titles from Tupelo Press

Silver Road: Essays, Maps & Calligraphies (hybrid memoir), Kazim Ali

A Certain Roughness in Their Syntax (poems), Jorge Aulicino, translated by Judith Filc

Flight (poems), Chaun Ballard

The Book of LIFE (poems), Joseph Campana

Fire Season (poems), Patrick Coleman

Sanderlings (poems), Geri Doran

Calazazza's Delicious Dereliction (poems), Suzanne Dracius, translated by Nancy Naomi
     Carlson

Hallowed: New and Selected Poems, Patricia Fargnoli

Leprosarium (poems), Lise Goett

Hazel (novel), David Huddle

Darktown Follies (poems), Amaud Jamaul Johnson

Dancing in Odessa (poems), Ilya Kaminsky

domina Un/blued (poems), Ruth Ellen Kocher

Phyla of Joy (poems), Karen An-hwei Lee

At the Gate of All Wonder (novel), Kevin McIlvoy

Boat (poems), Christopher Merrill

The Cowherd's Son (poems), Rajiv Mohabir

Marvels of the Invisible (poems), Jenny Molberg

Canto General: Song of the Americas (poems), Pablo Neruda, translated by Mariela Griffor
     and Jeffrey Levine

Lucky Fish (poems), Aimee Nezhukumatathil

Ex-Voto (poems), Adélia Prado, translated by Ellen Doré Watson

Mistaking Each Other for Ghosts (poems), Lawrence Raab

Intimate: An American Family Photo Album (hybrid memoir), Paisley Rekdal

Thrill-Bent (novel), Jan Richman

Dirt Eaters (poems), Eliza Rotterman

Good Bones (poems), Maggie Smith

What Could Be Saved (novellas and stories), Gregory Spatz

Kill Class (poems), Nomi Stone

Swallowing the Sea (essays), Lee Upton

feast gently (poems), G.C. Waldrep

Republic of Mercy (poems), Sharon Wang

Legends of the Slow Explosion (essays), Baron Wormser

Ordinary Misfortunes (poems), Emily Jungmin Yoon

See our complete list at www.tupelopress.org